THE POLITICS OF NONASSIMILATION

THE POLITICS OF NONASSIMILATION

The American Jewish Left in the Twentieth Century

DAVID R. VERBEETEN

NIU Press / DeKalb, IL

Northern Illinois University Press, DeKalb 60115
© 2017 by Northern Illinois University Press
Printed in the United States of America
26 25 24 23 22 21 20 19 18 17   1 2 3 4 5
978-0-87580-753-9 (paper)
978-1-60909-212-2 (e-book)
Cover design by Yuni Dorr
Composed by BookComp, Inc.

Library of Congress Cataloging-in-Publication Data
Names: Verbeeten, David Randall, author.
Title: The politics of nonassimilation : the American Jewish left in the
    twentieth century / David Randall Verbeeten.
Description: DeKalb : Northern Illinois University Press, 2017 | Revised
    version of the author's thesis (doctoral)—University of Cambridge, 2012.
    | Includes bibliographical references.
Identifiers: LCCN 2016021240 (print) | LCCN 2016021505 (ebook) | ISBN
    9780875807539 (pbk. : alk. paper) | ISBN 9781609092122 (ebook)
Subjects: LCSH: Jews, East European—United States—History—20th
    century. | Jews, East European—Cultural assimilation—United States.
    | Immigrants—United States. | United States—Ethnic relations. |
    Bittelman, Alex, 1890–1982. | American Jewish Congress. | New Jewish
    Agenda (Organization)
Classification: LCC E184.353 .V47 2017 (print) | LCC E184.353 (ebook) |
    DDC 305.800973—dc23
LC record available at https://lccn.loc.gov/2016021240

To my grandparents, Magda Fodor and Frank Fleischmann,
Ruth Rotenberg and Mathijs Marinus Verbeeten—survivors all.
And to my parents, Judy and Bernard, who helped me along this path.

Contents

Acknowledgments

ALL THE OVERSIGHTS IN THIS work are mine, but all the credit is not. As this book is based on my doctoral thesis at the University of Cambridge, I would like to thank Dr. Christopher Brooke and the late Dr. Emile Perreau-Saussine, who supervised my work, and I would like to recognize the financial assistance I received from Pembroke College and Canada's Social Sciences and Humanities Research Council. I appreciate the time and efforts of the archivists who facilitated my research, especially Jan Hilley of the Tamiment Library at New York University; of the former members of New Jewish Agenda who corresponded with me about their past activities; and of the staff, reviewers, and editors at NIU Press. I am grateful to Paul E. Gottfried for having recommended the original thesis for publication.

Introduction

In his introduction to the anthology *Essential Papers on Jews and the Left*, Ezra Mendelsohn, a historian of Eastern European Jewry and its worldwide diaspora, noted that the "left, however it is defined, has had a profound impact upon the modern Jewish community." It has, in all its varieties, constituted a salient and at times controversial feature of modern Jewish life. It may even provide a basic continuity to Jewish political history in the modern period, as affiliation with the Left ostensibly relates individuals and communities across time and geographic space. Even as the facts of this modern Jewish political attraction and attachment may be "easy to demonstrate," they are, Mendelsohn has cautioned, "perhaps not so easy to explain."[1]

This book is an effort at explanation. It seeks to determine the nature and sources of left-wing ideologies and movements among American Jews and to do so by exploring pertinent cases as well as the contexts in which those cases were situated and formed. It focuses on the record of Eastern European Jewish immigrants and their descendants in the United States, with occasional glances at European precedents or coeval developments. Its subject matter is a cycle of three "generations" over a period of transformation in Jewish life: the "First" being the Eastern European immigrants to the United States at the turn of the twentieth century, whose formative years occurred around the time of and after the First World War; the "Second" being the children of those immigrants, who generally came of age during the interwar period and matured throughout the Second World War; and the "Third" being the grandchildren, a larger number of people over a broader period of time, yet distinguished herein by birth after the Second World War. The geographic focus is primarily but not exclusively on the state and city of New York, where a majority of Russian Jewish immigrants settled or lived at some point, remaining to this day the largest concentration of Jews in the United States, if not the world.

Generations constitute a fitting periodization, despite the overlapping and irregularity of lifespans, for the very reason that American Jewish left-wing leanings, as a distinct phenomenon, have been ostensibly independent of the major events that may conceivably separate one epoch from the next. Generations are also a common device within American Jewish historiography. As this generational cycle commences with the fact of immigration from Eastern Europe, which had a definite start and finish, not least due to the 1921 and 1924 US immigration laws, the schema is not open-ended. Each generation was characterized by some important shared features, cultural if not entirely chronological. It may be noted generally that a Jewish individual of the First Generation was likely born in the Russian Empire, spoke Yiddish, and worked, for some time at least, as an industrial laborer. A member of the Second Generation, even if born as the major migration from Eastern Europe to the United States was ongoing, likely knew English better than Yiddish, had an orientation that was more exclusively domestic rather than split between the United States and the original homeland, and was probably never a part of the working class as his or her parents had been. Finally, a member of the Third Generation was a part of the baby boom and its common experience.

A wish to grasp that which may unify these generations motivates this work. The persistence of a distinct Jewish Left over an entire generational cycle and beyond calls for investigation and explanation. The time frame comprises much of the twentieth century. Such a scope sacrifices some historical detail, but a sole focus on any one narrow period would obscure the longevity of the phenomenon in question and thus fail to provide a comprehensive account. The American Jewish Left has certainly changed over time in its causes and concerns, along with the Left in general, but as an orientation it has remained a comparatively disproportionate fact of Jewish life, especially in the United States. It has done so against all expectations to the contrary and against standard models, which tend to emphasize (and not without empirical foundation) socioeconomic status, along with ethnic difference, as important factors in political conduct and preference.[2]

Eastern European Jews as a whole bucked the basic trends of the American party system in the twentieth century. As immigrants they were not unique in gravitating toward the Democratic Party in the 1920s and 1930s, although their earlier third-party radicalism was fairly exceptional. Even before the Civil War, the Democrats were the party toward which gravitated those who did not belong to the country's hegemonic group of white, bourgeois Protestants.[3] Eastern European Jews, however, remained committed and decidedly liberal Democrats when others did not. In the twentieth century, as outsiders have tended to become insiders, through social mobility and recognition, they have usually become more Republican. Catholic immigrants from Europe, who arrived in the United States at the same time as most Jews and faced similar travails, underwent this process during and after the Second World War. By comparison with most other coeval immigrants, Jews began much further to the Left and remained further Left even after attaining unprecedented affluence and acceptance. This "pattern prevails despite concerted efforts to shift Jews to the political right" by a small yet vocal number of Jewish neoconservative intellectuals and through "a major Republican outreach to Jews" from the 1980s up to the present.[4]

Each generation of American Jews of Eastern European provenance faced a distinct set of circumstances and challenges, yet the majority of each generation, to varying degrees of intensity and with certain important exceptions, oriented itself toward the left wing of the American political spectrum, toward the administrative state, varieties of socialism or welfare liberalism, multiculturalism, and eventually permissive social codes. Partisan loyalties tend to demonstrate continuity from parents to children, yet they are also likely to "erode and become susceptible to political shocks" over time. The partisan loyalties of southern whites, Kenneth D. Wald observed, reversed "almost at the moment that the national Democratic Party embraced the cause of racial integration in 1964," and "this is precisely the problem" with conventional explanations of American Jewish liberalism that look back to Europe or the experience of the First Generation without taking into account that the Jewish Left "has weathered the political shocks that might well have produced the kind of realignment long sought by neoconservatives."[5] The persistence of the phenomenon suggests that conventional theories may have been insufficient all along.

Most of these theories are invoked and summarized in the recent book *Why Are Jews Liberals?*, by Norman Podhoretz, a prominent American Jewish neoconservative intellectual.[6] Podhoretz traces the Jews' marked predilection for the Left back to the Enlightenment and the period of emancipation in Western and Central Europe in the eighteenth and early nineteenth centuries. According to Podhoretz, in this time the Jews' "great enemy—the kings and nobles who ruled the state—joined forces with the Church to keep the Jews from achieving equal rights before the law." In turn, when Eastern European Jews migrated to the United States at the turn of the twentieth century, they brought this memory with them, and it was reinforced by the circulation of antisemitic ideas "in the upper echelons of the Wasp [Anglo-Protestant] patriciate." "In America, as in Europe," Podhoretz maintained, "it was the conservative upholders of the old order who were hostile to the Jews, whether they were rich or poor and whether they had immigrated from Germany or from Eastern Europe." What is more, the Jewish immigrants endured poverty and hardship, "huddling together in a latter-day ghetto on the Lower East Side of Manhattan and clinging to one another for dear life," even as "the best the great majority of the Jews working in the needle trades could hope for was . . . modest improvements in their condition." They turned to the leaders of the labor movement for solace, all of whom were "Marxists who had brought their ideological convictions from Russia to America."[7]

Podhoretz's account is not entirely accurate and involves considerable apology. The body of this text offers a detailed correction. First, Podhoretz's version errs in its assumption that Eastern European Jews, prior to their migration to the United States, had been part of the "Enlightenment dialectic" of social integration and assimilation.[8] Most Eastern European Jews arrived in the United States as a traditional, religious population. Some came with Marxist beliefs, but they were for years a small minority, and the reasons for the success of these radicals within their community require clarification. The development of a radical sub-culture among Jews in the United States was *sui generis* and paralleled rather than proceeded from Russian developments. What is more, the much smaller number of American Jews from Germany, who had migrated well before the "Jews from the East" and who had typified the "Enlightenment dialectic" in Europe, often became Republicans in the United States and were not known for radicalism.

Second, the Republicans were not a European-style party of the Right, of throne and altar. For much of the twentieth century they approximated, at least in rhetoric and image, a bourgeois, classical liberal party. Through the First World War those Jews who voted for a mainstream rather than a radical third party went Republican as often as Democrat. In its southern constituency, the Democratic Party was a bastion of genuine conservatism rather than the reverse,[9] and in its northern constituency—especially Catholic immigrants and "the Church" as well as the working class and African Americans—it was (and remains) home to the most antisemitic elements in the country.[10] Even as Republican presidents and other officials in the first third of the twentieth century denounced publicly the persecution of Russian Jews under the czar and promoted (German) Jews to high office, such actions did not hinder radicalism among Eastern European Jews or their (re)alignment toward the Democrats during the presidencies of Thomas Woodrow Wilson and especially Franklin Delano Roosevelt. Some have attributed this movement in part to Roosevelt's promotion of Russian Jews under the New Deal, but as Irving Howe recognized, the Democrats by this time were rewarding a preexisting loyalty, even as Republicans "neither owed nor paid many debts to the [Lower] East Side."[11]

Finally, this same Lower East Side of Manhattan was not the hopeless place that Podhoretz describes. Jews arrived in the United States with relatively more skills than other immigrants and experienced unprecedented mobility, not just after the Second World War, as is the conventional wisdom. Despite the initial hardships they faced, along with many others, Jewish immigrants were known for their socioeconomic advance as early as the turn of the twentieth century.[12] Many if not a majority of Jewish immigrants moved out of the working class and the Lower East Side within fifteen to twenty-five years. By the 1940s their children had already become one of the wealthiest groups in the country. What is more, Jewish radicalism emerged as a predominant force within the community *after* this rapid process of uplift had begun, and it cut across class lines.

Podhoretz's narrative invokes antisemitism to interpret the Jewish Left. But even though, as Leonard Dinnerstein has observed, "in no Christian country has antisemitism been weaker than it has been in the United States,"[13] Jewish radicalism and subsequently Jewish liberalism (which, as Podhoretz notes, has often resembled moderate or democratic socialism)[14] was just as if not more pronounced in the new world than the old. The United States provides a compelling context for an exploration of the Jewish Left, which came to characterize both American and European Jews, precisely for this reason. Even as an analysis of conditions in Europe can easily be overshadowed by antisemitism, especially in light of the Holocaust, it is much harder to place antisemitism at the center of an American study while being rigorous about historical sources and chronologies as well as about statistical data. Without denying its relevance, this book demotes antisemitism from its customary pride of hermeneutic place. The Jewish Left was not simply anti-antisemitic.

American Jews have demonstrated considerable preoccupation with antisemitism, but as noted above the Democratic Party was objectively just as if not more likely to harbor antisemites than the Republican. Jews have been subjectively prone to project antisemitism on to those they disfavor politically and to excuse such sentiments among those they favor. If more Jews have regarded Republicans as antisemites, that is in part because more Jews have been and remain Democrats. In surveys, Jews have regarded neither Democrats nor Republicans as overtly or predominantly antisemitic, but even so tend to regard their party of choice as being less antisemitic than its rival: Democratic Jews believe Republicans are more antisemitic; Republican Jews believe Democrats are more antisemitic. Perceptions are mediated by preexisting political commitments. They are also subject to considerable volatility from year to year.[15]

The causal relationship between antisemitism and the American Jewish Left is ambiguous. There is no obvious positive correlation between left-wing activism in the United States and concerns about antisemitism. If anything, studies, both historical and statistical, tend to suggest a negative correlation, and for good reason: Jews who have feared gentiles or have had serious status insecurity as a minority have not typically wanted to attract the kind of adverse attention that may attend unconventional or undue political agitation.[16] Left-wing activism has often engendered or exacerbated anti-Jewish feelings among some non-Jews, a fact of which at least some left-wing Jews have been aware. What is more, despite the significant decline of antisemitism since the Second World War, Jews have remained the most liberal or left-wing white ethnic group in the United States, even more so than many visible minorities.

Rather than antisemitism, the Jewish Left is far more decisively correlated with secularization. The most basic fact about the Jewish Left across time and place is that it has been especially if not exclusively prevalent among more secular yet still ethnically committed Jews and, more specifically, secular ethnic Jews of Eastern European provenance. On the one hand, the Jewish Left was not (and has not been) disproportionately pertinent to the experience of those who have observed devoutly the biblical commandments and assented to rabbinical authority. Such orthodox Jews have tended toward conservatism, *vis-à-vis* both the Jewish community and the wider society. They have also demonstrated antagonism to left-wing forces in many instances. On the other hand, highly assimilated Jews—those who have converted and intermarried or have become thoroughly and unselfconsciously bourgeois, as did many German or Central European Jews in the United States, if not Europe—have also demonstrated less attachment to the Left.

Given this fundamental demographic fact, which persists to this day, Geoffrey B. Levey has described the demographic distribution of the American Jewish Left as a "curvilinear pattern," peaking between the poles of orthodox commitment and communal detachment.[17] This most basic and consistent fact points to the functional dimension of the Jewish Left for those secular ethnic Jews from Eastern Europe who have predominated within it: in the United States, if not elsewhere, the Jewish Left was not just politically expedient but rather socially useful in the renovation and retention of a secular ethnic Jewish identity.[18]

In *Jazz Age Jews*, historian Michael Alexander makes similar note of a utilitarian foundation to American Jews' ideological expressions. He observes that for Jews born in America in the early twentieth century, "in any way calculable by socioeconomic statistics, five hundred years of alienation had ended."

> At least so it would seem. Yet as this generation took its place among other middle-class groups in American society, some of its members displayed a peculiar behavior that did not correspond to their new social positions: They acted as though they were increasingly marginalized. What is more, many identified themselves with less fortunate individuals and groups, people who remained in America's economic, political, and cultural margins. Jews did this by imitating, defending, and actually participating in the group life of marginalized Americans. I call this behavior *outsider identification*, and it is a paradox in the psychology of American Jewry. As Jews moved up, they identified down.[19]

The concept of marginality has been used credibly to explain the Jewish Left in the United States and elsewhere, but it is Alexander's emphasis on dimensions of self-marginalization that comes closer to the argument in this book. According to Alexander, Jews shared with other European immigrants a basic experience as newcomers, but they were the "only group that, as a group, identified with people more marginalized than themselves." This tendency made for a "long career of self-marginalization on the part of the children of the great migration." Ceasing by and large to observe Judaism's traditional commandments or to live under rabbinical authority, American Jews were still influenced by and acted out a "lived religion" of secularized theological concepts of exile and covenant and sacralized historical legacies of persecution. Jewish identity had historically been "fused with outsider status." It was "threatened by perceived social integration," Alexander observes, and so "to halt such integration, Jewish communities revitalized their social distinctions from time to time, *intentionally* impairing their economic, political, and cultural relations with gentiles." Thus, when "Jews were succeeding, they identified with those who were not." In this way, upwardly mobile "Jews met the obligation of their own definition of themselves as a marginalized people."[20]

Three major figures from interwar New York City, "who marked themselves off from American society and were celebrated by their Jewish peers for doing so," illustrate Alexander's contention. First, Arnold Rothstein became king of the gambling underworld. He was "exalted" by the Yiddish press "for being a trans-gressive power," and excused by the Anglo-Jewish press "by finding sources for his behavior in the oppression of Jews in Eastern Europe," despite his middle-class upbringing in Manhattan. Second, Felix Frankfurter became the most vocal champion for murdering anarchists Nicola Sacco and Bartolomeo Vanzetti. They "were political outsiders, and thus became a Jewish cause," much more so than an Italian one. Finally, Al Jolson and other Jews revived blackface and ragtime in American theater and cinema, to great popular acclaim. They depicted African Americans "for their own ends" so as "to see in African-American life their own story of exile and slavery."[21]

Alexander focuses on the early members of the Second Generation. This book extends the scope to include both their parents and their children, who demon-strated similar tendencies. It explores the Jewish Left across much of the twen-tieth century as a politics of nonassimilation. If, as contemporary historian of American Jewry Jonathan Sarna has insisted, the tension between assimilation and the maintenance of Jewish identity is "probably the foremost challenge of American Jewish life,"[22] then this book emphasizes the extent to which, more than other groups of appropriate reference, American Jews from Eastern Europe placed their ethnic identity before conformity to the country's once hegemonic Protestant bourgeoisie. Various left-wing ideologies served as both vehicle and content for ethnic assertion and self-fulfillment: vehicle, by criticizing bourgeois conformity and standards as well as advocating pluralism or multiculturalism; content, by doing much to validate the self-image, informed by "lived religion," of Jews as outsiders in exile and alienation with a unique moral insight derived from this condition. Each chapter of this book engages directly with those authors who have insisted to the contrary that the Jewish Left reflected a desire to assimilate.

The efforts of three generations—broadly, Jewish immigrants from Eastern Europe, their children, and their grandchildren or baby boomers—to express and assure a whole and undiminished ethnic identity in the United States are explored in the three following chapters. Each chapter includes an introduction and a conclusion, and its main body is divided into two parts. The first part of each chapter describes the life or affairs of persons—whether an individual or an organized group of individuals—who reveal much about their respective generation. This part also provides contextual information about the Jews' socioeconomic status and their political proclivities by comparison with others in each respective period. The second part analyzes and interprets that life or those affairs in relation to Jewish identity.

The First Generation is explored through the case of Alexander Bittelman, who was born in Ukraine in 1892, moved to New York City in 1912 during the peak period of Eastern European Jewish migration to the United States, and went on to become a founder of the American Communist Party after the First World War. The outsiders with whom Bittelman and his peers identified were the working class and the poor. The Second Generation is explored through the case of the American Jewish Congress, which came together in 1918 and launched significant campaigns against felt discrimination within civil society before, during, and especially after the Second World War. The outsider identification here was primarily with African Americans. The Third Generation is explored through the case of New Jewish Agenda (NJA), which was founded in 1980 and criticized Israel from within the Jewish community. This case reveals the functional dimension of Jewish liberalism in reverse. When the organization criticized Israel, it was ostracized by the American Jewish community and its establishment, indicating the limits of the broad political orientation that they otherwise shared in kind if not degree. New Jewish Agenda, ironically, identified with the Palestinians as an oppressed people.

These cases have been chosen for a number of reasons. Notably, they have been overlooked (Bittelman), understudied (the American Jewish Congress), or unexplored (NJA). This dearth of scholarly attention may be explained by many causes, about which it would be unduly speculative to make any definitive claims, but at least one plausible factor is that information on these figures or groups is by and large confined to various archives. What is more, the archival collections on the American Jewish Congress and NJA have not been cataloged in full. The laboriousness of archival research, especially in non- or semicataloged collections, may have deterred scrutiny. All the same, the archival foundation of this text enhances the contribution to the various fields on which it touches, including Jewish, American, intellectual and radical history. It also accounts for the structural decision to move from individual (Bittelman) to organization (American Jewish Congress) to organization (NJA), as the choice of cases was affected by the limitations that the available archival material imposed. Nonetheless, all these cases have in common the fact that they have allowed for a thorough and novel investigation not only of their own affairs, but also of the political commitments of their respective generations. The relatively shorter space devoted to NJA is a reflection of its relatively shorter period of operation; this third and final case also builds on the arguments and data as laid out in the preceding chapters.

In seeking to explain the American Jewish Left, this study, with its longitudinal scope and archival emphasis, does not mean to deny or do without those other factors that are regularly cited within the literature as etiologically relevant, including antisemitism. Many of these factors are addressed in detail in the following chapters, and many would seem to be causally significant and even necessary. The functional dimension, however, may alone be sufficient to explain the phenomenon's transgenerational longevity and relative prominence. In pursuing such an interpretation of the American Jewish Left, moreover, there is no intention to impugn the contemporary sincerity of the actors under scrutiny. This work does not seek to judge philosophical perspectives, but to explain an ethnic phenomenon. It distinguishes between third-party justification and first-party motivation. A functional account or "utilitarian justification of an action may be," Roger Scruton has observed, "*inseparable* from a third-person viewpoint. It cannot be made part of the 'first-person' outlook which generates action. It will not, then, be a reason for the agent to do what he does, but only an endorsement of his action in the eyes of an observer."[23]

Alexander Bittelman, the Communist Party, and the First Generation

A Radical Life

Alexander Bittelman was a laborer and radical activist in the Russian empire as well as an immigrant to the United States in the early twentieth century. Some aspects of his upbringing and resettlement overseas were shared by most of the First Generation of American Jews of Eastern European provenance. As a prominent and important figure within the American Communist Party—its chief theorist in his own and others' estimation—he was extreme in his commitment and convictions, yet not entirely unlike many of his peers in the United States who became known for their unconventional political tendencies.[1] Bittelman's life provides insights into the radical movements of which he was a part and into the factors and motivations that made Eastern European Jews like him a pronounced element and force in those movements.

Bittelman left behind a large number of writings, including a massive, detailed autobiography of nearly fourteen hundred pages, as well as other lengthy texts on topics of personal and professional significance and interest. These documents provide considerable information about his personal life and political activities as well as musings on his Jewish identity. Despite his literary prolificacy and the important role he played in the American Communist Party, no published account of his life has been produced. Outside of the most specialized tomes on the history of American communism, in which the focus is on Bittelman as a radical rather than as a Jew, he has gone almost entirely unmentioned and unnoticed within Jewish studies. An investigation into his life provides an opportunity to learn about a committed member of the American Communist Party as well as about the First Generation and the possible sources and nature of its political behavior.

The main resource for this investigation is Bittelman's unpublished autobiography, "*Things I Have Learned*."[2] This document is straightforward and lucid in its description of people and places and its construction of events and moods. Its language is clear and emotionally direct. It brings grand history down to earth by way of personal experience and suggests relatively uncomplicated reasons and motives for the social and political behavior of the author as well as others of similar background and conditioning. Any autobiography may engender concerns about memory and bias. Such concerns do not, however, negate the usefulness of such narratives as primary sources. An autobiography may be cross-referenced with and contextualized by other sources, both primary and secondary, to measure its accuracy or to point out errors in judgment or recollection. In this vein, it may be noted of Bittelman's autobiography that on those occasions when it has been referred to by experts, it has been cited for its vivid descriptions and its general commensurability with known episodes and chronologies.[3]

In comparison with what has been a principal discourse within the field of Jewish studies—which tends to present Jewish communists as being communists before Jews, if Jews at all—Bittelman's case indicates otherwise.[4] It helps to rectify a tendency in the discipline by demonstrating that Bittelman's Jewishness was a formative inspiration for his radical outlook as well as an abiding preoccupation of his political and social life until his death at the advanced age of ninety-two. His radicalism emerged out of Jewish predicaments and Jewish feelings, including a childhood that was informed by Judaism and themes of exile, alienation, and messianic redemption. He gravitated toward the Left as a vehicle for ethnic assertion and communal autonomy, and he imagined a future revolutionary society as one in which a state-managed and state-promoted multiculturalism would prevail against bourgeois expectations of Eastern European Jews' integration into the gentile world as individuals rather than as a group. His radicalism was, he came to realize, a kind of inverted nationalism by a member of a minority.

From Berdichev to Manhattan and Occasionally Back Again

Bittelman was born Usher-Anshell Bittelmacher on January 9, 1890, in Berdichev, Ukraine, to Avrom-Wolf, a shoemaker, and Deborah, an illiterate yet pious woman. Soon after his birth the family moved to the port city of Odessa, where they lived in a Jewish neighborhood for the next ten years. Throughout that time his parents considered migrating abroad to London, Paris, or New York, where relatives lived, yet they were daunted by the prospect of change and adjustment to new surroundings. An attempt by the father to settle in London at the turn of the century proved a disappointment, resulting in his return to Odessa after only seven months, an example of the kind of return migration that was more frequent than later imagined.[5] By 1900 the family had relocated back to Berdichev. In both Odessa and Berdichev, Bittelman attended Hebrew schools, where he learned about the Old Testament, the Prophets, and the Talmud. He later remembered the envy he felt toward the more affluent students, but he retained positive recollections of the synagogues and religious ceremonies in both cities.

Bittelman's first decade was not unduly eventful, but his early imagination was suffused with thoughts and images of the suffering and persecution of the Jewish people. This sense of oppression came less through direct experience than through the evocations of his elders, who mixed discussion of recent events, such as the pogroms of the early 1880s, in which a family member had been killed, with biblical legend and messianic expectation. A beloved grandfather, Samuel, left the greatest mark in this regard. The old man taught his grandson about Rabbi Moses—Bittelman's first and greatest hero, "the hero of all my heroes"—"who liberated the Jews from Egyptian slavery" and brought them out of exile to the promised land. In this schema, Czar Alexander III was another pharaoh, who inflicted cruelties on the Jewish people, including the restrictive May Laws of 1882, and whose death in 1894 was consequently welcomed. He was, as Bittelman heard from those around him, "that monster of a czar" and "the murderer, enemy of Israel." The belief that the czarist regime organized and condoned pogroms against Jews—"He always timed his pogroms for Passover"—was shared by the Bittelmachers.[6] Such views were widespread throughout the Pale, and though not always accurate, they allowed Jews to make sense of local events in terms that they readily understood.[7]

Tropes of exile, slavery, and redemption were transmitted to Bittelman such that oppression, first of Jews and then of others like them, constituted a lens through which he came to see the world. The familial loathing of the czar was early translated into rebellious sentiment against gentile authority and even gentile society, with which he had little contact as a Yiddish-speaking boy. The "cruelties of Alexander III and his advisor, especially towards the Jews, was more than enough to make me hate all autocracies and tyrannies," he wrote. "I was quite definitely a republican having heard from my father of such countries, as France and America, where the people were getting along very well without Czars and without Kings and where the Jews were not oppressed and persecuted." By the age of ten, "I had already acquired a strong sense of injustice in the world: the existence of rich and poor, strong and weak, Jews and their persecutors, especially the Czar; and also an equally strong sense of identity with the poor, to which I belonged, with the weak and powerless, and with the Jews, of course."[8]

Whereas his pious and traditional grandfather was relatively passive in the face of perceived hardship and maltreatment, Bittelman seems to have internalized and then secularized his grandfather's and his parents' messages, rendering them into a mentality of active protest. This shifting of the axis of attribution and retribution was common among diasporic Jews in the age of their emergence from their medieval structures of life—the age of so-called emancipation. Why were Jews degraded?

Why were they unproductive? Why did they have a low or marginal social status in the world of the gentiles? Reading Jewish memoirs and writings from the period, Benjamin Harshav has observed of contemporary American Jews, "we are amazed at how wretched, dirty, degenerate, illiterate, or ugly our ancestors appeared—only three or four generations ago."[9] There was a set number of archetypal answers to such questions. As the sociologist John Murray Cuddihy observed:

> As far as the condition of the Jews goes, at any given time the need for "betterment" due to "degradation," "inferiority" (call it what you will) can be either affirmed or denied. If it is affirmed, then it will be explained by the past. The traditional, observant Jew will explain it as part of sacred salvation history—that is, it is a punishment for Israel's sins. The secularizing, intellectual Jew will turn this theodicy inside out, forging it into an instrument with which to blame the Gentile. The older, intrapunitive theodicy becomes an exteropunitive sociodicy: "You made us what we are today," the secularist intelligentsia of the Diaspora insists, indicting the Gentile West.[10]

The young Bittelman presents a model case of this psychic transformation. His secularization led to his rejection of messianic anticipation or meekness as the correct response to felt Jewish adversity or inferiority. "Why doesn't God do something to our enemies? Why does he let them do what they are doing to us?" he would ask his grandfather. The old man would reply: "We remain in Exile, dispersed and persecuted. The Creator sees it and does not seem to do anything about it. Why? Because of our sins and transgressions. . . . We pray to God to have mercy on us, to shorten our sufferings." The grandfather felt similarly about Zionism; he "held very definite opinions. He would say: you don't come to the Creator of the World and try to prod him along."[11]

Such views were fairly typical of traditional Eastern European Jewry of Bittelman's grandfather's generation.[12] For Bittelman, however, they proved insufficient. About God he would ask, "Why is He doing nothing to protect His people from pogroms and all other persecutions?" As a rejoinder was not forthcoming, Bittelman began to conclude "that, if You, the Creator of the World, does not see fit to put to right some of the wrongs in human life and relations, we shall try to do it without you. We meaning the workers and all the poor people." This tendency was reinforced when Bittelman, compelled to drop out of Hebrew school and to find work, apprenticed to a printer at the age of eleven, successfully "participated in my first economic strike . . . in the summer of 1902" with the help of an older colleague, who also introduced him to the notion of class struggle and the writings and philosophy of Tolstoy.[13]

By age thirteen, Bittelman had become a member of the General Jewish Workers' Union in Lithuania, Poland, and Russia—commonly known as the

Bund—founded in Vilna in 1897 as a Marxist party of the Jewish proletariat.[14] It was an organic development. Bittelman was enrolled by his father's friend Isaac, a glove maker, who gave exhortatory speeches to small groups of men in the Bittelmachers' house. When the young Bittelman heard Isaac speak, "Naturally, I couldn't yet know or fully understand the program and theory of the Bund." Nonetheless, Isaac's words fit into Bittelman's received Jewish paradigm, enabling him to make immediate sense of Isaac's heartfelt declamations against "the injustices and brutalities of the entire existing social and political systems"; "socialism, revolution and republic were to me . . . dream-images of some bright and joyful future, something like what would happen when the Messiah arrived." Bittelman was notably impressed by "the way that he [Isaac] would speak of the sufferings of the Jewish workers as Jews":

> According to him, the Jewish workers in Czarist Russia were carrying a double burden: the burden of exploited workers which they shared with all other workers in Russia and the burden of an oppressed and discriminated and persecuted nationality. Never before had I seen the special Jewish miseries in the Czar's empire in quite that light.[15]

For the young Bittelman, the Jews were oppressed, as were the workers, by the same czarist regime that had persecuted his grandfather. Such basic thoughts are repeated throughout Bittelman's memoirs. They constituted an example of what Michael Alexander has called "outsider identification," whereby Jewish self-perceptions of exile and alienation were projected onto members of other groups deemed to meet this definition.[16] They sum up the mental trajectory of Bittelman's adolescent initiation into an adversarial social, political, and cultural orientation, a trajectory ostensibly shared by many of his peers.[17] Jewishness and socialism were early fused in Bittelman's mind. His conflation of the interests and causes of the Yiddish-speaking Jewish masses, on the one hand, and the workers and their supposed representatives, including eventually the Soviet Union, on the other, remained a crux of his worldview for his entire life, at times engendering cognitive dissonance when the two did not obviously or immediately coincide.

Already in adolescence Bittelman was aware that the more moderate Bund, to which he remained committed, and the general Russian Social Democratic Labor Party, to which he was attracted, were often at odds on the issue of Jews. Notably, he was "troubled by the differences between the Bund and most of the party leaders on the so-called national question." The latter's argument in favor of Jewish assimilation as progressive "didn't appeal to me at all. Why can Lenin's Russian workers and Kautsky's German workers cultivate their own national languages and literatures and art without . . . hurting working class solidarity?" After all,

"I knew I was a Jew; I wanted to continue to be a Jew; and I wanted a Jewish national cultural life." That such aspirations constituted "a nationalist, a reactionary, an anti-socialist proposition" according to Vladimir Lenin, Karl Kautsky, and others—"All of this was very hard to take. But what do you do about it? You continue to be a loyal member of the Bund and do your best to fight for freedom and socialism. And that was what I tried to do."[18]

Thus, Bittelman remained a Bundist, even as he increasingly sympathized with the Bolsheviks due to their uncompromising revolutionary zeal. The two seemed to go together in his mind. His logic was simple:

> As to the differences between the Bund and the Zionists, that didn't interest me at all. The Bund's answer to the Jewish problem in Russia—full equality of civil and political rights in a democratic republic coupled with national-cultural autonomy—this was to me fully satisfactory. And the way to achieve that was the revolutionary overthrow of the Czarist autocracy. Following that will be the socialist revolution which will solve *all* problems. And there will be no more a Jewish problem.[19]

In pursuit of this vision, Bittelman had become a Bundist activist by the time he was fifteen, participating in demonstrations, attending classes, and joining an armed Jewish self-defense group. Even though he and his father journeyed to Paris in spring 1905 to assess possible resettlement of the family there, Bittelman's ardor was such that he left his father after only a few months, returning to Berdichev so as to help organize trade unions and strikes and to oppose anti-Jewish violence. (His father gave up on France and returned home in early 1909.) Over the next seven years Bittelman operated in this capacity for the Bund in Berdichev and other cities throughout Russian Ukraine, including Odessa, where he faced the hostility of middle-class Zionists. He was jailed and released several times, but he remembered most such episodes as "exciting, interesting and instructive," in part because the political prisons to which he was sent "weren't so bad" and were often "in reality more in the nature of a permanent and continuing debating assembly or congress or a club rather than a jail." Of his banishment to and exile in the remote arctic hamlet of Yuroma from summer 1909 to summer 1910, Bittelman reminisced: "My experiences in the little village of Russia's Far North remained forever a bright and warm moment in my memory and feelings."[20]

Although the Russian penal system is depicted as harsh, often by foreigners, Bittelman's rather sanguine recollections of his incarceration were neither inapt nor simply the product of nostalgia for youthful exploits. Political prisoners in late imperial Russia were treated with more leniency than other criminals, and they usually "faced their punishments without great fear." What is more, "one of the key advantages of the prerevolutionary Russian prisons was the ability of prisoners to read and write, or 'to further their political education,' as they often put it. [They] were allowed to have any publications except those prohibited in public libraries or journals appearing in the previous twelve months."[21] Bittelman began his study of Karl Marx in Yuroma. He considered *Capital* to be unduly obscure and was "on the verge of giving it up several times in the course of our study," yet in later years, "I found my early studies in Yuroma to have been quite helpful."[22] Like many, his Marxism was an *ex post facto* rationalization of a preexisting set of prejudices.[23] His socialism was not a science, as he once insisted, but rather, as he recognized later in life, a kind of faith: "From the very beginning, from the very time I first heard Isaac speak of it to the Berdichev shoeworkers at the memorable meetings in my father's house. . . . It was a belief and a faith in an ideal. Marxism showed me how to get there. Marxism did not take away my belief and faith in the ideal."[24]

In his memoirs Bittelman described his encounters with the agencies of the despised czarist regime more as corrupt and overbearing than as willfully vicious—an irony of which some radicals later became aware after the establishment of a far harsher and more inhumane Soviet penal system.[25] When Bittelman wrote to the governor of Archangelsk, after a year in Yuroma, requesting to complete his exile in the nearby town of Mezen, he was permitted to leave, "despite all expectations." Mezen proved more suited to Bittelman, not least because there were other Jews and Bundists there with whom he could speak Yiddish. In the hamlet of Yuroma he had missed above all a familiar and warm popular Jewish culture or *yidishkeyt*:

> It was amazing to realize how much I had missed the Jewish environment without being conscious of it. Of course, on second thought, I understood perfectly that this was natural. After all, I grew up in a Jewish environment and for most of my conscious life up till then, I mingled very little with the non-Jewish environments. . . . Perhaps the novelty of the different environments, the interesting new people and experiences, the good friendship and comradeship . . . perhaps all of that obscured from my consciousness for a while the feeling of separation and loss. But it was there, alright. . . . The meeting and brief sojourn with my Bundist comrade—Samuel, was his name—precipitated my realization of how much I had been missing my so-called natural milieu. Even talking Yiddish with Samuel, who knew Russian very well, was an exciting experience.[26]

Bittelman returned to the *yidishkeyt* of Berdichev in early 1911, after finishing his political exile with "quite a few jolly parties with drink and song aplenty."

Despite hopes of settling down permanently in that majority-Jewish city, he began to consider emigration overseas due to an increasing awareness of his "approaching hour for military service." His anxious parents encouraged him to leave. Letters from "old comrades, who had left for America several years back . . . encouraging some of their friends to join them" were an additional inducement, being "very enthusiastic about the city of New York" and "the large and great socialist movement in America . . . in which Jewish workers took a very active part." In the fall Bittelman opted to go "away very reluctantly in a rather unhappy frame of mind. America's image was not attractive to me. It was a land of selfish, egotistic people, bent on making money—dollars—and nothing else."[27] All the same, he went, evading the czar's army, with a ticket purchased, as was common, with passage money supplied by friends who were already resident in New York.[28]

Departing from Antwerp, Belgium, on the *Vaderland*, Bittelman arrived at Ellis Island in early January 1912. He recalled that the passengers on his ship "were mostly younger people," and "the majority were Jews."[29] This demographic observation is not surprising. His journey may have been subjectively made for immediately personal reasons, but Bittelman objectively took part in a vast movement of people that significantly affected the course of Jewish history. He immigrated during the peak decade before the outbreak of the First World War, when more than one and one-quarter million Eastern European Jews arrived in the United States, a majority of whom settled in the city of New York and nearby areas.[30] Perhaps more surprising is Bittelman's depiction of his experience crossing the Atlantic: "The ten days of sailing passed very quickly. I enjoyed every minute of it."[31] Bittelman's descriptions of Ellis Island and the officials by whom he was interviewed for admission into the country are also positive, notwithstanding that he informed them quite openly of his political activities and imprisonment in Russia.[32]

The young immigrant's early years in the United States were encouraging, despite emotional qualms over becoming American, because "my Jewishness, my feelings of identification with and belonging to the Jewish people, was with the Jews of Russia." Upon his arrival Bittelman met up and stayed with friends from New York's large "Berdichev colony," and he gradually established contact with the "social and cultural environment of the Jewish socialists and trade unionists."[33] He did not pass through the Lower East Side—the famous crowded immigrants' ghetto in Manhattan—but immediately rented a flat in Harlem, which he "considered a center of the advanced immigrant youth."[34] He found employment as a typesetter, quickly achieving higher wages by moving from firm to firm. Within two years he had been admitted to Cooper Union, and soon thereafter he became a civil engineer, ceasing to be a laborer and beginning to move into the middle class in terms of his material and occupational profile. Bittelman's mobility was swift, and while it was more rapid than many of his peers', it was not entirely exceptional. As Arcadius Kahan observed of the economic progress of Eastern European Jewish immigrants who arrived in the United States in the period from 1890 to 1914:

> Despite their initial disabilities of language and skills, each cohort of Jewish immigrants caught up in earnings with the native American workers of the same age and in similar occupations within 10–15 years. This is a record of achievement that is all the more remarkable when we consider that the real earnings of natives were also rising during these years.[35]

No other group of immigrants flourished more in the United States, under its system of government and socioeconomic organization, than did the Eastern European Jews. Kahan's study is limited to the period before 1914, because after the First World War the Jewish working class, whose existence had been maintained due to ongoing mass immigration, began a terminal decline in sync with the decline in the number of new Jewish arrivals and then their exclusion from the country after the imposition of entry restrictions in the 1920s.[36] In 1916 the Lower East Side held around 353,000 Jews; in 1935 it held 98,000.[37] Immigration was not the only factor in this process; New York was not alone in the transience of its Jewish proletariat. As Bernard Harshav noted of interwar Eastern European Jews and their settlements worldwide: "A new Jewish proletariat was formed in Warsaw, Kharkov, New York, Tel Aviv, and other cities, encouraged by ideology and social pressures, but it dissolved everywhere within one generation."[38] Observations of a similar nature were made by contemporaries.[39] Jews were nowhere an enduring proletariat.

This is not to deny the First Generation's hardships. Conditions for many, especially on the Lower East Side, were arduous. They are and were well recorded. Yet what was true of the conditions in Jewish districts of New York City and other urban industrial conglomerations was usually equally if not more true of other white ethnic neighborhoods. As one contemporary declaimed: "Pathetic descriptions of the dirt, misery and squalor of the Ghetto are common. . . . The fact is usually disregarded that there is a great deal more dirt, misery and squalor in Italian, Irish and other kindred 'ghettos' of Manhattan Island."[40] What is more, the denizens of these "kindred 'ghettos'" did not experience the rapid mobility of their Jewish counterparts, who, even when "causal factors are controlled as completely as the [historical] data allow," were more mobile.[41] The Jews "throve in their crowded tenements—in a shorter time than any other group, the Jews left the tenements."[42] Eastern European Jews on the Lower East Side were healthier (even more so than native-born Yankees), relatively well paid, and more adept at reestablishing the institutional nexus of communal life than all other immigrant groups.[43] Half achieved white-collar status after fifteen to twenty-five years in the United States.[44] Finally, they did not have to contend with the dangerous antisemitism that was prevalent in parts of Eastern Europe. Disdain for and discrimination against Jews existed, but analogous sentiments were also expressed toward or by other immigrant groups, whose members did not by and large behave politically in the same way as the First Generation.[45]

Promising developments and relatively favorable conditions in the United States did not—as they did not in Bittelman's case—obviously mitigate the emergence among Yiddish-speaking Jews of a "culture of protest, which became their hallmark."[46] Even as Jews prospered in the New World more quickly and fully than did other immigrant groups, and eventually even more than natives, they also dissented more often and openly. As historian Hadassah Kosak has emphasized, Eastern European Jews "were new immigrants who, despite their recent arrival in the United States, were determined to participate as self-conscious actors in social and political struggles. They demanded, at all times, full economic and political rights for themselves and their community." The First Generation was not made up of "passive historical agents overwhelmed by industrial capitalism. On the contrary, the community's political culture was pervasive, distinctive, and influential."[47]

The most conspicuous and constant expression of this political culture was socialism, and Jews from the Russian empire were, with the possible exception of the far smaller cohort of Finns, the most consistently and persistently radical of all immigrant groups. Irish immigrants were almost entirely immune to socialism, and Germans, who are often credited with importing a social-democratic tradition to the United States, were only radical in parts, such that "we cannot speak of an affinity between Germans [as a whole] and socialist voting."[48] By comparison, "even though Russians [Jews] tended to concentrate in urban and working-class counties, where we would expect socialist voting to be highest, the overall coefficient for Russians is positive despite control variables tapping these influences." This result is "particularly impressive, because New York, which has been the focus of intensive case study, does not exert undue influence on these results."[49] Radicalism emerged in most Jewish settlements. What is more, there was no obvious, direct correlation between Jewish radicalism, on the hand, and class or economic need, on the other. According to Daniel Soyer, Jewish "immigrant socialists promoted the proletarian cause, even as they aspired to leave the proletariat behind." This disjuncture "between the social ideals and personal goals of many Jews" eventually meant that "outside of New York and the other large manufacturing centers, the Jewish labor movement itself often consisted entirely of small businesspeople."[50]

Radical tendencies within the Yiddish-speaking population were in evidence as early as the mid-1880s, when the mayoral candidate Henry George, and later the Socialist Labor Party (SLP) that backed him, received a significantly disproportionate percentage of an otherwise small Jewish vote.[51] By the mid-1890s Jews had come to rival German immigrants as the predominant ethnic group in the SLP.[52] By this time, moreover, the mainstream American press was reporting on the radicalism within the immigrant Jewish community, often with notable disapproval. The *New York Times* opined in 1893:

> The boys and callow youths of the Russian-Jewish quarter, weaned on the pestiferous milk of Nihilism and dynamite throwing, long insanely to demolish law and order and the police, as American boys and youths long, with equal insanity, to go out West and kill Indians. . . . On these depraved, diseased, diabolical natures the appalling nonsense of creatures like [Emma] Goldman falls like alcohol on a kindling flame.[53]

After 1901 the incipient radical propensities of the First Generation were largely redirected to the Socialist Party of America (SPA), which split off from the SLP in that year and soon surpassed this rival predecessor to embody the dissident American Left for the next two decades. Much of the SPA's early support came from rural western states, but Jews were notable in the party's leadership from its inception and became increasingly numerous in the rank and file during and after the First World War.[54] This demographic shift was reflected in the portion of the party's membership that was located in foreign-language federations, to which many Jews belonged: nearly one-sixth in 1912, nearly one-third in 1918, and over one-half in 1919 (out of around 110,000 persons in that year).[55] As Daniel Bell noted, "The rising strength of the Socialist Party in the urban East, and particularly in New York, was due in great measure to the high tide of European, and particularly Jewish, immigration. These new immigrants—again particularly the Jewish group—provided the sinews which sustained the American Socialist Party until 1932," after which it was largely undone by the attraction of the New Deal.[56]

For himself, Bittelman joined the Harlem branch of the SPA's Jewish federation at the "end of 1914 or beginning of 1915"—not long after having studied civil engineering—and soon became its secretary.[57] The Jewish Socialist Federation (JSF) had around five thousand members at that time, behind the Finnish and German sections, although many Jews participated in the party's other branches.[58] The JSF was, as Bittelman noted aptly, "not of the largest in the Socialist party but one of the more important," given its connections to the large Jewish garment unions and other prosocialist Jewish organizations, including fraternal orders.[59] These institutions were an important part of the radical Yiddish subculture of the First Generation, and they became "the financial backbone and chief orga-nizational props of the Socialist Party."[60] During the 1910s and early 1920s—the "Golden Age of Yiddish Socialism"[61]—Jews became "the party's single largest repository of electoral support."[62] This was so even though most Jewish immi-grants were neither naturalized nor registered to vote as late as 1920, and even though many chose to back conventional candidates in practice due to strategic and material considerations, despite endorsing socialism in principle or in other contexts.[63] As a contemporary recalled of this dual consciousness, "Election Day was one thing and being a member of the Socialist Party was another," because the "politicians who got the petty things done for the Lower East Side were not the socialists," but the Democrats of Tammany Hall.[64]

During the golden age as much as half of the Jewish vote in numerous New York and other elections went to various socialist candidates. Many of these candidates gained office, including one congressman in 1914, Meyer London, a Jewish immigrant.[65] In 1920 the socialist presidential candidate, Eugene Debs, of whose reputation Bittelman was aware even in Berdichev, received nearly 40 percent of the total Jewish vote—a record level of Jewish support for a third-party candidate, then and since—as compared to a national 3.5 percent.[66] Of the 915,000 votes cast for Debs—also a record for the SPA, then and since—more than 200,000 came from New York State, and more than 130,000 came from New York City alone (in itself larger than any state vote).[67] The First Generation probably made up most of this latter number, as the SPA and its candidates "never made any real headway in any section of New York City not dominated by Jewish Americans."[68] Jewish unions, renowned for their militancy, played a role in producing such electoral outcomes by promulgating radical socialist ideas and viewpoints and promoting various socialist candidates. They were power-ful entities in their interwar heyday. Whereas the Jewish-dominated garment industry's rate of unionization increased from 17 percent in 1910 to 58 percent in 1920, American manufacturing's average rate of unionization in 1920 was 23 percent, and the structurally similar yet Catholic-dominated textile industry's rate was 15 percent.[69]

Bittelman was very much a part of this radical Yiddish subculture. He knew well that the revolutionary socialism to which he was attached was neither pop-ular nor effective in the United States as a whole. This awareness did not cause him to reassess his political loyalties, but "to seek the reasons" for the SPA's lack of success "in the inadequacies of policies," which could be rectified.[70] Bittelman quickly devoted himself to this course. Within a year of joining the JSF—which, to Bittelman's satisfaction, "enjoyed . . . a large measure of autonomy in matters of language, cultural activities, press and internal affairs of organization"—he began writing articles for the section's Yiddish-language weekly, *Di naye velt*

(*The New World*), which was edited by a former Bundist, Yankev Salutsky (later J. B. S. Hardman). The articles focused "on the 'war aims' of the warring powers" and on the positions of the mainstream and radical parties in relation to American neutrality toward and then entrance into the First World War. Bittelman supported Wilson's policy of neutrality, for he, along with most of the First Generation, "wished with all my heart for the defeat of Russian czarism" by imperial Germany.[71]

When the United States did enter the First World War on the side of Britain, France, and Russia in April 1917, Bittelman was disappointed by this development yet consoled by the antiwar resolution that the SPA passed at an emergency convention in St. Louis, Missouri, the next day.[72] He recognized, however, that there were some within the SPA who were more antiwar than others.[73] There were those who were vehemently and actively opposed, and there were those, "mostly among the leaders" and the Anglo-Saxon native born, who "didn't like the war but were not prepared to do anything worth while to build an effective opposition to it," in part due to attachment to England and in part due to governmental pressures and intimidation.[74] Bittelman sided with the former and viewed the latter as lax. For him, the St. Louis convention constituted "the first distinct indications . . . of a new political and ideological current and grouping in the Socialist party which later crystallized into the Left Wing of 1918, the group that subsequently organized the Communist party of America."[75]

The incipient split, precipitated by the American involvement in the First World War, was deepened and widened by the Bolshevik revolution later that year, which was greeted with enthusiasm in many Jewish quarters, both in New York and elsewhere.[76] For Bittelman, this revolution was and remained "the greatest event in this century":

> I had no doubts about the greatness of the revolution itself, about its being a revolution for socialism. . . . Nor did I have any doubt that socialists everywhere, including America, would have to study very carefully the lessons of the Bolshevik revolution; and to do so, not just for academic purposes, but in order to learn how to make use of these lessons to promote the cause of socialism in the United States.[77]

Bittelman viewed the Bolshevik coup "as a historic opportunity to spread the socialist revolution," as did most within the SPA's various foreign-language federations. A "feeling of an approaching storm was especially aroused in us," Bittelman recalled, "by the widespread strike struggles and sharp industrial conflict in the years when the left wing was taking shape—1917, 1918, 1919. We talked a lot about Seattle . . . [and] also about the General Strike in Winnipeg."[78] This sense of urgency typified the left wing of the SPA, which diverged from the older, more staid leadership on the means to, if not the ends of, socialism. As one of the party's leaders, Morris Hillquit (né Hillkowitz), emphasized: "The division was not brought about by differences on vital questions of principles. It arose over disputes on methods and policy, and even within that limited sphere it was largely one of emphasis rather than fundamentals." The "newly baptized 'Communists' have not ceased to be Socialists," he averred. All the same, "they are wrong in their estimate of American conditions, their theoretical conditions and practical methods, but they have not deserted to the enemy. . . . When the hour of the real Socialist fight strikes in this country, we may find them again in our ranks."[79]

Bittelman came to share many of these views later in life, reconsidering above all his erstwhile commitment to the Leninist "theory of the dictatorship of the proletariat" and the concomitant idea that the democratic socialist "experiment must be conducted exclusively by people who are convinced of the need of such an experiment and are determined to make it succeed."[80] In the excitement of the immediate postwar period, however, he and others regarded allusions to the exigencies of American conditions and procedural proprieties as an evasion of revolutionary commitment in a period of impending global revolt.[81] Bittelman viewed the Democratic Party as no different than the Republican, and he insisted that the SPA was made up of elements "who have submitted to a bourgeois point of view" on the crucial issues of property, government, and class.[82]

Unperturbed by any incongruity in the fact that he, a foreign-born alien, was seeking the radical transformation of his very recently adopted country,[83] Bittelman early became an advocate, from within the JSF's Harlem branch, of immediate socialist revolution and centralized technocratic rule—by himself and those like him, for "we couldn't very well share party leadership with the Right or the Center. We had to have it all to ourselves." In support of this position, he published, along with several friends, "a declaration" in *Di naye velt* in early 1919.[84] This document brought Bittelman to the attention of the coalescing left wing of the JSF and subsequently a position as the editor of its small newspaper, *Der kamf* (or *The Struggle*).[85] He later remarked of this promotion that "to have myself in the position of an editor—AN EDITOR—was no small thing in my life. I felt bigger and more important and, for all I knew, my behavior may have shown that change and not always from the most sympathetic side."[86]

Such jejune reminiscences convey some of the pettiness and fantasy that characterized the left wing of American socialism, about which Bittelman later lamented.[87] Due in part to such traits, the various factions of the left wing proved remarkably incapable of cooperation.[88] With incessant jockeying for small authority, power, and status—Bittelman himself was always wary of and vigilant against any real or perceived attempts by others to usurp his influence—it took years and manifold debates, meetings, and conventions, as well as considerable intervention by Moscow, for a unified American communist party to emerge from the breakup of the SPA in the aftermath of the Bolshevik revolution. Even then, internecine disputes and rivalries persisted interminably. Bittelman covered these twists and turns in significant detail in his memoirs. His autobiographical account may be compared, and generally very well for factual and chronological accuracy, to a pamphlet that he published on the subject in the 1930s, *Fifteen Years of the Communist Party*, and to academic tomes on American communism by specialists. As Bittelman summarized in that pamphlet:

> The formative period in the history of our Party appears as a development from Left Socialism to Communism. The essence of the development consisted in this, that the Left Wing of the Socialist Party (1918–1919) was gradually freeing itself from vacillation between reformism and ultra-Left radicalism by means of an ever closer approach to the positions of Marxism-Leninism.[89]

An official break by the left wing with the SPA occurred in summer 1919, by which time many of the more extreme foreign-language federations had been expelled or suspended from the party, whose membership was thereby greatly reduced. In June a conference was held in New York City, which "was to decide the future course of the Left Wing."[90] There Bittelman decided to lead his own left-wing faction out of the JSF, eventually forming the Jewish Communist Federation (JCF).[91] In September he and his comrades attended a follow-up convention in Chicago at which not one but two organizations—the Communist Party (CP) and the Communist Labor Party (CLP)—were created. Bittelman was elected to the central executive committee of the former even as some of his comrades, including those who managed *Der kamf*, joined the latter. As a result, Bittelman founded and began to edit his own Yiddish-language monthly, *Di funken* (or *Sparks*). Soon after these propitious developments, however, the anti-red "Palmer raids" began, which by early 1920 had the effect of "driving our party—and the Communist Labor party—underground" and so, counterproductively, making "us feel considerably more important for the future of American socialism."[92]

This repression caused a significant drop in the membership of the communist parties, from as much as forty thousand to ten thousand, but did not bring the two groups together.[93] "From the moment of their separate births," historian Bryan Palmer has written, "the large Communist Party adhered to a conception of itself as the anointed vanguard of American communism, rebuffing attempts on the part of its rivals to foster unity."[94] The leaders of the CP, largely members of European foreign-language federations, like Bittelman, doubted the Marxist intellectual credentials of the more pragmatic heads of the CLP, who were mainly English speaking and more native born (although both parties' bases were overwhelmingly alien in composition).[95] They also felt antagonized by the CLP's demands "for the abolition of the autonomous rights of the leading bodies of the federations." Bittelman desired unity, but "I wasn't at all prepared to sacrifice the federations, to help liquidate certain of their autonomies in the party structure and, above all, their political and ideological influence on the leadership of the party." He wanted to have "the English-speaking fellows in and at the head of the party and the federations setting the party's ideological and political course." His preference, he considered, "may have been influenced in part by my outlooks and experiences in the Bund in Russia."[96]

Squabbling between the two communist groups continued through May 1921, "when the Communist movement finally became united" at the behest of the Comintern.[97] A new weekly publication, *Der emes* (or *The Truth*), replaced *Di funken* as the party's Yiddish-language organ.[98] (*Der emes* was the name of the Yiddish-language communist paper in Bolshevik Russia.) Discord persisted, however, as the formally united party was in turn divided between those who wished to remain a covert underground organization and those who wanted the underground apparatus to merge with and liquidate itself into the party's above-ground, public legal front, which by December 1921 had taken the form of the Workers' Party (WP). Bittelman, along with James Cannon and others, was a liquidator; his undergroundist opponents were arrayed in what became known as the Goose Caucus.[99] Seeking to resolve what fast became a fierce internal dispute, Bittelman traveled with Cannon to Moscow in May 1922 to gain the support of the Comintern "for our side in intra-party differences."[100]

Bittelman's "first visit to Soviet Russia was a memorable event in my life." His two main purposes on that trip were to aid Cannon against the Goose Caucus before the Comintern and to "establish contact and collaboration between the Jewish Communists of the American party with the Jewish Communists of the Soviet party." In so doing, he came across a number of notable individuals, including Grigory Zinoviev, Karl Radek, Leon Trotsky, Joseph Stalin, and Antonio Gramsci, and became friendly and fairly intimate with the heads of Jewish communism in the Soviet Union, many of whom had been "leading members" of the Bund. With these former Bundists he "had many get-togethers, chats and discussions."[101] Bittelman also traveled to Berdichev to visit his family. As such, he participated in "a larger movement of [American Jewish] tourists to the Soviet Union" during the interwar period, many of whom were socialists, eager to witness the new revolutionary society in the making.[102] Like many other Western radicals, who "tended to confirm their preconceptions" and "were ready to be impressed" in the Soviet Union,[103] Bittelman was pleased and enthused by what he saw, notwithstanding the "awfully depressing stories" of the Ukrainian famine about which he heard from his parents and his poor reception by an anti-Bolshevik aunt.[104]

Returning to New York City before Cannon in fall 1922, Bittelman was chagrined to discover there "a new comrade in our midst, in the leading circles of the party. His name here was John Pepper," though he had been known as Jószef Pogány in his native Hungary (where he had been a member of the short-lived, disproportionately Jewish, Bolshevik regime of Béla Kun).[105] Pepper "was the official representative of the Communist International to the American Community Party," remembered as short, arrogant, proud, and power hungry by Whittaker Chambers.[106] Bittelman's resentment and frustration at the intrusion of this strong-willed "stranger" resounded in his memoirs. He wrote petulantly of "Pepper's coming" that it "had been a deliberate move to undermine my influence and standing in the Jewish Buro," and what is more, that "Pepper and his friends had to get the Jewish section under their own influence and this meant, under the circumstances, to get the section out of the influence of Bittelman and his friends."[107] As the "Jewish Federation was one of the most important of the foreign-language groups" in the WP, Bittelman sought to retain his control of it.[108]

By the fall of 1922 the JCF had grown in prestige and size through the incorporation of the JSF, which, under Yankev Salutsky and Moyshe Olgin, had finally left the faltering SPA in December 1921. These men had helped set up *Di frayhayt* (*Freedom*) in April 1922, which superseded *Der emes. Di frayhayt* not only "attracted the most impressive array of poets and fiction writers of any Yiddish newspaper" in the country, but also became an important communist organ in its own right.[109] At various points in its existence it surpassed the party's principal English-language newspaper, the *Daily Worker*, in circulation. It was frequently a key source of funds for the CP and often subsidized the operation of the *Daily Worker*.[110]

As with the JCF in general, the relative strength of *Di frayhayt* reflected the relative strength of communism among the First Generation. Few Jews, and few other Americans, were communists, but a disproportionate number of communists and fellow-travelers in the United States were Jews.[111] The early membership of the CP was demographically diverse, including many Finns and South Slavs, notwithstanding that a majority were foreigners from the eastern half of Europe. The Jewish element within the party was the most stable and dedicated, and it would expand most over time even as overall membership increased during the decade of the Great Depression. As Nathan Glazer noted in his study of the social bases of American communism, "It was from New York that the cadres came; it was New York that was steady and dependable, while the trade-union leadership and industrial membership was often in danger of defection and softening."[112]

Other areas of Jewish concentration outside of New York, like Boston and Los Angeles, also resulted in Jewish predominance in local CP branches.[113]

Overall, secular ethnic Jews constituted a sixth of the small party membership in the 1920s and around half by the late 1930s and through the 1940s.[114] Being more educated and white collar than their non-Jewish counterparts, they also produced leaders at a higher rate than all other immigrant groups, constituting on average more than one-third of the members of the various central committees between 1921 and 1961.[115] The American CP was so unusually middle class—a fact that "differentiated it from almost every other Communist Party in the Western world"—precisely because it "was so heavily Jewish," with many "Jewish doctors, dentists, and lawyers."[116] As with socialism, Jewish support for communism was not obviously directly related to class or economic need.

The CP and its affiliates never had more than a hundred thousand official members at any one point, but turnover was high, and perhaps a million people passed through the ranks.[117] Sympathy for communism, like other radical ideologies and movements, was also more widespread among the First Generation than formal indicators of commitment alone suggested. Murray Rothbard, later a noted libertarian thinker and participant in the American "Old Right," recalled of the milieu of his upbringing that "the middle-class Jews of New York whom I lived among, whether family, friends, or neighbors, were either Communists or fellow-travelers in the Communist orbit." The "one great moral question in the lives of all these people was: Should I actually join the Communist Party and devote the whole of my life to the cause, or should I remain a fellow-traveler and 'selfishly' devote only a fraction of my energy to communism?"[118] Most Jews who may have sympathized with communism or the Soviet Union in some capacity chose to pursue their own personal interests rather than devote themselves to a socially suspect ideology in the American context of the time; however, they helped to create a communal sentiment that was favorable to the ideals of communism as well as to the Soviet regime, which took the lead in the fight against Nazi Germany after 1941.

Communist enthusiasm typified small segments of the First Generation, but as Irving Howe explained, "If the number of card-carrying Jewish Communists in the early twenties was small (perhaps fifteen hundred in all the garment unions, for example), their influence in the Jewish labor movement was large."[119] Jewish unions or unionists, concentrated in the garment industry in the 1920s and in white-collar civil service sectors like the American Federation of Teachers (AFT) by the 1930s, constituted notable sources of support.[120] Into the 1940s, Jewish voters continued disproportionately to back communist or communist-endorsed candidates. The first communist to hold public office in the United States, Peter V. Cacchione, was elected in 1941, and then again in 1943 and 1945, to the New York City council from Jewish Brooklyn. In these years another communist,

Benjamin J. Harris, joined the council from Jewish and black Harlem. In 1948 the heavily Jewish Twenty-Fourth Congressional District in the Bronx elected the communist-endorsed labor candidate, Leo Isaacson. In that year also, 10 to 15 percent of the Jewish national vote, compared to 2 percent of the general electorate, went to the communist-endorsed Progressive Party candidate, Henry Wallace. About one-third of Wallace's votes came from Jews.[121]

By 1948 the CP was in the habit of endorsing socialist or "progressive" yet noncommunist candidates for office. Throughout the 1920s, however, the pursuit of such a "united front" policy proved a major point of contention. Soon after James Cannon had returned to New York from Moscow in late January 1923 with a directive from the Comintern against the Goose Caucus (the CP was dissolved into the WP in April), new lines of division began to form within the party around this very issue.[122] Some, including Bittelman, who had given up on the belief that the United States was verging on revolutionary upheaval in the Roaring Twenties, wanted to exploit their public legal position to penetrate trade unions and other socialist third parties so as to maximize communist influence.[123] William Z. Foster led the circle that supported this agenda, founding the Trade Union Education League to further its goals. A German American, Charles E. Ruthenberg, led the more revolutionary circle that opposed such "syndicalism" as a reformist deviation.[124] This struggle made up "the axis of the internal life of American communism" into the next decade.[125]

In September 1923 the headquarters of the WP relocated to Chicago, and at Cannon's urging, Bittelman left the JCF and moved to that city so as to bolster Foster's forces within the executive. Bittelman was recruited for his theoretical knowledge of Marxism-Leninism and was expected "to assume new responsibilities in general party work as a member of its national leading body."[126] Foster's circle dominated the party for the next two years, but the Comintern ultimately came down in favor of the program of Ruthenberg and his colleagues. In August 1925 the Comintern ensured that they took the leadership of the party. Cannon moved away from Foster's circle as a result (and eventually out of the party) even as Bittelman moved closer. Neither Bittelman nor Foster had the "appetite for going along willingly with these new leadership arrangements." In September Bittelman traveled again to Moscow with Foster, joined this time by their wives, to plead his faction's case. "On this second trip to the land of the socialist revolution," Bittelman wrote, "I met Stalin face to face in direct dealings."[127] Stalin "made no commitments," but after several meetings with Zinoviev and Nikolai Bukharin it was decided that Foster's group would "assume complete charge of the party's trade union work" and Ruthenberg's group would "remain in control of the party's leadership." Returning to New York via Italy in early 1926, neither Bittelman nor Foster was entirely satisfied "with the outcome of our trip."[128]

Conflict within the party continued. After Ruthenberg's death in 1927, leadership of his faction passed to his protégé, Jay Lovestone (né Liebstein). In August 1928 Bittelman went to Moscow again, attending the Sixth Congress of the Communist International (Comintern) as part of the American delegation, and he argued on that occasion, as the *de facto* leader of Foster's circle, especially vehemently against Lovestone's position.[129] His vehemence proved counterproductive. In March 1929, at the Sixth Convention of the now renamed Communist Party of the United States of America (CPUSA), Stalin himself resolved the incessant and unconstructive intra-party factionalism by sending orders that Bittelman and Lovestone, perceived as bad factionalists, be banished from the American party to Moscow.[130] As Lovestone's nexus was to be replaced by men from Foster's faction, and as the CPUSA as a whole benefited in its operation from this diffusion, Bittelman felt reconciled to his tem-porary "withdrawal from the American party."[131] In summer 1929 he dutifully went to work for the Comintern in Moscow, focusing on anticolonial propaganda, even performing a mission to India in 1930.[132] He recalled earnestly of his journey to Bombay that when passing through the Suez Canal and along the Sinai peninsula, he was "positively reliving the Biblical story of the Exodus."[133]

By late 1931 Bittelman had returned to the United States, tired and sick. His doctor advised that he move to southern California to convalesce, where he devoted himself for three years to the study of and writing on Marxism and related subjects, producing a number of texts, some of which were published as pamphlets by a party-affiliated printing house.[134] Despite the opportunities that the Depression ostensibly afforded communist agitation, Bittelman remained aloof from the CPUSA, in part because he sensed that he was unwanted within the fold, for the "internal balance in the leadership was still very delicate." He also failed, as did many within the CPUSA, to recognize "the serious progressive possibilities that were inherent in the First New Deal, which covered the period of 1933–35."[135] In February 1934 Bittelman published, along with another Eastern European Jewish immigrant, the pamphlet *Leninism: The Only Marxism Today*, in which he condemned "reformist-socialism" as "the main social pillar of the bourgeoisie" in a time of "declining capitalism."[136] As late as April 1935 Bittelman proclaimed that Franklin D. Roosevelt had broken his insincere promises to end poverty, asserting that "plenty for all in the United States who toil is not a dream but a practical possibility. But only under socialism, as the first phase of Communism. The Soviet Union is proving that."[137]

Such attitudes closely followed the dictates of the Comintern's Sixth Congress in 1928, which had discouraged cooperation with noncommunists, including socialists and *a fortiori* New Deal Democrats. Instead of seeking to work with other left-wing forces, the party hoped to radicalize the proletariat outside of the structures of the New Deal so as to "build up a broad united front 'from below' under Communist leadership." Members of the CPUSA engaged in industrial organization through their own Trade Union Unity League, even though this hard-core policy of "class against class" caused the group to remain "isolated from the mainstream of American progressive political life"—to Bittelman's retrospective regret.[138] At the time, however, he maintained that the New Deal was but "a sharper turn of the American bourgeoisie towards fascization and war."[139] The Democrats under Roosevelt may have favored "relief and a certain measure of social security," but they were "inadequate relief and less than inadequate measures of security."[140] These programs were "fraudulent," a "caricature of old age pensions and unemployment insurance" to mislead and mollify the masses.[141]

It was only after the Comintern's Seventh Congress in 1935, which encouraged communist parties worldwide to cooperate "with all progressive elements in the struggle against fascism,"[142] that Bittelman, ever attentive to Moscow's official line, "took a fresh look at the New Deal and found in it major opportunities for social progress and for the advance of American labor to influence and leadership in the nation." By this time he had returned to New York City from California and was assisting the CPUSA in the production of party propaganda and theory. He forever felt pleased by the "splendid and very useful role" that he and other communists played "in the New Deal developments of 1936–1939."[143]

In adopting a popular front orientation, members of the CPUSA began to operate within the mainstream labor movement.[144] Experienced communist organizers were notably invited to take part in the Committee for Industrial Organization (CIO), established in 1935, as "part of a broader New Deal electoral coalition centering around Franklin D. Roosevelt."[145] By 1937 Bittelman was advocating "the further advance and consolidation of the forces of the People's Front"; he praised the trade union work of the CIO and lambasted "big business" for seeking "to break the New Deal, to destroy Roosevelt, to stimulate further the offensive of reaction."[146] He enthused that the popular front offered "the road toward making a mass party out of our organization." The "Republican Party is not . . . the same traditional Republican Party. . . . [It] has become the center of reaction and fascism," even as the new Democratic Party, "under pressure from the independent struggles of the masses of the country . . . is moving generally in a progressive direction."[147]

There were disputes within the party over whether the CPUSA was losing its militancy, Marxism, and independence by affiliating too closely with the CIO, but the dominant personality within the leadership at that time was Earl Browder, who embraced the New Deal "wholeheartedly."[148] The party clearly gained from its more open orientation amid the disconcerting state of domestic and international affairs. Between 1935 and 1939 membership in the CPUSA rose from thirty thousand to a peak of around ninety thousand.[149] During these years, moreover, the party experienced notable successes in establishing a presence in the unions of key industries, both Jewish and gentile. Yet "strangely enough," Nathan Glazer observed, "the professional membership rose even faster than the working-class membership." In large part, Jewish New Yorkers engendered this discrepancy, joining the party more often than members of other groups, despite their more white-collar occupational profile.[150]

These positive developments notwithstanding, Bittelman's intimate involvement with the CPUSA did not endure. In late 1941 he was dismissed from his position as propagandist and theorist. The party's other foremost figures, Bittelman explained, "seemed to think that I didn't . . . function harmoniously" in the leadership. The Russian Jewish émigré was criticized, and not for the first time, as "too rigid in my views and attitudes—obstinate and stubborn—in plainer language" and as "a very poor member of a collective leadership—a bad team worker, in plainer words."[151] In his autobiographical account, Bittelman admitted that he often lacked restraint and moderation, yet he failed to convince his colleagues of the extenuating circumstances behind some of his more obstreperous conduct. He was simply too familiar in his behavior, and it bothered his peers that he failed to appreciate "the hierarchical structure of party leadership and of strict lines of commands."[152] Despite this setback, Bittelman did not depart from radical life. He was sent back to the world of Jewish communism—to the offices of *Di frayhayt*, which were located in the same building as, but three floors up from, the offices of the CPUSA.

The JCF, along with all foreign-language federations, had officially ceased to exist after 1925, when the CPUSA (then the WP) had sought to Americanize its image. In the 1920s (and beyond), American communism had been widely perceived as a largely non-native and overly Jewish movement.[153] This perception was considered adverse to the party's ambitions and perhaps even its tenets. In 1925 the WP had set out to "Bolshevize" its organizational structures by centralizing authority in the English-language section and eliminating the independence of the foreign-language federations. These moves caused a sharp drop in membership at the time, but did not altogether alter the actual quotidian operation of the party.[154] Ethnic fractions continued to function as social entities and ancillaries, and cultural cleavages and loyalties persisted.[155] Further, by the time of Bittelman's return to *Di frayhayt*, foreign-language groups had been "rehabilitated" as part of the party's popular front policy, following the Comintern's Seventh Congress in 1935. The CPUSA wanted as many recruits as possible to aid the Soviet Union in the antifascist struggle, and by 1937 appeals to nationality and ethnicity were once again legitimate as a basis for enlistment.[156]

As part of this general struggle, Bittelman reorganized the offices of *Di frayhayt* into a new procommunist, party-affiliated body—the Morning Frayhayt Association (MFA)—of which he was secretary and also the *de facto* leader.[157] From 1941 until 1950 he remained "actively and joyfully" in communist agitation as specifically geared to the Jewish community. His ten years as an active participant in American Jewish life were a "valuable and fruitful experience," as well as "totally absorbing and gratifying." Bittelman felt fulfilled: the MFA proved a homecoming, a return "to my native environment and to numerous old friends and co-workers. But it meant much more than that":

> I knew how dangerous the rise of fascism had become especially to my people, how essential it was for all American Jews to unite, regardless of politics and ideology, to join the rest of the nation in common action against that danger, and most particularly to help win the war against the fascist axis. I felt, therefore, in high spirits as I prepared to assume my responsibilities.[158]

For all Bittelman's awareness of the Nazi menace to Jews and for all his attention to world affairs, he claimed to have been entirely unprepared for "what had actually happened to the Jewish people—my own people."[159] During the war he argued in favor of Jewish unity across class lines and geographic boundaries, proclaiming that "every passing day sees the physical annihilation of large numbers of Jews in the Hitler-occupied territories. It is for this reason that the struggle for Jewish unity is fundamentally a struggle for helping to hasten victory [and] save the Jewish people from physical annihilation."[160] Notwithstanding such contemporary pronouncements, he later reflected that his grasp of Nazi terror "was nothing, absolutely nothing, as compared with what was happening and had actually happened to the Jews of Europe."[161] In his memoirs Bittelman expressed significant guilt over his failure to foresee and to act, to "arouse and organize the Jews for the survival of Jews as Jews." He consoled himself by contending, and not without some justification, that most diasporic Jewish leaders, "in all ideological and political movements," had similarly failed and that perhaps many of these individuals felt a like sense of personal culpability and despondence.[162]

The Holocaust prompted Bittelman to a greater commitment to Jewish communist work and to "Jewish national survival," which were complementary rather than contradictory endeavors in his mind.[163] His contribution to these causes, however, was interrupted by his arrest in mid-January 1948 for subversion under the Smith Act of 1940.[164] Federal authorities found Bittelman and his wife in Miami Beach, Florida, where they "were spending the severe winter months," as they did every year,[165] "in an expensive apartment," as pointed out by *Time* magazine.[166] Bittelman was released on bail a few days later, returning to New York City to prepare for his hearings and to the offices of the MFA to continue his Jewish communist work. Despite "feeling happy about the part I personally played in bringing about my party's decision favoring the establishment of a Jewish Homeland in Palestine," Bittelman's relations with the MFA deteriorated over the next two years, in part due to his support for a binational Arab-Jewish state and an internationalized Jerusalem, against the more fervent Zionism of his colleagues.[167] By 1950, having further fallen out with the MFA, Bittelman returned to the CPUSA's headquarters, three floors down. He recalled: "Those were difficult days. Going away from Jewish life and work in the Jewish field was like tearing myself away from something very precious and valuable."[168]

They were also very "difficult days" for the CPUSA as a whole, whose belea-guered national committee welcomed Bittelman back into the general fold without much enthusiasm. By the early 1950s the CPUSA had become exter-nally extremely isolated, even as it remained internally divided if not paralyzed between die-hard Stalinists and revisionists.[169] The party's leaders were being indicted and jailed as subversives, even as Bittelman's own case remained before the courts.[170] Its membership and publication rolls were contracting. Its contacts with an increasingly conservative labor movement, including the CIO, were being severed. In short, the gains of the New Deal era and the Second World War were being lost with the end of the American-Soviet alliance and the advent of the Cold War. For Bittelman, "those years—1951, 1952, 1953, 1954—were some of the unhappiest years of my entire life."[171] If any good came out of the debacle, it "was an intensified effort by the party leadership to make fully clear, theoretically and politically, the party's position on 'force and violence.'" To avoid further prosecu-tion, by 1954 the CPUSA began to explore "a program embodying the position of peaceful transition" to socialism.[172]

By this time, however, Bittelman had already been indicted by a court in Manhattan for "conspiring to teach and advocate the violent overthrow of the US government."[173] In his defense, yet to no avail, he attempted to blame American antisemitism for his conversion to communism and to insinuate that this prej-udice was the true motive behind his prosecution. These charges were not, as Melech Epstein, a former colleague, observed, "anywhere near the truth," but rather "the party line," which encouraged Jewish communists to "drag in the issue of anti-Semitism before congressional hearings and in court proceedings."[174] In his memoirs, Bittelman made no mention of antisemitism in relation to this episode—or any part of his life in the United States. Resentment and anger were instead directed against the government for having designated him an alien and for having sought to deport him on that basis. Bittelman had never officially taken out American citizenship, despite forty years of aggressive political radicalism in the country, but he felt himself to be, "truly so, more genuinely American and a better American than my legal persecutors," lackeys of an imperialist regime. Unlike the said lawyers, Bittelman believed himself to be "contributing to the best of his abilities to the progress and happiness of the American nation."[175]

Upon appeal, Bittelman was spared deportation, but he was sentenced to three years behind bars. In December 1954 he entered a federal penitentiary in Atlanta,

Georgia; less than thirty months later he was released from a second penitentiary in Lewisburg, Pennsylvania. It was during this last incarceration of his long life that Bittelman underwent a "spiritual development" and finally became, in his estimation, a "real philosopher."[176] This final stint in jail proved a sobering experience. Bittelman underwent an epiphany, precipitated by Nikita Khrushchev's revelations about Stalin's dictatorship and personality cult at the Twentieth Congress of the Soviet Communist Party in February 1956. The political prisoner learned of these revelations from his wife and from delayed copies of the *New York Times*.

Like many other Western communists, Bittelman was devastated by Khrushchev's and subsequent disclosures about the Soviet Union.[177] Of course he had known of Stalin's bogus trials and executions, including of some of his own acquaintances and friends; of the brutality and famine that attended upon the collectivization of agriculture; and even of the gulag penal system. Bittelman categorically denied that any leading communist was innocent in this regard: "I really felt embarrassed when I read in Khrushchev's speech of March 8th, 1963, that he didn't know of Stalin's misdeeds. . . . Impossible. Just plain impossible." The truth is that "we all endorsed and supported the actions of the Stalin leadership."[178] At the time Bittelman had accepted such actions, taking them "into my stride as a matter of inevitable development." It was only "in later years, much, much later, I had to come to some very difficult and painful conclusions about this moral blow to Communism." Even the mysterious disappearance, in the early 1930s, of his own brother, Samuel, who had had the misfortune of being a supporter of Trotsky under Stalin, did not disrupt Bittelman's worldview or cause him to reflect upon the operation of his preferred regime: "I have to say it right here," he confessed, "I had no inclination to probe into the matter too deeply."[179]

In 1956, for reasons that Bittelman could not fully explain, Khrushchev's speech destroyed his complacency and confidence. Of the supporters, perpetrators, and apologists of Stalin's tyranny, Bittelman asked himself again and again, "Where was their conscience? Where was their Communism—yes, the moral substance of Communism?" He himself had been a Stalinist, and thus "my responsibility is clear and so is my guilt. There is no getting away from that."[180] On the spurious trial and execution of Bukharin in particular, whom Bittelman had met on his trip to Moscow in 1925, he reflected at length:

> I stop and take a mental look at myself. And I say: What about you? True, the matter wasn't in your hands. It wasn't you who killed him or ordered his killing. But you learned about it after it had happened and you approved of it. You wrote and spoke of Bucharin [*sic*] as an enemy who had to be destroyed. How do you explain that? Where was your own heart and Communist conscience? Well, for the heart, there is no answer. . . . But for the mind, there is.[181]

The answer, Bittelman came to believe after forty years of activism, was that he and other socialists—going all the way back to Karl Marx himself—had never differentiated between communist politics and communist ethics. Despite having become a socialist at the age of thirteen in Russia, it occurred to Bittelman only fifty years later in the United States that "at no point in my experience have I come across a full realization that conflicts between politics and morals in Socialist and Communist practice are AT ALL POSSIBLE. . . . I had not the slightest notion that anything in Socialist and Communist practice can be morally wrong if it is politically right."[182] Bittelman's lifelong mentality had been quite simple: socialism was absolutely and entirely good (as well as in the best interests of secular ethnic Jews, whether they knew it or not), and therefore everything that was done in its name, especially by the Party, was "automatically" good, including coercion and even violence. It was an epiphany of some moment for Bittelman to realize that "the use of force by Communists is not always a progressive force."[183]

Bittelman struggled with such thoughts. He never completely resolved the cognitive dissonance that they engendered. He accepted that Stalinism was not simply the product of one man's persona, but "the basic and truly decisive element was a set of political and theoretical ideas and concepts, Marxist and Leninist in origin."[184] All the same, he remained a Marxist and continued to consider himself a communist—of a more humane and mature disposition.[185] He still dismissed bourgeois anticommunism as so much hypocrisy and cant, for the West with its "capitalism" and "imperialism" was morally just as reprehensible if not worse than Stalin's Soviet Union, having produced fascism, racism, "the crimes of colonialism," and "the threat of thermo-nuclear war." At the same time, he recognized that a "comparison between the treatment of myself by the agencies of the capitalist-imperialist government of the United States" and "the treatment of Communist dissenters, such as Milovan Djilas, in lands governed by Communists" was highly unfavorable to the latter. Bittelman was sentenced to "only three years" for a lifetime of subversion as an alien in the United States, whereas "in socialist Yugoslavia, led by Communists, Djilas is put away for more than ten years merely for writing an anti-Communist book, assuming it was anti-Communist":[186]

> And under Stalin's leadership in the Soviet Union, Communists were legally killed for having been found guilty—wrongly so, as in my case here—in conspiring to overthrow by violence the Soviet system. Well, all I can say at this point: it is not easy to live with these thoughts.[187]

Bittelman's way out of this intellectual and emotional conundrum was to make a distinction between "the real and the ideal"—between facts and values—to which intellectual discovery he devoted an entire chapter in his autobiography.

He concluded on the basis of this distinction that socialism is "a noble and beautiful ideal . . . that . . . can never become identical with the real." Nonetheless, all men must, with the help of communists and other political leaders and technocrats, "strive to approximate that ideal as closely as possible." In this endeavor, they must keep in mind that "no program which ignores or violates the principles of Communist ethics can lead to Socialism and Communism. . . . This is where I rested. From this I have no intention of departing."[188] Bittelman did not explore how or whether his newly determined "Communist ethics," emphasizing the means to various ends as much as the ends in themselves, differed from conventional bourgeois morality.[189]

When Bittelman left prison in 1957 and returned to New York City and the CPUSA, he attempted to convince the party of the correctness of his new convictions, including support for a "peaceful transition to socialism" and a radically expanded welfare state.[190] He wrote many letters and articles as well as a lengthy typescript, "*A Communist Views America's Future*," in which he presented and argued for these ideas and policies.[191] His overtures were not well-received by the CPUSA, whose isolation had only become more severe after the Twentieth Congress in 1956. In late 1960 Bittelman was expelled from the party, to which he had devoted his entire adult life, for being a revisionist.[192] He continued to consider himself a communist of a modified sort, to defend the Soviet Union from unduly harsh detractors, and to interest himself in left-wing politics.[193] His days of radical activism, however, were more or less over. He was already an old man. He retired to his suburban home in Croton-on-Hudson and spent the last two decades of his long life in obscurity, writing his autobiography and other reflective works.[194] He passed away in 1982.

"Progressive Jewish Nationalism"

As a founding and leading member of the American Communist Party, Alexander Bittelman was unique. As an Eastern European Jewish immigrant with a radical disposition and orientation, he was not. Few Jews, just as few gentiles, in the United States supported communism; nonetheless, a disproportionate number of American communists were Jews, and these Jewish communists, like Bittelman, emerged out of a distinct social milieu. Bittelman was an outlier even among his peers, but he belonged to a discrete ethno-religious population whose political mean was (and to a considerable extent remains) skewed to the left of the political spectrum, both absolutely and in comparison with groups of appropriate reference. Even though most members of this First Generation avoided or even opposed revolutionary communism, many if not a majority became advocates of socialism or other types of radicalism—from which Jewish communism, as

Bittelman's case demonstrates, was an outgrowth—in a country in which such ideologies and movements at the time had little support.[195] Why were Eastern European Jews in the United States so leftist?

In his autobiography Bittelman wrote of his socialism as a vehicle and a validation for a secular ethnic Jewish identity against the modern bourgeois arrangement in which "equality was granted to the individual and not to Jews as a group or cultural entity."[196] In reflecting on his Jewish communist work within the MFA during the 1940s, he emphasized that he and his colleagues "took a strong stand against what we called 'bourgeois assimilation.' By this we meant all those currents in Jewish life which project assimilation as the solution—the desirable solution— of the Jewish question":

> We didn't criticize individual Jews who sought assimilation as their own way out of their own problems although we took sharp exception to the refusal of some of those Jews to join the fight for equal rights and for our rights as a distinct ethnic group or "national minority." That was it: we viewed the Jewish community in the United States and the other lands, except Palestine, as "national" minorities and on that basis we called for a united Jewish struggle for the democratic rights of that minority and for the further development of a progressive Jewish culture. All of that we conceived as an organic part of the cultural growth and development of the whole American nation.[197]

Bittelman also came to the realization that such resistance mediated ethnic consciousness:

> Looking at the whole thing in retrospect, it is quite clear to me that our resolution [against bourgeois assimilation], and my own thinking on the Jewish question, were definitely at variance with the established Marxist attitude on the eventual disappearance of the Jewish people as a people. . . . We were fighting for Jewish survival, not only physical against Hitler's "final solution," but for cultural and spiritual survival as a people. Without realizing it, we were really projecting the idea of a progressive Jewish nationalism.[198]

Bittelman wrote his memoirs after the Holocaust, when many radical Jews wondered whether they should have been more committed to the Jewish colony in Palestine and less to Marxism or the Soviet Union.[199] Nonetheless, his conclusion that socialism manifested a resistance to assimilation or even the inverted nationalism of a disempowered minority "without realizing it" need not suggest a retrospective projection onto the past of present preoccupations, but rather the possibility that the function of Jewish radicalism operated best in conjunction with true devotion. To suggest a third-person function is not to deny the first-person commitments of individual actors to their chosen causes. Bittelman was, without a doubt, a true believer in socialism, but at least until after the Second World War, he assumed the interests of socialism and Jewishness to be largely coincident. When socialism came into conflict with his Jewishness, Bittelman, among others, underwent considerable cognitive dissonance and even ideological reassessment.

Bittelman's contention that the radicalism of the First Generation manifested a reaction against if not resistance to bourgeois assimilation is supported by the trajectory of its development. Eastern European Jews tended to become radical as they came into contact with modern or modernizing bourgeois societies. Radicalism was not, as some scholars have claimed, just an import to the United States from czarist Russia, where conditions had been far less favorable for Jews.[200] Bittelman did arrive in his new country with pronounced left-wing loyalties after considerable agitation against czarist autocracy, but he was not typical in this regard. Most Eastern European Jewish immigrants tended to be fairly traditional and quietest, notwithstanding that they may have been less conservative than their peers who, demonstrating less initiative as well as less independence from the staid rabbinical elites of the shtetlach, remained in the Pale of Settlement. On this point, Tony Michels has noted that "contrary to the old misperception, Eastern European Jews did not import a preexisting socialist tradition to the United States. As of the 1880s only a tiny number of Jews in the Russian Empire . . . knew anything about socialist ideas before coming to America."[201]

Harry Burgin described the earliest immigrants in his "*History of the Jewish Workers Movement*" of 1914 as follows:

> The great majority of the Russian immigrants in those days were a raw, ignorant group. It was difficult to make contact with them. They were so ignorant that they didn't know the difference between a missionary and a socialist. At Essex Street, which was the center of the Jewish quarter, it was perilous to walk through holding a lighted cigarette (this is forbidden to the Orthodox Jews) on the Sabbath. The one who showed himself with a cigarette suffered for his lack of decorum. In this atmosphere of ignorance and darkness the spirit of the weekly "Jewish Gazette" ruled without hindrance; it was published by the deceased Kasriel Sarasohn. This newspaper attacked the socialists and told huge falsehood [*sic*] concerning the socialist meetings. They attacked the meetings, first, because they took place Friday afternoon, second, because cigarette-smoking took place, and third, because both men and women attended them. The paper spread libelous statements about the character of the socialists and claimed that they were not different than missionaries. . . . For many years, the "Jewish Gazette" continued in this manner against the socialists and unions. However, the forward-looking workers continued on their way.[202]

As Burgin, a contemporary, knew, only a few committed radicals were to be found among the early cohorts of immigrants. These radicals, moreover, faced competition from more conservative forces for the hearts and minds of the Eastern European Jewish masses. The fairly religious, conservative, and pro-Republican gazette of the aforementioned Kasriel Sarasohn maintained a larger circulation than any other Yiddish-language broadsheet until 1910, when it was superseded by the famous socialist organ *Forverts* or *Jewish Daily Forward.*[203] Only after 1910 did a radical subculture became predominant within the First Generation. In Michels's words: "A distinct movement of Yiddish-speaking Jewish workers did not come into existence until the mid-1890s and did not gain a following until early in the twentieth century, almost two decades after the Jewish labor movement arose in New York." As such, it is the case that "'the Jew' had not always been a radical; the Jew had become a radical in New York and other American cities. Eastern European Jews knew this. Invariably, newcomers were amazed by the assertiveness of New York's Jewish population."[204]

By 1910 the Jewish community had become well established, more secure, and more prosperous, even as the American economy was advancing, providing average citizens with amenities that were largely unknown to their counterparts in Europe. The Golden Age of Yiddish socialism, which took off around that time and in which Bittelman participated eagerly, emerged not in the earliest days of settlement—those of greatest disorientation and dislocation—but after Jewish immigrants had established a "complex, loosely structured but relatively self-contained Yiddish-speaking community and sense of family." Jewish radical movements and ideologies, Gerald Sorin has emphasized, "did not grow out of a desperate anomie," nor "out of poverty and hardship alone."[205] Further, Jews were not compelled *faute de mieux* to join marginal socialist and communist parties because mainstream counterparts in the Northeast, especially the Republicans if not the Democrats, excluded them. They were courted by both parties, and often more assiduously in the beginning by the Protestant-dominated Republicans than by the Catholic-dominated Democrats.[206]

Radical positions became common after 1910, for by then a critical mass of Eastern European Jews had left the insulation and certainty of rigid orthodoxy. Just as Bittelman became more secular in Ukraine in the early 1900s, so did many of his peers in the United States at around the same time.[207] These processes were independent though parallel events in each country. Secularization initiated modernization and thus Jewish radicalization, which was ostensibly a reaction to modernization. Bittelman embodied this trend.[208] A working-class experience may have been necessary as well as formative, but it was not sufficient. Bittelman's life in the United States, as an individual and as a Jew, improved by most objective indicators of well-being and even by his own subjective appraisal, but such propitious personal developments did not impede his radicalism in that country. By contrast, orthodox Jews remained relatively immune if not hostile to left-wing movements and ideologies, both in the United States and Europe.[209] The orthodox rabbinate, however, lacked the institutional infrastructure to project its power beyond the Pale and did not retain its influence in the New World.[210] Rabbinical efforts to establish a communal authority structure or *kehillah* in New York City failed for a number of reasons, not least because America's democratic norms and institutions meant that "anyone who did not like its decisions refused to be bound by them."[211]

Secularization exposed young Eastern European Jews to the modern or modernizing societies around them and to the pressures and expectations of their erstwhile Christian oppressors. The development of an adversarial attitude to these societies and their Christian character has often been attributed to traditional antisemitism.[212] In the United States in the first half of the twentieth century, invocations of antisemitism are not without merit, but they would seem insufficient as an explanation for Jewish radicalism for a number of reasons. First, without denying the reality of antisemitism, it was far less prevalent in the United States than in Central or *a fortiori* Eastern Europe and hardly ever dangerous, yet Jewish radicalism was even more pronounced in new American diasporic centers like New York City than in the old Pale of Settlement, where established rabbinical elites sought to contain such sentiments even as explicitly Jewish parties vied for the Jewish vote.[213] According to historian Joseph Frankel, socialism among Russian Jews at the turn of the twentieth century was influenced by events among the First Generation in New York City, rather than the other way around.[214]

Second, the hostility or rejection that Yiddish-speaking Jews may have experienced in American Protestant-dominated civil society was not obviously greater than that experienced by European Catholic immigrants. Given their larger numbers and the deep antipapist animus within broad segments of the Protestant population, Catholics often preoccupied nativists more than Jews did.[215] With their biblical evocations, Jewish immigrants often fascinated and received the special sympathy of Protestant reformers.[216] Of course both Jews and Catholics were marginal to America's hegemonic Anglo-Protestant bourgeoisie, which was associated with the Republican Party. Marginality is a comprehensive and powerful concept by which to explore the political behavior of minorities. It has been applied productively to the Jewish case, as to others.[217] In their overwhelming affiliation with the Democratic Party since the mid-nineteenth century, European Catholics did fit the mold in their own way.[218] All the same, despite sharing a certain status as outsiders and a certain propensity for counterhegemonic forces, European Catholic immigrants were not as radical as the First Generation.

Third, Western or Westernized Jews in the United States did not by and large behave politically in the same manner as those from Eastern Europe, despite (or because of) having far greater social contact with bourgeois Christian society. For the relatively small number of German Jews, who preceded the First Generation by several decades in their immigration to the United States and whose more gradual modernization had begun before that of their Russian counterparts, radicalism was not notably attractive. Despite producing a number of politically and socially dissenting individuals of renown, German Jews in the United States were often Republican and fairly conformist and were often dismayed by the Eastern European Jews' radicalism, which they, like the orthodox rabbis, attempted to curtail.[219]

These groups—orthodox Jews, European Catholics, and German Jews—ostensibly differed from secular Eastern European Jews in their compliance and compatibility with modern social arrangements. To pass as and among Americans, Jews were expected to differentiate not just between private and public spheres—the basic bourgeois division—but also concomitantly between their religion and ethnicity and between their Yiddish subculture and the rest of society. Catholics had to differentiate between church and state.[220] This prospect proved an enormous adjustment for a people that had been in Europe "one of the most familistic societies known."[221] In the words of Harshav:

> Individuals who experienced the change in their own bodies and souls paid an extraordinary price for leaving their hometown, their parents' home, their childhood language, their beliefs, their ways of talking, and for the conquest of new modes of behavior, a new language, new traits, new conventions, and beliefs.[222]

The modern encounter was not without considerable loss of status and humiliation. Maurice Samuel, a prominent intellectual of the First Generation,[223] described the encounter:

> In the Roumanian village of my childhood the Jew felt himself to belong, quite justly, to a higher order. In the great modern city to which we migrated the feeling of superiority vanished. The shock was extraordinary. We were, at first, as grasshoppers in our own eyes. Here were schools for everyone, running water in all houses, public baths, newspapers which everyone read, public libraries, universities, lectures, theatres, and above all, a dazzling vastness of gentile life. Where was our medieval system now?[224]

Samuel, a Zionist rather than a Marxist, explained the challenge of embourgeoisement:

> The Jews are probably the only people in the world to whom it has ever been proposed that their historic destiny is—to be nice. This singular concept has played such

an important role in recent Jewish history that it almost characterizes an epoch. As applied to an individual, the word *nice* indicates a pleasing absence of character. It is the best that a man can be without being anything. As applied to a people and to its historic role, the word rises to a sublime and solemn fatuity. For a people consisting of nice individuals and of nothing more is not a people at all; it is a loose association of fourth hands at bridge; it is a protracted Sunday afternoon call; it is a subdued cough in the Hall of Fame.

The problem was that the "nice Jew . . . has . . . talked himself out of his soul": "Nothing remains for a man in this desperate position but to surrender his identity . . . and, consciously or unconsciously, that is the intention behind the theory of niceness."[225] Bittelman concurred: "A Jew is not," he insisted, "just a person who chooses to call himself a Jew but a living organ of a national entity, of a living Jewish national group":[226]

> I see the main difference between the assimilated Jew and the non-assimilated Jew from the standpoint of Jewish national character in the following: in the former, the national character is not allowed to express itself freely and to become manifest whereas in the latter the Jewish national character enjoys full freedom.[227]

For the orthodox, who remained apart from civil society, the issue of bourgeois assimilation was moot. Their faith also helped inure them from the shame of "recognizing themselves as disgracefully backward" due to their "contact with a superior civilization" emanating from the West.[228] For European Catholics, having more associational ties than Protestants yet less intensely communal ties than Eastern European Jews, the problem was less acute. They recouped some status from their social, cultural, and economic subordination in the United States, moreover, by sharing in the country's Christian (albeit Puritan) heritage. Catholics also heeded their clergy, who warned believers against radicalism.[229] Finally, for German Jews, whose more gradual modernization predated that of the "Jews from the East," the problem was resolved to a considerable extent by a readier and fuller accession to bourgeois standards. German Jews tended to present themselves in public as individual American citizens of the Jewish faith, as a denomination akin to Protestantism.

As a largely secular or postorthodox community, Central European Jews provide a revealing index of comparison to Eastern European Jews. In their greater acquiescence to bourgeois standards, German Jews, especially in the United States, where antisemitism was less prevalent than in Europe, became socially quite respected and respectable as well as economically very successful. E. Digby Baltzell, chronicler of America's bygone "WASP" elite, recalled that in his fashionable Philadelphia neighborhood before the Second World War, the "few fashionable families of German or Sephardic Jewish origin had married Episcopalians for several generations."[230] German Jews strove to blend into civil society, adopting the prevailing manners of public life and civil interaction. They were, Lionel Trilling observed, "likely to be envied and resented by East European Jews for what would have been called their refinement."[231] In modern society, Eli Lederhendler has written, "the familiarity of strangers could not be presumed," and so "it was necessary to be educated in the outward forms of civility, even if one happened to be naturally good-hearted and moral." This "Anglo-Saxon civility . . . was basic to the fabric of American life," but it "was especially foreign to the Jew newly arrived from Eastern Europe, precisely because of its differentiation between inner feelings and outward expression."[232]

Such a bourgeois differentiation fit poorly with *yidishkeyt*. Members of the First Generation knew each other as a close community of brothers and sisters, not as polite strangers in the civil realm of citizens. The gap between the First Generation's actual and accepted social behavior, however, often resulted in ecological tension. As Hadassah Kosak has noted, "in the tightly defined area" of Jewish immigrant neighborhoods, "private and public spaces merged, to the considerable consternation of outsiders. . . . The community's occupation of public spaces contravened widely accepted notions of social behavior as sanctioned by the law and civil society."[233] Bittelman rejected bourgeois standards and despised the modern division of labor, which he viewed as little more than "exploitation, oppression and persecution."[234] In his social life he vacillated between premodern forms of "mechanical" solidarity (the immediacy of *yidishkeyt*, which he had missed so much during his exile in Russia's Far North) and revolutionary fraternity (in which all were "automatically" comrades).[235] Bittelman was even moved to the MFA from the CPUSA due to his undue and overbearing familiarity. In general, social relations between Jewish radicals, typically intellectuals, and their gentile counterparts, more likely blue collar and hands-on, were, to the extent that they took place, often fraught.[236]

American German Jews looked down on Russian Jews for their political defiance and social awkwardness. They, not just bourgeois gentiles, excluded Eastern European Jewish immigrants from polite company as "too uncivilized."[237] The German Jews' stereotypical attitudes toward the newcomers were summarized by Lloyd P. Gartner:

> The new immigrants were primitive and clannish, unwilling to take on American ways, insistent on maintaining "Asiatic" and "medieval" forms of religion and social life. "Culture" and "refinement" could not be found among them. They demanded charity as a matter of right without appreciation for what they received. They were

unduly aggressive and assertive and embarrassed the painfully acquired good name of the American Jew. They had a disturbing penchant for unsound ways of thought, especially political radicalism, atheism, Zionism, and held to a form of speech which could not be called a language.[238]

In turn, the Eastern European Jews tended to denounce the inauthenticity of the German Jews. According to the "traditional German-Jewish school of thought," Bittelman averred, "Jewishness was identical with Judaism," but "that philosophy has been proven hopelessly wrong and very costly to the German Jews." It had led to "a steady atrophy of Jewish national consciousness and feelings, a break-away from popular Jewish identities, a virtual disappearance of a conscious struggle for Jewish survival." Bittelman maintained that "the Jews of each country and nation have much to contribute to the glory and greatness of these countries and nations and to do so as citizens and nationals, but also as Jews."[239] "Bourgeois nationalism and assimilationism," Bittelman informed the CPUSA in late 1946, in a report that he prepared for a special national conference "on the Jewish question," were reactionary. American communists had "erred in not sufficiently resisting the pressures of bourgeois nationalism and assimilationism, as well as underestimating Jewish work." They ought to recognize that "all Jews belong to an oppressed and persecuted people" and to support the "struggle against assimilationism as a bourgeois ideology which reflects the imperialist pressures of Anglo-Saxon domination."[240]

Bittelman used the language of anti- or decolonization, but the "pressures of Anglo-Saxon domination" were the prevailing social expectation, and the Jews' rapid mobility made their accession all the more urgent. In part, integration into civil society at the level of the individual was meant to mitigate the potential for intergroup conflict and animosity. After all, as Bruno Bauer asked Karl Marx in the age of Jewish emancipation in Germany in the early nineteenth century: Why should Christians treat Jews as free individuals if Jews do not treat Christians as such?[241] In addition, such integration was meant to bring Jews into closer contact and thus "organic" solidarity with other members of society who were not their ethno-religious peers.[242] Having eschewed the sumptuary legislation and control of the Catholic and Jewish Middle Ages,[243] modern society, separate from the state, assumed of stranger-citizens an inner-directed restraint and moderation, deriving from a general if diffuse sociability, for its autonomous operation.[244] If Jews lacked regular noncommercial interaction with non-Jews, would they come to demonstrate toward stranger-citizens the social sensibilities and moral sentiments—the civility—on which bourgeois civil society presumed to rely?

(Marx's 1843 response to Bruno Bauer—"On the Jewish Question"—dealt with the problem of a (self-)segregated group in the increasingly deregulated socioeconomic spaces of the modern state.[245] Bauer argued against the full political emancipation of Jews in imperial Germany, criticizing the necessarily public nature of the Jews' *religion* as precluding them from acting as free individual citizens. Marx retorted by shifting to the unfortunately public nature of the Jews' *material livelihood*, an early example of his superstructure-base methodology and rejection of idealism.[246] In his essay Marx conceded to the antisemites that Eastern European Jewish merchants were antisocial and so uninhibited.[247] He used vitriolic language to describe Jews, a group with whom he was commonly associated, willingly or otherwise, due to his birth.[248] Many scholars have consequently contended that Marx was a "self-hating" antisemite.[249] Marx concluded his essay, however, by suggesting that the Christian bourgeoisie, with its civil courtesies and decorum, was in fact, underneath such appearances, no better than the pariah Jewish merchants from the Prussian marches, with their overt "selfishness" and "haggling." The Christian bourgeoisie was "too gentlemanly, too spiritual, to remove the crudeness of practical need other than by raising it into the blue heavens," but all the same, the "practical spirit of the Jew has become the practical spirit of the Christian people" in so-called civil society.[250]

The debate surrounding Marx's alleged antisemitism misses the ironic construction of his famous polemic and ignores the rhetorical strategy [in relation to his ultimately strong support for Jewish emancipation[251]] behind his emphasis on the "similarity between Jews and Gentiles, as against Bauer who stressed their differences."[252] This emphasis calls into question not Marx's alleged antisemitism, but his objectivity in comparing the Christian bourgeoisie of his hometown with the immigrants who made up the majority of the Jewish population of Trier at the time he was writing.[253] Marx's close friend Wilhelm Liebknecht contended that the philosopher's "whole life was a reply and a revenge" against the social humiliation of his native German Jewish father's coerced conversion to Christianity.[254] The sumptuary tinge to Marx's German Jewish socialism differed from Bittelman's more ethnic coloration.[255])

In the context of modern encounter and bourgeois pressures, the appeal of socialism for the First Generation was manifold. As an antibourgeois posture, socialism evaded civil society and its differentiating structures. Further, as an antibourgeois moral critique, socialism simultaneously justified this evasion. Why defer to a social order that was so unjust and imperfect? Finally, socialism promised to re-regulate, in part or in whole, the modern state's deregulated or self-regulating social spaces, with their daunting and unfamiliar codes of conduct. Under socialism, Jews would self-actualize as whole individuals—as part of a Yiddish-speaking community—without ecological conflict. By reducing the distance between state and society, socialism would manage interpersonal and especially intergroup relations.[256] Bittelman expected a socialist regime to afford a system of multiculturalism *avant la lettre.*[257] As he had envisioned already in his adolescence as a Bundist activist in Berdichev, after a socialist revolution "in a Russia free of the Czarist autocracy there will be established special governmental institutions in charge of all cultural affairs of the Jews. Yiddish would be recognized by the state as the national language of the Jewish people."[258] After decades in the United States he continued to adhere to the same goal. The "struggles for Jewish survival," he insisted, "require the systematic cultivation and development of the American Jewish community as a distinct ethnic or national entity" that was also, without contradiction, "fully integrated in the vital processes of the American nation."[259]

This anticipation was largely fulfilled, greatly reinforcing Bittelman's worldview. In the first two decades of its existence the Soviet regime established an "affirmative action empire," administered by its massive technocratic bureaucracy. According to Terry Martin, "Russia's new revolutionary government was the first of the old European multiethnic states to confront the rising tide of nationalism." It responded "by systematically promoting the national consciousness of its ethnic minorities and establishing for them many of the characteristic institutional forms of the nation-state."[260] The Bolsheviks may have outlawed the Bund and absorbed the majority of its personnel during their consolidation of power, but they fulfilled much of its mandate *vis-à-vis* secular Yiddish-speaking Jewry. As David Shneer has observed, "in the 1920s, the Soviet Union was the only country in the world to have state-sponsored Yiddish-language publishing houses, writers' groups, courts, city councils, and schools."[261] The Soviet Union suppressed Judaism, but it backed a Yiddish-based secular ethnic Jewishness. Bittelman was not alone among the First Generation in his appreciation of the Bolsheviks' efforts on behalf of secular Jewish culture, including its Yiddish-speaking alternative to Hebrew-based Zionism: Birobidzhan, a swampy territory in the far east of Siberia.[262]

During his trip to the Soviet Union in 1922, when he journeyed to Moscow with James Cannon to argue against the Goose Caucus before the Comintern, Bittelman personally witnessed the reality of Soviet multiculturalism. He met with the representatives of Russian Jewish communism, including the formidable former Bundist Esther Frumkina:

> These people looked to me very happy and also proud of the great things they were doing. This mood of cheer and optimism I found prevalent in several other Jewish circles in Moscow. I was invited to a number of comradely parties where I met Jewish writers, poets, actors and political workers, and in all of these gatherings I felt the same mood of pride and hopeful expectation.[263]

These leading Russian Jewish communists informed Bittelman of the "role of former members of the Bund in the life of the new socialist state in general and about Soviet Jews in particular."[264] There was considerable antagonism expressed toward former Bundists who had set themselves against the Bolsheviks. There was discussion of the efforts of the Soviet government to resettle declassed Jewish merchants on land in agricultural colonies, notably in the Crimea.[265] Bittelman was impressed above all by the cultural ferment, which he was told about and to which he was exposed firsthand:

> The brightest picture of Soviet Jewish life at that time I found on the cultural front. It was so in Moscow. It was so in my Berdichev and also in Kiev. . . . The Soviet government was obviously doing everything in its power to assist the free expression of the national cultural needs of the Jewish people. Most of these, if not all, were in Yiddish, the language of the Jewish masses, the language which was to me, too, very precious. Already in Moscow I thought I could sense the beginning of a genuine Jewish cultural renaissance in literature, poetry, art and the theatre. This, by the way, was the feeling of all the Jewish men and women with whom I came in contact.[266]

Frequenting Moscow's Yiddish theater, which "proudly asserted and celebrated Jewish identity,"[267] was a highlight for Bittelman. Here, he believed, was a country in which secular Jews could go to the Yiddish theater at night and help build a socialist state during the day. Here, he imagined, was a country in which secular ethnic Jewish culture was funded and promoted by the state even as social antisemitism was outlawed and Jews could excel unfettered.[268] For Bittelman and other Jewish radicals, this was the model for America and the world.[269] Nonetheless, the dream of having emerged from the nightmare of history did not last. Soviet multiculturalism—the regime's promotion of all its minority cultures—had implicitly operated on the suppression of the Russian majority culture. By the end of the 1930s, in preparation for war against Nazi Germany, Russian nationalism was rehabilitated and reinvigorated.[270] By the end of the 1940s the Soviet regime had turned on its former Jewish supporters, eradicating the very Yiddish culture that it had but recently done much to advance. Soviet Jews began to be subjected to forcible assimilation and Russification.[271]

Bittelman was slow in coming to terms with the Soviet destruction of Yiddish culture and the Soviet persecution of Jewish individuals after the Second World War, even as he had justified the Nazi-Soviet non-aggression pact of late 1939 as a prudent geostrategic maneuver, warranted by Western duplicity.[272] As Nathan Glazer noted, "Yiddish culture had been for many years the chief point with which" Jewish communists in the United States "argued the virtues of the Soviet Union with non-Communists of the immigrant generation."[273] Bittelman's cognitive dissonance on Stalin's anti-Jewish policies was, in addition to his support for binationalism in relation to the new state of Israel, a prime reason for his being pushed out of the MFA in 1950. The other leaders of the MFA perceived more quickly and clearly the new negative reality for Soviet Jewry, but as late as December 1949, Bittelman could celebrate Stalin's seventieth birthday by proclaiming that

> Stalin will be honored by the Jewish masses in the United States—for his historic contributions to the solution of the national question in general and of the Jewish question in particular, for his leadership in the fight against anti-Semitism, for outlawing anti-Semitism, for full equality of rights of the Jewish masses, for his world leadership in the fight against fascism, for his leadership in the defeat and military destruction of Nazi fascism in the last war.[274]

As Bittelman had believed since boyhood, the interests of secular ethnic Jews and of socialism coincided, such that "Jewish life in America can be built only on progressive foundations."[275] Bittelman remained committed to this conflation until 1956 (if not beyond), at which point, as part of his overall reassessment of his loyalties and prejudices, he confronted Stalin's antisemitism and the state of affairs that prevailed for Jews in the Soviet Union after the Holocaust, when Yiddish culture and its most creative elements were liquidated "in violation of the humane and humanitarian impulses and values of mankind's moral ideals which are part of Communist morality."[276] Of all Stalin's crimes, it was the dictator's anti-Jewish policies that Bittelman considered the worst and the most inexcusable and by which he was most deeply affected, troubled, and mystified:

> By bits and pieces, through rumor and suggestion, I began to learn of the great Jewish tragedy that was played out by the actions of the Stalin leadership. For some reason, which I am unable to explain, I had known nothing about the attempts made by the Stalin leadership at the forcible liquidation of Jewish cultural life in the Soviet Union as well as Jewish cultural creators. This was a new shock to me, in certain respects, deeper and more painful than the shocks I received from the first news of the general re-evaluation of the Stalin leadership by Khrushchev. . . . My mind was numbed. I simply couldn't absorb the fact that Jewish writers, poets and artists . . . great creators of Jewish culture, devoted friends and supporters of Socialism and the Soviet state and sincere lovers of their homeland; I couldn't—I refused—to understand why these people were murdered by a Communist leadership of a Socialist government. I kept on asking myself—for Heaven's sake, why? What could they have been guilty of to deserve death? . . . I remember having wept bitter tears, in secret, hidden even from my own [wife] Khavelle. I felt ashamed but I couldn't help it.[277]

The Holocaust and the ultimate failure of Soviet socialism to accommodate Jews as a Yiddish-speaking community impelled Bittelman to reconsider the prospects of Jewish continuity in the diaspora. He produced a large unpublished typescript on the subject, *"Jewish Survival: A Marxist Outlook,"* in which he argued that Stalin's latter-day policy "of accelerated and forcible Jewish assimilation in the Soviet Union" was "wrong theoretically from the standpoint of Marxist philosophy and Marxist theory"; "wrong politically because it rendered a dis-service [*sic*] to the cause of socialism in the Soviet Union and the world"; and "wrong morally because the terroristic measures of repression and liquidation . . . violated all precepts of socialist ethics and morality."[278] Stalin and the Soviet leadership failed to recognize the "distinct Jewish national character" and "the potential progressive role this factor is destined to play in the life of mankind."[279] They "never fully understood the active and creative role of the *subjective reaction of Jews against assimilation.*"[280] This resistance by secular ethnic Jews was good for the entire world:

> The struggle for the democratic ideals of social justice is the very essence, the very heart, of the progressive life of all nations and peoples at the present juncture of their history. . . . If nations and national groups have social missions to perform, and history shows that this is so, then the historic mission of the Jews is to help promote the advance of mankind in this epoch *to the final realization* of the democratic ideals of social justice in the lives of all mankind.[281]

Bittelman's understanding of the Jewish Left as mediating a resistance to assimilation is not without controversy. Within the relevant literature, a principal explanation for Jewish radicalism maintains that it manifested a yearning among Eastern European Jews to acculturate and assimilate into the non-Jewish societies with which they came into increasing contact as they secularized and left the medieval shtetlach of the Pale. According to this view, socialism's emphasis on class over nation and its universalism and internationalism appealed especially to Jews because it seemed to promise them a more neutral space in which to achieve a much-desired integration into the non-Jewish world.[282] The fact that orthodox Jews, who were obviously committed to Jewish continuity, were rarely socialists has been used to bolster this argument. Given the predominance of this discourse, Michael Berkowitz, in his studies of the First and Second Generations in the United States and Britain, has written of his efforts "to look against the current of a *supposedly* overwhelmingly imperative towards acculturation."[283] Just such an imperative was emphasized by Will Herberg, who put forward a socialism-as-Americanization thesis, and reiterated by Moses Rischin.[284]

In this vein Melech Epstein, an ex-communist American Jewish historian of American Jewish communists, claimed that his contemporary, Alexander Bittelman, was a "semi-assimilationist." Like his peers, Epstein maintained, Bittelman adopted positive attitudes toward Jewishness merely when it suited Moscow for him to do so, such as during the Second World War, when Bittelman led the MFA out of expedience and backed Jewish causes only as part of the CPUSA's antifascist campaign.[285] According to this view and indeed the official party line, the foreign-language branches of the American socialist and communist parties were merely tactical entities through which "to reach out to foreign-speaking voters"—as non-Anglophone workers, rather than as members of separate ethnicities.[286] According to Epstein, the JCF in particular, which Bittelman established after his split from the SPA in 1919, tended to put the interests of socialist revolution before the interests of Jews *per se*. This was supposedly demonstrated by the Jewish communists' refusal to take "special action" on behalf of those Eastern European Jews affected by the civil war in revolutionary Russia, seeking instead to aid the revolutionary Soviet forces and all victims of counterrevolution.[287]

Bittelman's career does not support the contention that he was a "semi-assimilationist." He explicitly rejected bourgeois assimilation and preferred to perceive a coincidence between the interests of socialism and Jewishness throughout his decades of activism. Bittelman addressed himself to Epstein's charge, fully aware that he was misrepresented by fellow Jews who, though radical by comparison with other Americans, were not quite as radical as himself. "Our opponents in the labor and socialist movements," Bittelman wrote in his memoirs, "seized upon" the Jewish communists' decision not to cooperate with the relief body of the Joint Distribution Committee during the First World War "to represent us almost as enemies of the Jewish people":

> Of course, we were not opposed to Jewish relief work, although we viewed even this task in the light of the unfolding socialist revolution in Europe . . . which was in our eyes the real and radical "relief" to the ruined and suffering Jewish masses of that part of the world. Yet we were prepared to engage in the collection of relief funds in the United States provided this was not totally controlled by our political opponents in the labor and socialist movements.[288]

When Bittelman had been the secretary of the Harlem branch of the JSF, prior to his establishment of the JCF, he had done much to organize on behalf of war-torn Jewry, a major concern of his generation. In 1915 and 1916 he had used his influence in the JSF to cooperate with the Joint Distribution Committee, helping to organize "mass collection-days in one of the largest Jewish communities of New York city." Of these events, moreover, he had fond memories, recounting with pride and satisfaction that "hundreds of young men and women, the Jewish youth, as well as older ones, took part as volunteers in these collections—door to door—for relief for the Jewish war victims."[289] One of these volunteers was Eva "Khavelle" Shapiro, who later became Bittelman's beloved wife. Bittelman married her on December 31, 1917—"the year of the Bolshevik revolution," he emphasized portentously—with a rabbi and "according to most of the traditional Jewish rules."[290]

Notwithstanding cosmopolitan protestations, endogamy was the norm among American Jewish communists. For Bittelman, marrying a non-Ukrainian Jew—Eva was "a Litvak" (from Lithuania)—was practically exogamy.[291] As Paul Lyons noted in his history of Jewish communists in Philadelphia:

> Evidence of the importance of ethnicity in general and Jewishness in particular permeates the available record. Many Communists, for example, state that they could never have married a spouse who was not a leftist. When Jews were asked if they could have married Gentiles, many hesitated, surprised by the question, and found it difficult to answer. Upon reflection, many concluded that they had always taken marriage to someone Jewish for granted. The alternative was never really considered, particularly among Jewish men.[292]

Bittelman's commitment to Jewish causes continued after the Bolshevik revolution. Notably, as a socialist representative at a Jewish labor conference in New York City soon after the issuance of the Balfour Declaration of November 1917, Bittelman "voted in favor" of a "resolution endorsing in some way the idea of a Jewish Homeland in Palestine." From the other Jewish socialists in attendance, "there was some criticism of my conduct but not very much and not very severe."[293] During the Second World War, moreover, Bittelman argued in favor of recognizing the Jewish community in Palestine and its desire to fight on the battlefield, insisting that such recognition did not entail acceptance of "Zionism as a nationalist ideology, nor Zionism as a political movement."[294] Bittelman's ambivalence toward Zionism typified many if not most of those Jewish radicals who were meant to be committed to class struggle above national concerns.[295]

Bittelman was not against Zionism *per se,* but rather opposed to its bourgeois elements and above all its intention to solve Jewish problems in Eastern Europe by moving Jews to Palestine, which he viewed, at least prior to the late 1940s, as both craven and unfeasible. He was not alone in these relatively prosaic and pragmatic attitudes.[296] He claimed to disagree with the ultimate goal of Zionism, "but I couldn't feel hostile to the program itself":

> I reasoned: since there seem to be Jews who want to go to Palestine, settle there and try to make it a national homeland for themselves—let them. I wasn't going to prevent them from doing so because I could see nothing especially wrong in the Palestine aspiration from the standpoint of Socialism, provided that could be done without injuring

the Arabs and without entangling the Jewish people with the imperialists who were dominating and oppressing the Middle East and its peoples. This was a rather naive and utopian view of Palestine but that was my attitude to it for many years.[297]

What was true for Bittelman was true for others. There is little empirical proof to indicate a positive relationship between radicalism and acculturation or assimilation. General evidence suggests a negative correlation. The most radical Jews tended to be the most insular, and their radicalism naturally reinforced their insularity. This is not altogether surprising in that there were obviously better ways to integrate into existing American society than to espouse ideologies and to join movements that were committed to its overthrow, radical restructuring, or extensive reform and were highly critical of prevailing social values, norms, and institutions. For Eastern European Jewish immigrants to aspire to transform "American society so that they could dissolve into it on their own terms"[298] did not amount to a striving for integration into a concrete social reality but rather to a deferral of a resolution of their status into an abstract future.

By contrast, Murray Rothbard, quoted in the preceding section for his blunt description of the communist milieu of his youth, attributed some of his later conservatism or libertarianism, both absolutely and in relation to his peers, to the fact that his father, an immigrant from Warsaw, Poland, differed from his relatives in his "intent not only on quickly learning English," but also "abandoning Yiddish papers and culture and purging himself of any foreign accent." Rothbard's father did not become a socialist who read an internationalist newspaper that just so happened to be in the Yiddish language yet wrote of the universal proletariat and Americanization; he made "a determined effort to integrate" his family "into American life," both politically and culturally, moving away from Jewish residential concentrations to Staten Island.[299]

As a general rule, acculturation and assimilation tended to undermine radicalism even as ethnocentricity tended to reinforce it. American Finns provide a case in point. In the United States, the first generation of Finns was even more radical than that of Eastern European Jews. In the early 1920s the Finnish-language federation of the WP—a party in which Bittelman was at the top during those years—constituted nearly half of the membership, far ahead of the official Jewish contingent. (The Finns' significance to the organization was less vital than the Jews', because Finns were a smaller community in the United States, less educated, and more rural in their distribution.) Like Jews, Finnish immigrants experienced discrimination and initial hardship in the United States; also like them, many were enthused by the Bolshevik revolution and the Soviet sponsorship of Finnish culture within the framework of a revolutionary society in East Karelia. Some Finns even returned overseas to great fanfare in order to help build the "new society."[300]

In studying the radicalism of Finnish immigrants, Peter Kivisto noted that "part of the rich social life provided by both church and radical Finns was designed to attract youth and to keep them from seeking entertainment in the larger society." Despite the putative internationalism of socialism and communism, radical Finnish clubs tended to operate as ethnic networks and to resist efforts at ethnic desegregation by central headquarters. What is more, "at the very point when Finnish American leftists had overcome the linguistic and some of the other cultural impediments to incorporation into distinctly American radical organizations, they experienced a general withdrawal from socialism." It was the "ethnic character of their organizations provided a protective shell from those external influences that tended to undermine the influence of socialist ideology."[301] In the United States, ethnocentricity and radicalism were complementary, not contradictory, whatever the nostrums of official doctrine.[302]

Finns differed from Eastern European Jews in that they experienced a faster and more comprehensive Americanization. By 1945, Kivisto concluded, "the saliency of ethnic identity and working class identity had dissipated for a majority of Finns."[303] The most thoroughgoing indicator of this acculturation and assimilation was intermarriage. Whereas the American Jewish rate of endogamy (including German Jews, who were more likely to out-marry than *Eastern European Jews*) was 98.82 percent in 1900 and still 96.1 percent in 1950, the rate among Finns was less than 50 percent by the late 1920s, with urban Finns—and almost all American Jews were urban—more likely to intermarry than geographically and culturally isolated rural Finns.[304] As a contemporary, John Kolehmainen, observed, this rate of out-marriage among Finns was not the result of a lack of suitable partners within the ethnic community. The explanation for the phenomenon "must be sought in the psychological condition of the young," who rebelled against their elders' customs and traditions, because "they disliked the exactions of [a] dual existence": the "difficulties of trying to be a Finn, on the one hand, and an American, on the other, became onerous" for them.[305]

Finns were largely Protestant. Unlike Jews, they did not have a long experience as a diasporic minority and their identity was not informed by a theology of separation. These factors made Finns more susceptible to Americanization even as they rendered Eastern European Jews more resistant. As William Berlin observed:

> For Jews, the tension between old and new was probably even more complicated than it was for other immigrants. It was more acute because Judaism implied separation from the nations of the world. . . . Jews have been a people who have seen their existence as a refutation of ordinary history . . . The immigrant Jew was more likely to be conscious of his past and conscious of a distinct identity than were other newcomers. Jewish experience had fostered alienation from the ways of the Gentiles, but

it also encouraged an awareness of a unique history and tradition. . . . The immigrant Jew, in certain respects, may have wanted to remain a stranger.[306]

The tropes of a Jewish lived religion, including secularized theological concepts of exile and alienation and sacralized historical memories of real or imagined persecution, did reinforce the radicalism of the First Generation. Messianism, Will Herberg contended, "permeated the thinking and feeling of believer and unbeliever alike, even those who felt compelled to reject it as a doctrine along with the faith in which it is grounded."[307] As Gerald Sorin has demonstrated, radical Jews of the First Generation actually came disproportionately from the ranks of those who "were sons and daughters of rabbis, cantors, Hebrew school teachers, Talmudic scholars, or who had had rabbinical or advanced Jewish schooling."[308] As a young boy, Bittelman imbibed Jewish religious culture in his parents' household, especially from his grandfather. He imagined a future socialist world in terms of the messiah and interpreted the status and hence cause of the workers—as outsiders and victims of the czar—in terms of felt Jewish suffering and received notions of exile, alienation, and eventual redemption.

Many radical Jews did believe that left-wing ideologies and movements reflected Judaic values, and there is a strong sense in which Judaism's emphasis on the Jews' own exile, alienation, and affliction segued well with socialism's stated concern for the poor, oppressed, and ostracized. Bittelman, for instance, deemed his fellow Jews to be especially "rich in moral and spiritual capacities for the ideals of social justice" due to their ancestral religion and historical experience.[309] Whether there was an objective link between radical politics and traditional Judaic values—a view likely to be denied by orthodox rabbis if not belied by their greater conservatism—is moot. Radical Jews subjectively subscribed to this view and reified it. Radical motifs of "social justice" were incorporated as normative content into secular ethnic renovations of Jewish identity that went beyond an increasingly obsolete orthodox observance.[310] This secular ethnic identity filled the space that was opened up by the Jewish Left's evasion and moral criticism of bourgeois society. In this way, left-wing movements and ideologies acted as a substitute for the old religion, and thus, even in the United States, where a socialist revolution was most improbable, as a vehicle for group cohesion and ethnic assertion against the destabilizing and disesteeming pressures of modernity.

Of this, Bittelman was not unaware. "Religious attachment and identity," Bittelman admitted, "did not appeal to me" or most of his peers. The "old and traditional role of Judaism as the mainstay of Jewish survival had come to an end long ago."[311] All the same, the Jewish labor movement and its causes had become an important secular medium for Jewish identity:

That Judaism and its institutions are inadequate for a full expression and development of Jewish life in the United States has been recognized for a long time by
many groups and social classes in the American Jewish community. The first ones
to bring into being secular movements and institutions of a distinct Jewish national
character were the Jewish workers, radical and Socialist-minded wage earners, men
and women, mostly immigrants from Eastern Europe. With the growth of these
movements and institutions came a veritable Renaissance of American Jewish culture in the Yiddish language. This was something new in Jewish history and in the
history of the American Jewish community. . . . It was an expression of American-
Jewish secular culture and a powerful force in the growth and development of the
American Jewish national group.[312]

In his study of the *Forverts* or *Jewish Daily Forward* (*JDF*), the quintessential institution of the First Generation, and its founding editor, Abraham Cahan,
Israeli historian Ehud Manor came to a similar conclusion. During the First World
War, "Cahan released unequivocal statements both in English and in Yiddish
regarding the *JDF*'s role as an 'Americanization agent.'"[313] Such claims were reiterated by contemporary scholars—like Mordechai Soltes, who tellingly subtitled
his interwar study, *The Yiddish Press,* "An Americanizing Agency"—and have persisted to the present day.[314] Nonetheless, Manor's probing of "various aspects of
Cahan's Americanization project" reveals that the editor, "instead of easing the
natural alienation of the Yiddish-speaking immigrant to this new environment,
actually aggravated it." Indeed, his paper's "description of the American way of life
was quite negative."[315] Cahan was basically pessimistic about the First Generation's
experience in the United States.

Abraham Cahan understood the modern transition that the First Generation
was undergoing in the United States. In his Yiddish-language autobiography, he
described the process as follows:

> I knew that the hundreds of thousands who were living down there [on the Lower
> East Side] were ingathered refugees. With one gigantic leap these hundreds of thou-
> sands had jumped from a medieval world into the twentieth century, from evil
> despotism—right into a free republic, from a familiar *shtetl*—into the most seething
> metropolis. And the Jewish soul could not take it. The old customs, the old faith and
> the old morality—all this collapsed. Much of what the old life had bred, that which
> Jewish fears had borne and Christian hatred had nurtured now disappeared. . . .
> Amidst this chaos of a new Jewish life, amidst the ruins of the old Jewish customs,
> there was born an authentically Jewish working class and we, Jewish Socialists, who
> now stand at the infant's cradle, must create a new morality, a new public opinion
> and a new literature.[316]

Cahan was also aware of the often degrading difficulties of the Jews' integration into an alien civil society, as a deregulated or self-regulating space that operated according to daunting rituals of conduct, including the mediation of economic activity through social formality. Cahan devalued such trifles, emphasizing his moral, spiritual superiority against his civil inadequacies. Speaking through the eponymous protagonist of his English-language novel, *The Rise of David Levinsky*, Cahan wrote:

> One day I had lunch with the head of a large woolen concern in a private dining-room of a well-known hotel. He was dignifiedly steel-gray and he had the assurance of a college professor or successful physician rather than of a businessman. He liked me. . . . He addressed me as Dave. There was a note of condescension as well as of admiration in this "Dave" of his. It implied that I was a shrewd fellow and an excellent customer, singularly successful and reliable, but that I was his inferior, all the same—a Jew, a social pariah. At the bottom of my heart I considered myself his superior, finding an amusing discrepancy between his professorial face and the crudity of his intellectual interests; but he was a Gentile and an American.[317]

According to Manor, the *JDF*, which had by and large given up on advocacy of revolutionary socialism by the early twentieth century—as indicated by its discrete and later overt cooperation with bourgeois capitalist elements within the American Jewish community, especially German Jewish representatives—adopted a "basic pro-alienation attitude." The "method was quite simple: the fostering of an antagonistic attitude toward American reality under the respectable flag of socialism." *Forverts* was not ultimately defined by fervent belief in a socialist utopia as much as by this "pro-alienation project." The *JDF* was, Manor has asserted, "led by a man who could not face reality. In a word, Cahan led his admiring crowd to a politics of non-politics."[318] Cahan sought to evade the basic and difficult social facts with which the First Generation was confronted and attempted to justify doing so through moral criticism: "Cahan belonged to those who perceived socialism not as a tool for more accurate political thinking and acting, but as a vague, moralistic and pious ideological structure," which served "as an individual moral compass for some kind of self-righteousness and self-esteem."[319]

By dint of its evasion and moral criticism, Manor has maintained, *Forverts* was, contrary to the conventional narrative and the "empty slogans" of its own editor, more of a "barrier" than a "bridge" to Americanization. In *Assimilation in American Life*, Milton M. Gordon put forward various criteria for integration.[320] In relation to most of these criteria, Manor has observed, the *JDF* was nonaffirmative. It "did not encourage its supporters to participate in the cliques, clubs and institutions of host society on a large scale." It did not promote intermarriage.

It certainly did not develop "a sense of nationalism based exclusively on the host society." What is more, it tended "to dismiss anti-Jewish prejudice as anti-Semitism, which is too abstract a generalization, especially when made by a supposedly progressive institution." Finally, even though it urged "Jewish immigrants to obtain citizenship," it did so not "as a token of social integration" so much as a "basic political tool in value and power conflict."[321]

Cahan and his *Forverts* were not atypical. The general tendency was the reverse of that posited by the dominant academic discourse: more radicalism was related to less acculturation or assimilation. An extreme case is provided by Bittelman's own Communist Party, whose Yiddish-speaking members were often almost entirely isolated from American life: socially, culturally, economically, politically, and residentially. The Yiddish branch of the CP-affiliated International Workers Order (IWO) was so insular that by the late 1940s, when the Federal Bureau of Investigation (FBI) sought to shut it down as a subversive organization, it "was forced into the role of an employment agency for Yiddish-speaking members who were contemplating leaving the party. In order to help them, the FBI would canvas the Yiddish community for persons and businesses willing to give them employment."[322] These individuals had never learned English properly, having existed within a self-contained, parallel, radical, Yiddish-speaking world, which in its intense separatism re-created the socio-spatial reality of its members' immediate, premodern, orthodox forebears. David Horowitz, a "red-diaper baby," described the world of his parents:

> What my parents had done in joining the Communist Party and moving to Sunnyside was to return to the ghetto. There was the same shared private language, the same hermetically sealed universe, the same dual posturing revealing one face to the outer world and another to the tribe. More importantly, there was the same conviction of being marked for persecution and specially ordained, the sense of moral superiority toward the stronger and more numerous *goyim* outside. And there was the same fear of expulsion for heretical thoughts, which was the fear that riveted the chosen to the faith.[323]

That a countercultural position should impede acculturation would seem fairly self-evident. As such, a larger question is not so much whether the First Generation's radicalism facilitated a kind of nonbourgeois assimilation—it did not—but why so many, against common sense and empirical evidence, insisted upon this interpretation of the phenomenon. This disciplinary bias may be explained to a considerable extent by the fact that many Jewish historians have felt the need to apologize for the adversarial and antisocial nature of Jewish radicalism. It may in turn be placed within a larger historiographical tendency to write of American radicalism more broadly as a "morality tale of seduction and betrayal."[324] As Tony Michels observed, "socialists intended to build a new society, not adapt to the existing one." In "dismissing this goal as youthful excess bound to give way to 'Americanization,'" historians have failed to take socialism seriously, flattening "the radical Jewish experience into a larger story of harmonious interaction between Jews and American society."[325]

Many contemporary Jews understood that Jewish radicalism fanned antisemitism and later Jewish historians transmitted this concern through their work.[326] As early as 1910 Meyer London, the future Jewish socialist congressman, recognized that a sensitivity to stereotypes often inhibited radical Jews from voting for radical parties: "Why, the would-be socialist voter was asked, Send a Jewish immigrant to Congress when the American working men do not . . . ? If you should send a socialist to Congress, they will exclude the Jews from America and adopt a strong immigration law."[327] These concerns only intensified during the interwar period and especially during the Cold War, as secular Eastern European Jews were increasingly accused of subversion and became identified with a murderous Soviet tyranny. The fact that many Jews were undeniably associated with domestic radical parties proved increasingly embarrassing and discomfiting for many Jews in the United States—including those who were themselves socialists and communists.

A common face-saving measure was to assert that radical Jews were not really Jews at all, often by reverting to a religious definition of Jewish identity despite the fact of the strong secular ethnic self-conceptions and commitments of most post-traditional Eastern European Jews in the United States. Even Bittelman preferred to regard a Jew who had "committed most unspeakable moral crimes" in czarist and then revolutionary Russia as "a Jewish apostate, renegade, *meshumad*."[328] Some radical Eastern European Jews were indifferent or even antagonistic to their ethno-cultural backgrounds, but this was not typical in the United States.[329] Social animosity against and suspicion of Jews, which Jewish radicalism tended to exacerbate, often engendered efforts at exculpation.

As an example, Baruch Charney Vladeck, a prominent member of the First Generation and its radical subculture—he was a socialist alderman and a manager at *Jewish Daily Forward*—published a manifesto with two bourgeois American German Jews in 1935, in which he denied the charge, propagated by the Nazis, of "a so-called Jewish communist link." "If the Jews," the manifesto declared, "are to be condemned because there are some communists among them—*men who have never in the slightest degree concerned themselves with Judaism*—then there is not a people on earth that might not with equal right be condemned."[330] Vladeck was justifiably afraid for his fellow Jews in Europe at this time, but he privately admitted what he publicly denied. "The Communist Movement," he noted in a letter to the SPA's leader, Norman Thomas, in 1934, "is particularly strong in New York, and more particularly so in the Jewish Unions."[331] What is more, Vladeck himself journeyed to the Soviet Union a year *after* his manifesto and still "could say with conviction that the Soviet Union represented a great social achievement."[332] Vladeck was not, because of his radicalism and sympathies for the Soviet Union, unconcerned with Jewishness, but rather distinguished by his commitment to the Jewish masses.[333] All the same, Jewish Democrats and Republicans denied the Jewishness of Vladeck—because he was a socialist (who had once openly supported Bolshevism)—just as Vladeck denied the Jewishness of men like Bittelman—because they remained avowed communists.[334]

Bittelman *qua* communist never denied his commitment to Jewish identity and Jewish interests, but he did declare his commitment to universalism and internationalism. There was, Joseph Frankel emphasized, a "strong pull towards universalism" among Jewish radicals in the United States.[335] Many scholars have interpreted such declarations of universalism and internationalism as corroboration of the socialism-as-Americanization thesis. Bittelman, however, did not understand his internationalism as implying a desire for acculturation or assimilation:

> I was an internationalist, alright, ever since I became conscious of the meaning of internationalism. But my understanding has been and continues to be that real internationalism is attained only through merger with one's own people. I mean genuine and consistent internationalism in art, in the sciences, in politics and in statesmanship. Internationalism means friendly, brotherly, intercourse and relations between nations and peoples on the basis of true equality. It means respect for each other's national cultural characteristics and a sincere desire to learn from one another. *It does not mean* one people merging with another; it most certainly excludes the possibility or desirability of members of one people deserting their own and seeking merger—assimilation—with another. This was my understanding of internationalism ever since I joined the Bund in 1903 and became a Socialist.[336]

For Bittelman, internationalism implied multiculturalism. He believed in *yidishkeyt* and maintained that "building the American nation and building the Jewish community has been and is, for the mass of American Jews, one single and indivisible task." It was the assimilationist German Jews who were "both bad Americans and bad Jews."[337] Other radical Jews, including communists, who were putatively the most universalist and, according to some, the most assimilationist, agreed. Internationalism, according to Israel Amter, a fellow founder of the CPUSA, and his wife, Sadie van Veen, meant the peaceful cooperation of all nations and mutual respect between them.[338] Internationalism did not imply assimilation.

It was "among the better-situated Jews, small businessmen and professionals" that they perceived "a marked tendency toward assimilation." To advance their businesses or careers, such Jews strove to obfuscate their Jewishness and to blend in and so were "victims of, or affected by, [a] form of latent anti-Semitism."[339]

Whatever the dictates of the doctrines to which Jewish communists and others adhered, this understanding of internationalism matched up well with the actual behavior of most radicals of the First Generation. The "statements of internationalism notwithstanding," Irving Howe wrote, "early radicals wanted to keep within the familiar bounds of the immigrant culture, for even when scoffed at on the East Side, it was still the place where they felt most at home. The great world they dreamed of conquering was actually the world they were least prepared to visit."[340] Marxist prescriptions about "the eventual disappearance of national differences and distinctions" were rather moot to the extent that socialism did not presently make undue demands upon secular Jewish identity or undermine secular Jewish communal life, even as it facilitated a more immediate evasion of bourgeois society and criticism of its standards of conduct.[341]

In Bittelman's experience, "the 'eventual' began to merge in my thoughts with the 'eternal' and the 'infinite'. Some day it [the disappearance of national differences and distinctions] will come but that day is so far away that, for all the purposes of the present and many more historic epochs, that day doesn't exist."[342] In Bittelman's candid words:

> I have rejected the old Marxist idea that the Jewish people are destined to disappear as a people by assimilation and merger with other peoples and nations and that this would be good for everybody. The truth is I never felt altogether happy about this proposition. Ever since I became familiar with and understood this Marxist position on Jewish survival, which was very early in my life—I must have been 15 and 16—while a member of the "Bund," I couldn't quite warm up to it. I accepted it as a "historic inevitability" but I couldn't make myself do much to give history a hand in that particular job. On the contrary, wherever and whenever I could do something to influence Jewish life, I would devote my efforts towards helping Jews being Jews and living as Jews—as progressive, forward-looking, revolutionary socialist-minded Jews. In doing so, my conscience wasn't at all bothered by thoughts that I might be obstructing "the historic inevitability." No. I reasoned like this: whatever was bound to happen to the Jews "historically" and in the future, as long as there were Jews in the world, especially in my immediate environment, THERE IS A JEWISH PEOPLE in the world, even though not a nation, in the Marxist meaning; and myself being of that people, and a Socialist, I have to do all I can for the alround [sic] progress and happiness of that people, even when my social activities happened to take me outside the special realms of Jewish life.[343]

When socialism did clash with Jewishness, the former usually gave way to the latter among radical Jews, suggesting the ultimate order of priority. In the United States, as Arthur Liebman documented meticulously, the "actions and policies taken by Left parties on Jewish issues and on matters concerning Jewish interests, whether advertent or inadvertent, affected the degree and level of support that they received from Jews."[344] As Arthur Goren demonstrated in his study of congressional elections on the Lower East Side, socialist candidates did well only "when due recognition was given to the local interests of the ghetto" and to specific Jewish concerns.[345] As early radical parties in the United States valued Jewish support, they were more careful to placate their Jewish constituents *qua* Jews than were their European counterparts, who had much broader bases of popular support.[346] Through the 1940s Bittelman argued in favor of his party's outreach to Jews *qua* Jews and its adoption of Jewish causes.[347] But cracks emerged and could not be entirely covered up. The most contentious issue between radical parties and radical Jews proved to be Zionism, both before and after the independence of Israel.

Zionism and socialism tended to attract the same Jewish individuals. (Moses Hess, it is well known, was the first Jewish communist—mentor to Karl Marx—as well as the first Jewish Zionist.[348]) Of course Zionism was "particular" in its orientation, and socialism was "universal"—a polarization about which a great deal has been written in the literature on twentieth-century Jewish political history.[349] Notwithstanding ideological differences, "particular" Zionism and "universal" socialism had a basic structural resemblance in that both rejected individual bourgeois assimilation into civil society and sought instead a collective solution to the problem of secular Jewish integration in the modern world. Zionism validated Jewish collective difference; socialism subsumed it under a class variable. In the diasporic context, socialism proved preferable to Zionism because like Zionism, it resisted bourgeois assimilation, but unlike Zionism, it did not thereby legitimate nationalism as such. As a dispersed minority with a legacy of maltreatment, most Eastern European Jews feared and resented the nationalism of gentiles. The First Generation's internationalism was, Frankel recognized, "more exactly antinational"—above all *vis-à-vis* non-Jews.[350]

The establishment of Israel in 1948, which many radical Jews supported—and often with more zeal than Bittelman, who advocated binationalism—complicated this "antinational" stance. It rendered overt the ethnic preoccupations of *soi-disant* Jewish universalists. As a socialist and later a communist, Bittelman had never been a fervent Zionist. He was not adamantly opposed to Zionism *per se*, but he "did not believe that the establishment of a Jewish homeland in Palestine—or in any other part of the world, for that matter—was the complete answer to the problems facing the Jewish people as a people no matter where they lived."[351] For Bittelman, socialism, including a state-sponsored multiculturalism, provided the more comprehensive answer to these problems. After the Second World War, the Holocaust, and the establishment of Israel, which Bittelman considered "a landmark" in his life, his support for Zionism became more direct.[352] He hoped that the Jewish state "might become a very important factor in the struggle for national liberation throughout the Near East."[353] His support soon raised a difficult question for someone at the head of a party that tended to condemn nationalism as mere chauvinism.[354]

To maintain ideological consistency, Bittelman began to distinguish between socialist—good, anticolonial, progressive—and bourgeois—bad, imperial, reactionary—nationalism, just as he had sought to distinguish between socialist and bourgeois morality. According to Bittelman these kinds of nationalism differed as follows:

> Socialist nationalism, which leads to the creation of classless societies, brings to creative national life the entire nation, not only a ruling class, as is the case with bourgeois nationalism. The second basic difference is that socialist nationalism leads to ever closer friendship and collaboration between nations, whereas bourgeois nationalism tends to create divisions and rivalries between nations and, with the rise of capitalist monopolies and imperialism, progressive bourgeois nationalism becomes transformed into chauvinism and "master-race" nationalism. The third basic difference is that socialist nationalism is *international* which bourgeois nationalism never was and never could be. Socialist nationalism is in reality the *national* realization of the principles and ideals of *internationalism* by specific nations, peoples and all types of national entities.[355]

Labor Zionism, Bittelman asserted, was socialist nationalism—it was "good nationalism, pride and happiness in the active identification with one's own people and true brotherhood between nations and peoples building their lives on the principles of equality and fraternity."[356] Zionism was an anticolonial nationalism that fought against bourgeois Western imperialism in the Middle East. Arab nationalism was also, in Bittelman's estimation, quite possibly good socialist nationalism, anticolonial and anti-imperialist. Bittelman was disconcerted by "a quarrel in which BOTH SIDES ARE RIGHT, a quarrel between peoples which had all the reasons in the world to be good friends." He was troubled by the Arab refusal to recognize Israel, just as he was troubled by the "tragic Arab refugee problem." All the same, he supported the "new Jewish nationalism, which is in full harmony with the best ideals of internationalism. . . . I think it is good for the Jews, for non-Jews, for mankind and its future in Communism." What is more, if Arab nationalism proved insufficiently "progressive" and the Arab countries kept to "the idea of driving Israel into the sea," then Bittelman knew his allegiance:

"To Israel I don't have to appeal. Here—if I had the opportunity—I would FIGHT, for I am a Jew and I carry responsibilities for what Jews are doing in Israel and everywhere else."[357]

Things Learned

Alexander Bittelman was a moderately significant figure within the radical Yiddish subculture of the First Generation and within American radicalism more generally. His life spanned more than nine decades, and his radical career coincided with most of the major events of the twentieth century, from the First World War and the Bolshevik revolution through the Second World War, the Holocaust, and the Cold War. Over this long and tumultuous period, Bittelman's basic political orientation and goals remained constant. From his initiation at the age of thirteen into the Bund in Russian Ukraine through his expulsion at the age of seventy from the American Communist Party, which he helped found and lead, Bittelman consistently perceived or chose to perceive a coincidence of interests between socialism and Jewishness. For Bittelman, socialism was to be a vehicle for an undifferentiated Jewishness. In the early Soviet Union it seemed, at least at first, to offer Eastern European Jews both full cultural and communal expression and full social admission and opportunity. In the United States it enabled Jews to evade and criticize bourgeois society and its alien standards of conduct even as it provided the normative foundation for the renovation of Jewish identity into secular ethnic forms, with an emphasis on identification with other outsiders of pathos, like the proletariat.

Bittelman's life and career, and his candid account of both, counter the view that radical Jews were more radical than Jewish, if Jewish at all. Bittelman was both a dedicated communist as well as a proud Jew. Bittelman was more extreme in his radicalism and more devoted in his activism than most of his peers, but his very zeal and commitment cast into starker relief the dilemmas and choices that Eastern European Jews faced in their contact with the modern Western world. His case, though in many ways unique, does suggest plausible reasons for the political behavior of the First Generation as a whole and does correspond well to general empirical evidence and statistical data, including the negative correlation between degrees of radicalism, on the one hand, and social integration and bourgeois assimilation, on the other, as well as the positive correlation between Jewish support for left-wing parties and left-wing parties' support for narrow Jewish interests.

This chapter considers the functional dimension of American Jewish radicalism in relation to the preservation and assertion of a premodern ethnic identity within a hegemonic bourgeois context. In so doing, it denies neither the subjective beliefs of the social actors themselves nor other commonly cited causal factors, such as the First Generation's relatively limited working-class experience or its felt discrimination. Nonetheless, it analyzes those beliefs and factors in relation to other groups of appropriate reference, both Jewish and gentile. This comparative approach reveals the intensity and durability of the First Generation's radicalism. A working-class experience and antisemitism may have been necessary for the emergence of the radical Yiddish subculture in New York and other American cities, but alone they are insufficient. Bittelman's proletarian youth in the Russian empire, where antisemitism could and did take violent form, certainly influenced his worldview and informed his turn to socialism (any personal experience of American antisemitism goes unmentioned in his memoirs), but it was his commitment to secular ethnic Jewishness, along with a certain "pro-alienation attitude," that ostensibly impelled his radicalism and that of his peers even as they experienced favorable socioeconomic conditions or mobilized into white-collar positions. Resistance to bourgeois assimilation, about which Bittelman wrote frankly, was a decisive factor in the development and perpetuation of the radical phenomenon of the First Generation of Eastern European Jews in the United States.

2

The American Jewish Congress
and the Second Generation

A Common Experience

The American Jewish Congress was founded by members of the First Generation along with individuals of German or Central European background. In due time it became a significant institution of the Second Generation, reflecting much of the experience and representing many of the concerns of the children of the Eastern European, Yiddish-speaking immigrants who came to the United States at the turn of the twentieth century. Its most active and successful years—after the Second World War and through the 1960s—coincided with the maturation of the great bulk of this largely native-born and English-speaking population. The Second Generation, Deborah Dash Moore has written, had "in common the experience of growing up American in Jewish immigrant homes." They were not so much a "compact group in time," given the duration of the Great Migration, as individuals with "a similar point in space in their relationship to each other and to their immigrant parents." They were "a cultural generation, not a chronological one."[1]

The American Jewish Congress, as Joshua Zeitz has noted, was the Second Generation's "most liberal mainstream advocacy group." It "represented the left wing of the organized Jewish community," but it also "fell squarely within the liberal consensus, and its politics reflected the community's outlook."[2] This concurrence was no mere coincidence, for the Second Generation of American Jews did follow the First in registering as a notably politically idiosyncratic group according to various criteria. As a popular organization that mediated this tendency and demonstrated a certain generational continuity, the American Jewish Congress provides an institutional lens through which to explore the Second Generation's persistent and relatively disproportionate commitment to decidedly left-wing if not entirely radical causes.

At the American Jewish Historical Society at the Center for Jewish History in Manhattan, the main archival source for this chapter, there are two hundred processed boxes as well as one thousand unprocessed or semiprocessed boxes (this chapter draws mostly from the former) on the American Jewish Congress covering the many decades of its existence from 1918 to 2010. The sheer size of this collection suggests the wide scope of the organization's activities. The specific focus of this chapter is the American Jewish Congress's campaigns against discrimination, prejudice, and racism during and after the Second World War. American Jews' movement into the Democratic Party in the 1920s and especially 1930s and their enthusiasm for Franklin D. Roosevelt and his New Deal constituted the crucial context out of which emerged their postwar preoccupations, as manifested within the American Jewish Congress. Despite the extensive primary materials and a number of secondary works, no study (to this author's knowledge) has encompassed the relationship between the origins and early concerns of the American Jewish Congress during the interwar period, on the one hand, and its efforts on behalf of domestic civil or human rights during and after the Second World War, on the other.

Several scholars have invoked the influence and importance of Jewish identity to account for the Second Generation's political orientation and expression. In comparison to Stuart Svonkin, who has located the source of the American Jewish Congress's fixations in Jewish insecurity and the Holocaust, this chapter, with its consideration of the prewar context, suggests that these factors were important yet not entirely decisive.[3] They catalyzed several tendencies, but they were not their original or sole source. In contrast to Marc Dollinger, who has described the Jewish community's dedication to American "liberalism" as a manifestation of an ongoing "politics of acculturation" and a yearning for "social inclusion,"[4] the annals and activities of the American Jewish Congress indicate impartial conformity to prevailing social expectations. These traits typified the organization from its inception just after the First World War to its suspension of activities in July 2010 due to insolvency.[5]

Pays légal

The American Jewish Congress first convened in Philadelphia on December 15, 1918, for five days.[6] The idea for such a convocation, however, predated this session by many years. Calls for the establishment of a representative Jewish congress to unite and coordinate the efforts of the many competing Jewish groups in the United States were made by various individuals around the turn of the twentieth century, most notably Rabbi David Philipson of the Union of American Hebrew Congregations in 1903, who urged that attention be paid to the needs of the growing number of Eastern European Jewish immigrants in particular and the difficulties of Eastern European Jewish life in general.[7] The impetus for concerted action proved insufficient at the time, not least because the established German Jewish elite, seeking to co-opt the uncouth masses, set up their own American Jewish Committee in November 1906, following several pogroms in Russia, "to defend Jewish interests" domestically and around the world in a quiet and diplomatic fashion.[8] The American Jewish Congress, as a democratically elected body of representatives that would augment the voice of immigrants against the German plutocracy, only emerged against the misgivings if not opposition of the American Jewish Committee, and the relationship between the two organizations remained fraught for decades, revealing much about their respective constituencies.

The outbreak and dislocation of the First World War renewed pressure for an American Jewish congress. The American Jewish Committee began to consider a Jewish brief for the postwar peace conference as early as August 1914, but other individuals and groups did not wait for these elite German Jews to resolve matters at their own discretion through their customary backdoor channels.[9] American Zionists, seeking to attract new members and to garner greater institutional clout, initiated the drive for an American Jewish congress under the banner of intracommunal democracy and openness.[10] They were joined by "recent immigrants possessing almost every conceivable radical philosophy."[11] The American Jewish Committee approved of neither Zionists nor radicals, but decided to cooperate in a fashion with the forces behind the congress movement in order to moderate its course. The American Jewish Committee recognized that public opinion among the Russian Jewish masses was increasingly against German pretensions to communal dominance, not least because of a propaganda campaign in the Yiddish press that led more and more Jewish bodies to proclaim themselves in favor of a congress in 1914 and 1915.[12]

These proponents did not ignore the American Jewish Committee, given its wealth and social connections. The contemporary status of Central European Jews in the United States meant that even the congress movement was fronted by Stephen S. Wise, a Reform rabbi whose family came from Budapest, and Louis D. Brandeis, a prominent jurist and soon to be a US Supreme Court justice, whose family hailed from Prague. These men lent prestige to the congress movement, providing the Russian base with confidence to proceed against the vested influence and power of the American Jewish Committee.[13] They also facilitated communication between the two blocs. After failed efforts at unity throughout 1915 and early 1916, Brandeis secured the agreement of fellow jurist Louis Marshall, the American Jewish Committee's dominant personality, to a congress. In private meetings in July and August 1916, Brandeis conceded that the prospective American Jewish Congress would not be a permanent entity in competition with the American Jewish Committee; it would pursue a limited mandate for a postwar settlement, then cease to exist. In turn, Marshall conceded the name of "congress" (rather than conference) and democratic elections, with some reserved seats for national organizations.[14]

The two men compromised on the issue of nationalism, an enduring point of contention. Whereas the congress movement had previously resolved to consider not just "equal rights, civil, political, religious, in all such lands where these rights were denied them" but also "national rights in all such lands in which national rights were or are ought to be recognized," the committee that emerged from the Brandeis-Marshall exchange to organize the American Jewish Congress replaced "national rights" with the vaguer conception of "group rights" and only tangentially recognized Jewish interests in Palestine.[15] A congress was to be called, Marshall wrote,

> exclusively for the purpose of defining the methods whereby in cooperation with the Jews of the world, full rights may be secured for the Jews of all lands, and all laws discriminating against them may be abrogated. It being understood that the phrase "full rights" is deemed to include:
> 1. Civil, religious and political rights, and in addition thereto
> 2. Wherever the various peoples of any land are or may be recognized as having separate group rights, the conferring upon the Jews of the lands affected, of such rights, if desired by them, and
> 3. The securing and protection of Jewish rights in Palestine.[16]

This compromise disappointed the Zionists, the "backbone of the [congress] movement," but their opposition was overcome and preparations for a convention proceeded.[17] Postponed from its original date of convocation in November 1917 due to America's entry into the Great War in April, the American Jewish Congress first sat in mid-December 1918, within weeks of the cessation of hostilities in Europe. The gathering issued a restrained endorsement of the Balfour Declaration, even as Marshall qualified the nature of that commitment in statements to the press.[18] As official policy, the American Jewish Congress adopted a bill of rights, written by Marshall, whose contents it hoped "to insert in the treaty of peace as conditions precedent to the creation of the new or enlarged States."[19] The enumerated rights included "national rights" in order to ensure amity among the various segments of the American Jewish Congress, but Marshall explained to a disconcerted Reform rabbi:

> We are dealing with Eastern European conditions, not those which prevail in the United States or in England, France and Italy, where the populations are practically homogenous and where the term "national" has reference to a political, as distinguished from an ethnical, unit . . . It is not for us in the United States to determine the wisdom of that conception. . . . The paragraph to which you have referred means merely that if any of these [minority] groups is accorded national rights . . . then every group shall have an equal claim.[20]

In the end, the minority treaties made provision for cultural expression rather than national rights. As the *de facto* leader of both the American Jewish Congress's and American Jewish Committee's delegations to the Paris peace conference, Marshall was "perhaps more responsible for the Minority Treaties than any other man," but he worked behind the scenes to secure their passage, the first and most important of which was signed by Poland on June 28, 1919.[21] As Naomi Cohen has noted, Marshall and colleagues from the American Jewish Committee made their case well before the American Jewish Congress "filed its brief" on June 9, rendering the latter "a purely academic document."[22] The treaties themselves proved unenforceable and were largely ignored by the new nation-states of Eastern Europe: the League of Nations lacked means of enforcement, not least because the Republican US Congress refused to participate, despite the urging of the Democratic president, Woodrow Wilson;[23] the American Jewish Committee, whose leader was a lifelong Republican, did not go "on record in support of the league";[24] and the American Jewish Congress, despite its admiration for the League, adjourned *sine die* on May 30, 1920, upon its delegation's return from Paris, as per the agreement between Brandeis and Marshall.[25]

The first phase of the American Jewish Congress came to an anticlimactic end. The loss of a sense of crisis after the war vitiated commitment among the rank and file. Even after the American Jewish Congress reconvened in May 1922 as a permanent body with more expressly Zionist aims,[26] it proved incapable of mobilizing mass interest or raising satisfactory funds, often suffering fiscal deficits in the following years.[27] The focus in the 1920s on Eastern Europe and Jewish life there did not galvanize the Second Generation to concerted action. The American Jewish Congress sent or joined fact-finding missions to Poland and Romania, whose Jews were perceived to be doing poorly and treated unfairly, and to the Soviet Union, whose Jews were in need of material aid and freedom of conscience.[28] Efforts to involve agents of the American government in bringing pressure to bear on these sovereign states were unsuccessful. The American Jewish Committee lamented the American Jewish Congress's tactics, whose protest meetings and public denunciations it felt were too militant.[29] Neither the American Jewish Congress nor the American Jewish Committee effected much change in the lives of Eastern European Jewry, although both bodies distributed funds to distressed communities.

For young American-born Jews, the concerns of the American Jewish Congress seemed remote from their daily lives. Unlike their parents, who knew both Europe and America, they only knew America, and unlike their counterparts in Eastern Europe, young American Jews were doing very well. They were in fact the most upwardly mobile population in the United States. In 1900 around 60 percent of Jews were industrial workers and 3 percent were professionals; by the 1930s less than 14 percent were industrial workers (the number was higher in New York City due to the larger foreign-born population), yet 13 percent were professionals, even as the remainder engaged in white-collar occupations, with a plurality in trade.[30] Most members of the Second Generation grew up in increasingly comfortable middle-class surroundings, moving from one new and better neighborhood to another.[31] Few were on course to repeat their parents' blue-collar experience, notwithstanding their parents' socialist ideology or leanings.[32] Already by 1900 Jews were overrepresented in institutions of higher learning, white-collar occupations, and the professions. This overrepresentation continued in a very pronounced fashion throughout the interwar period and beyond, resulting in some consternation among the Anglo-Protestant elite.

By 1920 Manhattan's City College and Hunter College were 80–90 percent Jewish; Columbia and New York University were 40 percent Jewish, if not more; and Harvard was 20 percent Jewish. As Stephen Steinberg noted in his study of the topic, "Without its pejorative implications, the notion of a 'Jewish invasion' would not be inappropriate for describing the trends in these institutions" on the East Coast.[33] Most exceptionally, Jewish lawyers constituted 26 percent of new bar admissions in New York City between 1900 and 1910, 36 percent between 1911 and 1917, 40 percent between 1918 and 1923, 56 percent between 1924 and 1929, and 80 percent between 1930 and 1934; this proportion declined to 50 percent at the end of the 1940s, but stabilized at 65 percent during the 1950s.[34] New York City had the largest concentration of Jews in the United States (and indeed the world), and law was the profession most attractive and accessible to them; nonetheless, the basic trajectory of rapid economic mobility characterized other American cities with large Jewish populations, as well as other professions.[35]

The social life of the Second Generation boomed in the 1920s. Making up more than a quarter of the population of the country's consistently largest city, "the immense numbers of New York Jews decisively influenced the character of Jewish group life." According to Moore, "sheer size gave New York Jews tremendous psychological security and triggered an amazing complexity of institutions."[36] As Eastern European Jews spread throughout New York City, most going to Brooklyn and the Bronx, they built many synagogues and community centers. Often the two went together, as few members of the Second Generation followed traditional or orthodox Judaism; most "synagogue centers" operated as ethnic fora where "cultural Zionism," among other expressions, became important.[37] Jews also established their own domestic courts and, given the state's limited role in this area prior to the New Deal, set up their own network of social services.[38] Similar developments may be observed among other dense Russian Jewish concentrations in the United States.[39]

The public schools constituted an essential social experience for the Second Generation, as most would attend a local branch. From the 1910s the number of Jewish teachers grew such that schools in Jewish neighborhoods, to which Jewish teachers had themselves assigned preferentially, often became demographically homogeneous venues that encouraged Jewishness and even Jewish political causes and engendered strong and often extracurricular pupil-teacher and parent-teacher relationships.[40] The percentages of teachers entering the New York City school system who were Jewish were 22 in 1914, 26 in 1920, 44 in 1930, 56 in 1940, 65 in 1950, and 59 in 1960.[41] Second Generation Jews demanded that the public schools acknowledge Jewish ethnicity, respect Jewish holidays, and remove national symbols with Christian associations. They regarded "Americanization activities as the most threatening to their sense of identity" and sought to have Yiddish and then Hebrew included within the general curriculum (they succeeded in the case of the latter, on the basis of the civilizational significance of the biblical text, but not in the former). Jewish parents and teachers "changed their children's schools from agents of Americanization into instruments of democratic pluralism."[42]

The American Jewish Congress's campaigns in the 1920s on behalf of Eastern European Jewry may not have induced the Second Generation, confidently and safely busy with everyday existence and success, to active engagement, but its leaders' domestic political sympathies did reflect the masses' evolving political preferences. Notably, Stephen S. Wise, a popular Reform rabbi and founder of the "Free Synagogue," was a proponent of the first American Jewish Congress and president of the second with few interruptions from 1923 until his death in 1949, during which time he was the "most impressive [Jewish] public figure in Washington."[43] A nominal Republican and "progressive" at the turn of the century, he became a Democrat in the 1910s in support of Wilson, who in turn became close to Wise, endorsing the idea of the American Jewish Congress and later the Balfour Declaration.[44] Wilson's diplomatic internationalism (the League of Nations) and incipient welfarism appealed to Wise, as they did to many members of the First and especially Second Generations, who gave him a majority of their votes in 1916 if not 1912.[45] Wilson, Wise proclaimed, would bring about the "re-birth of the Party you represent" in the name of progress.[46]

This process of electoral (re)alignment continued through the 1920s, a decade of otherwise national Republican dominance; the Jewish community evinced notable support for Al Smith, the Catholic Democratic governor of New York from 1923 to 1928 and Democratic presidential candidate in that last year, when he received almost three-quarters of the Jewish vote.[47] Both Wilson and Smith ostensibly attracted Jews because they took the Democratic Party in the direction of what became known as American "liberalism"—ultimately involving the expansion of the role of government—so distinguishing that party more clearly in

purpose and ideology from the Republicans, who remained nominally more committed to the separation of the state from civil society.[48] The federal elections of
the 1910s and 1920s proved early indicators of Eastern European Jews' absorption
into the Democratic fold, which occurred more quickly in New York City than
in other places with sizable Jewish populations, like Chicago and Boston, where
nearly total Irish Catholic control (and corruption) of the Democratic machine
kept many Jews away.[49]

Of all the American Jewish Congress's endeavors in the 1920s, the establishment at the very end of the decade of several commissions to study perceived
discrimination against American Jews in workplaces and universities predicted
well its future focus. Proposals to investigate prejudice and racism and simultaneously to encourage tolerance and Jewish culture had been made for some years
within the American Jewish Congress, not least because of the antisemitic propaganda of Henry Ford and the Ku Klux Klan, but a lack of funds and internal
conflicts had impeded forward movement.[50] A minor incident in the small town
of Massena in upstate New York in September 1928 precipitated matters.[51] As
Morris Frommer observed in his detailed account of the early American Jewish
Congress, the commissions that were then formed "and their subsequent reports
must not be minimized, for it was the first time that the Jewish Congress emphasized the importance of scientific and authoritative studies to combat prejudice."
What is more, "a concerted effort was made to use those studies to direct and
condition Jewish public opinion to a changing environment."[52]

By 1930 the American Jewish Congress had established the Commission on
Economic Problems (CEP) to coordinate its efforts in this regard.[53] The "work of
the Commission covered" the following areas:

1. Investigation and adjustment of complaints
2. Job placement through established agencies
3. Cooperation with non-Jewish leaders and agencies
4. Education of employers through conferences
5. Legislative work for remedial measures
6. Research in the Jewish contribution to the economic life of the community
   and the extent to which discrimination exists.[54]

The chairman of the CEP was Wise's protégé from the Free Synagogue, Jacob
X. Cohen, an engineer-cum-Reform rabbi, born on the Lower East Side at the
end of the nineteenth century to Eastern European immigrants.[55] Cohen helped
to organize the CEP after many years of his personal "fight on discrimination
against Jews, Negroes and other minority groups in the fields of employment and
education."[56] The various surveys and studies that he produced for the American

Jewish Congress from 1930 purported to confirm that discrimination in these fields persisted and posed a serious menace to the Jewish individual as well as "to the true spirit of our American ideals."[57]

The work of the CEP continued throughout the Depression and the Second World War, but the American Jewish Congress's attention was again distracted from purely domestic pursuits by Adolf Hitler's rise overseas. Having dismissed the Nazis as rabble-rousers in the 1920s, Jewish groups in the United States and Europe were caught off guard by Hitler's ascension.[58] The American Jewish Committee advocated circumspection, in line with Germany's "leading Jews," who told a delegation from the American Jewish Congress in October 1932 to mind its own business, for "Hitler would never come to power."[59] Even so, the American Jewish Congress was under pressure from various American constituencies to act in some positive, public way, and when Hitler did become chancellor in January 1933, its executive committee passed a resolution two months later to "sponsor a series of meetings to voice the protest of the American people against the outrages committed against the Jewish citizens of Germany."[60] On March 27, 1933, a mass rally under the auspices of the American Jewish Congress filled up Madison Square Garden in Manhattan; tens of thousands took part, and written protests, including some by Christians, were lodged in other parts of the country and around the world.[61]

Despite this showing of support, momentum in the campaign against Nazi Germany was not maintained, in part due to "organizational rivalries."[62] The American Jewish Congress and American Jewish Committee, among others, continued to bicker. "Even in the face of Hitler," Frommer observed, "American Jewish leaders could not trust each other," and "aside from the creation of a number of committees, the Congress did very little to counter effectively the Nazi onslaught, and even those committees either did not meet or proved to be totally ineffective."[63] The American Jewish Congress failed to raise sufficient funds from the American Jewish public, even as it dithered in its sponsorship of a boycott of German goods, the idea of which, though likely impractical in implementation, had captured the Jewish community's moral imagination.[64]

Lack of accomplishment in relation to the Nazi threat has led some historians to deplore the dismal conduct of American (and especially American-born) Jews during the Holocaust and others to question whether anything but military victory would have been advantageous in the given context. As in the 1920s, the Second Generation was preoccupied domestically. It endured the Depression and was later involved in the American war economy, even as few grasped fully at the time the fact of the genocide that was perpetrated in Europe in the 1940s.[65] Nonetheless, some refugees from Nazi Europe recalled with shock and dismay the parochial self-absorption, even insouciance, that they encountered among many

American Jews during that decade, who were doing materially quite well and were not obviously interested in survivors' stories of suffering.[66]

A notable factor that kept the American Jewish Congress from behaving in a more determined and vociferous manner during the Second World War was its leaders' strong endorsement of Roosevelt and his New Deal—his "program of social justice," in the words of Wise.[67] Like others, Wise refrained from undue public criticism of the president and his foreign policy, even when the Democratic administration failed to pursue a proactive strategy of aiding Jews under Nazi tyranny.[68] Historian William Rubinstein has declaimed that the "American Jewish community could have threatened to direct its large voting strength to the Republican Party at the 1942 and 1944 elections if the Roosevelt administration was not prepared to take some determined action to rescue whatever portion of European Jewry it could."[69] More members of the Second Generation devoted their time and energy to the implementation of Roosevelt's New Deal, in which they played a central and highly visible role, than to anti-Nazi agitation.

American Jews were extremely enthusiastic about Roosevelt. The mood of the Second Generation in the 1930s was summed up famously in a Yiddish rhyme by the Tammany-connected judge Jonah F. Goldstein, who observed that American Jews lived in three *velten* (worlds): *die velt, yene velt, un Roosevelt* (this world, the world to come, and Roosevelt).[70] In 1932 Roosevelt received 82 percent of the Jewish vote; by 1944, it was over 90 percent.[71] As such, Roosevelt entrenched and completed the process of American Jews' passage into the Democratic Party, which had begun as early as the 1910s with Wilson and gained ground in the 1920s with Smith. In addition, Roosevelt's enormous appeal mobilized hundreds of thousands of previously unregistered Jewish citizens to become voters.[72] By the 1950s, "Jews were the most heavily and consistently Democratic of all ethnocultural groups in the United States."[73] The alliance that Roosevelt cemented between American Jews and the Democrats remained a feature of American Jewish life into the twenty-first century.

The Jewish vote was not class based then or later. It "transcended all economic cleavages."[74] What is more, American (and especially American-born) Jews lived through the Depression in relative comfort, being more white collar than other groups and thus more insulated from economic vicissitudes, which most affected laborers and the industrial sector.[75] In this regard, Jews were notably better off than urban Catholics, most of whom remained blue-collar, poor, and subject to Protestant animus, yet whose fewer wealthy members were still more likely to vote Republican. Urban Catholics had a long tradition of Democratic voting, and large majorities cast their ballots for Roosevelt in the 1930s and beyond. They were an essential electoral mainstay of the New Deal, without which it may have floundered. Their loyalty, however, was above all to the local party machine and to Al Smith, who initially endorsed Roosevelt. They were not especially dedicated to the latter, whose economic policies they found congenial yet whose foreign and social policies and Anglo-patrician background they often suspected. Some Catholics expressed their disapproval by voting for William Lemke's quasi-fascist Union Party in 1936.[76] By the 1940s Catholic disillusion with Roosevelt resulted in increasing defection to the Republican Party. In 1944 New York City's Italian and Irish vote for Roosevelt fell below half.[77]

Despite its small numbers, the Second Generation's prominence in and steadfast commitment to the New Deal, by contrast, led some of its opponents, including the notorious antisemitic priest and radio broadcaster Charles E. Coughlin, who backed Lemke, to make repeated, derogatory references to a "Jew Deal."[78] Jews were prominent among Roosevelt's advisers and administrators, and many young Jewish lawyers drafted and then defended before the courts key pieces of New Deal legislation, often having been guided into such regulatory work by the Harvard professor and later Supreme Court justice Felix Frankfurter, himself a founding member of the American Jewish Congress, a noteworthy Zionist, and a long-standing friend of the president. According to legal historian Peter Irons, Frankfurter "most directly put his stamp on the New Deal lawyers" as "mentor of the 'Happy Hot Dogs' whom he stuffed into New Deal agencies."[79] Along with Frankfurter, some of these "Happy Hot Dogs," many of whom were Jewish, were involved simultaneously in some way with the American Jewish Congress.[80] A number of them would also come to join the American Jewish Congress in the early 1940s or after the Second World War, when the organization expanded its antiprejudice campaigns.

As a body conceived originally as an organization in defense of Jewish rights, the American Jewish Congress had always looked to law as an important instrument in the international arena. The use of lawyers and litigation to bring about preferred changes in the domestic sphere, however, emerged most obviously out of Jacob X. Cohen's CEP, which, though it was sidelined within the American Jewish Congress before and during the war due to the urgent crisis in Europe, had continued to operate and conduct research. Cohen published many pamphlets on the topic of social and economic discrimination during the 1930s, but the most important, because most well-known, was his 1937 tract, *Jews, Jobs, and Discrimination*, which, according to his wife and biographer, "drew country-wide, even world-wide comment."[81] Therein, Cohen covered the situation in various major industries and professions, alleging the existence of ongoing discrimination against Jews, which was—at least in the case of public utilities, like the New York Telephone Company—in "plain violation of the Civil Rights Law of New York State (Laws of 1933, Chapter 511, Section 42)."[82] Cohen also put forward a "program for meeting discrimination," wherein he proclaimed his belief that "only a specialized, local agency, established as a bureau, and adequately supported by the community, can do the work properly":

> One of the chief functions of the bureau envisaged here would be to receive the complaints of victims of discrimination. The intercession of a respected third party of community standing will often produce tangible results in a situation which otherwise might be considered hopeless. In Greater New York and vicinity the Congress has an interesting record of such cases, cleared up by a process of systematic investigation and tactful intercession.[83]

A version of this proposed bureau emerged in June 1941 with Executive Order 8802—"the first executive order on civil rights since Lincoln's Emancipation Proclamation"[84]—whereby Roosevelt mandated the creation of the President's Committee on Fair Employment Practice (COFEP).[85] This agency was reorganized in May 1943 through Executive Order 9346 and was better known as the Fair Employment Practices Commission (FEPC).[86] The COFEP/FEPC was set up to monitor compliance with executive antidiscrimination instructions to the burgeoning wartime defense industry, with its many lucrative federal contracts.[87]

The immediate pressure behind the establishment of this regulatory body had been brought to bear by the African American labor leader A. Philip Randolph, head of the union of the Brotherhood of Sleeping Car Porters, who threatened a march on Washington in the summer of 1941 unless black workers' grievances over jobs in the growing military-industrial complex were addressed.[88] Even though "the initial movement to create the FEPC was all-black, the FEPC was not," Kevin M. Schultz has observed, "just a civil rights advocacy for black people, and it had attracted the support and imagination of numerous liberal Americans."[89] The American Jewish Congress was one such source of support, and it backed Randolph's drive.

The American Jewish Congress joined the Coordinating Committee of Jewish Organizations Dealing with Employment Discrimination in War Industries, which "was created to further the purposes of Executive Order 8802" and was chaired by a prominent "congressionist" from Chicago, Claude A. Benjamin.[90] At a public hearing of the FEPC in New York City on February 16, 1942, Jacob X. Cohen, on behalf of the American Jewish Congress and the Coordinating Committee, provided testimony and evidence of discrimination against Jews in the defense industry; he presented a survey of job placements for this industry in major newspapers, of which between one-quarter and one-third apparently expressed religious bias in some way.[91] Cohen also "testified at a number of hearings in the House of Representatives and in the Senate."[92] By 1945, with the help of the Coordinating Committee, Jews had filed about 10 percent of all complaints with the FEPC; the vast majority were filed by or on behalf of African Americans.[93]

Jewish individuals and groups were so keen about the FEPC that the Coordinating Committee, as Merl E. Reed noted in his classic study, "harbored hopes of becoming a semiofficial arm," an aspiration that "far exceeded anything the blacks proposed." As early as 1942, the Coordinating Committee "proposed that specially deputized representatives of private agencies collect information and make follow-up contacts with companies cited by the FEPC for discrimination. It also pushed for the creation of community councils to act as representatives of the committee." Despite a chronic shortage of staff and attempts by Jewish personnel to facilitate such a partnership, these proposals were not readily received by the FEPC. The Coordinating Committee, Reed mused, "somehow failed to understand that government agencies could not take the chance that investigations might be carried out by untutored individuals or by private zealots who, under the imprimatur of an official agency, might turn such activities into witch hunts."[94] Notwithstanding such formal impediments, activists of the Second Generation, including those from within the American Jewish Congress, remained procedurally central to the FEPC:

> Jewish leaders spent untold hours preparing memoranda and communicating with the FEPC, and their organizations provided research data, complaints, witnesses, and a variety of services. Many of those who worked in the FEPC offices were Jews. Their national network of organizations and groups, like those of the black community, could be relied on to rally behind the FEPC with letters, telegrams, petitions, or other forms of support. The blacks and the Jews, one with numbers and resolve, the other with political influence and resources, both well organized, became the main legs of FEPC support. These relations greatly benefitted both the agency and its clients.[95]

Historians have debated the extent to which the FEPC attained its goal of effecting change in the composition and operation of the marketplace, not least because of its narrow application to war-related industry. As "the first administrative agency established in the United States to protect and enforce the rights of all Americans to equality of opportunity in employment," the federal FEPC "was the forerunner of state fair employment practices laws, which were a giant step forward . . . for civil rights."[96] All the same, the FEPC was not terribly potent. First, despite sympathy for the principle of nondiscrimination, Roosevelt had issued Executive Order 8802 under pressure and without obvious "determination to stand firmly behind it." Further, the FEPC lacked the power of statutory law, so "could not directly penalize firms, managers, or unions that failed to comply."[97] As

legal scholar Arthur Earl Bonfield observed, the FEPC "suffered from the disabil-
ities of numerous administrative frictions, inadequate authority, financing, and
personnel. It also lacked distinct, clear organizational position and was shifted
several times from one federal agency to another."[98] Finally, the FEPC expired
automatically in June 1946, notwithstanding efforts by A. Philip Randolph and his
allies to render the commission into a permanent body and to enlarge the scope
and nature of its activities as well as its powers of enforcement and appropriation.[99]

The American Jewish Congress participated eagerly in these and related
efforts.[100] In August 1945 it hired the New Deal lawyer Will Maslow to lobby on its
behalf for the continued existence and eventual expansion of the FEPC, from which
agency he had just come.[101] Maslow had prior ties to the American Jewish Congress.
During his time as the "bright, intense, and aggressive" director of field operations
at the FEPC, he had "met frequently with Jewish leaders" and had even "prepared
a list of organizations affiliated with" the Coordinating Committee, which included
the American Jewish Congress, encouraging his colleagues "to establish close and
friendly relations with them."[102] Nonetheless, his dealings with black coworkers at
the FEPC, about some of whom he had a "low opinion" and by whom he was viewed
as unqualified in the field of race relations, were often strained.

As a result, after Maslow joined the American Jewish Congress, it "remained
almost completely outside of the pressure structure erected by [Randolph's]
National Council for a Permanent FEPC" at the federal level.[103] Maslow focused
his attention and the resources of the American Jewish Congress at the state level,
which proved more amenable to FEPC-style legislation. "Coincident with the
effort to enact a federal statute," Maslow wrote, "were the efforts to adopt analogous state laws. The trickle of such bills in 1941 and 1943 sessions of the legislatures
became a flood in 1945."[104] By 1963 twenty states had "passed laws substantially
similar in general approach and design to that first [NY] act," although schemes
for enforcement varied.[105]

In this endeavor, Maslow operated as director of the American Jewish
Congress's Commission on Law and Social Action (CLSA), which grew out of
Jacob X. Cohen's CEP at the end of the Second World War.[106] The CLSA was established officially by the executive committee on November 29, 1945.[107] The new
commission's chairman from 1945 to 1955 was Shad (né Isadore) Polier, who was
somewhat unusual among his peers for having been born and raised in South
Carolina, yet whose professional development was not atypical.[108] He had attended
Harvard Law School in the late 1920s, where he had been Felix Frankfurter's student, to whom he was indebted "for the realization of the function of the law in
society."[109] He subsequently became an activist for black rights, preparing briefs
in the early 1930s for the famous Scottsboro case, in which "black youths were

sentenced to death on an allegation of rape against two white girls." In the late 1930s he became a New Deal litigator. He was also the husband of Justine Wise, Rabbi Wise's daughter, from 1937.[110]

The "basic aim" of the commission over which Polier and Maslow presided was, according to a founding member, Alexander H. Pekelis, who wrote its *de facto* "constitution" in 1945, "full equality in a free society." This goal was to be achieved by the further extension of the apparatus of the state into the civil sphere and the partial if not full abrogation of those "private governments" and "private groups" that were unfortunately "exempt from the requirements of fairness" by an unduly constricted interpretation of the American Constitution.[111] In Pekelis's estimation, the most important contemporary measure in the "struggle for Jewish equality at home, equality in law, and equality in fact" was the potential "enactment of fair employment practice statutes in the states of New York and New Jersey," which would apply to half of American Jewry.[112]

As part of a larger coalition that included blacks, Catholics, and labor unions, the CLSA played a key role in the formulation of the relevant statutes in New York, whose Ives-Quinn bill, applicable to all employers of more than six people, whether private or public, became the "model" on which similar legislation across the country was "patterned."[113] Republican Irving M. Ives was the chair of a temporary commission that New York State's legislature set up in April 1944 after much lobbying to make "studies of practices of discrimination" as well as "recommendations designed to eliminate such discrimination."[114] Democrat Elmer F. Quinn joined him in January 1945 to propose the permanent State Commission Against Discrimination (NYSCAD) with comprehensive powers of enforcement.[115]

After considerable public controversy and despite opposition from many Republicans and some Democrats, who maintained that Ives-Quinn "offers a remedy worse than the disease,"[116] New York's Law Against Discrimination passed the houses of government, receiving the sanction of the liberal Republican governor, Thomas E. Dewey, on March 12, 1945.[117] For its part, the American Jewish Congress not only provided evidence and applied pressure in the right places, but also drafted a bill that informed the subsequent law, which was written up officially by Charles H. Tuttle of NYSCAD.[118] There are similarities in language and structure between Tuttle's bill and the earlier "bill introduced February 1944 by Senator William F. Condon in the New York State Senate to provide for a state board of fair employment practice." This bill had been framed by a judge, Nathan D. Perlman, who was head of the American Jewish Congress's Commission on Law and Legislation, which predated yet merged with the CLSA.[119]

Jews were "the religious group that contributed most, both early and late," to such antidiscrimination laws.[120] They were instrumental in New Jersey and

Massachusetts, which were the first states to follow New York in the enactment of such legislation.[121] In the former, "the staff functions of the state Committee against Discrimination in Housing [were] provided by the Newark Jewish Community Relations Board"; in the latter, "all but one of the major civil rights bills in Massachusetts were drafted by" the American Jewish Congress's New England branch. As Duane Lockard observed in his relatively contemporary study of the subject, "Jewish religious and social organizations and their leaders deserve much credit for the initiation of hundreds of civil rights campaigns. In every state there is evidence of some major contribution from Jewish groups," including the provision of money and personnel for sundry activities:

> Much of this assistance has come through the Commission on Law and Social Action, a subdivision of the American Jewish Congress. From its headquarters in New York [it] has issued a steady stream of publications, correspondence with state and local groups, and legal and strategic advice to local Jewish organizations, ad hoc committees, and individuals involved in civil rights work. From that office came original drafts of bills that were to become laws in dozens of places. . . . Individual Jewish leaders in nearly every state have been significant participants, many of them active for twenty or thirty years.[122]

In the decade after 1945 the American Jewish Congress was involved in scores of cases before various courts, including the Supreme Court.[123] "The American Jewish Congress actively embraced the role of 'gadfly,'" Stuart Svonkin has noted. "In many of the instances where state and city civil rights laws were passed"— often through the American Jewish Congress's intervention—"CLSA lawyers were among the first to lodge complaints against discriminatory employers, landlords, real estate developers, and schools."[124] By 1946 the CLSA had established its right to file complaints with NYSCAD on behalf of aggrieved parties, including non-Jews, arguing that "a ruling by [NYSCAD] that it will entertain complaints only from individuals directly discriminated against places the burden of effectuating the purposes of the Act upon an underprivileged group, usually lacking legal or financial resources" and that "no group could be more directly concerned with and 'aggrieved' by discriminatory practices in employment against a particular religious minority than one organized for the purpose of safeguarding the economic and other democratic rights of that minority."[125] By 1950 the CLSA alone had "filed 186 cases with [NYSCAD] since its creation"[126] out of a total of around 7,000.[127]

Arguing for its standing before a district court in Southern California at around this time, the American Jewish Congress invoked the Jewish heritage of social justice and identification with the oppressed:

In the three decades of its existence the American Jewish Congress, on frequent occasions, has represented the democratic interests of the Jewish people before the courts, legislatures and administrative tribunals of the State and Federal Government. Its work, however, has never been confined to the interests of the Jewish people alone. We believe, indeed, that the [*sic*] Jewish interests are inseparable from those of justice and that Jewish interests are threatened whenever persecution, discrimination or humiliation is inflicted upon any human being because of his race, creed, color, language or ancestry.[128]

The many domestic legal campaigns of the American Jewish Congress during and especially after the Second World War were ostensibly more immediately popular with the Jewish masses than its earlier international diplomacy. These campaigns segued with the postwar "Jewish support for the civil rights struggle," in which "examples of Jewish participation, large and small . . . can be drawn from every Jewish community."[129] The years from 1945 to 1964 have been called the "golden years" of a black-Jewish alliance on civil and human rights in the United States.[130] Surveys of the Second Generation for much of this period indicated overwhelming support for such measures.[131] The American Jewish Congress benefited from the widespread enthusiasm. Its finances improved in the late 1940s and kept pace with inflation for several decades.[132] Even though it was less successful in raising funds in a time of general Jewish philanthropy than some other major communal organizations, including the American Jewish Committee and the Anti-Defamation League (ADL), its preferred strategy of legal activism remained relatively inexpensive to practice until around 1980, when "an exorbitant increase in the cost of litigation," due to structural factors beyond its control, "made it almost impossible for the American Jewish Congress to continue to engage in the direct sponsorship of legal cases."[133]

At its peak, the American Jewish Congress was able to partake in a larger civil rights movement that "successfully swayed popular sentiment" in favor of "a relatively broad scope, comprehensive, and enforceable national fair employment law." Several of its leaders, including Will Maslow and Rabbi Joachim Prinz, were involved in planning the March on Washington of August 1963, at which Martin Luther King Jr. gave his famous speech, "I Have a Dream."[134] This event precipitated passage of the Civil Rights Act of 1964, which the American Jewish Congress hailed as "the most far-reaching civil rights measure enacted since the post-Civil War days."[135] More important, the Civil Rights Act had grown out of successive, frustrated attempts to set up a permanent FEPC during the Truman, Eisenhower, and Kennedy administrations, and it was "modeled in basic design and approach on the New York experience."[136] The American Jewish Congress had helped to shape this "New York experience" through its lobbying for the original

state legislation against discrimination and its establishing of important precedents in the courts.

New York's Ives-Quinn bill helped Shad Polier win a suit that he brought
against the Arabian American Oil Company (Aramco) in the mid-1950s for "violations of the State Law Against Discrimination" due to a refusal to hire Jews "for
positions in Saudi Arabia." NYSCAD dismissed the petition, but the CLSA "commenced a proceeding" in the Supreme Court of the State of New York.[137] After
several years and much recrimination, Justice Henry Epstein decided in favor of
the plaintiff, ordering Aramco on July 15, 1959, to "stop asking applicants in New
York State questions about their religion so that the company could comply with
Saudi Arabian barriers against Jews."[138] NYSCAD appealed the decision,[139] but it
was upheld.[140] After several rounds of disputation,[141] the CLSA could report in
1963 that Aramco was finally "complying with a state order to stop discriminating
against Jews."[142] The Aramco suit was one of many relating to prejudice in employment that the CLSA took up either as plaintiff or *amicus*.[143]

Housing was an another area of concern for the CLSA.[144] In a report that
the American Jewish Congress produced with the National Association for the
Advancement of Colored People (NAACP), a quasi-Jewish organization at the
time,[145] housing was characterized as "the strongest and most tenaciously defended
bulwark of racism in the country."[146] Notably, in June 1947 the American Jewish
Congress and the NAACP, in conjunction with the American Civil Liberties
Union (ACLU), sponsored a legal challenge by three black war veterans against
the Metropolitan Life Insurance Company, whose sprawling housing development in southeast Manhattan—Stuyvesant Town—excluded blacks from rental
contracts (*Dorsey v. Stuyvesant Town Corporation*). Simultaneously, Shad Polier,
in his capacity as a taxpayer, sued the mayor's office (*Polier v. O'Dwyer*).[147] Both
plaintiffs argued that Stuyvesant Town was not a truly private enterprise, because
it had received subsidies in the form of tax exemptions.[148] Both cases were dismissed (the first was appealed to a higher court yet lost again) on the basis that
the project in question had received municipal aid to redevelop slums; it was thus
only public until the time of occupancy, after which it reverted to full private own-
ership and could choose tenants on its own terms.[149]

The American Jewish Congress did not prevail in the court of law, but it did
make strides in the court of public opinion. The rulings over Stuyvesant Town
engendered public protests in the form of "meetings, petitions and polls" against
Metropolitan's racial policy and catalyzed the enactment of "fair housing" laws.[150]
In June 1950, two weeks after the Supreme Court refused to hear *Dorsey*, two
councilmen—the black Democrat Earl Brown and the Jewish Republican Stanley
M. Isaacs—"introduced a CLSA-drafted bill designed to bar discrimination in
all public or publicly assisted housing in New York City, including Stuyvesant

Town."[151] Under media scrutiny, Metropolitan's chairman, Frederick H. Ecker, allowed that it would admit several black families into Stuyvesant Town even before the passage of Brown-Isaacs.[152] This bill duly became law in February–March 1951 and was extended to cover private housing in December 1957.[153]

Stuyvesant Town influenced the course of similar legal action against the Jewish developer William Levitt, whose post–Second World War suburban subdivisions or "Levittowns" also denied access to blacks yet received default insurance on mortgages through the Federal Housing Administration, a New Deal agency. In a campaign that lasted nearly a decade and in which the CLSA played a supporting role,[154] New Jersey courts ruled against Levitt in 1959, "enforcing a decision made outside the community, and, like most nonpolitical decisions, it was not favored by the community's majority." As with Stuyvesant Town, Levitt began to admit blacks to his developments to avoid negative publicity prior to the outcome of his (unsuccessful) appeal.[155] In response to such trials, various states over the subsequent years would pass "fair housing" laws, some drafted by the CLSA, and provisions to this effect were incorporated into the Civil Rights Act of 1966 and 1968. Levitt himself testified in the latter's favor before Congress in 1966; he sought uniform coverage across his industry, arguing that "no builder will desegregate his community unless all builders are required to do so."[156]

The American Jewish Congress may have been most preoccupied by discrimination in higher education. Throughout the interwar period, Jacob X. Cohen's CEP had denounced repeatedly the perceived restrictions on Jewish students in the Ivy League. These charges came to a head in March 1946, when Rabbi Wise, with the help of his son-in-law, Shad Polier, as well as others in the CLSA, sued his *alma mater*, Columbia University, for purported discrimination against Jews in medicine.[157] Although they failed to get the courts to revoke the institution's tax-exempt status, Columbia changed its methods of admission anyway.[158] Pursuing this matter in New York State's legislature, the American Jewish Congress pressed for "fair education" laws against the express wishes of most educators, who preferred voluntary rectification to state-enforced resolution and denied antisemitism at their institutions.[159] By dint of its advocacy, which included various studies "in the field of discrimination in education" as well as model drafts of suitable bills, the American Jewish Congress helped to secure passage of relevant legislation in 1947 and 1948, through which public universities were also established.[160]

In a coeval incident, in the fall of 1946 the CLSA filed an *amicus* brief in support of Mexican American parents in California, who some months earlier had brought suit against their school board due to its segregation of their children on the basis (or pretext) of linguistic needs (*Westminster v. Mendez*).[161] The school district argued for the separate-but-equal doctrine as upheld in 1896 by the Supreme Court (*Plessy v. Ferguson*). The parents, led by a black lawyer from the NAACP,

Robert L. Carter, employed a strategy that had been devised for the organization in 1930 by Nathan Margold, a member of the Second Generation, a New Dealer, an activist for Amerindian rights, and the protégé of Felix Frankfurter: they maintained that separation necessitated inequality in actual fact if not in theory.[162] Alex Pekelis presented "scientific" research before the bench, much of it funded and carried out by the American Jewish Congress and other Jewish groups, to back this claim.[163] He also invoked the lessons of Nazi Germany.[164] On April 14, 1947, the case was ultimately decided in favor of the plaintiffs on a narrow technicality rather than Pekelis's evidence.

Westminster vs. Mendez "had important ramifications for the battle against segregation"[165] and "directly affected the strategy used by the NAACP in *Brown v. Board of Education*."[166] This case proved groundbreaking for the future course of intergroup and race relations in the United States. At the urging of Esther Swirk Brown—a Jewish housewife-cum-activist from Merriam, Kansas, who had earlier campaigned against the poor conditions in the public school near her black maid's house—the NAACP filed suit in February 1951 against the board of education in the town of Topeka on behalf of Oliver Brown (unrelated). This man's daughter attended a segregated facility.[167] With Esther Swirk Brown as an intermediary, a case was put together by Carter and a Jewish attorney from New York, Jack Greenberg, who had ties to the American Jewish Congress and later worked with the CLSA.[168]

The American Jewish Congress's Commission on Community Interrelations, which cooperated with the CLSA, financed, conducted, and disseminated "scientific" inquiries that purported to demonstrate the detrimental psychological effects of academic segregation, which imbued minorities with a sense of inferiority and thus undermined positive attitudes to learning. This as well as similar work by the American Jewish Committee—its Studies in Prejudice Series—would influence the outcome in *Brown*.[169] The United States filed an *amicus* brief written by a Jewish socialist, Philip Elman, who was a former law clerk of sitting Supreme Court justice Felix Frankfurter.[170] The court's final, unanimous (due, according to Elman, to the exhortations of Frankfurter) decision in March 1954 overturned *Plessy*, providing impetus for racial integration across the United States.[171] For its own part, the CLSA had filed an *amicus* brief when *Brown* reached the Supreme Court in late 1952.

As in the past, the American Jewish Congress invoked elements of a "lived religion" to justify its participation:

> Through the thousands of years of our tragic history we have learned one lesson well: the persecution at any time of any minority portends the shape and intensity of persecution of all minorities. There is, however, an additional reason for our interest. The special concern of the Jewish people in human rights derives from an

immemorial tradition which proclaims the common origin and end of all mankind and affirms, under the highest sanction of faith and human aspirations, the common and inalienable rights of men. The struggle for human dignity and liberty is thus of the very substance of the Jewish tradition.[172]

Only a few years later, a leading, long-standing figure within the American Jewish Congress ended up at the center of the beginning of the push for desegregation in the North, a project to which the organization pledged its "full support and cooperation."[173] As Jennifer de Forest has noted, despite the greater scholarly attention that has been paid to the popular white resistance to the enforcement of *Brown* in the South, including the "dramatic events" in places like Little Rock, Arkansas, "local resistance to desegregation may have been less visible in the North, [but] it was nevertheless both pervasive and persistent." Following *Brown*, efforts to get the Jewish-dominated New York City board of education to address "systemic . . . inequities in the city's school system" were hindered by various forms of obstruction "not unlike some of their more notorious counterparts in the South."[174] After two years of organization, nine frustrated black mothers—the "Harlem nine"—decided to act. In September 1958 they pulled their children out of class and established their own unaccredited, alternative school. A month later the mothers were charged with violating the state's compulsory education law.

Two of the cases were soon assigned to the court of Rabbi Wise's daughter and Shad Polier's wife, Judge Justine Wise Polier, head of the American Jewish Congress's women's division and a friend of Eleanor Roosevelt.[175] She absolved the parents in December, asserting in her conclusion that they "have the constitutionally guaranteed right to elect no education for their children rather than to subject them to discriminatorily inferior education."[176] Polier's ruling "was hailed as the first northern decision against de facto segregation."[177] It affirmed "a parent's right to confront the educational bureaucracy over perceived inequities" and so "fueled the tumultuous movement for the community control of New York's schools that began in the 1960s."[178] In the midst of this movement in 1964, a black journalist, Chuck Stone, wrote to Shad Polier to express his appreciation:

> You have risen in my estimation . . . now that I have learned that you are married to Justine Wise Polier who, in my opinion, was the first person in America to give the freedom fight a true boost by her ruling in the "Harlem Nine" case in December 1958. Only last night, my wife remarked that people forget that the "Harlem Nine" started this whole thing.[179]

By 1964 the *de facto* segregation in New York City's school system had increased many times over: as the black population increased, pervasive discrimination in the housing market produced school districts that were racially homogenous and materially quite unequal.[180] As this system was largely controlled by the Second Generation, hopes of challenging an arrangement that provided black children with "discriminatorily inferior education" brought black parents into conflict with their ostensible allies in civil and human rights. Notably, African Americans in the Ocean Hill-Brownsville section of Brooklyn, an erstwhile solidly Jewish neighborhood, sought more black teachers for schools that were now filled with black students. Rigid union guidelines and contracts, however, tended to hinder such desired innovations.

In mid-1968 the black governing board of the Ocean Hill-Brownsville school district unilaterally and without due authority "transferred" nineteen mostly Jewish teachers, replacing them with African American educators. The district's teachers staged a walkout in protest and solidarity, and three strikes ensued later in the fall after failed arbitration. The stoppage lasted seven weeks, "which turned out to be the longest school strike in American history up until that point." The entire system was crippled, and "what began as a dispute between the Ocean Hill Governing Board and the teachers' union soon turned into a struggle between Black spokesmen and the predominantly Jewish teachers' union."[181] The Jewish head of the United Federation of Teachers (UFT), Albert Shanker, a one-time member of the Socialist Party of America (SPA) and an activist with the Congress of Racial Equality (CORE), defended the prerogatives of unionized teachers.

Cheryl Greenberg has observed that in so doing, Shanker "sought to change the calculus from racial quotas and community control to black attitudes toward Jews." Shankar believed in the antisemitic impetus of his black critics, but he overlooked the socioeconomic factors that precipitated the clash between black radicals and the UFT. He emphasized class over race and upheld colorblindness and universal standards against ethnic quotas.[182] Like other liberal Jews, he was disturbed by the growth in black nationalist consciousness and demands in the late 1960s. In support of his position, Shankar went so far as to distribute anonymous leaflets, ostensibly written by an African American militant, in which Jews were referred to as "Middle-East murderers of colored people" and "bloodsucking exploiters."[183] The ACLU and others accused Shanker of fomenting racial tensions, but he concurred with the ADL when it proclaimed antisemitism to be "at a crisis level in New York City" in early 1969, notwithstanding its "assurances six months earlier that there was no organized anti-Semitism in New York, and its even more recent report that African-Americans were less anti-Semitic than whites."[184]

The Ocean Hill-Brownsville episode was a symbolic flashpoint in an ongoing disruption of the legacy of the golden years during the 1960s. Surveys tended to reflect, albeit crudely, this rapid breakdown. Most white New Yorkers continued to profess a commitment to integration, yet by the late 1960s a significant majority of Jews as well as Catholics believed that the pace of racial change was occurring "too fast" and that African American demands were not entirely justified. Many Jews and Catholics denied that blacks faced discrimination in housing, education, or wages. Very large majorities admitted that they would be upset if more blacks moved into their neighborhoods or if a friend or daughter married or dated an African American. Racist views were shared by large numbers of Jews as well as Catholics, many of whom maintained that blacks had less ambition, looser morals, and less intelligence, and bred more crime than whites. Many blacks in turn expressed unflattering opinions of Jews. Notably, degree of religiosity tended to determine sympathy for blacks among Jews: in almost all surveys, orthodox Jews tended to have the least favorable opinions of blacks and secular ethnic Jews the most. Furthermore, the Second Generation tended to express more concern for blacks than the Third.[185]

The mid-1960s proved a decisive turning point in black-Jewish relations. The shift was precipitated by rapid growth in the North's African American population after the Second World War and especially after the 1950s. Up through the Second World War, most American blacks still lived in the rural South, and outside of a few major Northern cities, "most white Americans . . . had probably never seen a Negro in person."[186] In New York City, blacks were around 6 percent of the population in 1940, nearly 10 percent in 1950, 14 percent in 1960, and 21 percent in 1970. In absolute numbers, the city's African American population increased by over one million persons between 1940 and 1970—from 485,000 to 1,668,000.[187] Similar demographic booms occurred in many northern urban centers.[188] The American Jewish Congress kept itself informed of these developments.[189]

Both blacks and Jews experienced disappointment in their encounters with each other. Concrete proximity tended to undermine the tendency toward abstract affiliation and projection from afar of a mutual minority interest. Up close, it was not clear what Jews, one of the wealthiest groups already by the 1940s, had in common with blacks, one of the poorest, or what kind of equality or social justice—terms in constant use by the Second Generation—this discrepancy constituted. Jewish invocations of shared suffering were increasingly challenged by blacks, who became liable to point out that anti-Jewish persecution and violence, unlike antiblack racism, was a collective memory of European rather than American experience.[190] They were also called into question by the "appalling level of opportunism" among Jewish businessmen, especially real estate agents in new black ghettoes, of which the American Jewish Congress was aware due to its commissioned studies of the problem.[191]

Despite its ongoing civil and human rights advocacy, the Second Generation seemed to have more in common with other whites in its actual behavior toward blacks. *De facto* segregation in education was matched by *de facto* segregation in residential and recreational arrangements. Jews did not simply engage in so-called white flight; they were often the first white group to do so. Catholics, by contrast, tended to stay, in part because they had less means to relocate.[192] By the early 1970s, moreover, local Jews organized against Mayor John Lindsay of New York City when he sought to build low-income housing in a predominantly Jewish area of Queens. Residents complained openly of their fear of black crime and violence. This "fear is so ingrained," wrote Mario Cuomo, a lawyer brought in to mediate, "that even if unjustified (and I don't believe it can fairly be said that it is totally unjustified) it must be assuaged somehow." Local Jews proved uninterested in the deeper causes of black poverty.[193] "Once the civil rights movement focused on the North," Marc Dollinger has written, "its meaning to many urban Jews changed. For many northern Jews, the struggle for racial equality in the South fostered a benevolent self-image."[194]

The American Jewish Congress and other Jewish organizations attempted to remain philosophical about these developments. Shad Polier insisted that Jewish discrimination against blacks was not racism, for Jewish intentions were allegedly different from those of other whites:

> Political categories have never influenced us in the American Jewish Congress; human beings have. But you have to remember that Jews are human too. They often act out of selfish motives. Education has been the key to the Jew's success in American and when busloads of Negro children are sent into their schools Jews are frightened. They do not object because the children are black; it wouldn't matter if they were green. They object because these children are often unprepared and because educational levels fall. The Jew who objects to desegregation realizes that these children have been the victims of inferior ghetto schools and is ashamed himself for objecting. That is why so many of these Jews contribute to the American Jewish Congress and allow us as an organization to initiate programs they are opposed to as individuals. A paradox? Of course it is; but you can understand the paradox when you realize that even the most selfish Jew feels ashamed when he acts outside of his heritage.[195]

Notwithstanding such exculpations, the American Jewish Congress's priorities tended to shift along with the Second Generation's. By the mid-1960s the American Jewish Congress recognized that a certain apathy toward integration (at least in its own neighborhoods) and antiracism had overcome the Second Generation.[196] Even the unflagging activist Will Maslow, who had published a probing indictment of northern *de facto* school segregation in 1961,[197] announced his resignation from CORE five years later.[198] Maslow cited the "tepid and ambiguous response by CORE to a vicious anti-Semitic outburst" by a certain Clifford A. Brown, a black CORE official, who lambasted Jews and praised Hitler because of the "delaying tactics" of his "school board in ending de facto segregation." Maslow was not placated when CORE disavowed the statement and ordered an investigation. He promised to continue anyway "my efforts in the struggle against racism to which I have devoted a good part of the last twenty years," yet both he and the American Jewish Congress showed signs of some disengagement from the black cause if not the broader agenda of civil and human rights.[199] The "realization that intergroup conflict could occur between members of minority groups, not simply between a unified band of minorities and some amorphous majority," Svonkin has observed, "forced the leaders of Jewish agencies to look for new intellectual models and strategies."[200]

Nonetheless, some within the American Jewish Congress supported affirmative action or reverse discrimination policies throughout the 1970s, on the basis that Jews would be classified among whites as a whole rather than as Jews, and as such would not be adversely affected. Discrimination against Jewish individuals *qua* Jews was wrong and "we must always oppose" it, not least due to significant Jewish overrepresentation in the upper echelons of American life by this time, but discrimination against white individuals *per se* in favor of blacks and other designated groups amounted to social justice and would "make of us no more than a part (and a small part at that) of the white majority which is today resisting correction of inequality." Paul S. Berger and Joseph B. Robison of the CLSA argued against those who asserted "that any measure based on race that is designed to correct past discrimination violates American Jewish Congress policy. This is not true. Nothing in our past pronouncements bars consideration of race in devising corrective measures."[201]

By the late 1960s and the early 1970s, in part due to the Six-Day War of 1967, a greater focus on Israel and the plight of Soviet Jewry began to appear within the American Jewish Congress and the Second Generation as a whole.[202] These new concerns accelerated certain communal tendencies away from the black cause. Even the stalwart and energetic Poliers wavered, shifting their intellectual focus over the course of the 1960s. In 1963 they harshly criticized the editor Norman Podhoretz for his unkind essay on African Americans and their advocates among "white middle-class liberals" in the pages of his magazine, *Commentary*.[203] In 1964 Shad Polier wrote of his regret about the "increasing anti-Semitism among Negroes," yet also of his equal worry "lest Jews react to it by alienating themselves from the struggle for racial justice" in which they had played and continued to play such a prominent role. The "victim" of such bitterness "will not be the Negro," but "the Jew—corrupted and scarred because he will have forsaken the most precious precepts of his religion."[204] A year later, in an interview with the *Jewish Daily*

Forward in his townhouse on the "aristocratic East side, where selected American families . . . still live lavishly," he repeated his call for Jews to keep up "their eternal tradition of helping the persecuted and suffering people."[205]

By the 1970s, if not earlier, the Poliers and other members of the American Jewish Congress had begun to express dismay at black and general left-wing sympathy for the Palestinians since the Six-Day War as well as umbrage at the increasing comparisons between Zionism and European colonialism, if not racism.[206] Justine Wise Polier evinced especial interest in the affairs of Israel.[207] In December 1970 she criticized a group of American Quakers for publishing "a sad and disheartening document" on the Middle East, which was worse than "blatant attacks against Israel," for "the theme of peace is persistently obscured and distorted by notes of anti-Jewish prejudice," of which the authors were disturbingly "unconscious" and "unaware." This was supposedly demonstrated by their "lack of understanding concerning the meaning of Israel to Jews throughout the world" and "the need for a Jewish homeland where Jews and their children could live as of right and not by tolerance." Why, even after the Holocaust, Judge Polier implored, "do the Friends not understand that Jews have the right to live without yielding to demands that they minimize their identity, accept tolerance with gratitude, and forego the right to justice, equality and manhood?"[208]

Despite these quandaries, the Second Generation did not change its political loyalties. Into the mid-1970s few Jews identified themselves as "conservative," even as more of New York City's white Protestants and Catholics were "turning to the right" in their attitudes toward municipal affairs.[209] Throughout the 1970s Jews continued to vote overwhelmingly for the Democratic Party. Even in the 1956 presidential elections, in which the Republican candidate, Dwight D. Eisenhower, received a significant minority of the Jewish vote, Lawrence H. Fuchs observed that it was quite possible "that Jewish voters for Eisenhower were something other than a manifestation of illiberalism. Literally dozens of Jewish voters indicated in their replies to open-ended questions that they thought Eisenhower was a liberal himself."[210] Reverting to form in 1960, over 80 percent of Jews voted for John F. Kennedy against Richard Nixon.[211]

In short, "most New York Jews clung stubbornly to political liberalism, long after many of them abandoned liberal positions on integration and urban race relations."[212] What is more, few members of the Second Generation recognized any "dissonance" between the goals of Jews in "Israel and the Dispersion."[213] For the American Jewish Congress, these goals remained one and the same. In her opening address to the organization's biennial convention in June 1970, Justine Wise Polier deplored anti-Zionism as a new form of antisemitism and declared: "Tonight we shall seek to understand the challenge of Israel to us as Jews, to America and to the world." The American Jewish Congress "has a heritage which requires this," she averred, because "it was born in a period when the rights of minorities in Europe had become a vision in the minds of its founders," who also "insisted on the right of Jews to live and govern themselves in their own homeland free of dependence on the sufferance of others":

> At the same time, the American Jewish Congress saw the moral imperative of Jewish teachings as requiring responsibility in the struggle to secure justice in this land not only for Jews but for all people. . . . There is no easy road to freeing this land from the blight of racism and there must be an enlistment for the duration of the struggle to uproot and end this curse. No seasonal engagement will suffice. . . . There is no majority in America today. There are many minorities, both silent and vocal, both heard and unheard. There is urgent need for more listening and more communication between every one of the minorities if greater understanding is to be achieved in the struggle for a better America. . . . [Only] such an America can contribute to the making of a world in which respect for other peoples will replace the threats to contain, to dominate or to destroy those with whom we disagree.[214]

Pays réel

At the time and since then, American political scientists have commented upon the unusual political profile of the Second Generation. Unlike all other groups, Wesley Allinsmith and Beverly Allinsmith observed in 1948, among whom "politico-economic orientation" can be "predicted from . . . occupational status," American Jews were exceptional.[215] Jews were closest to Congregationalists in their occupational status, but "in 1944, less than a third of the Congregational major-party vote went to Roosevelt, compared to 92 percent of the Jewish vote."[216] By the 1950s Jews were more urban, prosperous, white collar, and educated than all other Americans, even surpassing the well-off Episcopalians. This gap only widened in subsequent years and decades.[217] Such socioeconomic status has tended and continues to denote Republican affiliation. Nonetheless, as Nathan Glazer and Patrick Moynihan observed of the Second Generation in their well-known book *Beyond the Melting Pot* from the 1960s: "What attracts Jews is liberalism, using the term to refer to the entire range of leftist positions, from the mildest to the most extreme."[218] Why was the forcefully upwardly mobile Second Generation so left wing?

In seeking to understand the "liberalism" of the Second Generation, which expressed itself through the American Jewish Congress and its various commissions, the "constitution" of the CLSA, written by Alexander H. Pekelis and approved by Rabbi Wise, offers insights. Therein, Pekelis declared "in some detail and with utmost candor, the ideological fundamentals that underlie this program of ours." He made clear that in contrast to those Jews who "would be content if every single Jew—or at least those in the United States—were permitted to enjoy full and genuine political, economic and social equality" by becoming "perfectly assimilated into the rest of the population, at most professing their right—should some of them so desire—to profess their own religious beliefs and worship according to their rites," the American Jewish Congress did not share this "viewpoint."[219]

In this introduction, Pekelis was making a not-so-subtle reference to the American German Jewish community and its representatives in the American Jewish Committee. Indeed, it was against this latter, politically neutral organization that the American Jewish Congress had first come together. Many within the American Jewish Committee had in turn opposed the very idea of an American Jewish Congress. The philosophy that guided the early American Jewish Committee was suggested by its leading figure, Louis Marshall, in 1923:

> I disagree totally with Mr. [Israel] Zangwill's intimation that the Jews of this country should unite for political action, or that there should be such a thing as a Jewish vote in the United States. The thought cannot be tolerated that the citizens of this country shall form racial or religious groups in the exercise of their civic and political functions. The citizens of the United States constitute one people, and there can be no divergent interests among them so far as government is concerned. . . . It is the glory of our country that before the law all men are equal, that every member of the state owes unqualified loyalty to it, that its laws must be free from discrimination, and apply equally to all citizens. . . . It is therefore inconceivable that a government of laws and not of men, such as ours is, can exist if the electorate is divided and subdivided into a multitude of segments or blocks, each considering merely its own interests. . . . For centuries their ancestors in foreign lands suffered from the consequences of an enforced segregation of this character, and they would not be so fatuous as to create voluntarily a condition which in effect would establish an American ghetto.[220]

The American Jewish Congress was from the beginning in open opposition to these formulations. The initial impetus for its creation came from Zionists, who subsequently led the organization. Those Central European Jews who directed the interwar American Jewish Congress were considered unusual by their own community in this regard. Stephen S. Wise's future wife's Bavarian family, his biographer wrote, attempted to scuttle their marriage, not least because he was "a leader of that crazy Zionist movement."[221] Louis D. Brandeis, from Louisville, Kentucky, befuddled his peers in affirming that "loyalty to America demands . . . that each American Jew become a Zionist,"[222] according to the logic by which America represented democracy and democracy "proclaims that each race or people, like each individual, has the right and duty to develop" fully.[223]

In such opinions these men and others were informed directly by the theories of their friend Horace Kallen, who was a foremost exponent of "cultural pluralism" in the United States as well as a Zionist and a firebrand within the early American Jewish Congress.[224] In an address to a convention of the American Jewish Congress in 1933, in which he chastised the American Jewish Committee as the "chief obstruction to [Jewish] unity," Kallen looked back in time and praised "emancipation" for opening the "doors of the ghetto" and enabling Jews, "as separate and distinct individuals, to enter fully into the common life of their respective countries":

> But in the long run it brought not only opportunity to the individual, but destruction to the social and cultural unity of Israel. An increasing multiplicity of Jewish sects, classes and movements replaced the organic oneness of Jewish life. The word "Jew" lost its single and unambiguous meaning. . . . "Emancipation" set up a disintegrating and centrifugal movement among the Jews of the world. . . . The consequences [thereof] were not truly healthy.[225]

Kallen wished for a return to Jewish unity and whole, premodern, even medieval community, which would yet be in full harmony with modern American and international "democracy." A decade later Pekelis concurred, criticizing "the ultra-individualistic spirit pervading the Renaissance, the Revolution, and the Emancipation":

> Jewish equality and Jewish distinctiveness, the integrity of the Jews as a people and their dignity as individuals comprise the twofold but indivisible aim of [the] Congress. We would reject individual equality if its price were renunciation of our collective individuality. We would do so not only because equality conditioned on uniformity is not genuine equality but also because we believe that, by acting otherwise, we would betray our place in human history and our duty to mankind.[226]

In effect, the American Jewish Congress set itself against bourgeois assimilation, which located Jewish integration at the level of the individual rather than the group, demanding that Jews differentiate between private and public spaces, between their religion and ethnicity, and between wider society and their own ascribed community. It did so in order to preserve what it felt to be an authentic Jewish identity. Like much of the Second Generation, however, it chaffed at the social liabilities that came along with this failure to conform. Through the middle of the twentieth century, Protestant-dominated, American civil society predicated bourgeois admission and opportunities on bourgeois assimilation, which involved general sociability and the common manners that derived therefrom as well as a concomitant emphasis on private religious identity at the expense of public ethnicity. As Will Herberg explained in his famous treatise on American integration or Americanization, *Protestant, Catholic, Jew*:

> Of the immigrant who came to this country it was expected that, sooner or later, either in his own person or through his children, he would give up virtually everything he had brought with him from the "old country"—his language, his nationality, his manner of life—and would adopt the ways of his new home. Within broad limits, however, his becoming an American did not involve his abandoning the old religion in favor of some native American substitute. Quite the contrary, not only was he expected to retain his old religion, as he was not expected to retain his old language or nationality, but such was the shape of America that it was largely in and through his religion that he, or rather his children and grandchildren, found an identifiable place in American life.[227]

Given the fundamentally ethnic character of their identity, secular American Jews ostensibly knew difficulties of adjustment to this social code. The Second Generation tended to experience and define the link between bourgeois admission and opportunities and bourgeois assimilation, which applied to Jews as well as Catholics and other groups, as so much arbitrary discrimination. In his youthful memoirs, Norman Podhoretz referred to wider society's unwritten social expectations as the "brutal bargain" that his cohort faced; social integration was felt as a denaturing and often humiliating process.[228] In setting up the CEP at the end of the 1920s, Jacob X. Cohen suggested this dilemma as his motivation when he deplored that many Jews "have learned to pass" as bourgeois Christians in order to gain access to certain firms and forms of employment, a fact that he considered insupportable and self-effacing.[229]

Protestations about discrimination must be placed within the context of the Second Generation's obvious socioeconomic success. Jews were to be found at the highest tiers of American life in the interwar period, not only in the private economy but also at all levels of the various branches of government. By the mid-1930s, in the midst of the Depression, they were overrepresented markedly in the professions and white-collar occupations generally. In New York City, where they were around 30 percent of the population at the time, Jews made up half of the physicians, managers, and proprietors, and two-thirds of the lawyers and dentists. In the country as a whole, in which they were around 3–4 percent of the population and 9 percent of the students at professional schools, Jews were 16 percent of those in training for medicine and 25 percent in pharmacy, law, and dentistry. As more native-born Jews lived outside of New York City, Jewish professionalism was even more prominent in many smaller settlements like Buffalo and San Francisco, where half or more of all the resident Jewish men "were rendering medical, dental and legal services in the late 1930s." Almost no members of the Second Generation anywhere were unskilled laborers.[230]

Given such numbers, it is not surprising that Cohen's research for the CEP was not always empirically rigorous. He often inferred prejudice without positive proof. For example, in his most well-known study from 1937, he charged the secretary of New York State's board of medical examiners with bias on the basis that non-Jewish applicants to New York City's medical schools were four times more likely to be admitted than their Jewish counterparts. Nonetheless, more than two-fifths of admissions were still Jews, as they put in more than three-quarters of all the applications.[231] Cohen did not consider reasons other than antisemitism for the discrepancy between Jewish applicants and matriculates, such as the very strong cultural emphasis within the Jewish community on professional careers, which may have resulted in more unqualified candidates among the Jewish pool. Much of Cohen's research involved surveys of and subjective appraisals by Jews of their sense of the (un)fairness of American institutions; surveys by others indicated that members of the Second Generation were more likely to blame external factors like discrimination and the "American capitalist system" for their failures, even as "most other Americans tended to internalize responsibility, considering their narrowed straits evidence of their own deficiencies."[232]

Cohen and others within the American Jewish Congress also tended to overlook or dismiss the discrimination against gentiles that existed within the Jewish community—including informal restrictive covenants in housing against selling to non-Jews[233]—which in their own case was accepted as normal ethnic networking, nepotism, and self-preservation. Given the asymmetry in social and economic power between Jews and gentiles in the United States in the interwar period and subsequent decades, such discrimination was not usually debilitating for most Christians. Nonetheless, Jews did come quickly to control large swaths of New York City's economy and to establish ethnic niches within it. By 1937 Jews owned close to two-thirds of the metropolis's 34,000 factories, of its 104,000 wholesale and retail establishments, and of its 11,000 restaurants and lunchrooms. Jews were also two-fifths of the builders and four-fifths of the speculators in real estate.[234] Most Jews, Moore has written, "entered the building industry with little or no previous experience," yet this industry, which boomed after the First World War, "soon acquired an ethnic Jewish flavor":

> In Brooklyn and the Bronx, Jews rapidly became predominant in apartment house construction. Indeed, by the middle of the decade large segments of the building trades constituted areas of self-contained Jewish activity. Working out of a home

office, usually the dining table, many Jewish builders relied on a favorite Jewish architect to design their buildings. A handshake between a Jewish building and his Jewish contractors often sealed their agreement. The contractors in turn usually employed Jewish workers, especially in the "Jewish" trades.[235]

Discrimination by the Second Generation was reciprocated by gentiles and to more devastating effect, especially in the higher echelons of the economy, which remained largely Protestant. That practices of exclusion existed was recognized by Christians as well as Jews. Even those gentiles who sympathized strongly with the Second Generation's dilemma expressed reservations about their social conduct, which they believed hindered their relations with gentiles, especially Anglo-Protestants, and thus their social reception. The sociologist Talcott Parsons insisted that "the main explanation" for antisemitic bias, which he deplored as un-American, was "envy"—for "Jews as a group have shown superior ability" in those fields "that are highly valued by our society"—but he still regretted their "aggressiveness," "self-assertion" and "obnoxious qualities," supposedly a product of their psychological insecurity and thus mental instability as a minority, as well as their clannishness and "resistance to assimilation," putatively a self-defense mechanism from centuries of European persecution.[236]

Many scholars have explained the Second Generation's political "liberalism" as a direct result of antisemitism, and many contemporary Jews along with the American Jewish Congress did evince considerable concern with this sentiment. Antisemitism, which peaked in the United States during the Depression, is necessary to explain the Second Generation's political preoccupations, but it alone is not sufficient. The relationship is ambiguous. First, other groups, including Catholics, faced similar social pressures and sometimes even more hostility than Jews, yet they proved less ideological and more pragmatic in their political affairs. They demonstrated less concern for other outsiders, like blacks, and were more likely to eschew Democratic partisanship in response to changes in their socioeconomic position. Second, studies have tended to show that "feelings of true minority status reduce the sense of effectiveness in external political affairs and reduce the amount of political activity." As Edgar Litt discovered of the Second Generation, "feelings of ethnic affiliation are significantly and inversely related to both indices of liberalism. Jews who feel socially and psychologically subordinate because of their ethnic affiliation are least likely to be tolerant of political non-conformists and altruistic toward other deprived groups."[237]

It was precisely this charge that the militant American Jewish Congress leveled repeatedly against the more circumspect American Jewish Committee. The former contrasted its fearlessness of antisemitism against the latter's alleged fearfulness in order to account for their differences in operation and ethos. These differences diminished over time, as the American Jewish Committee, for a number of reasons, became increasingly less German and amateur and more Eastern European and professional in staff and membership, but they remained noticeable into the 1950s if not beyond.[238] Even though these two Jewish organizations were often preoccupied with the same problems, they tended to differ in their preferred methods of resolution. In a thinly veiled strike, the American Jewish Congress condemned the American Jewish Committee in the late 1940s for recommending the "silent treatment" as a "technique for dealing with certain rabble-rousers":

> It is only a few years since the same group accepted it as a basic technique for combatting all problems of racism, discrimination and anti-Semitism. A dogmatic insistence that all problems in this field could be solved by the intervention of influential individuals rather than by organized public action, the universal insistence that it was harmful to stimulate public discussion of such problems, the practice of coping with them through "front" and non-sectarian groups rather than in the name of the Jewish community—these were the principles that were applied over the entire field of community relations.[239]

Notwithstanding such dismissive characterizations, the American Jewish Committee was proactive in the field of intergroup relations in the 1940s and 1950s, even though it preferred "soft" methods of persuasion rather than "hard" methods of coercive litigation. Notably, the American Jewish Committee focused on propagandizing against prejudice.[240] Borrowing from the field of commercial advertising, it sought to use mass communication—radio, television, film, posters, and pamphlets—to inform the core (Anglo-Protestant) American majority about the various minority groups within the country, in the belief that positive knowledge would correct negative stereotypes and bring about amity.[241] Education was also emphasized. Notably, the American Jewish Committee along with the ADL funded, *inter alia,* the Bureau of Intercultural Education. This agency sought to "foster training in better human relations at the grassroots levels of elementary and secondary schools and colleges," on the assumption that young people were relatively free of bias and could be taught to respect cultural diversity.[242]

The very research produced under the auspices of the American Jewish Committee, however, did not always back up the view that "soft" persuasion could correct undesirable social practices, not least due to the nature of prejudice. The dominant theory of prejudice within the field of intergroup relations during and after the Second World War considered such sentiments to be a mental malady, rather than a product of socioeconomic factors, such as competition for status and resources. This psychopathological model of prejudice was most famously propounded in *The Authoritarian Personality*, which was published in 1950 by radical Jewish émigrés from Nazi Germany, funded by the American Jewish Committee as part of its Studies in Prejudice Series.[243] In the conclusion to this tome, the authors contended that previous "measures to oppose social discrimination" had not been terribly successful, because "rational arguments cannot be expected to have deep or lasting effects upon a phenomenon that is irrational in its essential nature."[244]

Activists within the American Jewish Congress implied their agreement with the authors of *The Authoritarian Personality* when they eschewed "soft" persuasion in favor of the "hard" power of the law to alter social mores. In 1951 Maslow wrote that "the effort to utilize law as a catalyst of social change still encounters resistance,"[245] but he expressed satisfaction that social scientists were increasingly rejecting William Graham Sumner's outdated dictum that "stateways cannot change folkways"[246] in favor of Gunnar Myrdal's conviction that "we are entering an era where fact-finding and scientific theories of causal relations will be seen as instrumental in planning controlled social change."[247] According to Maslow, the (CLSA's own) record of achievement in this regard lent credence to Myrdal's prediction and proved that "no other technique of social control promises as quick, durable, and meaningful results as well-conceived and vigorously enforced civil rights legislation."[248] In fact, the law would just as likely modify social mores as social mores the law. "It seems reasonably clear," Maslow and his colleague, Joseph B. Robison, wrote in 1953, "that legislation not only affects patterns of behavior but, by changing the situations in which we live, may also change beliefs and attitudes."[249]

The American Jewish Congress saw in the greater reluctance of the American Jewish Committee to turn to the courts—especially on sensitive issues of church-state separation, in which the CLSA's Leo Pfeffer played a nationally vital role—an exaggerated and needless fear of antisemitism. By contrast, it understood its own more confrontational style as adherence, in the words of the same Leo Pfeffer, to a "position on the basis of fundamental principle rather than of temporary or immediate considerations of expediency."[250] The American Jewish Committee, with its greater representation in the South and Midwest, where fewer Jews lived, conceded its concerns over antisemitism, but also emphasized its respect for bourgeois privacy and its regard for the sensibilities of non-Jews. Commenting on a controversial church-state case in Dade County, Florida, from the 1960s, Charles Wittenstein of that region's American Jewish Committee recalled that Pfeffer "could never resist the chance to stick it to us":

> [He] also used to make it quite clear that he thought we knew nothing about standing up for the rights of Jews, that we were too fearful, afraid of what the Gentiles would think. [The] "fear factor" is not something I believe is fair. We just thought Miami was the wrong place to agitate non-Jewish opinion. . . . What [the] Congress didn't realize was that you didn't run down from New York and tell these people

what to do. You have to prepare a community for a major change, to talk with them, deal with the issues. . . . You don't say, "Do what I say or I'll sue," which was how the Congress did business. We were more sensitive to local considerations. . . . Sometimes Leo, as gifted and talented as he was, could just be so overbearing.[251]

If members of the American Jewish Congress were not "sensitive" to the feelings of Christians, it was in part because they were unlikely to know many very well. The Second Generation in the United States constituted one of the most residentially clustered and socially insular populations in the country.[252] As late as 1961 the sociologist Gerhard Lenski could relate with some surprise that while white Protestants ranked with Catholics as the most widely scattered groups, Jews ranked with and even above black Protestants as the most concentrated:

> The fact that the coefficient for the Jewish group was even higher than for the Negro Protestants is especially remarkable, since Negroes are so severely limited in their choice of residential areas both by finances and by out-group hostility. . . . One can only conclude that the magnitude of the coefficient is one more indication of the communal spirit [among Jews].[253]

Unlike blacks, the residential separateness of the Second Generation was "shaped less decisively" by prejudice than by "Jewish associational networks." According to Moore, "seldom did Jews choose a new home solely in response to discrimination." They were simply "happiest living near other Jews."[254] In the case of New York City, as the Second Generation abandoned Manhattan in the 1920s for Brooklyn and the Bronx, moving to more spacious homes and leafy streets, its ethnic concentration did not go down but up.[255] In 1920 around half of the city's Jews lived in neighborhoods that were at least 40 percent Jewish in population; by 1925, that number was 64 percent; and by 1930, it was 72 percent.[256] The same phenomenon held true elsewhere. As Judith Kramer and Seymour Leventman noted in their sociological investigation of a typical "North City":

> The second-generation community, located in the better neighborhoods of the city, emulated the structure of the general community with a multitude of institutions parallel to those of the larger society. Yet it retained its fundamentally ethnic character. It was, in effect, a gilded ghetto whose social life was carried on exclusively with Jews of appropriate status. The institutions were all middle-class, but the participants were all Jewish. The social distance between the minority community and the general community had yet to be bridged. As a result of both exclusion and exclusiveness, second-generation Jews were well insulated from any but impersonal economic relations with non-Jews. The gilded ghetto thus furnished the prerequisite of social segregation essential for conformity to its special values.[257]

This "social distance" between Jews and everyone else did not prepare Jewish youth well for mixing in wider civil society. "The Jewish community enclosed one," reminisced Irving Howe, "not through choice as through experience and instinct, and often not very gently or with the most refined manners."[258] It also produced paranoia and an intense sense of alienation. "As a Jewish child in a Jewish neighborhood," recalled Israel Kugler, later the Second Generation head of the socialist Workmen's Circle, a Jewish fraternal organization that was founded by the First Generation, "the street reaction was to shun all churches and to regard the Christians, the 'Goyim', as our collective enemy."[259] As they matured, the Second Generation discovered "often through bitter experience, that the accent, dress and manners learned in their neighborhoods precluded easy access into the American mainstream."[260] Isolation from the norms of the wider, Protestant-dominated civil society and from social contact with gentiles made many Jews appear to other Americans as uncivil, lacking in obligation, and unduly materialistic.[261] The unscrupulous conduct of the Jewish pariah-cum-parvenu was a notably common literary theme, especially among Jewish writers themselves.[262]

(In the early socialism of the prominent American journalist Walter Lippmann, John Murray Cuddihy detected a sumptuary motivation akin to that of another German Jew, Karl Marx.[263] In 1922, in the pages of the *American Hebrew*, Lippmann warned his fellow up-and-coming Jews against their "conspicuousness":

> [The Jew] needs more than anyone else to learn the classic Greek virtue of moderation; for he cannot, even if he wishes to, get away unscathed with what less distinguishable men can. For that reason the rich and vulgar and pretentious Jews of our big cities are perhaps the greatest misfortune that has ever befallen the Jewish people. They are the real fountain of anti-Semitism. They are everywhere in sight, and though their vices may be no greater than those of other jazzy elements in the population, they are a thousand times more conspicuous.
>
> Moreover, they dissipate awkwardly. It happens that the Jews, for good or evil, have no court or country-house tradition of high living, and little of the physical grace that just barely makes that mode of life tolerable. When they rush about in super-automobiles, bejeweled and be-furred and painted and overbarbered, when they build themselves French chateaus and Italian palazzi, they stir up the latent hatred against crude wealth in the hands of shallow people: and that hatred diffuses itself. They undermine the natural liberalism of the American people.[264])

The Second Generation's encounter with the Ivy League provided a prominent stage on which the dilemma and dynamics of its social embourgeoisement (or lack thereof) played out. It was in fact the perception of restrictions on Jews at elite colleges that constituted the *fons et origo* of the impetus behind the establishment of the American Jewish Congress's CEP in the 1920s and later the CLSA.[265] Informal quotas against Jewish students at many Ivy League universities had been suspected by the Jewish community for some time, but became a topic of public debate when Harvard's president, Abbott Lawrence Lowell, announced openly his intentions in this regard in 1922. By an explicit allowance, he hoped to limit Jews to 15 percent of the student body, a proportion that they had since surpassed and seemed set on further outpacing. Lowell's proposed quota was ultimately rejected by his colleagues, some of whom were Jewish, including Felix Frankfurter, but more nuanced mechanisms of diversifying enrollment away from the Northeast did eventually accomplish his goal.

In the first part of the twentieth century it was relatively easy to pursue higher education in the United States. Early Jewish overrepresentation was as much a product of a predilection for learning as it was of easy standards and minimal fees, even at prestigious institutions.[266] The Ivy League especially did not emphasize academic rigor so much as "genteel dissipation." It was a collection of "gentlemen's colleges."[267] A contemporary, Frederick Rudolph, observed that

> what mattered for so many young men was not the course of study but the environment of friendships, social development, fraternity houses, good sportsmanship, athletic teams. The world of business was a world of dealing with people. What better preparation could there by than the collegiate life outside the classroom—the club room, the playing field, where the qualities that showed what stuff a fellow really was made of were bound to be encouraged.[268]

The Second Generation often proved uninterested in these pursuits. Whereas "the first German Jews who came were easily absorbed into the social pattern," the Russian Jews were not. "At the turn of the century," Samuel Eliot Morison wrote in his history of Harvard, "the bright Russian Jewish lads from the Boston public schools began to arrive. There were enough of them in 1906 to form the Menorah Society, and in another fifteen years Harvard had her 'Jewish problem.'"[269] Eastern European Jewish students were resented as stiff competition, but also disdained for disrupting the Ivy League's social life. They were seen as unpleasant and insufficiently deferential intruders, and many German Jews, some of whom were members of the American Jewish Committee, empathized with the Anglo-Protestant elite's complaints about the Second Generation's manners and sociability, if not with racial restrictions.[270] Of his experience after the Second World War at Yeshiva University, which was ostensibly established in response to the partial exclusion of Jews from the Ivy League,[271] Paul Gottfried, the son of a German-speaking Hungarian refugee from Nazism, recalled that even at a wholly Jewish institution Russian Jews did not mix easily:

As soon as I arrived, I felt a massive cultural barrier separating me from my new classmates, who were preponderantly from Brooklyn and Queens . . . and seemed to carry with them the social gracelessness of having grown up in a transported Eastern European ghetto. . . . They . . . showed a clannishness that extended even to their fellow Jews. The few Sephardic and more numerous Austro-German Jews in their midst, even if they came from "the City," had trouble fitting into the dominant society.[272]

The hurdles that some Eastern European Jews faced at the Ivy League colleges were ostensibly put in place to avoid these frictions, even as they were hardly insurmountable.[273] As one dean put it, "We do not want to make our college a Ghetto."[274] Some Jews challenged the characterization of the Second Generation as uncouth, but "the popular reputation of colleges with a majority of Jewish students, such as the City College of New York, reflected these assumptions."[275] Indeed, the most famous alumni of City College, including many later neoconservative intellectuals, were not known for gregarious pastimes on campus, but for fierce, bitter, and very public quarrels about the merits and demerits of Stalin versus Trotsky, which raged between two alcoves in the cafeteria.[276]

Such political radicalism, for which Jewish students were notorious even at Harvard, was another important reason that elite institutions sought to curtail their numbers.[277] Fears that Jews would alter the ethos of the establishment's infrastructure were pervasive. They also proved prescient, for Jews, especially after the Second World War when their institutional presence expanded markedly, did contribute to the de-Christianization, secularization, and "liberalization" of American academia and public culture. David Hollinger has maintained that Second Generation intellectuals followed this course in genuine service and devotion to rational social "science";[278] however, as Andrew Heinze has shown in the case of the discipline of psychology, neutral "science," once having sapped Christianity or Anglo-Protestant hegemony, often gave way to assertions of a secular ethnic Jewishness that had been close to the surface.[279] In due time, moreover, some of these Jewish intellectuals "played an important role in persuading a much larger public of the merits of the 1960s student activists," who were themselves disproportionately of the Third Generation.[280]

As suggested by their subsequent preeminence in the American academy, discrimination did not "reduce overall Jewish attendance at postsecondary institutions," even if "it did limit their numbers at the more elite private schools of the East."[281] Individual Jews who were denied entrance at Harvard could and did go elsewhere. The "extent and significance of quotas should not be exaggerated," Stephen Steinberg cautioned. They were "not a serious disability." They were social rather than economic in nature. Unlike in Europe, no one in the United

States questioned "the right of Jews to a college education" or to attend private Ivy League schools. The issue was rather "the right of certain Eastern colleges to preserve their unique character, which was Protestant and upper-class."[282]

Members of the Second Generation disputed that right more persistently and tenaciously than perhaps any other group in the country, and their own civil and human rights campaigns, which were the quintessential expression of their "liberalism," grew out of such social predicaments. They may not have been held back by occasional discrimination or social exclusion, but they deeply begrudged the message that they were—as whole, undivided, and authentic Jews—unwanted in better bourgeois company.[283] Unlike blacks, "theirs was not a struggle for basic political, economic, and educational rights, but for good will, freedom to develop further, and respect."[284]

The Second Generation's "liberalism" responded directly to the kinds of aggravation that the Ivy League epitomized. A main thrust was to decouple bourgeois admission and opportunity from bourgeois assimilation by subordinating the modern division between the state and civil society to so-called social justice, about which term American Jews were especially passionate. Seeking to cover up or diffuse perceived social delicts with legal edicts, Jews appealed over and against the concrete *pays réel* below, in which they suffered the indignities of a retained pariah status, to the abstract *pays légal* above, in which they were equal citizens before the law. As the men within the American Jewish Congress understood, anti-Jewish prejudice in the United States was not a public, state-condoned affair, as it was in parts of Europe, but a private, subtle one. As Pekelis wrote in the CLSA's "constitution" by way of elucidation:

> The children of the Jew who escaped from Russia, where the state barred him from state-controlled medical schools, have nothing to fear from the state of New York or that of Massachusetts. If these states operated medical schools, more than one constitution would guarantee non-discriminatory admission. Unfortunately, most states do not operate medical schools. And against those persons who do operate these schools and determine their admission policies, the Constitution does not run.[285]

The solution to this problem was to lessen the distance between the state and civil society in a manner favorable to Jews (and other designated minorities) rather than in the manner of the czar. According to Pekelis, the situation that the Second Generation faced *vis-à-vis* an independent civil society would remain "true unless . . . we are able and willing to extend the basic philosophy, if not the direct application, of our Constitution and subject to its power not only the political microcosms but the social microcosms as well. Such a course of action is big with hope and danger."[286] Likewise, Maslow contended that prior to the creation of the FEPC in 1941, "little attention had been devoted to preventing discrimination in employment or trade unions. This neglect was due in part to the then prevailing constitutional doctrine that the state could only regulate those industries affecting a public interest":

> The basis for this judicial attitude is a rigorous distinction between the agencies of the state and discrimination by "private" institutions. As to "private" discrimination, the courts assert that they are powerless in the absence of statute and that constitutional guarantees are applicable only to acts of the Government. *This doctrine must be discarded.*[287]

In short, if Anglo-Protestants tried to keep unassimilated Eastern European Jews out of their private realm of bourgeois decorum and privilege, then some of those same Jews would quite literally legislate their way in, without submitting to the disgraceful deracination of "*yahudim*" (prototypical German Jews). The earliest Jewish "civil rights" campaign in New York State attempted to accomplish this very thing. Confronting exclusionary advertising for and practices in places of accommodation and amusement—hotels, clubs, and so forth—Jews in the early 1900s sought an amendment—the Saxe Amendment—to the 1895 New York State Civil Rights Act to outlaw such discrimination as much as possible. In his capacity as a private individual, rather than as a representative of the early American Jewish Committee, Louis Marshall took part in this campaign, yet was chastised for so doing by several of his German Jewish peers, above all from outside New York City, who held up the sanctity of free association and contract.

No matter how hurtful it was, Rabbi Max Heller of New Orleans contended, "when all is said and done the refusal of social intimacy is a human right, one of the sacred rights of privacy which society must safeguard and dare not infringe upon." Anglo-Protestant exclusion was "simply the throes of assimilation. To the feelings of those people our assimilation has not yet progressed to the point of perfect social acceptability. Let us have patience." Rabbi Julius Morgenstern of Cincinnati was even more forthright and hostile to the proposed amendment and condemned vulgar "Jewish social climbers":

> It is safe to say that there is a Jewish influence behind this bill. It is not the negro, nor the Chinese, nor the Indian, who seeks his way into summer hotels where he is not wanted. It is against Jews, and Jews alone, especially in the State of New York, who often seek to force their way into just those resorts in which they are not wanted. The mere fact of their exclusion makes the particular resort more desirable and whets their ambition to force their way, into the forbidden circle.

Morgenstern believed education and edification, on the part of Jews as much as others, would resolve the matter in due time, yet was even more adamant than Heller in asserting his view of the true nature of civil rights in the meantime:

> I believe it to be a natural and inherent right of the individual to determine just whom he does like and wishes to associate with and whom he dislikes and does not want to associate with. I must admit that some people I do judge as a class and base my likes and dislikes from a social standpoint upon the consideration of them as a class. I have never invited a negro to dine with me, and probably will never do so. I do not associate with them nor do I wish to do so. I believe I have a constitutionally legal right to select my own social associates, and if I feel this way with regard to the negro, then I must accord the same right to the anti-Semite to feel the same way toward the Jew.[288]

Both proponents and detractors have agreed with Morgenstern that many of the "civil rights" sought by Jewish groups, including the American Jewish Congress, were without solid constitutional or legal foundation at the time. Of the fair employment legislation from the 1940s, Arthur Earl Bonfield, despite his sympathy for such measures, admitted that political "experience has been a far more persuasive teacher than logic and has been responsible for most of the relevant legislative process."[289] Libertarian legal scholar and critic Richard Epstein has likewise noted of Title VII of the 1964 Civil Rights Act, which enshrined the antidiscrimination principle in private employment and gave rise to "affirmative action," that there "is no adequate theoretical foundation" for such laws. They are not part of the modern, liberal, bourgeois "social contract tradition," in which "the control of force was [the] overriding theme," but rely on expansive police power, thus having engendered a "massive apparatus of state control over private behavior."[290]

In legal terms, Epstein has observed, such laws were the direct if inverted heirs to the Jim Crow regime, for "under the Civil Rights Act, the distinction between private and government discrimination is rendered largely, if not wholly, irrelevant."[291] With this the American Jewish Congress agreed, and explicitly so. In ruing the "neglect" within his profession of "the potentialities of the law in helping to break down racial bigotry and its chief objective manifestation, discrimination," Maslow of the CLSA conceded:

> This neglect *unfortunately* is not shared by our southern legislators. The entire apparatus of Jim Crow is employed by them to prevent the white from ever encountering the Negro except in a role which symbolizes inferior status. Southern segregation laws are designed to emphasize this inferior status and to drive home at every

opportunity the lesson that the white race is a superior one. The South has always believed that law *does* affect folkways.[292]

The CLSA did not simply seek to ensure that blacks and other minorities could exercise without hindrance traditional civil rights such as those established immunities from the state's coercion or interference within the private sphere. It also wanted to invest them with a new set of human rights that would, through the state's police power, secure certain social outcomes and arrangements or provide certain entitlements in the name of social justice (as defined by well-positioned Jews rather than, presumably, southern racists). This distinction as made here—between civil and human rights, between immunities and entitlements—is blurred more within American law than the commonwealth tradition, but it did not go unrecognized by Jewish lawyers.[293] It informed the aspirations of the American Jewish Congress as well as the political proclivities of the community that it represented.

The sundry legal campaigns of the Second Generation had operated on (and against) the said distinction since the early twentieth century. As with the agitation for the Saxe Amendment, Jewish groups strove to curtail, and often succeeded in curtailing, the exercise of existing civil rights—freedom of association, contract, and eventually speech (when it was inimical to Jewish interests and therefore classified as "hate")[294]—in the name of the higher moral imperative of the "human right" of nondiscrimination. (The American Jewish Congress used the terms *civil* and *human* rights interchangeably throughout the interwar period and beyond.) The lawyers of the CLSA frequently drew attention to this distinction, seeking a language by which to express it. When they invoked "civil rights," they did not mean the defense of personal liberties, but the provision of "intergroup equality"[295] by bureaucratic administration that eschewed deference to modern bourgeois conceptions of privacy and transcended a preoccupation with collective bourgeois social standards.[296] In the words of Will Maslow:

> The discrimination attacked by the National Association for the Advancement of Colored People has largely been governmental action—the acts of school boards, of jury commissioners, of state legislatures. The anti-Semitism that vexes the Jew in the United States is, however, that of private groups, of personnel managers, resort owners, admissions committees, or rabblerousers, almost entirely non-governmental and hence not subject to the majestic prohibitions of the Fifth and Fourteenth Amendments. Although these may be "private governments" in the power they wield to deny employment or educational opportunities, their acts do not fall within the accepted categories of legal wrongs. Before these private groups can be sued, *new laws have to be created* making their conduct unlawful.[297]

Maslow's vision, shared by his colleagues, calls into question the nature of American Jewish "liberalism" as well as the claims of Louis Hartz that the United States is exceptional in its adherence to classical (Lockean) liberal principles.[298] The example of the Second Generation lends credence to those who have viewed American "liberalism" since the New Deal as a euphemism in the American context on the basis, as Upton Sinclair informed Norman Thomas, head of the SPA, that "the American people will take socialism, but they won't take the label."[299] As Bernard Johnpoll observed, the New Deal signaled the death knell of the SPA, not because its former adherents were suddenly attracted to bourgeois principles and arrangements, but because Roosevelt's programs became so popular "among the very people to whom the socialists hoped to appeal."[300] As Melvin Dubofsky noted, the Second Generation devoted itself to the Democratic Party in the 1930s, because with the New Deal "younger Jewish-Americans could have their reforms without bearing the stigma of Socialism."[301]

Several advocates within the American Jewish Congress, especially within the CLSA, had been socialists in their youth and in many ways remained so. Will Maslow, Shad Polier, and Justine Wise all had some radical affiliations in their pasts, as did many of the best and brightest members of the Second Generation, who, like the First, filled up the rolls of the radical groups in the country, above all the Young People's Socialist League (YPSL).[302] In later life, Jack Greenberg of *Brown* fame recalled forthrightly of his fellow Jewish "civil rights" lawyers: "We were social activists. Back then we'd call them socialists; now you'd call them liberals."[303] As such a statement implied, the movement of Jews into the Democratic Party signified not the end of their socialism but its transmutation into a mainstream vehicle and a semantic shift to go along with it. The point at which a Jewish socialist diverged from a *soi-disant* Jewish liberal was not always self-evident.

This lack of clarity extended to the voting booth. In the 1930s and 1940s many Jews who supported Roosevelt and the New Deal actually cast their vote for the American Labor Party (ALP), which was set up in the spring and summer of 1936 by older Jewish socialists "to provide President Roosevelt with a second ballot line in New York State" against the SPA, which had been backed by 200,000 people there, mostly Jews, in 1932.[304] Acting as an electoral intermediary, the ALP allowed Jews "to pull the lever for Roosevelt and Lehman [the Jewish Democratic governor] without compromising their ideological convictions" or endorsing the notoriously corrupt and largely Catholic machine of Tammany Hall.[305] Its greatest popularity was achieved in the 1937 mayoral election, when the ALP received over two-fifths of New York City's Jewish vote. In both the 1936 and 1940 presidential elections, the ALP received one-fifth of the Jewish vote.[306] In 1944 half of Roosevelt's Jewish support came through the ALP and another left-wing intermediary, the Liberal Party.[307]

Eschewing revolutionary commitments and repudiating the socialist and communist parties, the ALP backed those mainstream candidates, usually Democrats but sometimes "liberal" Republicans, who it believed would, within the existing system, expand the role of the state in society for the purposes of welfare, planning, and "civil rights." The ALP's program, Moore has observed, "represented the political ideology espoused by most second generation Jews by 1940":

> The move to liberalism from a background in which respect for radical ideology was embedded and even institutionalized in the community required only a gradual transition. Second generation Jews, too, created a milieu in which their liberalism was as intrinsically Jewish as had been their parents' radicalism.[308]

It was in its orientation to an expansive state that the Second Generation resembled the other major elements in and behind the New Deal, which, for often differing reasons, looked to the police power of an enlarged bureaucratic apparatus, not just to resolve the economic crisis of the 1930s, but also to advance various interests against a faltering civil society during the Depression. They formed an antibourgeois coalition, whose individual parts, moreover, were often significantly more antisemitic than the largely Republican, Anglo-Protestant bourgeoisie.[309] The New Deal held out the promises of wealth distribution for the poor and African Americans; of stronger unions for workers; of cartelization and less competition for many of the largest banks and industries; of ongoing accommodation of Jim Crow for southern racists; of more corporatist economic reforms for Catholic immigrants; of agricultural subsidy for Protestant farmers; and of greater cultural expression for and recognition of "minorities," including Jews.[310]

In the Jewish case, the Second Generation's orientation to the state as an interventionist bureaucratic apparatus—which would, among other things, protect and promote cultural pluralism—demonstrated a basic continuity with the First, for whom the coercive, technocratic, Bolshevik regime was recognized and celebrated from afar in its first two decades as the sponsor of *yidishkeyt*. If the Yiddish-speaking First Generation had criticized and evaded American civil society, fantasizing about a revolution that would sweep it away, then the English-speaking Second Generation sought to hedge it in on many sides. The American Jewish Congress, Maslow affirmed, "has sought *to enlist the forces of social control* in a nation-wide struggle against racism," using "the courts, the administrative agencies, and the legislatures" as well as "an aroused community to strike down racial and religious discrimination in employment, education and housing." It did so "not merely out of selfish concern to protect the interests of any one minority," but to complete and perfect American democracy through pluralism.[311]

Like Maslow, Jewish intellectuals, following Brandeis and especially Kallen, tended to interpret cultural pluralism as the very essence of American democracy, which they understood not as local self-government "by self-conscious peoples," but as socialization of citizens "by experts with 'progressive' social views."[312] The "challenge of racism in this country," David Petegorsky of the American Jewish Congress averred after the Second World War, "does not come either from the organized hate groups or from our failure to develop an adequate 'climate of opinion' with regard to prejudice and intolerance. The threat lies rather in the imperfections and shortcomings of our democratic system." As such, "the real job of combating racism and anti-Semitism is that of completing our unfinished American democracy" through the establishment of an interventionist welfare state that would do away with such evils. Petegorsky spoke of "democratic" rights rather than civil rights to describe a world without private prejudice.[313]

Here was an important inner link between the Second Generation's eagerness for Roosevelt and his New Deal, on the one hand, and its legal campaigns and social engineering, on the other. By establishing the administrative authority and bureaucratic instruments, the former was a prerequisite for the implementation of the latter. The Democrats, Shad Polier reminded his colleagues as late as 1960, remained more willing than Republicans to use the state apparatus to intervene in and so reform civil society to ensure "enforcement powers which are essential to any meaningful effort to eliminate discrimination in employment" and other areas of private life.[314] As Stuart Svonkin has observed:

> The notion that the government had a legitimate interest in regulating the relations between employers and employees grew out of innovations introduced during the New Deal and World War II, particularly the National Labor Relations Board [NLRB] and the President's Committee on Fair Employment Practice. It is extremely significant that CLSA attorneys Will Maslow and Joseph B. Robison—who helped to promote the contention that state commissions against discrimination should be empowered to intervene in "private matters" such as employment, housing, education, and accommodations—had previous experience as staff members of these federal agencies.[315]

Shad Polier, the director of the CLSA and later of the American Jewish Congress, had also worked as a lawyer for the NLRB, which had been established in 1934 as a replacement for the National Labor Board of 1933 (struck down by the Supreme Court as unconstitutional), and was both led and disproportionately staffed by lawyers of Jewish background.[316] In the late 1930s Polier helped to prosecute the Weirton Steel Company of West Virginia for alleged violations of the Wagner Act of 1935, which endorsed the autonomous organization of private-sector workers into unions.[317] In letters that he wrote to his wife, Polier referred disdainfully to the defense lawyer, Clyde A. Armstrong, as a Protestant hick, who in turn viewed Polier as a Jewish communist.[318] With its broad powers of enforcement and appropriation, the NLRB was subsequently viewed as the ideal model for the FEPC, to which entity some members of the former, most notably Maslow, migrated.

This movement of personnel, from one New Deal agency to another or from a New Deal agency to a left-wing group like the American Jewish Congress, resulted in what Stephen M. Teles has called the "liberal legal network." This network emerged out of Roosevelt's administration and came to challenge the "conservative, Republican WASPs who controlled the legal profession" until the mid-twentieth century, producing activist courts that did not obviously respect the modern separation of powers.[319] After the Second World War New Deal lawyers, many of whom were Second Generation Jews, entered law faculties, where they in time ensured a "near-absence of conservative voices," or set up firms in New York City and Washington, DC, where they guided bewildered clients through the regulatory maze they themselves had set up and therefore knew firsthand.[320] They formed key members of a "new class" that obviated the popular will in elections, which became "decreasingly important as sources of large-scale policy change," even as the political system became "increasingly sensitive to expert opinion, issue framing, and professional networks":

> Many of liberalism's achievements derived from the skilful use of power by a transformed federal bureaucracy, staffed by actors sympathetic to (or previously involved in) social movements. This system's advent gave liberal Democrats the ability to push their policy agenda even when the presidency was in the hands of Republicans. Shifts in attention driven by interest groups, the media, intellectual entrepreneurs, and litigators, became important drivers of cycles of policy change, independent of the electoral fortunes of the political parties.[321]

This trajectory of Jewish lawyers, including those who came to the American Jewish Congress, does not suggest that the Holocaust was decisive as an impetus behind their political views and activities, notwithstanding its subsequent importance to their self-conceptions or to their sense of vindication and urgency. The basic political orientation of men like Maslow and Polier remained fairly constant both before and after the war. Further, the American Jewish Congress's own anti-discrimination campaigns predated the European genocide by many years, originating out of the domestic rather than the international context, which latter never mobilized American Jewish opinion to the same extent. Finally, the militancy of the American Jewish Congress and its commissions did not suggest serious anxiety or a lack of confidence due to antisemitism, but rather disregard for the feelings of gentiles and determination in the pursuit of power and influence over them. In accusing the American Jewish Committee of kowtowing to antisemites in its relative moderation, the American Jewish Congress let it be known that this sentiment, although clearly a preoccupation, did not determine its behavior. In the late 1940s the American Jewish Congress was aware that residual antisemitism had collapsed after the Depression, yet remained wary.[322] By 1960 the president of the American Jewish Congress simply dismissed the forces of antisemitism as "too weak to cause concern" in the American context; the real concern was communal dissolution through tolerance and freedom, "an entirely new situation, unique in Jewish history."[323]

For the American Jewish Congress, the suppression of antisemitism was secondary to the construction of a pluralist America, in which Jewishness would not be subject to the pressures, costs, and rewards of bourgeois assimilation. Without denying the salience of antisemitism to the Second Generation and its representatives, this interpretation takes account of the fact that Jewish subgroups were not all equally attracted to what became known as American liberalism. Secular ethnic Jews of Eastern European provenance—the vast majority of American Jewry—were, as in the First Generation, the most likely to adhere to the political Left and to espouse its causes. Orthodox and German Jews remained relatively less sympathetic to such causes, by comparison with most American Jews if not the American population as a whole. The orthodox rejected assimilation of any kind but tended to resent less the liabilities of nonconformity, even as they feared for their own communities the kinds of social engineering that their secular counterparts intended for others.[324] German Jews were more likely to acquiesce to wider social expectations, identifying more fully with the Anglo-Protestant bourgeoisie and therefore voting more often for the Republican Party. In the case of "North City," around 40 percent of German Jews voted Republican, but only 6 percent of Eastern Europeans Jews did so.[325]

Eastern European Jews were especially attracted to the collection of views and values that informed New Deal liberalism, because this system not only made way for a degree of cultural pluralism, but also provided positive content to the Jewish identity that would be expressed in the reformed social order. During the 1960s regular and semiregular attendance at religious services was only around 10 percent for Jews, yet 50 percent for Protestants and 75 percent or more for Catholics.[326] The Second Generation's intense ethnic Jewishness was not rendered meaningful by observance of the commandments of Judaism, but rather by a "lived religion" that grew out of secularized theological concepts of exile and alienation and sacralized historical memories of persecution. Its tropes pervaded the Second Generation's consciousness. The sociologist Daniel Bell spoke for his "homeless radical generation," which had known the "loss of communal love," while reminiscing:

> We reject the basic values of American society as they stand. . . . Our roots are a
> Yiddish immigrant world from which we ventured forth each day and to return at
> night. It was a home that had, in its best moments, a warmth and quality of selfless
> sacrifice which shaped our ethics and defined our lives. It is a world that has faded
> and cannot be recreated. All that is left is the hardness of alienation, the sense of
> otherness. . . . The assumption of alienation is a positive value, fostering a critical
> sense out of a role of detachment; it is, if you will, the assumption of the role of the
> prophet. . . . This "otherness," for us, is a special role. It cannot exist within a terri-
> torial demarcation. It can exist, and with it the special historical quality of being
> Jewish, the quality of alienation, only as the attitude of the eternal stranger in a
> foreign land.[327]

This "lived religion" segued with the themes of an emergent American liberalism, expressing itself in the political sphere in what Michael Alexander has
called "outsider identification." According to the American Jewish Congress,
Jews *qua* Jews would only be safe and respected in a country in which all minorities were safe and respected, given the supposedly "unitary character of prejudice" within the collective psyche of the Anglo-Protestant bourgeoisie.[328] As
Jacob X. Cohen declared in 1944 in a speech before the NAACP in defense of an
expanded FEPC, "discrimination against any part is a threat against the whole."
Cohen affirmed then that "America is a multi-group society," whose "democracy"
is defined by "the right of differences to exist together harmoniously." "White
Americans," Cohen went on, "must be made to realize how they are stuffed
with contradictions. They serve democracy, with tall talk, but use all manner of
low devices to deny minority groups the rights proclaimed by democracy." The
"Negro" especially "is the victim of gross injustice," but "Jews have always cham-
pioned [his] cause," because "the principle of the dignity of man is [a] primary
teaching of Judaism" and informed the framers of the American Declaration of
Independence, Constitution, and Bill of Rights:

> I think of the parallels between the history of the Jews and that of the Negroes, and
> of the way the destiny of Israel and the fate of the Negroes have strangely dovetailed
> together. . . . The Jews spent many centuries in Africa, driven slaves of Egyptian task-
> masters. . . . The Negro people, brought against their will from Africa, were slaves
> in the New World.
>
> Today, we, together with other Americans, and supported by our comrades in
> arms from the United Nations, are fighting for democracy as soldiers on the military
> front. . . . This is as it should be. Your people and my people are toiling together,
> fighting together, yes dying together so that men may be free to work together, and
> live together, in tranquillity and equality.[329]

Delegates to the American Jewish Congress's biennial convention in 1960 continued to make similar statements. The then president, Joachim Prinz, emphasized that "only by rooting ourselves in our Jewish heritage will we be able to make a universal contribution to our country and to all mankind." According to Richard Cohen from the organization's public relations department, Prinz "urged recognition of the 'interdependence' between understanding of the Jewish heritage and the struggle for civil rights." The then retiring chairman of the American Jewish Congress's national executive committee, Justine Wise Polier, told the convention that for Jews "the teachings of justice to men, love of one's neighbor and love of the stranger are as inalienable as the right to worship God." "We, as Jews," she declared, "must find the ways of translating the application of the moral genius of our fathers to the world in which we live."[330]

Some have recognized in American Jews' outsider identification, especially with blacks, a means by which they used the causes of other groups to pursue their own agenda.[331] After all, the Second Generation projected its fixations onto largely imagined communities. The fact that the black-Jewish alliance began to break up soon after Jews and blacks came into closer everyday contact suggests strongly the validity of this argument. All the same, despite the function that may be discerned behind outsider identification and the Second Generation's liberalism as a whole, the sincerity with which many American Jews, including those within the American Jewish Congress, believed in their special connection to and responsibility for the persecuted and suffering, due to "prophetic Judaism" or historical experience or both, was very real and did determine their behavior. The phenomenon of black antisemitism proved agonizing or disorienting for many Jewish liberals.

The CLSA's Leo Pfeffer, who did more than perhaps any other single individual to de-Christianize the American public space through interminable court cases,[332] both affirmed his support for left-wing causes as a Jewish imperative and recognized the function in relation to his Jewish identity:

> I believe that ultimately there is no justification for Jewish survival unless there is that separateness, that outsidedness, that being the goad of the universal conscience. I don't think, realistically, that theology itself will long be adequate to maintain Jewish survival. To justify his survival as Jew the Jew should be the radical, the malcontent, the one who sparks revolutions. That, for better or worse, is his mission in society.[333]

Such an understanding of Jewish left-wing activism as constituting resistance to assimilation has not been universally accepted. Some scholars have interpreted the Second Generation's left-wing politics as, in the words of Marc Dollinger, "a quest for inclusion." In his recent and well-received account of American Jewish liberalism, Dollinger has recognized that "American Jews waged some of the most impressive liberal reform campaigns in American political history" and that "Jewish leaders represented the most influential liberal political constituency in America" despite their small numbers. According to Dollinger, "Jews used liberal politics to power their move from the margin to the mainstream of American life." When "faced with a choice between liberal politics and their acculturation," however, "Jews almost always chose the latter." In those "historical moments when Jewish social mobility clashed with a liberal political orientation, American Jews dissented from the dominant left-leaning trend."[334]

The general apologetic thrust to Dollinger's thesis, however, is best revealed in his analysis of the Jewish involvement in the black cause. Dollinger notes that northern Jews "chronicled impressive feats in the struggle for civil rights," yet acknowledges that "when the racial equality spotlight moved to the urban centers of New York, Chicago, Philadelphia, and Boston . . . acceptance into the surrounding non-Jewish society mandated that Jews adopt the prevailing social attitudes":

> Jewish children attended majority white schools, their parents joined racially segregated social organizations, and Jewish organizations adopted whites-only policies in their community centers, playgrounds, and swimming pools. Unwittingly, northern Jews had become part of the very system they were condemning. While they continued to vote Democratic, their newfound suburban lifestyle tempered their ideals.[335]

That Jews moved away from the black cause in deference to non-Jewish opinion is an unusual claim, for many segments of the Second Generation, as typified by the militancy of the American Jewish Congress, had long demonstrated and continued to demonstrate a conspicuous willingness to set themselves against and dissent openly from the still dominant Anglo-Protestant bourgeoisie,[336] even if, as Dollinger documents more persuasively, their ardor may have been dampened in wartime due to general anxiety (in line with Litt's aforementioned findings).[337] What is more, American Jews continued to live in considerable residential separation even in the suburbs, "largely out of their own desires,"[338] and they relocated there *en masse* only in the 1970s.[339] In keeping blacks out of their own communities from the 1960s, it is not clear with which gentiles they were seeking to ingratiate themselves.

Ostensibly closer to the truth was the accusation increasingly leveled by disillusioned blacks after the 1960s that Jews maintained a double standard between themselves and others, of which, moreover, they were not always aware because of a deeply held sense of moral superiority derived from their "lived religion." Secular ethnic Jews advocated bourgeois assimilation for blacks, yet not for themselves, not least because after the Second World War their "identity came to rely even more intensely on Jewish fraternization," rather than on any religious observance or positive culture. The Second Generation deplored in theory segregation's vices yet seemed to appreciate in practice its virtues. Seth Forman has more fully grasped the contradiction:

> At the very moment they [Jews] became aware that it was possible for them to "melt" away as an ethnic group they were refusing to do so, in part, through their involvement in the march for equal rights. The decision of the major Jewish organizations to pursue civil rights for all constituted a commitment to Jewish "otherness" through liberalism, while the same decision on the part of Black organizations and leaders constituted a commitment to black "sameness" (or at least black "similarity"). . . . The irony was that many Jews viewed the broader struggle to tear down the barriers to full integration as one way by which Jews could stave off complete assimilation.[340]

For himself, Dollinger provides no meaningful criteria of acculturation. The Second Generation's support for "a pluralist democracy that would value Jewish participation"[341] did not suggest an effort to further acculturation to the standards of the modern Anglo-Protestant bourgeoisie, but rather to render criteria of such acculturation moot. In helping to construct discourses on multiculturalism in which Americans were portrayed as a "propositional" people without a core culture or discrete traditions—an idea that though now dominant is historically false[342]—the Second Generation attempted to redefine American identity such that it did not—could not—conflict with its undifferentiated Jewishness.[343] What is more, in seeking to implement this understanding of American identity by opening the country's borders to all newcomers without distinction—culminating in their strong support for the 1965 Immigration Act—American Jews were not obviously seeking inclusion through acculturation or bourgeois assimilation, but inclusion by default.[344]

In this sought-after, end-of-history, pluralist America, moreover, the locus of accommodation was not conceived as the Jewish community, but the Anglo-Protestant or white Christian majority, which was required, as in the Soviet Union during the interwar period, to suppress its own hegemony, out of a sense of "obligation and guilt,"[345] so as to make way for the cultural expression or ethnic assertion of various minorities. As the American Israeli sociologist Charles Liebman observed of the Second Generation, "most Jews oppose intermarriage," and "Jewish parents will raise strong objections if their son informs them that he is marrying a non-Jewish girl." All the same, "if the son adds that his girl friend's parents also object to the marriage, the Jewish parents will either [be] outraged by their 'anti-Semitism' or else fail to understand what basis they have for raising objections." In general, secular ethnic "Jews want full acceptance as Americans, not as Jews":

> But they are scandalized by intermarriage, insist that a non-Jewish partner in a marriage convert to Judaism even when, as is usually the case, that partner no longer considers himself (generally herself) Christian. They support the State of Israel financially, politically, and emotionally when such support must surely raise the specter of dual national loyalty, if not outright disloyalty to America; but they are outraged by the idea that the State Department discriminates against Jews in its personnel policies.[346]

In this ambivalence, Jews were not alone, but the "intensity . . . is probably more pronounced among the Jews than in any other group in American society." By contrast, Catholic immigrants also resisted assimilation, but "their second and third generations are barely distinguishable as a separate group."[347] Liebman exaggerated on this last point, but he was not entirely off the mark. Upon attaining middle-class economic status (a generation after Jews) and greater social acceptance (after the Second World War), many upwardly mobile European Catholics, whose identities remained strongly religious and associational rather than simply ethnic or communal, increasingly viewed themselves as part of a white bourgeois majority and moved away from the Democratic Party on class lines.[348] For Jews, however, absorption into a broad "Judeo-Christian" conception proved less appealing, not only because of their suspicion of a formerly oppressive Christianity, but also because their identity was kept together by intense familism and exclusive fraternization rather than by personal religious observance.

Dollinger's thesis jars with the fact of the Second Generation's (self-)segregation as well as evidence that greater acculturation and social contact with gentiles correlated with greater conservatism or Republican voting rather than the reverse.[349] Nonetheless, it has a long pedigree. As early as 1926, Gedalia Bublick, a founding member of the American Jewish Congress, praised the Second Generation's Americanism by conflating Jewish ideals with the American Constitution (as did Jacob X. Cohen forty years later in his above-quoted speech before the NAACP). "It is a Jewish American creation," Bublick declared in the *Jewish Daily News*, because the Founding Fathers had followed "the old Hebrew books." As such, "We have our connection here, we are closely related to the present [Fourth of July] celebration. That which America presented to the world, is part of our soul, a part of our spirit." In response to such rhetoric, the journalist Nathan Zalowitz reminded readers of the *Jewish Daily Forward* of the empirical reality of a "voluntary ghetto" in the United States. It served "as one of our greatest bulwarks in our struggle against absorption in the maelstrom of Anglo-Saxon civilization," but also constituted "one of the potent causes of anti-Semitic feeling." Presenting contemporary data on Jewish residential concentration in New York and other cities, Zalowitz concluded:

> Four-fifths of the Jews in the United States practically have no social contact with the Gentiles who constitute 99% of the population of the country. This is a fact of the greatest significance. It means that for the overwhelming majority of Jews in America assimilation in any true sense is absolutely out of the question. It signifies that we are no nearer understanding our Gentile neighbors in this country than we were in the Old World. It means that despite the fact that we have attended American public schools and universities, read American papers and books, patronize the same theatres and subways and busses, we are kept and keep ourselves at arm's length from the bulk of the American population.[350]

If, as Nathan Rotenstreich maintained, "a Jew is a Jew when he is with other Jews,"[351] the Second Generation was quite Jewish. By extension, its members were not entirely American. That the Second Generation's political projects were mostly informed by ethnic Jewishness and its defense, rather than by American ideals, is suggested by contradictions in the American Jewish Congress's campaigns. The group proved rigid on the constitutional nonestablishment clause (the basis for the separation of church and state),[352] yet flexible on the constitutional interstate commerce clause (the pretext for the New Deal and so many antidiscrimination laws). It condemned efforts to purge subversives and communists (disproportionately Jewish) from various institutions in the name of civil rights (freedom of speech),[353] yet sought to have anti-Jewish critics sacked from academic positions or censored in the name of human rights (freedom from "hate").[354] It wished to de-Christianize public spaces in the name of church-state separation, yet defended Jewish public school students who wore religious paraphernalia to class and who demanded that noncompulsory secular events not fall on Jewish holidays.[355] Finally, it fought for a multicultural America in the name of social justice and antidiscrimination, yet backed an ethno-national Jewish state in the Middle East in the same language. In early 1948, for example, the American Jewish Congress published a statement, "urging all political parties in the coming elections to make plain their determination to support the United Nations partition plan for Palestine and to wipe [away] the evil of racial and religious discrimination at home and abroad."[356]

As in the First Generation, the sociological if not ideological nexus between the Jewish left and Zionism persisted into the Second Generation. The early American Jewish Congress attracted the support both of Jewish socialists or liberals and of Zionists. By contrast, the early American Jewish Committee, with its emphasis on bourgeois assimilation, tended to be less enthusiastic about either position. As mutual manifestations of resistance to bourgeois assimilation, American Jewish liberalism and Zionism were often combined in the same person. The American Jewish Congress's leaders were almost all both cultural pluralists (*vis-à-vis* the United States) and Jewish nationalists (*vis-à-vis* Palestine). Few were obviously cognizant of or bothered by any incongruity between these positions. From a Jewish perspective, they were flip sides of the same ethnocentric coin.[357]

This understanding of the sociology behind the Second Generation's political orientation explains, for instance, why American immigrants or *olim* to Israel after the Six-Day War of 1967, including those who settled in the West Bank and Gaza Strip, were almost all without exception "Democrats, Liberals, Independents, or unaffiliated." Like many of their peers, moreover, nearly half had "participated in peace or antiwar demonstrations" at home, and again like many of their peers, a vast majority believed that blacks in America had gone too far in their demands. There were fewer committed Republicans among these *olim* (around 2 percent) than among the Second Generation as a whole (around 10 percent).[358]

The bifurcation in American Jewish political thinking was expressed clearly by David Petegorsky in his address to colleagues at an American Jewish Congress convention in 1948, when he asserted, "We are profoundly convinced that Jewish survival will depend on Jewish statehood in Palestine, on the one hand, and on the existence of a creative, conscious and well-adjusted Jewish *community* in this country on the other." Such a community "can exist only within the framework of a progressive and expanding democratic society, which through its institutions and public policies gives full expression to the concept of cultural pluralism."[359] It was this insistence on "Jewish survival" as a pre-civil community, existing without liability in wider society, that motivated the liberalism of the American Jewish Congress and its supporters among the Second Generation, rather than a "quest for inclusion" via "acculturation."

In setting itself in the early 1950s against any "joint celebrations" of Christmas and Chanukah in public schools, with which arrangement some Jewish parents were content, and deploring "those who turn Christmas into a 'Jewish' holiday" by treating it as a secular national event, the American Jewish Congress explained itself explicitly:

> Try as parents may to raise their children in the notion that there is no difference whatsoever between them and their Christian friends, the differences are bound to reveal themselves. Jewish young men and women soon discover they belong to a different ethnic, cultural or religious group. . . . It is the fate of the Jew in the Diaspora to function as a minority, religiously and culturally. Only through the recognition of this basic fact can Judaism hope to survive. Only by the introduction of this awareness can the individual home become Jewish. The escape from it is Jewish self-negation and spiritual suicide.[360]

A Contribution to Change

In its adherence to third parties, radical politics, and *yidishkeyt*, the First Generation of Eastern European Jews in the United States tended to isolate itself and did not have a noteworthy impact on the rest of the country. The absorption of the Second Generation into the Democratic fold, by contrast, enabled its members to contribute to desired changes during the New Deal and to subsequent campaigns for civil and human rights. Reflecting the political concerns and sensibilities of many native-born American Jews, the American Jewish Congress was involved in these efforts on their behalf. The discrepancy in accomplishment between the American Jewish Congress's international diplomacy and its domestic pursuits during the interwar period and beyond indicates that its successes were determined not just by the exertions of its personnel but rather by the congruence of its preferred causes with broader social trends. The American Jewish Congress's antidiscrimination campaigns were part of a larger endeavor by various elements within American society in the mid-twentieth century to improve intergroup relations and to address the plight of African Americans.

This chapter traces the source of these campaigns to the social dilemmas of the Second Generation from the time before the Second World War and the Holocaust. It has sought to demonstrate the relation of these campaigns to the New Deal, about which the Second Generation was so enthusiastic and in which it played a prominent role. It was the New Deal that established the basis for the state's comprehensive intervention in civil society, and it was through expansive administration and its coercive instruments that the American Jewish Congress sought to preclude the Anglo-Protestant bourgeoisie from upholding a standard of assimilation to its norms and manners as the basis for social admission and opportunity in the private realm, by which arrangement the Second Generation felt disadvantaged, disabused, and denatured. The Second Generation understood such expectations as and tended to reduce them to arbitrary discrimination, which it claimed violated the precepts of American democracy.

The American Jewish Congress's stamina and intensity were ostensibly impelled and sustained by the earnest belief of its leaders that they were, through their activism in civil and human rights and related endeavors, meeting the dictates of their Jewish heritage, despite their relative nonobservance of Judaism's commandments. The Second Generation's identification with other putative outsiders, especially blacks, was a salient feature of its political activity and rhetoric. By championing black causes, many Jews paradoxically reinforced and reproduced their own distinctiveness even as they fought to bring down barriers to social integration. Despite their subjective sincerity in the promotion of black causes throughout the 1950s, the recalcitrance of many Second Generation Jews during the 1960s in complying with the policies of desegregation and antidiscrim-ination that they or their representatives had disproportionately advocated for the country as a whole resulted in bitterness on both sides. Whether the positions advocated by the American Jewish Congress, among other Jewish organizations, were meant for internal or merely external application continued to challenge American Jews and persisted into the Third Generation.

3

New Jewish Agenda and the Third Generation

Twice Removed from the Mainstream

New Jewish Agenda (NJA) came together in the summer of 1979 and was active from 1980 to 1992 as a "Jewish voice among progressives and a progressive voice among Jews."[1] The various local chapters of NJA were staffed and attended by a "diverse group of people [who] spanned several generations, and included students, professionals, Jewish secularists, the religiously observant, those with backgrounds in the non-Jewish Left, and people with strong ties to major Jewish organizations."[2] Notwithstanding this demographic variety, most of its leading members were the nonorthodox grandchildren of those Eastern European immigrants who came to the United States at the turn of the twentieth century or simply those who were born during or after the Second World War. In the words of one of its founders, NJA was "pretty much an age cohort of Baby Boomers."[3] As an organization whose membership was at core baby boomer yet not exclusively so, NJA emerged out of the social experience and political realities of the postwar Third Generation.

As a body that saw itself as more liberal or left wing than the American Jewish community and its establishment, which included the large advocacy organizations such as the American Jewish Congress, the American Jewish Committee, and the Anti-Defamation League, among others, NJA provides insight into the nature of the political attitudes and postures of the Third Generation not just by dint of its agreements, but also and more importantly by dint of its disagreements with that same community. New Jewish Agenda's disputes with the American Jewish "mainstream" suggested in reverse the continuing social function of the basic political inclinations that they both in large part shared. The Third Generation as a whole continued to demonstrate an anomalous preference for liberal or left-wing positions, as these were understood at the time, by comparison with other Americans of similar socioeconomic status. But NJA often pushed the logic of the American Jewish political tradition further than many Jewish individuals and groups of the latter half of the twentieth century felt entirely comfortable or happy with. This was most commonly and obviously so in relation to matters that pertained to Israel and the Middle East, the topic to which NJA devoted "at least 50% of our focus and resources," despite its commitment to a multiplicity of "progressive" causes, including gay rights, abortion, feminism, antiracism, and aid for refugees.[4]

Little of substance has been published on the activities of NJA, perhaps in part due to its ostracized status within the American Jewish community and establishment and in part because information about the group is concentrated in archives that have as yet not been cataloged.[5] This chapter relies heavily on archival sources from the forty-one boxes in the still unprocessed collection on NJA that reside in the Tamiment Library at New York University and on correspondence with past leaders and members of the now defunct group.[6] Given the scope of its activities, this chapter's main, but not sole, focus is on NJA's attitudes toward Zionism and the State of Israel, not least because its views thereon were most at odds with the rest of the Jewish community. As a result of its activities *vis-à-vis* the Middle East, NJA was criticized by opponents of varying political backgrounds as insufficiently Jewish, assimilationist, self-hating, or anti-Zionist. In response to such accusations, NJA emphasized repeatedly its commitment to Jewishness and the State of Israel and insisted that its positions were truly in line with Jewish values and Jewish political traditions as these had been understood in the United States for much of the twentieth century.

Further to the Left

In May 1979, at the invitation of Rabbi Gerry Serotta, about fifty Jews gathered for two days in New York City "to discuss and act on views which are both Jewish and also politically to the left of the public posture of the organized Jewish community."[7] Some of the participants, including Serotta himself, had been previously involved with Breira, an American Jewish group of largely elite intellectuals that had operated from 1973 to 1977 and had styled itself a "Project of Concern in Diaspora-Israel Relations." *Breira* was the Hebrew word for "alternative"; it played on the common slogan of *ein breira* or "there is no alternative," invoked by Israelis "to explain their situation, their attitude, and, increasingly, the policies of their government."[8] Breira came together in response to the Yom Kippur War of 1973 and the perceived lack of open debate within American Jewry on the topic of Israel. The group was devoted to peace in the Middle East and "what has come to be known as the two-state solution," a formulation that proved premature for most of the Third Generation and *a fortiori* the Second at the time.[9] Breira's demise, in large part due to communal hostility,[10] provided the impetus for Serotta's convocation, whereby self-styled progressive Jews could consider a new organization that would in some way take over from Breira, embodying and expanding upon its values and endeavors.[11]

Conversation at this initial convocation in New York City ranged widely, not least because Serotta was determined to give a new organization more breadth and thus more legitimacy and durability than Breira.[12] Consensus was not immediately reached on all subjects, but the Organizing Committee for a New Jewish Agenda (OCNJA) was formed out of a coalition of working groups to prepare for a national conference, set for late 1980, in which the goals and meaning of a progressive Jewish group would be determined. At the very beginning, however, a statement of purpose was released, whose message remained basically unchanged despite modifications to the text over the years:

> We are Jews concerned with the rightward drift of the public posture of the orga-
> nized American Jewish Community. We represent a broad spectrum of politically
> minded Jews who share views best characterized as "progressive." As Jews who
> believe strongly that authentic Jewishness can only be complete with serious and
> consistent attention to the just ordering of human society and natural resources of
> our world (Tikun Olam), we seek to apply Jewish values to such questions as energy
> policy, world hunger, peace in the Middle East, affirmative action, women's rights
> and Jewish education.[13]

In the run-up to the first national conference, which was held during the Christmas season in Washington, DC, the OCNJA "contact[ed] progressive Jewish groups and individuals throughout the United States" and abroad and published a newsletter "as a forum and resource for those interested people."[14] By late December 1980 more than two thousand individuals as well as fifteen multi-issue groups from different parts of the country had joined the OCNJA's mailing list.[15] The six newsletters that had appeared prior to this first national conference included letters and musings from a variety of individuals and groups, domestic and international, secular and religious, lay and academic. These contributions explored the possible meaning and scope of a progressive American Jewish group or applauded the efforts of the OCNJA to set one up.

A common theme in the newsletters was that American Jewry had lost some of its erstwhile enthusiasm for liberalism, which in the American context of the time had come to denote varying degrees of support for the welfare state, multiculturalism, civil and human rights, permissive or alternative social codes (increasingly in matters of sex, gender, and the family), and moderation in the prosecution of the Cold War. A letter of support was sent in by one Stephen Lerner of Charlotte, North Carolina:

> I am an organizer for the International Ladies Garment Workers Union in North
> Carolina and I feel very isolated from any progressive Jewish activities. In North
> Carolina the Jewish community is pretty conservative and business oriented.
> *Agenda* is a start in countering the swing to the right that some parts of the Jewish
> community seem to be undergoing.

Another was written by Daniel Soyer of Long Island City:

> I am looking forward to the conference and, I hope, to the founding of a new national
> organization of progressive Jews which will be capable of reversing the current con-
> servative, often chauvinist trends in the Jewish community. What is needed now is
> a broad based group with an unambiguously positive attitude toward the continued
> existence of the Jewish people . . . *and* a consistently progressive outlook in "general"
> politics and within the Jewish community itself.[16]

Rabbi Anson Layter expressed his wish that Jews in the diaspora might reach
out to peoples in the Third World, whose conceptions of Israel were, due to Arab
propaganda, largely focused "on the ideology and activities of the right-wing
Zionist parties" rather than on the country's anticolonialist and anti-imperialist
left-wing forces:

> By showing Third World peoples that many Israeli and Diaspora Jews share their
> concerns and criticisms, we might impart a sense of the internal dynamics of Israel
> and provide them with information about groups in Israel which they could support
> wholeheartedly.[17]

The general secretary of Israel's left-wing MAPAM party, Victor Shemtov,
gave his permission for OCNJA to add his name to the "international committee
of supporters":

> The Jewish people in Israel and the diaspora must deepen its national consciousness
> and commitment in seeking solutions for its own problems and those of the world.
> The voice of progressive Judaism, religious and secular, in all its political and reli-
> gious forms, must be heard so that higher Jewish values be applied in all spheres of
> life, in the diaspora and in Israel. . . . I am convinced that "AGENDA" could contrib-
> ute importantly in reshaping the Jewish people's political and spiritual life.[18]

That the Third Generation was becoming increasingly conservative or
Republican was in part substantiated by the results of recent presidential elections. Throughout the 1970s Republican candidates received over one-third of

the national Jewish vote, a considerable increase over the 1960s, during which Jewish support for the Republicans had never exceeded one-fifth.[19] In 1980, moreover, Ronald Reagan received close to 40 percent of the Jewish vote; Jimmy Carter received 45 percent, 20 percent less than in 1976 (around 15 percent of Jews voted for the independent candidate, John Bayard Anderson). Such an outcome, however, was likely an anti-Carter phenomenon, in part due to Carter's perceived ambivalence toward Israel, and did not in the end amount to the right-wing realignment against which NJA warned.[20] In 1984 support for Reagan dropped to 30 percent; the Democratic candidate, Walter Mondale, "received a higher level of backing from Jews than from Hispanics or members of trade unions. Only the blacks and the unemployed gave Mondale more support than Jews did."[21] Except for blacks, "Jews were the only group to shift against Reagan when he was gaining among all others." The presidential elections of 1988 between Michael Dukakis and George Bush produced similar results, as did congressional elections throughout the decade. Only the orthodox (less than one-tenth of Jewish voters) bucked such trends, with Bush receiving "85 percent of the vote in areas in Brooklyn and elsewhere inhabited by Hasidic sects."[22]

As such data indicate, American Jewry remained overwhelmingly liberal or left wing, despite some moderation in its Democratic partisanship from the highs of midcentury. All the same, NJA's first national conference did follow upon what proved to be a peak in Jewish support for the Republican Party in 1980, which resulted, both inside and beyond the new organization, in premature pronouncements about an imminent shift to the right among the Third Generation.[23] The sentiment at NJA's first national conference channeled the mood among *soi-disant* progressive Jews at a time when the United States, following "Carter's defeat" and the "devastating right-wing victories of November, 1980," was in the grip of "the forces of reaction" and the Jewish establishment and segments of the Jewish population had become unduly conformist and decreasingly committed to "justice, peace, and equality." The proceedings of the said conference were devoted to meeting the "immense challenge" of the "regressive policies of the current administration" so as to "fashion a better future for our children and grandchildren."[24]

Over five days of "mutual education" and "personal interaction" from December 24 to 28, seven hundred people (three hundred were turned away due to lack of space) came together and participated in "over 150 workshops, panels, caucuses, affinity groups, and plenary sessions, in addition to innumerable informal conversations."[25] The conference's program sought "the delineation through education sessions of a spectrum of Jewish progressive approaches to current social and political problems" over a remarkable range of topics, which included, among many others, "urban issues"; "energy, environment, and economy"; "reversing the arms race"; "world hunger"; "Jews, agriculture, and rural America"; "rights of gays and lesbians"; "refugees and immigration policy"; "animal rights, food policy, and vegetarianism"; "the Jewish elderly poor"; "unionization of Jewish teachers"; "the Jewish disabled"; "Israeli Arabs and Jews: cooperative efforts"; "feminism in Israel"; and "Jews and Hispanics."[26]

The OCNJA and later the NJA desired diversity not only in the scope of their concerns, but also in leadership and membership. The founding conference strove to be inclusive to bring together Jews of different backgrounds. The one requirement for involvement was that people "define themselves as 'left of center' politically" and "seek a Jewish identification which combines a concern for social justice with Jewish commitment."[27] Even though most conferees and future associates were nonorthodox, straight, young (in their late twenties and thirties), and middle class—for the simple reason that such traits overwhelmingly typified the Third Generation as a whole—NJA was still more diverse in its socioeconomic composition than perhaps any other Jewish organization of the period.[28] From the start, NJA applied its understanding of democracy by adopting a policy of affirmative action that sought to ensure or augment the female, homosexual, and working-class representation in its decision-making processes and entities. Balanced regional representation was also mandated for the "task forces" and other fora that emerged out of the founding conference. New Jewish Agenda's center of gravity would remain around New York City, but important personnel hailed from across the country, and local chapters within the national structure were found in every region.[29]

To some extent, such efforts toward inclusiveness simply took account of social changes in the United States, both inside and outside the Jewish community. Throughout the 1970s feminism, homosexuality, abortion, divorce, and decreased fertility all became more common or more open among the Third Generation as among Americans as a whole, even as all phenomena became the subjects of intense communal debate.[30] Jews also began to leave New York City in large numbers, disrupting the subculture that had existed there for more than half a century. The movement of Jews from the Northeast to other parts of the country, above all to the South and West, continued throughout the 1980s and NJA's existence.[31] In 1960, 67 percent of America's Jews lived in the Northeast and 14 percent in the Midwest. By 1991 these numbers were 49 and 11 percent respectively, and even within these areas Jews moved from older urban centers to newer suburbs. During this same period, and especially during the 1970s, New York State's proportion of American Jewry dropped from 46 to 28 percent of the total. The greatest gains—in the hundreds of thousands—were made in Florida and California, specifically the metropolitan areas around Miami, Los Angeles, and San Francisco. Smaller yet sizable gains were also made in Phoenix, Denver, and Atlanta.[32]

Regional, gender, and other diversity was reflected on NJA's interim council, which was chosen at the founding conference "to carry out a democratic process of platform development," with input from both the national and local levels. This body of thirty-five persons made sure to include "various groups which have been unrepresented or underrepresented in other Jewish organizations." Of those on the interim council, nearly half were women, over half came from thirteen states other than New York and New Jersey, and several were openly gay. There were also a number of radicals, some with past "New Left" affiliations.[33] This latter constituency was indicative of not only the general left-wing nature and thus appeal of NJA, most of whose leaders and many of whose members had had some experience with campus activism during the 1960s or 1970s, but also the important presence of Jewish baby boomers in the milieu of the New Left in those decades.

At the height of the New Left's activism in the mid-1960s, which had been a "mostly white student movement that promoted participatory democracy, crusaded for civil rights and various types of university reforms and protested against the Vietnam War," more than half of its cadres on American university campuses were Jewish.[34] The Jewish president of Columbia University's Students for a Democratic Society, Mark Rudd, later reminisced that this quintessential New Left organization at that institution was akin to a "Jewish fraternity."[35] According to Stanley Rothman and S. Robert Lichter, those who interpreted student radicalism as a product of a generic secularism suppressed the "relationship between Jewish ethnicity and radicalism, because Jewish Americans are differentially secular in their religious orientation." Indeed, the "often-noted association between secularism and new left radicalism is the product of a 'secular' Jewish heritage rather than a nonreligious upbringing *per se*." Jews who did not consider themselves to be unduly radical were still more likely to protest than non-Jews, even as they were more likely to come from upper-middle-class families.[36]

New Jewish Agenda tapped into the currents of the New Left not only in its Jewishness but also in its commitment to diversity as part of a general orientation to postbourgeois lifestyles and identities that were not restricted to traditional left-wing concerns with labor or even blacks. It also resembled the New Left in its emphasis on egalitarianism, antimilitarism, and countercultural criticism. It stood out, however, in applying this counterestablishment attitude to the Jewish community itself. In the "unity statement" that was formulated at the founding conference, NJA urged American Jews of all persuasions to come together "to join in dialogue" without "forced unanimity, intolerance or the stifling of dissent."[37] Above all, NJA insisted that Israel, an issue of especial interest to its membership, not be above censure. "All the draft positions considered at the Conference had in common support for the survival of a Jewish State of Israel, although sharing the premise that 'support' does not entail endorsement of the policies of a particular Israeli government, or the stifling of open discussions of alternatives in the Diaspora."[38] The "unity statement" encapsulated this position:

> We are committed to Jewish survival. Jews must have the rights to which every people are entitled: political independence and self-determination in Israel and full civil rights and cultural autonomy everywhere that Jews live. Survival, however, is only a precondition for Jewish life, not its purpose. Our agenda must be determined by our ethics, nor our enemies.

Over the next several months NJA set about applying these ethics, which mandated *tikkun olam*, "the repair and moral improvement of our world."[39] With the approval of the interim and later executive council, local chapters began to agitate across the country. Activities ranged from observances in several American cities of the nuclear bombing of Japan, which coincided in August 1981 with the Hebrew calendar's *Tisha B'Av* (Ninth of Av), commemorating the destruction of Jerusalem's temples, to petitions in favor of Dennis Brutus, an exiled, anti-apartheid, South African poet, who faced deportation from the United States due to infraction of the conditions of his work permit.[40] A chapter in Boston worked for "progressive" social change from within the Jewish community itself, interjecting itself in a labor dispute at a local Jewish hospital, which had used "union-busting services" and had failed "to implement Affirmative Action goals." Another chapter in Philadelphia protested outside a *soirée* hosted by a local Jewish congregation in honor of the "right-wing [though Democratic] ex-mayor Frank Rizzo."[41] In March 1982 NJA marched with "10,000 other New Yorkers" during Ronald Reagan's visit to the city and conducted a press conference with like-minded Christian leaders at which the National Council of Christians and Jews was denounced for presenting the president with a humanitarian award.[42] At around the same time NJA launched a letter-writing campaign to raise awareness of political repression and "disappeared persons" in a junta-ruled Argentina, not least because "Jews tend to be over-represented in segments of the population which are particularly hard hit by the repression, such as academics."[43]

In these early months NJA's only noteworthy public action on the Middle East occurred in response to the Knesset's passage of the Golan Heights Law in December 1981, whereby Israel formally annexed that territory, which it had conquered during the Six-Day War of 1967. The Manhattan and Brooklyn chapters staged a protest in front of the Israeli mission to the United Nations, "because of our deep concern for Israel, and our commitment to peace and justice for all peoples in the Middle East." A participant in this sidewalk demonstration, Rabbi Israel Dresner, who also sat on NJA's interim council, criticized the bill in an interview on Israeli television. Only in June 1982, with Israel's invasion of Lebanon, did

NJA bring a large part of its focus to bear on the issue of "contributing to peace between Israel and its neighbors and within Israel." As this issue constituted the highest priority for NJA's membership, according to an internal survey and general sentiment, the Lebanon war roused the group.[44]

New Jewish Agenda's opposition to the war in Lebanon was open, consistent, and immediate, making it unique among American Jewish organizations at the time.[45] Under the direction of its defense minister, Ariel Sharon, Israel invaded Lebanon on June 6 in pursuit of the Palestine Liberation Organization (PLO), which had a presence along the border between the two countries, causing disturbances there and elsewhere. Within days of that military deployment, NJA chapters across the United States had "taken part in a wide range of activities." The Detroit chapter held a memorial service for casualties at Temple Emmanuel. The San Francisco chapter held four educational forums on the conflict. The Cleveland chapter's opposition was featured on the national news. The Boston chapter held a teach-in at Arlington Church.[46] Notably, the Manhattan chapter held a protest rally before the Israeli mission to the United Nations on June 18. A participant, Jacob Bender, issued a distraught statement, which expressed feelings that were common among his colleagues:[47]

> I stand before you today as a Jew, child of centuries of cruelty and seekers of justice, and I stand before you today as a Jew in open opposition to the policies of the government of Israel and condemn the invasion of Lebanon. . . . Too many memories of pogroms and persecutions call to me from the night, too many visions of hatred and Holocaust and broken Jewish lives stand before me demanding truth, and the truth is that what Israel is doing today in Lebanon, and the West Bank, is an abomination. The invasion and the occupation have turned history on its head, making yesterday's oppressed, today's oppressor, yesterday's persecuted, today's persecutors.

Bender spoke for most within NJA when he insisted that Israel would not gain security "through the violence of conquest," but only through the "affirmation of peace and justice":

> Justice can only flow from the principle of the inalienable right of self-determination of all peoples, including Palestinians and Jews. . . . After these many long decades of violence, the cycle of violence must be broken. Two peoples live today in Israel and Palestine and it is only with the mutual recognition of the Palestinian and Israeli peoples that peace will finally come.[48]

Misgivings about the invasion of Lebanon, as well as about Israel's right-wing prime minister, Menachem Begin, who had come to power in 1977, thus overturning decades of Labor and left-wing dominance, were not only to be found within NJA. Doubts existed within the major American Jewish organizations, especially after Israel's military campaign passed beyond its proclaimed aim of routing Palestinian terrorists within certain territorial limits and moved north to the capital, Beirut, leaving considerable destruction and casualties in its wake.[49] Feeling the need for a unified front against Israel's increasingly numerous and vocal detractors, however, "no large American organization has come out against the Israeli action." What is more, those "groups that raise money for Israel," the *New York Times* reported at the time, "say contributions are exceeding projections since the invasion of Lebanon."[50] On the same day that NJA's Manhattan chapter held its protest rally before the Israeli mission, Menachem Begin addressed a gala dinner attended by prominent and wealthy American Jews at the Waldorf Astoria Hotel. This single event raised a record $27 million "for development projects in Israel."[51]

New Jewish Agenda challenged the stance of the American Jewish establishment, in part justifying itself by pointing to the unprecedented criticism of the invasion of Lebanon from within Israel itself, including an antiwar demonstration in Tel Aviv at the end of June, the first case in the country's history of opposition "by thousands of Israeli citizens while the fighting was still in progress."[52] It sponsored a half-page advertisement in the *New York Times* on June 30 (and later *The Jewish Post and Opinion*), appending six hundred American Jewish signatures, including those of thirty-nine rabbis, to an endorsement of a recent statement by Israel's Peace Now movement that called for an end to violence and mutual recognition between Israelis and Arabs.[53] New Jewish Agenda subsequently organized a petition campaign in support of the "Paris Declaration" of three prominent Jews—Philip M. Klutznick, a former American secretary of commerce; Nahum Goldmann, a founder of the World Jewish Congress; and Pierre Mendès-France, a one-time prime minister of France—who made a similar plea for accommodation on July 2. The petition was signed by "thousands of American Jews" and sent to notaries.[54]

Such conduct brought NJA some recognition from some segments of the Third Generation. Membership increased, as did income from dues and contributions, although these latter regularly fell short of organizational needs. By late 1982 NJA had twenty-three chapters and more than twenty-five hundred members across the United States, as well as $118,000 in funds.[55] Its earnest aspirations for expansion, however, were met above all by indifference as well as by hostility from more attentive elements within the American Jewish community. Notably, in early June a fraudulent mail campaign was begun by an unknown group, suspected to be the ultra-Zionist Jewish Defense League of Rabbi Martin David Kahane, which sent two unsigned letters to Jewish organizations across North America. These documents used the stationery of a defunct pro-Palestinian entity and suggested falsely that NJA had contacted and worked with this same entity to isolate and undermine Israel.[56] A more dramatic incident occurred in November, when three conservative rabbis from Massachusetts, to the chagrin of some of their peers, came together to excommunicate NJA's entire enrollment for their advocacy of the rights of Palestinians as well as homosexuals.[57] As a subtle indication of its ill repute, NJA was not included on the directory of national Jewish organizations in the *American Jewish Year Book* until 1986.[58]

These negative episodes annoyed yet in no way deflected NJA from its sense of mission. It continued in its activism, including its unpopular fault-finding of Israel. In its national platform, which was passed after much deliberation in late November 1982 at a conference in New York City at the Stoneworkers Union Hall, NJA reiterated its position on Israel:

> Our histories, traditions, values, and sentiments have created a connection between us and the Jewish State of Israel. We believe that the fate of the Jewish people in one part of the world is linked to the fate of the Jewish people in other parts of the world. . . . We affirm the right and necessity in democratic debate and open discussion regarding Israeli policies.

Against orthodox tradition, it also reasserted its commitment to homosexuals as well as feminism:

> New Jewish Agenda supports the struggle of Lesbians and Gay Men to lead lives of freedom and dignity. . . . Jewish religious tradition has neither condoned homosexuality nor accepted Lesbians and Gay Men as equal participants in Jewish communal life. However, Judaism is evolving, as evidenced by changes in women's roles. We reject the anti-Gay rights position of some Jews and Jewish organizations as antithetical to our Jewish heritage of respect for human rights.[59]

After the adoption of this national platform, several campaigns stood out from NJA's manifold pursuits through the mid-1980s, when the organization reached its peak, with around forty-five chapters, five thousand members, and $250,000 annually in funds, most of which came from grassroots donations, but some of which came from sympathetic pacifist or other left-wing foundations.[60] These campaigns included efforts to freeze Israeli settlement on the West Bank and to bring Palestinian speakers to local synagogues and other Jewish venues; to advance both women's rights and Middle Eastern peace by taking part in the United Nations' third Decade of Women conference in Nairobi; to disprove claims by the Reagan administration that the revolutionary socialist Sandinistas in Nicaragua were antisemitic; and to join the sanctuary movement that sought to provide displaced Central Americans with refuge in the United States.

In its readiness to denounce Israeli settlement in territories that had been conquered in the Six-Day War, NJA picked up where Breira had left off in the late 1970s. In accusing Israel of inflexibility *vis-à-vis* the Palestinians in the West Bank and Gaza, Breira had scandalized and incited the wrath of the major American Jewish organizations, for many of which it had become "an article of faith . . . that Israel should not give up an inch of occupied territory."[61] Of course the treaty that secured peace between Israel and Egypt in March 1979 did result in Israel's withdrawal from Sinai, to Egypt's benefit. Despite American diplomatic efforts, however, the status of the West Bank and Gaza had not been linked successfully to the status of Sinai, not least because of the PLO's refusal to recognize Israel. So relinquishment of Sinai convinced some elements within Israeli society of the need to ensure retention of the other conquered territories.[62] By 1983 there were more than 20,000 Israeli citizens in the West Bank, a tenfold increase from 1972, and many more in East Jerusalem. The rapid growth continued into the future, with 130,000 settlers in the West Bank alone (excluding East Jerusalem) by 1995 and nearly 250,000 by 2005.[63]

Observing these trends in the spring of 1983, NJA's Gordon Fellman argued that the Palestinians would either become second-class citizens as a source of cheap labor in an annexed West Bank or first-class citizens in an Israel that would consequently cease to have a Jewish majority and character. The only practical and humane option was to exchange land for peace. "Large numbers of people in Israel and the United States," Fellman warned, "seem unwilling to recognize the consequences of continued settlement and eventual annexation," even as most were simply ignorant of the realities on the ground. The "intention of the Agenda campaign is to spread information about real conditions."[64] This campaign involved a petition, ultimately signed by over one hundred Jewish community leaders and brought to the important General Assembly of the Council of Jewish Federations, which, "for the first time in its 52-year history," due to NJA's lobbying, "adopted a resolution on Middle East peace urging all parties" to be "flexible"—an "apparent reference to Israel's settlement policy."[65] The petition read as follows:

> We are American Jews committed to the security and well being of Israel. We join with the peace forces in Israel who call for a freeze of Jewish settlement activity in the West bank and who oppose all actions by the Israeli government designed to incorporate the West Bank and its population into the State of Israel.
>
> We believe that a negotiated exchange of territory for peace will contribute to Israel's long-term security, enhance its democratic character and promote justice for Israelis, Palestinians and all others who have suffered through this painful conflict.[66]

In order to facilitate the dissemination of this message, NJA decided in June 1983 to sponsor an Israeli-Palestinian tour in conjunction with the American Friends Service Committee as part of its objective of "humanizing the conflict and raising the issue of Jewish-Arab reconciliation."[67] Mordechai Bar-On, a former officer in the Israeli Defense Forces (IDF) and soon-to-be member of the Knesset, would speak alongside Mohammed Milhem, a deposed (by Israel) mayor of the West Bank town of Halhoul.[68] In the spring of 1984 Bar-on and Milhem traveled to seventeen cities across North America, showing audiences that "an Israeli and a Palestinian, each respected members of their communities, could publicly discuss the need for and possibility of a negotiated peace between their people [sic]." Local press coverage was extensive, and PBS aired a one-hour documentary special on the tour in October.[69] New Jewish Agenda followed up on the success of this tour in the following year by cosponsoring, again with Quakers, a tour by Dov Yermiya, the Jewish cochair of the Movement for Coexistence and Against Racism in Israel.[70] Over nine weeks Yermiya spoke to diverse audiences, both Jewish and Christian, in twenty-six American cities, about "growing anti-Arab racism in Israel and the IDF's immoral conduct in the 'war of choice' in Lebanon."[71] Other tours by other speakers were also subsequently arranged.

Through the auspices of NJA, Arab and Israeli women came together in July 1985 to share their stories in Nairobi at the United Nations' third Decade of Women conference. This forum was of especial interest to NJA, which sent its executive director, Reena Bernards, and national cochair, Christie Balka, as its representatives, for "the two previous conferences in Mexico City in 1975 and in Copenhagen in 1980 were seriously damaged by polarized discussion of the Israeli-Palestinian conflict."[72] Indeed, it was at Mexico City that delegates first passed a resolution equating Zionism with racism, subsequently corroborated in a vote at the United Nations General Assembly. Seeking to prevent a recurrence of such rancor,[73] NJA organized a workshop "where five hundred women hear . . . a dialogue that crosses the historical divide." Mary Khass, a Gazan who ran a preschool for refugee mothers and their children, and Lisa Blum, an Israeli peace activist, "each spoke of the position of women in their own societies," of "how the position of women is adversely effected by the continuing hostilities in the region," and "about the need for mutual recognition between Israel and the Palestinians."[74]

The Nairobi conference was not without acrimony—many Arab delegates proved less accommodating than Khass—but Reena Bernards considered it an improvement over previous events.[75] In a report that she and Balka prepared for NJA, they affirmed the "positive contact between Arab and Jewish women" in Kenya, which demonstrated an "effective way to empower people and work for peace" in the Middle East:

Many non-Arab, non-Jewish women who witnessed the Khass-Blum dialogue saw for the first time that there was an alternative to the paralysis and despair about the issue that took hold at the Copenhagen conference. Many saw in the Khass-Blum exchange a model for addressing this issue in their own communities.[76]

In confronting the controversy of the Middle East at Nairobi, New Jewish Agenda defied the strategy of the Reagan administration, whose delegation to the conference, led by the president's daughter, Maureen, had sought to avoid undue politicization of the event "by sticking to an agenda of narrowly defined women's issues." Balka and Bernards "maintained that discussion of the Middle East does have a role at a feminist conference, but that discussion should be well prepared and guided so that it can be a constructive one."[77] A similar oppositional stance was consciously taken by NJA against the Reagan administration in its nearly coeval campaign in relation to Nicaragua, which in 1979 had come under the control of the socialist, anti-American Sandinistas. In 1983 the Reagan administration and the Anti-Defamation League (ADL) began to accuse the Sandinista regime of antisemitism against Nicaragua's tiny Jewish population of around fifty persons, even though other major Jewish American organizations could not substantiate the allegations. New Jewish Agenda regarded such charges as a cynical ploy by the Reagan administration to draw "Jews to the right" with the help of Jewish neoconservatives, both before and after the overwhelming Jewish vote for the Democrats in the 1984 election, and "to enlist Jewish support for the Administration's bellicose policy towards Central America and particularly its efforts to topple the Sandinista leadership in Nicaragua."[78]

In the summer of 1984 NJA organized a Jewish Human Rights Delegation, including Rabbi Marshall Meyer of the University of Judaism in Los Angeles, formerly an activist against antisemitism and for "disappeared persons" in Argentina, to investigate the situation in Managua, Nicaragua's capital.[79] From August 12 to 17 this delegation met with "key government officials, representatives of human rights organizations, opposition groups and parties, members of the press, the US ambassador and members of the Nicaraguan Jewish community."[80] In a report on the expedition that it published in September, the delegation argued that the "current condition of human rights and civil liberties in Nicaragua presents a mixed picture" and advocated improvements in certain areas, but concluded that Jews *qua* Jews were not persecuted by the Sandinistas, despite anxiety among most Jewish citizens about the revolution:

> Charges of Nicaraguan government anti-Semitism cannot be supported; there simply is no body of credible evidence to suggest that the Sandinista government has pursued or is currently pursuing a policy of discrimination against Jews; or that Jewish people are not welcome to live and work in Nicaragua.[81]

Receiving communal and national press coverage, NJA felt pleased by the "success and impact" of its delegation, which "has shown that despite its size, Agenda can play an active and pivotal role in mobilizing progressive opinion within the American Jewish community." New Jewish Agenda noted that its efforts resulted in Elliot Abrams, the assistant secretary of state for human rights in the Reagan administration, admitting "for the first time that the government of Nicaragua does not have an official policy of anti-Semitism." What is more, Sergio Ramirez, a high-level Nicaraguan official, "told the delegation that [his] government was open to mutual initiatives towards the re-establishment of diplomatic relations between Nicaragua and Israel."[82] All the same, the issue continued to arouse debate within the American Jewish community. When Reagan and the ADL again accused the Sandinistas of antisemitism in 1986,[83] NJA found itself the subject of intense criticism in the pages of the now neoconservative Jewish magazine *Commentary*, which was sponsored by the American Jewish Committee.[84] It was lambasted for creating a false consensus about Nicaragua's Jews and apologizing for the Sandinistas.[85] Cynthia Aronson of NJA's delegation subsequently accused *Commentary* of blatant misrepresentation.[86]

New Jewish Agenda was not dissuaded by such detraction. It followed up on its investigation of the Sandinista regime by undertaking to aid those who had been harmed by the general instability in Central America as a whole, noting that "both US and Israeli government policies have contributed to the continuing state of war and poverty" in the region.[87] In the autumn of 1985 NJA raised funds for medical and other supplies to Central America and also sent a contingent of volunteers to Nicaragua to aid peasants in the coffee harvest.[88] By 1986 it had become involved in the sanctuary movement for refugees from El Salvador and Guatemala. Nearly one million people from those states, escaping violence and civil wars, crossed into the United States over the course of the 1980s, yet they were denied ready asylum. The Reagan administration maintained that these Central Americans were fleeing poverty rather than persecution, for any admission of governmental repression would have compelled the American Congress, under its own laws, to cut off further aid to the anticommunist and anti-Sandinista regimes in El Salvador and Guatemala.[89]

The sanctuary movement, which defied official federal policy and sought to safe-house Central Americans, was largely Christian in origin and composition. In April 1985 only 3 sanctuary sites out of 226 were provided by Jewish groups. By June 1986, however, 18 sanctuary sites out of 329 were Jewish, in addition to 5 provided by NJA alone. A year later the numbers had risen to 37 out of 399 in addition to 6 by NJA.[90] Along with the somewhat smaller Jewish Peace Fellowship, NJA played an instrumental role in "increasing the participation among Jews on the local level" in the plight of the Central American refugees.[91]

In April 1985 NJA had "initiated a campaign for Temples and Synagogues across the country to invite Central American refugees to their Passover seders in April 1985." For these seders, moreover, NJA prepared "an addendum to the Haggadah [Passover liturgy], specifically applying this issue to the Passover rituals," in which the suffering of Central American refugees would be linked explicitly to the suffering of Jews during their exile from Egypt and throughout their diasporic experience.[92] (New Jewish Agenda had in fact produced several such "alternative" Haggadot in the early 1980s in support of various victims, including Palestinians.)[93] A year later NJA distributed brochures to "raise issues and educate American Jews in communities and congregations throughout the country." It also sponsored three rabbis from Arizona, Wisconsin, and New York to spread the message of "providing support and protection for Central American refugees" and "the special Jewish obligation to 'harbor the stranger.'"[94] In 1987 forty-one synagogues pledged to open their doors.[95]

Grassroots enthusiasm for the sanctuary movement among average American Jews was not overwhelming, not least because the issue in no way affected their daily lives. In this particular instance, however, NJA did enjoy the endorsement of much of the American Jewish Reform leadership, including the Union of American Hebrew Congregations and the Central Conference of American (Reform) Rabbis.[96] Such cooperation, however, was not forthcoming for the causes that NJA emphasized through the turn of the decade. Most notably, NJA's sympathetic attitude toward the Palestinians during their uprising or *intifada* against Israeli occupation of the West Bank and Gaza, which broke out in early December 1987 and endured for several years thereafter, continued to isolate the organization within the American Jewish community and from the American Jewish establishment.

As had the war in Lebanon five years before, the *intifada* produced division within the Third Generation. The heads of many of the largest American Jewish organizations openly deplored Israel's strong-arm tactics in cracking down on the rioters, whom the world saw, with the help of graphic media images, as the abused underdog. "Jews Must Not Break Bones," a longtime supporter of Israel, A. M. Rosenthal, editorialized in the *New York Times*: "The enemies of Israel do use weapons against the unarmed . . . but Israelis cannot" due to their scriptures and their history.[97] Even the staunchly Zionist *Commentary* magazine observed that "never perhaps has criticism of the state of Israel by American Jews been so open, so wide-spread and so bitter as it is today."[98] After Yasir Arafat issued a statement rejecting terrorism on December 8, 1988, some surveys indicated that more American Jews approved than disapproved of the US State Department's eventual willingness to engage the PLO. As global sanctions of Israel intensified and as Palestinian actions became increasingly violent, however, their "basic solidarity with Israel reasserted itself." By the fall of 1990, moreover, the pressures on the American Jewish community and establishment relented as the commencement of the First Gulf War redirected world attention to Iraq; Israel regained American sympathy when attacked by Saddam Hussein's scud missiles, and the *intifada* lost its energy as the IDF endeavored to reduce casualties.[99]

Notwithstanding the debate that the *intifada* engendered among some segments of the Third Generation, NJA's position on the episode and on the Palestinians themselves did not render the organization much more welcome or much more mainstream among its institutional peers. By the winter of 1987 NJA did find itself in a somewhat better communal position than had been the case in its early years. It could report some lessening of hostility among local Jewish Community Relations Councils (JCRCs) toward the possibility that local NJA chapters would join, sit, and engage with them. By the late 1980s "many more chapters are seeking seats on their local JCRCs and many are finding their experiences as highly charged though more reasonable," despite the "often lengthy, sometimes arduous, and always highly politicized" process of application. In the early 1980s such efforts had been met by usually insurmountable "major opposition," especially from Zionists.[100] On the JCRCs and in other fora, however, NJA was received more readily on issues of common domestic concern, on which there was often a mutual liberal approach to resolving problems, than on Israel or the Middle East, on which such an approach tended to be suspended.

The *intifada* may have broadened the scope of debate within the Third Generation, which was compelled to ponder "the situation in the Occupied Territories, searching for explanations and solutions." But whereas "much American Jewish reaction has centered around specific policies, such as the indiscriminate and brutal beatings of Palestinians, we," Ezra Goldstein of NJA-Brooklyn observed, "have been able to place these events in a much broader historical and political context." As a result, NJA advocated comprehensive solutions to the conflict in the Middle East, including a Palestinian state under Arafat's PLO, that were still viewed as controversial if not treacherous by most American Jews.[101] "We have seen enormous movement by American organizations to our left and right towards acceptance of the formula we have advocated since our founding":

> Two states for two peoples. Most of these organizations, however, approach the two-state solution with an attitude far different from ours.
>
> To our right, Jewish groups (e.g., American Friends of Peace Now, segments of the AJ Committee and Congress) see a Palestinian state as the only available option, given demographic realities, the cost of the occupation, and the intensity of Palestinian nationalism. They offer this conclusion with a sense of resignation and pessimism.

To our left, many of the non-governmental organizations concerned with the question of Palestine have the same air of resignation. They have accepted two states either because they are committed to following the lead of the PLO or because they have concluded that accommodation with Israel is the only realistic means of achieving Palestinian statehood.

By contrast with these "negative attitudes," which have "led the right and the left to couch their acceptance of a two-state solution in a host of qualifiers," NJA stood "with a handful of Americans" and "no other progressive or Jewish organization in the United States" in propounding the message that "mutual recognition equals mutual liberation."[102] In support of this position, various local chapters of NJA held vigils across the country; a national petition campaign was launched, obtaining thousands of signatures;[103] and ads were successfully run in various local Jewish newspapers and other publications.[104] The *intifada* notably intensified a discussion within NJA itself over the advisability and desirability of American aid to Israel. Airing of this issue in particular further reduced the organization's credibility with the American Jewish community and establishment, and perhaps more important, added to internal schisms and existing strains, all of which helped to undermine the group's tenability.

Contention over the issue of American aid to Israel had existed within NJA for some time, but the *intifada* brought it to the fore.[105] Israel was an important recipient of American aid in the years after its independence in 1948 and especially after the Six-Day War in 1967.[106] Two discussion papers on this issue—one for and one against—were written prior to NJA's national convention in 1987, yet they were not circulated for a variety of reasons, including concerns over their divisiveness. Gerry Serotta wrote against addressing the aid issue within NJA:

> As the founder of NJA, I . . . feel I have the responsibility to warn others in leadership that any serious consideration of NJA advocating publicly aid sanctions against Israel will very likely mean the end of NJA's ability to work within the organized Jewish community. In addition, I believe it will lead to many resignations of individuals and of entire chapters. If NJA were not simply to seriously consider but went so far as to adopt such a position we would almost certainly be committing organizational suicide.[107]

Serotta emphasized that there was no tactical advantage in adopting a position against American aid to Israel, whatever the moral satisfaction for some. Notwithstanding such warnings, the issue resurfaced two years later at a subsequent national conference, at which papers on the subject of aid were circulated. Jon Weisberger of Columbia, Ohio, argued in favor of a call for reductions:

The *intifada* has put military aid, at least, on the national agenda. . . . To continue our virtual silence on the question means that we will be excusing ourselves from an important debate at precisely the time when our voices, Jewish and progressive, need to be heard. Military aid is essentially an ugly tool of national policy. . . . [The] suspension of aid on the grounds of human rights violations is an implicit recognition that stability and security cannot be achieved by denying justice. US military aid to Israel . . . is based upon neither justice nor security, at least as we would conceive them, but rather on the interests of aggressive elites in both countries.[108]

Gordon Fellman of Boston argued that the issue of aid was a distraction from the pursuit of peace, which was NJA's real mission:

I believe the time NJA spends on issues like US aid would be far better spent on figuring out how we can move the uncommitted, and how we can move the committed to rethinking their positions. The rest is, in my opinion, almost entirely tokenism—token issues, token protests, tokens left posturing.[109]

As in 1987, such arguments failed to result in a committed policy or platform.[110] No public stance was taken, but "the issue of aid to Israel epitomized" certain tensions within NJA, including the "conflict" between those who "were motivated by a pro-Israel approach, and those who were motivated by a pro-Palestinian approach" in their thinking about the Middle East. This "conflict" in turn overlapped with a vague yet noticeable division between NJA's East Coast and West Coast chapters, with the former being more "pro-Israel" and politically moderate and the latter being more "pro-Palestinian" and politically radical. "To overstate the case," one member has summarized, "the East Coast members were a bit more focused on being a progressive voice in the Jewish community, and the West Coast members were a bit more focused on being a Jewish voice in the progressive community."[111] Such distinctions were small in isolation, but they accumulated over time and added to organizational stains. In 1988 NJA's then executive director, David Coyne, announced his resignation, in part due to these strains:

I am burning out. . . . Most of the time my work at NJA has been a great pleasure, one of the best experiences of my life. . . . [But] some of my experiences have been very frustrating. As national organizations go, NJA retains a high degree of chapter autonomy and provides room for a wide range of political views. I have found myself exasperated by having overall responsibility for an organization in which I have had to defend sometimes conflicting activities and statements. That's tiring stuff.[112]

The sense of exhaustion to which Coyne gave voice was shared by others and was aggravated not just by internal schisms and ongoing ostracism and criticism from the Jewish community and establishment, but also and perhaps more decisively by growing and prohibitive debt, which doubled in 1987 and spiraled thereafter, notwithstanding fund-raising efforts.[113] In the early 1990s NJA notably called for a cease-fire in the First Gulf War against Iraq and hosted a conference on racism and antisemitism in Philadelphia, but its vigor was evidently sapped, as its activities dwindled in scale and scope.[114] By this time it had ceased to publish its newsletter. In 1992 ongoing financial crisis, coupled with mounting inertia and disarray, forced NJA to shut down its national office in New York and lay off its paid staff, effectively bringing the organization to an end.

Critics of the Community

New Jewish Agenda was an organization that saw itself and was seen by others as being to the left of the American Jewish community. The poor reception that members of the group found and felt among many of their ethnic peers and especially among the large, established Jewish organizations may suggest, as many claimed or predicted and as many within NJA bemoaned around the time of the group's founding, that the Third Generation had given up or was in the process of giving up on the left-wing or liberal political tradition of its forebears. Such forecasts were not by and large fulfilled.[115] Even as NJA remained to the left of most American Jews, most American Jews as a whole remained conspicuously to the left of other American groups of comparable socioeconomic status. Why, then, did NJA experience such rejection, and what did this friction between it and the Third Generation suggest about the nature and evolution of American Jewish politics after the 1960s?

New Jewish Agenda's isolation was above all the product of its position on Israel and the Middle East. Like Breira before it, NJA was ostracized due to its willingness to defy the "united front" of political support for Israel that American Jewry had maintained from the early 1950s.[116] As historian Rafael Medoff has observed, "individual NJA programs unrelated to Israel occasionally attracted the cosponsorship of local branches of major Jewish organizations, particularly the American Jewish Congress or affiliates of the Reform movement" as in the case of the sanctuary movement. New Jewish Agenda's credibility, however, was notably "damaged by its calls for Israeli acceptance of Arab territorial demands, including ceding control of parts of Jerusalem, and its willingness to cooperate with Arab-American groups that were unfriendly to Israel. Its controversial demonstrations aroused considerable ire in the community," as when it protested publicly against the Lebanon war and against Israeli treatment of Palestinian rioters during the *intifada*.[117] According to Hasia Diner, the "power of Israel to shape American consciousness led to the stifling of dissent within American Jewry" and so "compromised communal democracy and shattered even the semblance of unity."[118]

The "organized Jewish community usually wanted nothing to do with NJA," Ethan Bloch reminisced:

> If we were naive about the mainstream Jewish community, we were completely unprepared for the unbelievable intolerance for dissent found in that world. Our real crime, as it were, was ultimately neither image, nor naivete, *nor even leftist views*, but our explicit belief in the need to break the hegemony that the mainstream Jewish organizations had, and particularly to challenge the one-sided views they promoted in the 1980's about the Israeli/Palestinian conflict. . . . On non-Middle East issues our views were not always outside the pale, but our Middle East position often left us completely untouchable.[119]

In effect, NJA sought to apply to Israel and its community those values of social justice that many secular ethnic American Jews had insisted and continued to insist were thoroughly Jewish in derivation and inspiration in the domestic context and wider non-Jewish society. In NJA the ideology of the Jewish Left attained greater independence from its sociological matrix, exceeding the bounds of its social function as a vehicle of, justification for, and content of Jewish identity and ethnic assertion as a diasporic minority. New Jewish Agenda shifted the axis of criticism outside in, and both American Jewry and the Jewish state were necessarily found wanting. In so doing, NJA's members did not see themselves as acting in a manner contrary to the legacy of American Jewish politics, as their detractors claimed, but very much in line with it. If the First Generation had identified with the proletariat and the Second with African Americans, then NJA's protest on behalf of Palestinians, among others, as those who were downtrodden and dispossessed, was a fulfillment of American Jewry's political legacy. Few within the Third Generation cared to dwell on the irony, but it arose well before NJA came on the scene.

As Michael E. Staub has shown in his detailed study of the subject, "contests over Jewish liberalism—its legitimacy and its content—actually" went quite far back in the period after the Second World War.[120] Already by the late 1940s, some Jewish intellectuals began to question whether American Jewish identity had become too fused with a liberal political orientation and activism, and whether the former retained much substance beyond the latter. Eli Ginzburg, an economist at Columbia University, found it incongruous that so many American Jews in that decade were committed to "defense activities" against discrimination despite the historically relatively low levels of antisemitism in the United States and the ongoing decline if not collapse of residual anti-Jewish sentiments after the Depression and the war.[121] Such observations became more common in the 1960s in the context of the breakdown in black-Jewish relations. Rabbi Emil Fackenheim, a German refugee from the Nazis, denied that the discourses, narratives, and values of "prophetic Judaism," which touted left-wing causes of social justice, were scripturally authentic. He warned, moreover, that "the liberal Jew of today is in a dilemma," for he "might in the end have to choose between his Judaism and his liberalism."[122]

The Six-Day War of 1967, more than any domestic event, brought this dilemma to the fore. Throughout the 1960s, however, most members of the Third Generation ignored such theoretical quandaries, if they were aware of them at all. They flourished as established bourgeois patterns of life in the United States gave way to new social patterns. During the Cold War the apparatus of government and the bureaucratic state waxed under both Democratic and Republican administrations,[123] even as civil society and the traditional sociability and socialization that went on there waned.[124] Emphasis on a common Americanism and on Americanization gave way to a new multiplicity and appreciation for difference. Anglo-Protestant hegemony "stalled" and was in due time even suppressed as racism.[125] Whether such developments constituted a hypermodern hyperindividualism, in which common social norms were discarded as so many impediments to personal expression,[126] or a postmodern return to premodern social arrangements, in which closed communities related via external authority, remains unclear.[127] These developments did, however, remove many of those pressures for civil conformity and bourgeois assimilation that the First and Second Generations had found oppressive, unpleasant, and threatening. In this increasingly post-Christian environment, American Jewish (and all Western Jewish) life underwent a renaissance of communal esteem and individual success.[128]

The Third Generation very obviously gained on the already enviable socioeconomic status of its parents. In the 1950s Jews exceeded the non-Jewish median duration of education by 1.7 years, and 16 percent of them were college graduates versus 9 percent of gentiles. By the 1980s Jews had surpassed all other American groups, including well-placed Episcopalians, in their academic credentials. The Jewish-gentile gap in median duration was now 2.4 years, and every other Jew was a college graduate versus around 16 percent of gentiles. The discrepancy further widened into the 1990s. In terms of their income and earnings, Jews were already the wealthiest group in the United States by the 1950s, surpassing the affluent Episcopalians. By the end of that decade 78 percent of Jewish men were in white-collar occupations as opposed to 36 percent of all American men, and 83 percent of Jewish women as opposed to 55 percent of all American women.

By 1970, 54 percent of Jews were professionals and managers, versus 14 percent of non-Jews. In the 1960s their median household income was around 135–140 percent greater than that of non-Jews; by the 1970s it was over 150 percent higher; and by the 1980s it was over 170 percent higher. Even controlling for education and age, "Jews earn more" than their non-Jewish counterparts.[129] This discrepancy also widened into the 1990s.[130]

One consequence of this extraordinary achievement in a social context that elevated the status of minorities and even came to celebrate their cultural accomplishments and contributions was that any sense of beleaguerment, which had acted as a prop for Jewish cohesion, became ever more incongruous with social reality, thus relaxing the ethnic barriers between Jews and other (white) Americans. Throughout the 1980s many Jews continued to tell opinion polls that they worried about antisemitism, but to the extent that they gave it any thought such foreboding was habitual or self-serving and "bore no relation to any objective evidence."[131] Some within NJA were informed by the legacy of antisemitism, but few had direct experience with it or claimed to be driven primarily by it, if at all.[132]

Members of the Third Generation were often born in their parents' "gilded ghettos," but they were more likely to grow up in suburbs with at least some gentile neighbors, to attend public schools with a mixed (white) population, to enroll at universities outside New York City and even outside the Northeast, or to move into occupations that were unrelated to commerce or were traditionally non-Jewish.[133] More social proximity to (white) gentiles at various stages of life resulted in more social integration. The rate of intermarriage most obviously reflected this social rapprochement. The number of marriages of Jews to a non-Jewish partner rose from under one-tenth before 1965 to over one-third in the 1980s (and higher in the 1990s), with the least intermarriage in New York City and the preponderance of intermarriage at the time consisting of Jewish men and non-Jewish women.[134]

Given such trends, the American Jewish establishment began to express anxiety over the long-term viability of American Jewish life. These worries were not unfounded, but were often overstated. American Jews at the time remained a relatively cohesive population, especially in comparison with the weakening of ethnic ties and ethnic identity among Catholics and other white ethnic groups.[135] The vast majority of the Third Generation attached strong importance to Jewishness if not Judaism. During the 1980s surveys indicated that American Jews continued to see their coethnics as an extended family and to feel a special responsibility to them. Traditional and often unflattering images of gentiles persisted. Intermarriage remained somewhat stigmatized and discouraged, even as some non-Jewish spouses converted to Judaism or raised their children in the faith (although this phenomenon declined steadily from a peak in the 1950s or

1960s).[136] Even when Jews intermarried, moreover, considerable residential and occupational concentration usually endured and provided the Third Generation with a matrix for frequent fraternization. Most young Jews, especially women, still had mostly Jewish friends and many Jewish neighbors.[137] Other traits, such as lower rates of divorce and higher rates of self-employment, still distinguished Jews from non-Jews throughout the 1980s. As Calvin Goldscheider concluded in his study on the extent and nature of the Third Generation's integration:

> The Jewish community in America has changed; indeed has been transformed. But in the process, it has emerged as a dynamic source of networks and resources binding together family, friends, and neighbors, ethnically and religiously. As a community, Jews are surviving in America, even as some individuals enter and leave the community. Indeed, in every way the American Jewish community represents for Jews and other ethnic minorities a paradigm of continuity and change in modern pluralistic society.[138]

Above all, Jews differed from other Americans of similar socioeconomic status in their very marked liberal or left-wing political bias. Despite a general correlation between middle-class or upper-middle-class socioeconomic status and the Republican Party, Jews demonstrated little class distinction in their voting. As Milton Himmelfarb quipped famously in 1969, Jews earned like Episcopalians yet "voted like the Mexicans of the West and the Puerto Ricans of the East— the poor, the racial minorities."[139] Little had changed by the mid-1980s, despite many earnest Republican overtures to the Third Generation. Himmelfarb reiterated then that "Jews vote like Hispanics—*only more so.*"[140] Even when compared with *soi-disant* liberal Protestants, Jews remained more leftist in their strong self-identification as Democrats, in their strict views on the separation of church and state, in their acceptance of permissive social codes, and in their support for an interventionist state.[141] Even as Jews remained firmly within the Democratic camp, many Catholics, with whom Jews had "so much in common" in their historical experience as immigrants to the United States, broke away from the New Deal coalition as their social place and economic prospects improved during and after the Second World War.[142]

Some were dismayed by the persistence of Jewish liberalism in postwar America, in which Jews were both affluent and accepted as full, undifferentiated Jews.[143] For many within the Third Generation, however, liberalism had become synonymous with an understanding of Jewish identity, a connection to and affirmation of Jewishness despite or because of a lack of ritual observance and increasing social integration. That Jewish liberalism continued to serve some sort of function in relation to Jewish identity was suggested by its distribution, which remained basically unchanged from previous generations. Its greatest prevalence was among secular or Reform Jews, who tended to retain an ethnic identity yet were lax in their religious observance.[144] Left-wing sentiments and conduct did not typify the minority of traditionally orthodox Jews, whose numbers had been reinforced by the settlement of ultraorthodox or haredi refugees in the United States after the Holocaust.[145] What is more, even as German Jews ceased to exist as a distinct entity and voice within the Third Generation, having been absorbed into the larger Eastern European Jewish population or into the wider gentile world, those Jews who had converted to Christianity in the latter half of the twentieth century were almost half as likely to identify as liberals or Democrats and almost twice as likely to identify as conservatives and Republicans.[146]

Associates of NJA tended to link their left-wing activism to Jewish experience. Thus Michael Masch welcomed the formation of NJA as a group "whose primary purpose is discussion and action on public issues from a Jewish perspective":

> The Jewish community . . . needs a different organization, the kind of organization we may have it in our power to create, an organization that speaks to the issues from a position beyond Jewish defense, from the standpoint of justice and not merely the preservation of privilege, from the standpoint of Jewish values and not only Jewish self-interest, from the prophetic standpoint of Jewish idealism, and not just power politics.[147]

Ellen Willis of the *Village Voice* advised:

> I thought Agenda should base its politics not on abstract do-good impulses, but on an understanding of Jews' history as an oppressed people. My sense of Jewishness has less to do with any form of cultural separation than with the Diaspora Jew's historic role as critical outsider, living on the margins of dominant cultures, thus in a position to combine familiarity with skepticism.[148]

New Jewish Agenda's platform, adopted in November 1982, declared:

> Our history and tradition inspire us. Jewish experience and teachings can address the social, economic, and political issues of our time. Many of us find our inspiration in our people's historical resistance to oppression and from the Jewish presence at the forefront of movements for social change. Many of us base our convictions on the Jewish religious concept of *tikun olam* (the just ordering of human society of the world) and the prophetic tradition of social justice.[149]

David Coyne, an associate director in the mid-1980s,[150] justified his activism in NJA on behalf of gay rights by invoking the Jews' history "as a minority people within a relentlessly assimilating and homogenizing, predominantly Christian country":

> As Jews who celebrate the public expression of our Jewish identity, Agenda members can understand the principles of lesbian and gay pride that similarly produce an interest in public affirmation. The flight against the urge to "pass" can be a tough battle made the tougher by those both inside and outside the community who are offended by the public expression or our affirmation. "Why must she (or he) be so obviously Jewish (or gay)?" they ask. The joy we each feel in embracing our heritage, in expressing our love for who we are and what we are, is our best answer to their questions. "Because I am not ashamed! Because I am proud of who I am and of who my people are!"[151]

These sentiments were not unique to NJA. Surveys and studies indicated that throughout the 1980s the Third Generation, largely secular and ethnic in its composition, viewed support for social equality, welfare, pacifism, and pluralism or multiculturalism as not just in its self-interest as "outsiders, a religious and cultural minority in a heavily Christian country," but as fundamental to and a product of its heritage. Notably, despite the wariness and occasional animosity between blacks and Jews since the late 1960s, Jews continued to identify, far more so than other white Americans, with blacks and other minorities as mutual outsiders.[152] Such feelings were not by and large reciprocated.

In 1989 Julius Lester, a black professor and convert to Judaism, analyzed the phenomenon of Jewish liberalism and "outsider identification" with acute insight. "It is painful," he wrote in an article for *Reform Judaism*, cut out and filed by NJA, "to see how deeply Jews care about black-Jewish relations. It is not a caring shared by many blacks":

> Jews came to America seeking freedom from religious persecution. Blacks were brought to America to be enslaved. . . . From the very beginning, America represented diametrically opposed value systems to Jews and blacks. . . .
>
> When Jews maintain that they, too, are oppressed, blacks are incredulous. Jews are hurt and insulted that blacks are incredulous. Perhaps the two groups should understand that they may have very different notions of what it means to be oppressed. For blacks, oppression is physical and manifests itself, first, economically. . . . For Jews, oppression is social and psychological. It is the feeling of not quite belonging. . . . The black response to the social and psychological oppression of Jews is a shrug of the shoulders. . . .

Many Jews find this difficult to accept. Why? Because much of their identity as Jews is involved with seeing themselves as victims. There was a time in American history when it was easier for blacks to regard Jews as brothers and sisters among the oppressed of the earth. However, with the rise in Jewish affluence and the Six Day War, the image of Jew-as-victim ceased to match the reality.

The self-image many American Jews carry does not correspond to the objective reality. So important is the self image of Jew-as-victim that some Jews borrow such an identity through identifying with the Holocaust, with American blacks or with a variety of groups around the world fighting for what is described as "liberation."

Blacks do not need to borrow suffering from the past or from other groups. Anti-black racism stalks the land daily. Jews are fortunate enough that, in America, they do not have to live on terms of intimacy with anti-Semitism.[153]

Lester's invocation of the Six-Day War was apt. It was a seminal event in American Jewish life. Even as the war overturned the image of "Jew-as-victim" in the minds of many non-Jews, it paradoxically entrenched this image in the minds of members of the Third Generation, for whom Israel was an integral part of their "civil religion."[154] Both Israelis and American Jews themselves were stunned by the sheer "eruption of feeling" that the war and Israel's decisive victory engendered in the diaspora. "One could find the evidence everywhere," Melvin Urofsky recorded, "in the near obsession with Israeli news and personalities, in the spurt of Israel-related activities in Jewish communities, in the rise of *aliya* over the next few years, in the new and friendly attitudes of Israelis toward American visitors."[155] American Jews pledged $430 million in 1967 and closed ranks around their pervasive "fear that twice in their lifetime the Jewish people would be slaughtered."[156]

The Six-Day War reinvented the Israeli Jew as a hero and a bold fighter,[157] but in response the American Jewish establishment "decided to embark on an ambitious venture in Holocaust programming" in order to ensure ongoing support for Israel among Jews as well as non-Jews, ushering in a more pronounced "Holocaust consciousness." "Insofar as the Middle East imbroglio could be seen in a Holocaust framework," Peter Novick has written, "its complex and ambiguous rights and wrongs faded into the background," not least by connecting Arabs in general and Palestinians in particular with Nazism.[158] The promotion and rise of Holocaust consciousness among American Jews after the Six-Day War produced "an essential victim identity" that was extended to the Jewish state and was "reassuringly comfortable to all sorts of Jews who found it disturbing that Jews were no longer seen as victims or underdogs." By emphasizing Jewish suffering during the Holocaust and Israel's isolation in the Middle East, the secure, wealthy, and accepted Third Generation fulfilled the tenets of the old "lived religion" of exile, alienation, and marginality and kept itself within the "ranks of the oppressed" in a distinctly post-Christian "cultural climate that virtually celebrated victimhood" from the 1960s onward.[159]

Already in this decade, many young people of the Third Generation and even more so their parents were taken aback when elements within the New Left, especially African Americans, sided with Arab peoples and countries against Israel, characterizing the former as a colored and colonized people and the latter as an oppressive, white, imperial regime.[160] Notwithstanding its military triumphs, many American Jews perceived Israel as vulnerable. Many also viewed Israel as an extension of themselves and imagined that, as the Jewish state, it would embody their own brand of liberal politics, which was after all, in their own estimation, derived from Judaic values. As Steven Rosenthal has observed, "Israel's image as a secular, progressive, pragmatic, and democratic state accorded with American Jews' self-conceptions and provided a convenient way to present their identity to the larger society."[161]

The more radical Jews within the New Left—and later Breira, and then NJA—were received harshly by the American Jewish community and establishment, not because American Jews had become much more conservative or right wing in their domestic political orientation, as some believed or wished, but because these groups challenged the emotional substratum and social function of American Jewish liberalism, which crucially informed the identity of so many of their coethnics. These activist Jews argued that the Third Generation was more liberal in word than deed, that the Jewish community had become in actual fact, notwithstanding its Democratic partisanship, too comfortable and quite conformist.[162] Nowhere was this stance more controversial than in the case of Israel, and it was Israel—with the partial exception of disputes over racial integration and homosexuality, which remained somewhat controversial within the Jewish community throughout the 1980s—that constituted a crucial fault line that separated "left-wing" from putatively "right-wing" Jews in postwar America and that informed the emergence of neoconservatism among some Jewish intellectuals.[163] Otherwise, as Michael Staub has observed, "identifying where exactly the differences lay between left-wing and right-wing Jewish activist perspectives was not always so simple, not least because an ardent concern for Judaism [or Jewishness] sometimes led both sides to articulate similar concerns."[164]

The "left-wing" Jews called unwelcome attention to the fact that Israel, with its ethnonational, theocratic, and militaristic dimensions, did not quite live up to the multicultural, ultrasecular (or separationist), and pacifist standards that American Jews had for decades made their own and by which they had frequently and famously judged their own country. The "right-wing" Jews often responded that such radicals, in their criticism of their parents and *a fortiori* of Israel, had drifted away from the Jewish community and had ceased to concern themselves with Jewish survival.[165]

According to Arthur Liebman, when New Left Jews, like Mark Rudd, the important SDS figure, "commenced the solicitation of funds for the Palestinian resistance" after 1967, they demonstrated their own deracination. Through left-wing causes, Liebman argued, they were, like their Old Left antecedents, seeking "a way, at some unconscious level, of assimilating into and being accepted by American society" by joining an allegedly "universalistic movement."[166] Rudd's autobiography, however, describes his upbringing in an insular Jewish suburb and suggests, as formative for his worldview, the importance of his Jewish background as well as considerable hostility toward the diminishing elite of Anglo-Protestants as the "dumb goyim [non-Jews] who run this country."[167] Any sympathy for the Palestinians ostensibly emerged out of a general orientation toward those perceived as oppressed, which Rudd understood as the proper lesson of Jewish history, especially the Holocaust, as imparted by his community, rather than as a rebuff of this history.[168]

Critics of NJA likewise claimed that its leaders and members were assimilationist, "self-hating" and "anti-Zionist" for supporting a two-state solution to the conflict between Israel and the Palestinians as well as the right of Palestinians to designate the PLO as their representatives in their pursuit of self-determination.[169] In response to such denunciations, NJA reiterated over and over again not only its devotion to Israel but also the Jewish inspiration behind its activism. In a letter to the editor of the *Agenda* newsletter, NJA's Daniel Rosenblum lambasted the charge of "self-hatred" as a "fictitious diagnosis concocted by right-wing Jews," especially "in the pages of *Commentary*," "who wish to shame Jewish progressives into our publicly standing up for their views and struggling for recognition":

> In espousing progressive positions, we are doing nothing more than putting forward what we believe is best in the Jewish tradition, and we have every right and duty to be proud of that. We are expressing a deeper affirmation of our Jewishness than is expressed by Jews who, having lost all ethical links to their tradition, can cling only to a narrow particularism that sees as its only value an enforced unity which can merely ensure a temporary survival rendered hollow by its absence of ethical content.[170]

That the source of NJA's disapproval of various Israeli policies was a deep commitment to a certain understanding of Jewishness confused not simply most American Jews who paid any attention to the group, but also some Palestinians who worked with it. Thus, when Bria Chakofsky, NJA's cochair in the mid-1980s, introduced the PLO representative from Ottawa, Canada, Abdullah, to the national conference in Seattle in November 1985, she made the following statement:

> I am not here to express support for the PLO, or friendship for an organization that has much Jewish blood on its hands. . . . I am an American Jew, born in 1947—two

and a half years after the liberation of Dachau, five months before the founding of
the State of Israel. The history represented by these events has profoundly influenced my view of the world. As a Jew, I have a passion for justice; and it is hard for
me to believe that any non-Jews really care about the fate of Jews. . . . However, it is
precisely because I am a proud Jew committed to the survival and flourishing of the
State of Israel that I have chosen not only to participate in this conference . . . but
to introduce the next speaker. . . . I requested this place in the program because I
believe that the State of Israel, the Jewish people, and in fact all people, will be best
served by peace in the Middle East, and that the process of achieving peace can only
begin when enemies dare to talk.[171]

After the conference, Chakofsky felt compelled to write to Abdullah, who had
evidently reacted badly to the emphasis on Jewishness in her introduction of him:

I am writing to clarify some apparent misunderstanding concerning my introduction of you at the Middle East Peace Conference. . . . I felt a warm reaching out from
you to me as you left the podium after answering questions following your address
that Saturday and it is in that spirit that I am writing to you.

I have been told that you were shocked by my introduction and considered it a
trick! I can honestly tell you that it was in no way intended to trick or shame you or
anyone else. I spoke, as you yourself commented, from my heart. I am an intense,
Jewish, political woman and my introduction of you was, in part, an expression of
who I am. It had never occurred to me that the conference planners, or you, would
expect that a Jewish political leader could or would introduce a PLO spokesperson
without that political comment. . . .

It is my opinion that the introduction I made—both the act of introducing you
and the fact that I forthrightly addressed Jewish concerns in my introduction—
served both Jews and Palestinians well. Jews who speak out on behalf of the
Palestinian cause without also speaking out for Jews may make Palestinians feel
good, but I believe that they are not nearly the effective allies that Jews who also
speak strongly for Jews can be. I sincerely believe that, at the most basic level, there
is not an irresolvable conflict of interests between Jewish Israelis and Palestinians.[172]

Similar reasoning was used by figures within NJA to explain themselves to the
Jewish community and others during the Lebanon war. In *Commentary* magazine, the now neoconservative editor Norman Podhoretz bemoaned that "the war
in Lebanon triggered an explosion of invective against Israel that in its fury and its
reach was unprecedented in the public discourse of this country." American pun-
dits, primarily on the left, revealed their antisemitism, Podhoretz insisted, when
they focused on the imperfections of democratic Israel and ignored the more

regular abuses of its despotic Arab neighbors. Any such "criticisms of Israel that *are* informed by a double standard . . . deserve to be called anti-Semitic even when they are mouthed by Jews or, for that matter, Israelis."[173] Against such salvos, NJA shot back that as a Jewish state, Israel deserved, for its own good, to be held not to the admittedly woeful standards of the Arab world, but to the high moral standards that typified American Jewry's discourse and still (domestically) extant left-wing legacy. Its outcry over Lebanon did not derive from any self-abnegation, but from a deep sense of betrayal that Israel was no longer a "light unto the nations."[174] The Massachusetts chapter issued an official statement to this effect:

> As Jews, we look to Israel for many things. As a people, we have lived long years as a minority culture; in Israel Jews have created a place where our customs are understood without explanation, where we can celebrate our peoplehood and our religion without question. . . . The Jews, after surviving a brutal holocaust, regrouped to reclaim self-determination after it had been denied for many centuries. We see Israel as a haven. . . . As a people with a long concern for social justice, we look to Israel to uphold principles of freedom and self-determination.
>
> *Israel's brutal invasion of Lebanon betrays those hopes.* . . . We demand that Israel stop the senseless attacks. . . . We want security and self-determination for both Israel and the Palestinians, yet Israel's actions at this time will lead only to more hate, more violence, and less compassion from the other countries and peoples of the world.[175]

The Philadelphia chapter issued a somewhat more cautious statement:

> We are Jews committed to the survival of Israel as a Jewish state. Our Jewishness causes us to respond to the bloodshed in Lebanon. . . . We acknowledge that in the world that presently exists, Israel has had to behave as other nations. What can be possible though, is that as Israel wages war as the other nations do, we Jews can speak of the pain that the death and suffering cause us. . . . [We] acknowledge that Arab suffering is as real as Jewish suffering. We condemn all Palestinian acts of violence which may have provoked this current military escalation. In the same way we condemn the escalation.[176]

The Minneapolis chapter made it clear that its opposition to the invasion of Lebanon stemmed from an "unwavering" "support for a secure Israel," precisely because the war was not in the Jewish state's best interests:

> We defend Israel's unquestionable right to protect her citizens from armed attacks and terrorism, yet this invasion has been both morally indefensible and counter to

Israel's long-term interests. . . . The Judaic values on which Zionism is based—the
same values which have led so many Jews to fight for civil rights, take a leading role in
*labor struggles and care so well for our own people—*implore us to speak out now.[177]

By such statements, NJA denied the particular accusations of its detractors,
even as it belied the more general charge that criticism of certain Israeli policies
was usually if not necessarily antisemitic. New Jewish Agenda saw its position *vis-*
à-vis Israel as an extension of the political liberalism that "a majority of Jews still
shares" *vis-à-vis* the United States,[178] although it did not go as far as some Jewish
anti- or non-Zionists, who rejected the very notion of a Jewish state as antithetical
to the Second Generation's nondiscrimination principle and advocated instead a
binational Jewish/Arab state or multinational citizenship.[179] As indicated by the
Minneapolis chapter's statement above, the record of civil or human rights activism, in which the Second Generation and parts of the Third had played and in
some instances continued to play such a prominent role, was an important model
for NJA's leaders and members. Arthur Waskow, an older political radical and
later a Reconstructionist rabbi, who early joined NJA, represented this continuity
of causes in his own person.

Born in 1933, Waskow was a contributing editor of the New Left journal
Ramparts, in which he published "The Freedom Seder" in 1969, whose idea
"emerged from the moment of agony at Passover 1968 when Martin Luther King
had just been killed." This Passover Haggadah "brought together the age-old story
of the Exodus with tales of efforts of modern Jews and blacks and other people
toward their liberation."[180] New Jewish Agenda republished a "reincarnation" of
this document as "The Rainbow Seder" in 1984 in an anthology of such "progressive" Haggadot, *The Shalom Seders*. A concluding passage in "The Rainbow Seder"
reminded readers, "brothers and sisters," that "just as it was we, not our forebears
only, who were liberated in Egypt, so it is we, not our forebears only, who live in
slavery. Our slavery is not over, and our liberation is not complete. The task of
liberation is long, and it is work that we ourselves must do." During the service, all
were instructed to sing:

> No more killing
> No more hunger
> No more pollution
> No more racism
> No more sexism[181]

Waskow's retelling of the traditional exodus story in light of the black struggle inspired NJA to produce several of its own renditions. Within *The Shalom*

Seders there were two other "progressive" Haggadot: "A Haggadah of Liberation," a feminist text, which told "the stories of women's liberation—beginning with the freedom-minded midwives who were the first to resist the Pharaoh's murderous edicts"; and the "Seder of the Children of Abraham," a pacifist text, which "celebrated both sides of the family split that divided" Jews and Arabs, Israelis and Palestinians. In this latter text, "Pharaoh was transformed into the endless, oppressive war between the two peoples—liberation into the need for hope for both peoples to make a decent peace with one another."[182] In this liturgy Jewish suffering through the ages was compared to Palestinian suffering in the twentieth century. Both were slaves to their own fears, from which they required liberation:

> Today we are slaves of our fear. Jews are slaves to the fear bred of 2,000 years of Jew hatred culminating in the Holocaust; Palestinians are slaves to the fear bred of being homeless refugees and of living under an occupying power. Fear, insecurity, is the villain—our affliction. . . .
>
> Israel is both a metaphor and a reality. It is a metaphor for peace: next year may we all be at peace. Israel is the reality of a land which Jews and Palestinians both want. Next year may we share the land in peace.
>
> This year we are slaves, next year free men and women. As long as we are imprisoned in our own fears, not recognizing the rights of others, we are slaves. As long as Israel is an occupier operating from her fears, she cannot be healthy and is a slave. As long as Palestinians are not willing to recognize the rights of a Jewish homeland in Israel, they too are imprisoned in the slavery of fear. Next year may we recognize the needs of the other and be free.[183]

This Haggadah quoted from the Koran as well as from the written work or memoirs of Jewish survivors of the Russian pogroms and of the Holocaust, of Palestinian refugees, of Arab nationalists, and of prominent Zionists; these cited passages evoked common suffering and common hopes. The "Arab and Israeli look at each other," the narration lamented, "but they do not really see":

> Their vision is blocked by centuries of fear and violence. The Israeli sees not an Arab with a deep need to understand how this all came about, but rather a Cossack plunderer or a Nazi murderer. The Arab sees not a Jew whose need for physical security runs as deep as his soul, but rather a typical European colonialist, smug and self-righteous, whose only aim is to exploit at any cost. . . . Both the Israeli and the Arab are victims, victims of a past full of degradation and horror. That past is so awesome as to be ever-present, in every thought, ever emotion, every act. . . . The commonality of that oppression must be used as a key to opening up dialogue between these two peoples. Their common humiliation, common exploitation, common suffering must be realized.[184]

These Haggadot were quintessential expressions of the "outsider identification" that had characterized so much of American Jewish political discourse in the twentieth century and grew out of a "lived religion" that emphasized exile, alienation, and otherness. By expanding the ranks of victims to include Palestinians, NJA was not repudiating but mediating an important aspect of the American Jewish liberal or left-wing tradition—to the chagrin of most of its peers. An investigative report on the group by the American Jewish Committee noted that NJA's claims that "Palestinians yearn for sanctuary in their own sovereign state as they, like Jews, have been subjected to exile, dispossession, oppression and statelessness" alienated the group from American Jews and fueled "the animosity among more 'mainstream' Jewish organizations." As a result, NJA was "seen by many to be excessively pro-Arab, explicitly anti-Israel and overly critical in its substantive platform regarding Israel." It was simply not clear whether the group represented "dissent within, or disloyalty to, the Jewish community."[185]

Notwithstanding "mainstream" doubts as to NJA's suitability within American Jewish institutions and life, the group did embody the old nexus between the political Left and nonassimilation that had characterized previous generations. It was "important as a source of identity for many younger and some older but alienated Jews." The organization was, one of its founders has noted, "not an expression of assimilation" and certainly not of any self-hatred or anti-Zionism *per se*, as many of its opponents claimed, "but rather an expressive [*sic*] of intense affiliation with the concerns of the Jewish people and religion." In this (empirically accurate) opinion, it was assimilation, rather than the lack thereof, that correlated with any decline in American Jews' commitment to those "progressive causes" that their ancestors had conspicuously taken up. As such, even as NJA had no official policy on intermarriage, "the leaders who were married or eventually married had a higher percentage of in-married than the Jewish population as a whole," which was probably true of the membership too, for "it took a strong sense of Jewish identity for someone to affirmatively choose to affiliate with a clearly Jewish progressive group."[186]

Over time, more American Jews, especially the children of the baby boomers, became more open to the positions on Israel that NJA had pioneered. To the consternation of many older Jews, some of their children, invoking bequeathed political values, demonstrated more sympathy for the Palestinians and more skepticism toward various governments of Israel and their policies. After the Oslo Accords of 1993—which despite their ultimate failure saw Israel and the Palestinians for the first time recognize each other in face-to-face negotiations—acknowledging a two-state solution to the conflict in the Middle East and recognizing the PLO were no longer taboo among American Jewry. During the 1990s, moreover, the orthodox rabbinate in Israel continued to estrange and outrage many American Jews by its ongoing disparagement of their Jewish credentials. Notably, this rabbinate refused to recognize nonorthodox conversions to Judaism as the basis for applications for immigration or *aliyah* to Israel.[187]

Notwithstanding such developments, the quantity of American Jewish support for Israel did not decline during and after the 1980s. According to research by Steven M. Cohen, the "prevailing assumption that American Jews must have grown at least somewhat more distant from Israel during the turbulent 1980s" was not borne out by polling and surveys in the 1990s, which indicated stability in rank-and-file attitudes and a bit more critical detachment among elites.[188] There was rather some change in the quality of such support, especially among the children of the Third Generation. As Jonathan Sarna has noted, younger American Jews have not grown up with the projection and myth of a "utopian Jewish state" as shared by his generation of baby boomers. They have been exposed to the Middle East's "sordid realities" and Israel's "unloveliest warts" by the contemporary media.[189] Nonetheless, American Jews' attachment to Israel did not waver into the 1990s, even if the two-state solution and other platforms advocated by NJA did become more widely considered and accepted. As Peter Beinart has observed, many young American Jews had "imbibed" the liberalism of "American Jewish political culture" and "in their innocence, they did not realize that they were supposed to shed those values when it came to Israel." As such, many young American Jews were attracted to a "kind of Zionism that the American Jewish establishment had been working against for most of their lives."[190]

A decisive contest between American Jewry's support for Israel and its commitment to its brand of liberalism did not (and has not) come up. Unlike Jews in Europe and to some extent Canada, average American Jews by and large did not (and have not) had to contend with significant pro-Palestinian or anti-Zionist sentiments within the country's major left-wing or liberal party: non-Jewish Americans have remained consistently in favor of Israel over its Arab neighbors,[191] and perhaps more important, Jewish Americans have remained an important source of votes and above all private fund-raising for the Democrats.[192] As a result, American Jews were not, unlike some counterparts elsewhere in the Western diaspora, "pushed" to the right by the issue of Israel within the domestic political arena.[193] Contemporary successors to NJA, notably J Street, a lobbying group founded in 2008 as a "pro-peace" yet "pro-Israel" organization, have acquired an ambiguous status and experienced an ambivalent reception among many American Jews and their establishment.[194]

Full Circle

In NJA, the Jewish Left came full circle. During the 1980s NJA shocked its contemporaries when it held up the standards of the American Jewish liberal tradition to Jews themselves in the United States and above all in Israel. In so doing, NJA indicated that Israel fell short of those same standards and that much of the Third Generation felt uncomfortable with them as a mandate for internal application rather than external imposition. The harsh reception that NJA experienced among much of the American Jewish community and establishment revealed more about the political commitments of those latter constituents than about NJA itself. It suggested the ongoing utility of American Jews' marked liberal bias, which did not, despite many predictions and assertions to the contrary, change fundamentally throughout the 1980s or beyond, notwithstanding the increasingly multicultural society in which undifferentiated Jews were accorded full social respect, inclusion, and opportunity, and in which they knew unparalleled communal and individual advancement.

For Jewish baby boomers, liberalism and a sense of marginality remained fundamental to their self-image, despite or rather because of greater social integration and unprecedented affluence. For many the two were fused. As the neoconservative intellectual Norman Podhoretz bemoaned, "the 'Torah' of liberalism" has been, into the twenty-first century, the true religion of most American Jews, for whom the Republican Party has represented "apostasy."[195] New Jewish Agenda challenged the purpose of this posture by elevating the ideology to the same level or even above its social function, promoting for American Jews and *a fortiori* for Israel many of the same policies—including pluralism and pacifism—that American Jews had for decades demanded within and for the United States. As NJA discovered, such policies had not obviously been conceived in the American Jewish imagination in relation to their own community or the State of Israel.

Conclusion

THE MARKED LEFT-WING BIAS OF American Jews typified most of the twentieth century. It has also persisted into the twenty-first. Throughout the 1990s Jewish support for Democratic presidents went up from the level of the 1980s rather than down. Just days before the 2008 presidential elections, in which the Democrat Barack Obama faced off against the Republican John McCain, a survey of American Jewry's intentions at the ballot box confirmed the persistence of the "curvilinear pattern" of their political expression. Those many Jews who identified with (in the contemporary American context) the essentially ethnic and ritually lax denomination of Reform were most likely to want to vote for Obama—nearly four-fifths. Support dropped off among those Jews who had no affiliation or strong ethnic bonds and fell steeply to about one-quarter among the less numerous orthodox. Further, those Jews most concerned about Israel were more likely to prefer McCain, although this correlation was actually more pronounced among non-Jews.[1]

In the event, around 78 percent of American Jews voted for Obama, compared to 43 percent of whites in general and 67 percent of Hispanics, and compared to 45 percent of Protestants and 54 percent of Catholics. Only blacks, at 95 percent, proved more enthusiastic as a bloc. A similar, though somewhat less polarized result occurred in 2012, when Obama faced off against Mitt Romney. Reporting such electoral results in *Why Are Jews Liberals?*, Norman Podhoretz despairs that Jews had "fended off with wilful blindness and denial" Obama's past associations with putative antisemites and anti-Zionists and the greater number of such persons within the Democratic Party itself and on the left in general. They had also allegedly voted against their economic interests.[2] In the end, they sided with forces that wished "to transform . . . the very system in and through which Jews found a home such as they had never discovered in all their forced wanderings throughout the centuries over the face of the earth."[3]

Given this seemingly irrational behavior, Podhoretz concludes in exasperation that "liberalism" is not just a "substitute for religion"; "it is a religion in its own right, complete with its own catechism and its own dogmas and . . . obdurately resistant to facts that undermine its claims and premises." The ideological matrix of contemporary American liberalism "has not only superseded socialism as the religion of most American Jews, it has even superseded Judaism itself among many Jewish liberals who presume to speak in its name." In any conflict between "the Torah of contemporary liberalism" and "the Torah of Judaism," the latter "prevails" and the former "must give way." Overlooking the possible function of this new "faith," Podhoretz does not provide, for himself or others, a satisfactory answer to the eponymous question of his book, but simply hopes that "the Jews of America will eventually break free of their political delusions," even as he admits that "there is no sign that this will change in the foreseeable future."[4]

As this book has sought to demonstrate through its exploration of three generations of American Jews in the twentieth century, varieties of left-wing ideologies and movements have especial appeal to this population in that they have helped to mediate Jewishness in various ways. On the one hand, with their stated concern for the oppressed and downtrodden, they have afforded Jews in the safe and prosperous context of the United States an opportunity to meet their self-image as a marginalized people. They have facilitated an identification with other outsiders—whether the poor and proletariat, African Americans, or even, ironically, Palestinians—thus allowing Jews to live up to what historian Michael Alexander has termed their "lived religion," informed by secularized theological concepts of exile and alienation and sacralized historical memories of persecution. On the other hand, left-wing ideologies and movements have legitimized the very Jewishness that they have mediated.

In the era before the 1960s, when ethnicity was meant to give way to religious affiliation as the primary basis for Jewish identification in a civil society whose dominant bourgeois ethos emphasized integration at the level of the individual and a common cultural Americanism, antibourgeois postures allowed Jews to dispute and eventually help to overturn these social expectations. In the First Generation, foreign-born Jewish immigrants from Eastern Europe turned to radicalism to evade and criticize a modern civil society by which they felt humiliated or discombobulated. Notably, Alexander Bittelman from Ukraine helped to establish the Communist Party of the United States, looking forward to a revolutionary future or overseas to the Soviet Union at a regime in which cultural differences, including *yidishkeyt*, made no difference in society and were upheld and protected by the state. In the Second Generation, native-born Jews supported, defended, and helped to implement the New Deal, which empowered the state *vis-à-vis* civil society. On this foundation of enlarged administrative authority, the American Jewish Congress, among other groups, waged sundry campaigns against what they perceived to be discrimination and prejudice before and especially after the Second World War. They sought to use the courts and congresses to undo the felt oppressive link between bourgeois assimilation and bourgeois admission or opportunity so as to preserve and give expression to a whole, undifferentiated Jewishness.

By the time of the baby boomers of the Third Generation, a greater social recognition of ethnicity had emerged, but American Jews continued to support those forces that had advocated and still advanced pluralism and postbourgeois social innovations, despite their economic success and social acceptance. In seeking to fulfill their self-image as outsiders, moreover, they vied with other erstwhile or present-day marginalized groups for a position in the pantheon of victims that characterized postwar discourse and imagination, even as they became passionate about the Jewish state. In its harsh reaction to entities like New Jewish Agenda, which criticized some of the practices of American Jewry and above all Israel, the Third Generation revealed the ongoing functional importance of its liberal politics as an affirmation of its secular ethnic self-conception. The American Jewish establishment ostracized and at times condemned NJA, even as it was confounded by the group's claims that its criticisms of Jews in the diaspora and in Israel were the product of the very left-wing Jewish values that they otherwise tended to share, in principle if not always in practice, rather than their renunciation.

These putative Jewish values continue to inform American Jewish life and consciousness. In a corrective to Podhoretz's account of American Jewish liberalism, which "is meant to explain why Jews do not vote their self-interest," Rabbi David Wolpe argues that "it is because they vote their self-conception" that they are Democrats. "Jews identity with those who see themselves as on the margins: African Americans, immigrants, various minority groups."[5] Another reviewer of Podhoretz's book, Michael Medved, posits that "for American Jews the core of their Jewish identity isn't solidarity with Israel; it's rejection of Christianity":

> This political pattern reflects the fact that opposition to Christianity—not love for Judaism, Jews, or Israel—remains the sole unifying element in an increasingly fractious and secularized community. The old (and never fully realized) dream that Zionist fervor could weave together all the various ideological and cultural strands of American Jewry looks increasingly irrelevant and simplistic. . . . For many Americans, the last remaining scrap of Jewish distinctiveness involves our denial of New Testament claims.[6]

Such views come closer to the contentions within this text. Of course in the twenty-first century some, like Medved, have wondered what remains of Jewish distinctiveness in a country in which the lines between outsiders and insiders have become blurred and in which Jews ostensibly constitute an elite group. In *New York Magazine*, David Samuels has written of "how success has ruined the New York Jew." Has the very fulfillment of Jewish yearning in the twentieth century to render America into a pluralistic democracy undermined Jewish cohesion and identity in the twenty-first, rather than the reverse? Samuels observes:

> Today, it is hard to think of a single institution in the city that doesn't open its doors wide to Jews. . . . The ascendancy of the Jews of New York can be viewed as a

Hollywood-style triumph, but it can also be read as the tragedy of a group of brilliant outsiders who remade a city in their own image, only to cut themselves off from the roots of their tribal genius. . . . As the barriers of Jewish acceptance fell away, so did our connection to shared communal values and the traditions of intellectual work that formed the common cultural inheritance of our grandparents. New York Jews circa 2008 are wealthy white people whose protestations of outsiderness inspire blank stares or impatient eye rolling.

Samuels longs for a return to genuine outsider status and self-imposed (if need be) marginality. "Jews of New York City," he proclaims, "we don't have to go out like that"—like the old Anglo-Protestant elite who no longer inspire admiration or achieve great things:

Perhaps we can relinquish our fantasies of universalistic omnipotence and return to the prickly insularity that made us great. We can reopen delis and bakeries, and celebrate the wisdom of our sages who knew that worldly success is fleeting, and that the secret to happiness is fear of God, a bowl of hot chicken soup, and a rent-controlled apartment in Brooklyn.[7]

Samuels is not alone in bemoaning the perceived loss of Jewish distinctiveness in the United States, but he and others may overstate the case.[8] In their political profile at least, American Jews do remain rather discrete, albeit less so if controlled for their urban concentration. To the extent that left-wing politics have mediated Jewishness, moreover, as this text has striven to show, there is reason to believe that American Jews remain *relatively* ethnically robust and self-conscious. Recent studies do bear out this inference. In a detailed statistical monograph from 2005 for the American Jewish Committee, *Jewish Distinctiveness in America*, Tom Smith observes that, demographically and attitudinally, "Jews are the most distinctive of all ethnic/racial and religious groups" in the country—and no more so than in their political postures:

Demographically, Jews are especially distinguished by their older age, lower fertility, high socioeconomic achievement in terms of education, occupational prestige, income, and class identification, and concentration in large metropolitan centers in the Northeast. This distinctive Jewish profile has been around for some time, prevailing both for the parental generation and across recent decades.

Attitudinally, Jews differ most from non-Jews in general and other specific ethnic/racial and religious groups in particular on the topics of abortion rights, religion, sexual morality, partisanship/voting, suicide/euthanasia. . . . Also, differences were larger than average for the miscellaneous group, civil liberties, and child values. . . . Next, with lower than average differences were gender equality, inter-group relations, crime and firearms, psychological well-being/health, government spending and taxes, misanthropy, confidence in institutions, socializing, finances/jobs, and, lastly, social welfare policy.[9]

In the latter category—"lower than average differences"—the tendency was for non-Jews "to move in the same [liberal] direction toward the position held by Jews" rather than the reverse.[10] Given "the small and declining share of Jews in an over-whelmingly (98 percent) non-Jewish society," Smith avers, "what is striking is how distinctive Jews remain from non-Jews."[11] In his foreword to this same study, the American Jewish Committee's executive director, David A. Harris, emphasizes the importance of Smith's conclusions. "Why should we care about all of this?" he asks.

> We care because the numbers reveal an underlying strength of the American Jewish community: Despite our declining share of the overall American population, a high intermarriage rate, and a growing geographical dispersion, Jews have been able to retain a distinctive profile which bespeaks a unique core Jewish identity.[12]

In a survey of American Jews from 2006, Steven M. Cohen observes a sim-ilar pattern of communal strength coexisting with signs of weakness. On the one hand, Cohen finds, intermarriage between Jews and non-Jews has remained at high levels, at times exceeding one-half, since the 1980s. Intermarriage has become the most significant indicator of ethnic dissolution. American Jews may not marry gentiles out of any conscious desire to further assimilate or to renounce their Jewish identity, but such attenuation is the usual end result of exogamy. Jews who are married to gentiles are less likely (although not entirely unlikely) to raise their children exclusively in Judaism, to send their children to Jewish day schools, to volunteer in Jewish contexts, to keep kosher at home, to visit Israel, to have mostly Jewish close friends, to attend synagogue, to fast on Yom Kippur, to light Chanukah candles, to attend Passover seders, or to have their own children grow up to marry Jews. On the other hand, in-married Jews are much more likely to do or have all these things, and have, in comparison to their parents and intermarried peers, "become, as a group, relatively more engaged in Jewish life—more learned, more observant, and more communally active."[13]

American Jews have bifurcated between the intermarried and the in-married. It is this latter constituency that is bound to carry on American Jewish life, suggest-ing its enduring ethnic foundation. To the extent that in-married Jews are becom-ing more religious—whether autonomously or because orthodox Jews are having many more children—they may, Jonathan Sarna has noted, "pull" the center of Jewish gravity away from the Left sooner than many imagine.[14] What is more, to the extent that some left-wing groups in North America and Europe continue to question or even reject Israel's nationalist ethos, as Western countries themselves become increasingly multicultural and nonwhite, more American Jews may feel "pushed" to the Right. It is possible to discern the emergence of more right-wing Jewish voices in the diaspora. But as a majority of American Jews remains largely secular or Reform, yet still self-consciously ethnic, including many intermarried individuals, and as Democrats in the United States refrain from undue criticism of Israel, "the Torah of liberalism" may continue to predominate by fulfilling the same function as "the Torah of Judaism": to mediate Jewishness—not perfectly, but ostensibly well enough that "Jews are the most distinctive of all ethnic/racial and religious groups" in the United States in the early twenty-first century.

Notes

Introduction

1. E. Mendelsohn, introduction to *Essential Papers on Jews and the Left*, ed. J. Reinharz and A. Shapira (New York and London: New York University Press, 1997), 2.

2. A. Gelman, *Red State, Blue State, Rich State, Poor State: Why Americans Vote the Way They Do* (Princeton, NJ: Princeton University Press, 2008), 46–57.

3. L. Benson, "Ethnocultural Groups and Political Parties," in *Voters, Parties, and Elections: Quantitative Essays in the History of American Popular Voting Behavior*, ed. J. H. Silbey and S. T. McSeveney (Lexington, MA: Xerox College Publishing, 1972), 89–90.

4. K. D. Wald, "Toward a Structural Explanation of Jewish-Catholic Differences in the United States," in *Jews, Catholics, and the Burden of History*, ed. E. Lederhendler, *Studies in Contemporary Jewry* no. 21 (Oxford: Oxford University Press, 2005), 123. Despite having a communal prominence since the 1950s, neoconservatives have not been entirely politically representative of American Jews. Neoconservatism and its most prominent literary vehicle, *Commentary* magazine, have been covered in detail in other studies, including N. Abrams, *Commentary Magazine 1945–59* (London and Portland, OR: Vallentine Mitchell, 2007) and *Norman Podhoretz and Commentary Magazine: The Rise and Fall of the Neocons* (New York: Continuum, 2010); and B. Balint, *Running Commentary: The Contentious Magazine That Transformed the Jewish Left into the Neoconservative Right* (New York: Public Affairs, 2010).

5. Wald, "Toward a Structural Explanation of Jewish-Catholic Differences in the United States," 125.

6. Despite Podhoretz's subjective desire to see American Jews move beyond their liberal or left-wing political tradition, for which his narrative is in part a polemical inducement, his account of the origins of that tradition are not in themselves atypical even as it has received considerable recent attention. For detailed and annotated discussions of the strengths and weaknesses of the "conventional theories," most of which are reiterated by Podhoretz, see G. B. Levey, "The Liberalism of American Jews—Has It Been Explained?," *British Journal of Political Science* 26, no. 3 (July 1996): 369–401; and C. S. Liebman and S. M. Cohen, *Two Worlds of Judaism: The Israeli and American Experiences* (New Haven, CT: Yale University Press, 1990), 96–122.

7. N. Podhoretz, *Why Are Jews Liberals?* (New York: Doubleday, 2009), 30, 90, 97, 98, 100.

8. For the term, see D. Biale, M. Galchinsky, and S. Heschel, eds., *Insider/Outsider: American Jews and Multiculturalism* (Berkeley: University of California Press, 1998), 17–33.

9. J. Lukacs, *A Thread of Years* (New Haven, CT, and London: Yale University Press, 1998), 105.

10. R. D. King and M. F. Weiner, "Group Position, Collective Threat, and American Anti-Semitism," *Social Problems* 54, no. 1 (2007): 47–77.

11. I. Howe, *World of Our Fathers: The Journey of East European Jews to America and the Life They Found and Made* (New York: Simon and Schuster, 1976), 383.

12. T. Sowell, *Ethnic America: A History* (New York: Basic Books, 1981), 88.

13. L. Dinnerstein, *Anti-Semitism in America* (New York and Oxford: Oxford University Press, 1994), 245.

14. Podhoretz, *Why Are Jews Liberals?*, 123.

15. S. M. Cohen, *The 1984 National Survey of American Jews: Political and Social Outlooks* (New York: American Jewish Committee, Institute of Human Relations, 1984), 29. Cf. S. M. Cohen, *The Dimensions of American Jewish Liberalism* (New York: American Jewish Committee, Institute of Human Relations, 1989), 41.

16. H. L. Feingold, "American Jewish Liberalism and Jewish Response," *Contemporary Jewry* 9, no. 1 (September 1987): 38–39.

17. Levey, "The Liberalism of American Jews," 391. See also G. B. Levey, "Toward a Theory of Disproportionate American Jewish Liberalism," in *Values, Interests and Identity: Jews and Politics in a Changing World*, ed. P. Y. Medding, *Studies in Contemporary Jewry* no. 11 (Oxford: Oxford University Press, 1995), 76.

18. *Functional* is used throughout this text in the sense of "socially useful" and does not refer to the schools of functionalism within anthropology, psychology, philosophy or international relations.

19. M. Alexander, *Jazz Age Jews* (Princeton, NJ: Princeton University Press, 2001), 1.

20. Ibid., 8, 3, 5, 181.

21. Ibid., 1, 8, 59, 74–75, 136–37.

22. J. D. Sarna, ed., *The American Jewish Experience* (New York: Holmes and Meier, 1986), xvi.

23. R. Scruton, *A Short History of Modern Philosophy: From Descartes to Wittgenstein* (London and New York: Routledge, 2002), 239; emphasis in original.

Chapter 1

1. On Bittelman's status within the Communist Party, see W. Z. Foster, statement to national committee, April 15, 1951, in TAM/62.1/3/14.

2. A. Bittelman, "*Things I Have Learned: An Autobiography*," manuscript, 1962–1963, in TAM/62/3-4 (hereafter cited as TIHL).

3. See, for example, B. D. Palmer, *James P. Cannon and the Origins of the American Revolutionary Left, 1890-1928* (Urbana and Chicago: University of Illinois Press, 2007), 93–94, 418n7.

4. For a recent example of this kind of discourse, see Y. Slezkine, *The Jewish Century* (Princeton, NJ: Princeton University Press, 2004). Further examples are provided throughout the chapter.

5. Cf. J. D. Sarna, "The Myth of No Return: Jewish Return Migration to Eastern Europe, 1881–1914," *American Jewish History* 71, no. 2 (December 1981): 256–68.

6. TIHL, 8, 3, 17, 16, 11, 12.

7. T. R. Weeks, "Polish-Jewish Relations 1903–1914: The View from the Chancellery," *Canadian Slavonic Papers* 40, nos. 3/4 (September–December 1998): 233.

8. TIHL, 17, 30.

9. B. Harshav, *Language in Time of Revolution* (Berkeley: University of California Press, 1993), 4.

10. J. M. Cuddihy, *The Ordeal of Civility: Freud, Marx, Lévi-Strauss and the Jewish Struggle with Modernity* (New York: Basic Books, 1974), 147.

11. TIHL, 16, 15; emphasis added.

12. V. Karady, *The Jews of Europe in the Modern Era: A Socio-Historical Outline* (Budapest and New York: Central European University Press, 2004), 275.

13. TIHL, 31, 43, 41.

14. H. J. Tobias, *The Jewish Bund in Russia: From Its Origins to 1905* (Stanford, CA: Stanford University Press, 1972), xv, 60–69.

15. TIHL, 46, 47, 48.

16. M. Alexander, "Exile and Alienation in America," *American Jewish History* 90, no. 2 (June 2002): 165.

17. C. Weizmann, *The Letters and Papers of Chaim Weizmann*, ed. M. W. Weisgal (London: Oxford University Press, 1971), 2:A:306–7.

18. TIHL, 108, 111, 112.

19. TIHL, 109; emphasis in original.

20. TIHL, 131, 174, 134, 209.

21. J. Daly, "Crime in Late Imperial Russia," *Journal of Modern History* 74, no. 1 (March 2002): 91.

22. TIHL, 196, 197.

23. J. Barzun, *From Dawn to Decadence: 500 Years of Western Cultural Life, 1500 to the Present* (New York: Perennial, 2001), 588.

24. TIHL, 142–43.

25. Daly, "Crime in Late Imperial Russia," 100.

26. TIHL, 209, 210.

27. TIHL, 219, 225, 223, 235.

28. A. Ruppin, *The Jews in the Modern World* (London: Macmillan, 1934), 49.

29. TIHL, 238.

30. S. Kuznets, "Immigration of Russian Jews to the United States: Background and Structure," in *Perspectives in American History*, ed. D. Fleming and B. Bailyn (Cambridge, MA: Harvard University Press, 1975), 39, 112–13.

31. TIHL, 238.

32. Cf. Howe, *World of Our Fathers*, 42–46; I. Kopeloff, "First Days in America," trans. L. Wolf, in *Voices from the Yiddish: Essays, Memoirs, Diaries*, ed. I. Howe and E. Greenberg (Ann Arbor: University of Michigan Press, 1972), 193–201; and P. Adam, *Vues d'Amérique*, 10th ed. (Paris: Librairie Paul Ollendorff, 1906), 33–47.

33. TIHL, 270, 244, 245.

34. M. Epstein, *The Jew and Communism: The Story of Early Communist Victories and Ultimate Defeats in the Jewish Community, USA, 1919-1941* (New York: Trade Union Sponsoring Committee, 1959), 398.

35. A. Kahan, "Economic Opportunities and Some Pilgrims' Progress: Jewish Immigrants from Eastern Europe in the US, 1890-1914," *Journal of Economic History* 38, no. 1 (March 1978): 251.

36. Ibid., 235n1. According to the German Jewish leader Louis Marshall, who participated in proceedings on the matter, restrictions were not inspired by antisemitism. This charge was spread by Jewish Democrats for political advantage: "The bill related no more to Jews than it did to any other class of immigrants. Its adoption was largely due to the agitation of labor organizations." See L. Marshall, letter to F. Fuld, October 31, 1924, in *Louis Marshall: Champion of Liberty; Selected Papers and Addresses*, ed. C. Reznikoff (Philadelphia: Jewish Publication Society of America, 1957), 2:812–13.

37. L. Grebler, *Housing Market Behavior in a Declining Area* (New York: Columbia University Press, 1952), 254.

38. Harshav, *Language in Time of Revolution*, 47.

39. S. Gompers, *Seventy Years of Life and Labour: An Autobiography* (London: Hurst and Blackett, 1923), 153.

40. I. Rubinow, "Economic and Industrial Conditions: New York," in *The Russian Jew in the United States: Studies of Social Conditions in New York, Philadelphia, and Chicago, with a Description of Rural Settlements*, ed. C. S. Bernheimer (Philadelphia: John C. Winston, 1905), 118.

41. S. W. Model, "Italian and Jewish Intergenerational Mobility: New York, 1910," *Social Science History* 12, no. 1 (Spring 1988): 45–46. See also A. Godley, *Jewish Immigrant Entrepreneurship in New York and London, 1880-1914* (New York: Palgrave, 2001), 56–57.

42. N. Glazer, "Social Characteristics of American Jews, 1654–1954," in *American Jewish Year Book*, ed. M. Fine and J. Sloan (Philadelphia: Jewish Publication Society of America, 1955), 56:14.

43. D. Dwork, "Health Considerations of Immigrant Jews on the Lower East Side of New York: 1880-1914," *Medical History* 25, no. 1 (January 1981): 33; and National Liberal Immigration League, *The Immigrant Jew in America*, ed. E. J. James (New York: B. F. Buck, 1907), 111.

44. T. Kessner, *The Golden Door: Italian and Jewish Immigrant Mobility in New York City, 1880-1915* (New York: Oxford University Press, 1977), 169.

45. Dinnerstein, *Anti-Semitism in America*, 245.

46. H. Kosak, *Cultures of Opposition: Jewish Immigrant Workers, New York City, 1881-1905* (Albany: State University of New York Press, 2000), 2.

47. Ibid., 2, 1.

48. G. Marks and M. Burbank, "Immigrant Support for the American Socialist Party, 1912 and 1920," *Social Science History* 14, no. 2 (Summer 1990): 191.

49. Ibid., 183, 186.

50. D. Soyer, "Class Conscious Workers as Immigrant Entrepreneurs: The Ambiguity of Class among Eastern European Jewish Immigrants to the United States at the Turn of the Twentieth Century," *Labor History* 42, no. 1 (2001): 52, 59, 58. See also the documents in TAM/037/R-7325/1 that record donations by Jewish businessmen to Jewish socialist politicians; for example, J. M. Huber, letter to H. Berger, October 5, 1921.

51. M. Epstein, *Jewish Labor in the USA: An Industrial, Political and Cultural History of the Jewish Labor Movement* (New York: Ktav Publishing House, 1969), 1:149–52; and S. T. McSeveney, *The Politics of Depression: Political Behavior in the Northeast, 1893–1896* (New York: Oxford University Press, 1972), 60, 263–65.

52. H. Perrier, "The Socialists and the Working Class in New York: 1890–1896," *Labor History* 22, no. 4 (Fall 1981): 501. See also M. Hillquit, *History of Socialism in the United States* (New York and London: Funk and Wagnalls, 1903), 258; and F. Girard and B. Perry, *The Socialist Labor Party of America, 1876–1991: A Short History* (Philadelphia: Livra Books, 1993), 19, 88–92.

53. "Anarchists Mild as Lambs: Chased from Place to Place by the Vigilant Police," *New York Times*, August 23, 1893, 1.

54. H. Perrier, "Le mouvement ouvrier aux États-Unis et la guerre, 1889–1919," *Le Mouvement social* 147 (April–June 1989): 30; and A. Trachtenberg, ed., *The American Labor Year Book 1917–1918* (New York: Rand School of Social Science, 1918), 336–37, 340.

55. D. Bell, *Marxian Socialism in the United States* (Princeton, NJ: Princeton University Press, 1967), 79, 99.

56. Ibid., 97.

57. TIHL, 271. Cf. Epstein, *Jew and Communism*, 70.

58. I. B. Bailin, "Socialist Activities Among the Jews," in *The American Labor Year Book, 1916*, ed. A. L. Trachtenberg (New York: Rand School of Social Research, 1916), 1:139.

59. TIHL, 271.

60. Bell, *Marxian Socialism in the United States*, 98.

61. H. Perrier, "Socialists and the Working Class in New York," 502.

62. A. Liebman, *Jews and the Left* (New York: John Wiley and Sons, 1979), 48.

63. N. Carpenter, *Immigrants and Their Children, 1920: A Study Based on Census Statistics Relative to the Foreign Born and Native White of Foreign or Mixed Parentage* (Washington, DC: Government Printing Office, 1927), 260–63.

64. H. Roskolenko, *The Time That Was Then: The Lower East Side, 1900–1914; An Intimate Chronicle* (New York: Dial Press, 1971), 199. See also H. Rogoff, *An East Side Epic: The Life and Work of Meyer London* (New York: Vanguard Press, 1930), 16.

65. M. Dubofsky, "Success and Failure of Socialism in New York City, 1900–1918: A Case Study," *Labor History* 9, no. 3 (Autumn 1968): 371.

66. I. N. Forman, "The Politics of Minority Consciousness," in *Jews in American Politics*, ed. L. S. Maisel (Lanham, MD: Rowman and Littlefield, 2004), 153.

67. S. DeLeon and N. Fine, eds., *American Labor Year Book* (New York: Rand School of Social Science, 1929), 144–45.

68. N. Fine, *Labor and Farmer Parties in the United States: 1828–1928* (New York: Russell and Russell, 1961), 230.

69. L. Wolman, *The Growth of American Trade Unions, 1880–1923* (New York: National Bureau of Economic Research, 1924), 147, 138, 137, 141.

70. TIHL, 276.

71. TIHL, 271, 273, 276.

72. A. Trachtenberg, *American Labor Year Book 1917–1918*, 7–53.

73. Bell, *Marxian Socialism in the United States*, 100.

74. TIHL, 292–93.

75. TIHL, 290. Cf. J. Cannon, *The First Ten Years of American Communism—Report of a Participant* (New York: Pathfinder, 1973), 109–14.

76. T. Michels, *A Fire in Their Hearts: Yiddish Socialists in New York* (Cambridge, MA: Harvard University Press, 2005), 219; and A. Shapira, "Labour Zionism and the October Revolution," *Journal of Contemporary History* 24, no. 4 (October 1989): 626.

77. TIHL, 293, 294.

78. TIHL, 298, 310. Cf. P. K. Edwards, *Strikes in the United States, 1881–1974* (Oxford: Basil Blackwell, 1981), 1–51, 84–133; D. J. Bercuson, *Confrontation at Winnipeg: Labour, Industrial Relations, and the General Strike* (Kingston, ON: McGill-Queen's University Press, 1974); D. Montgomery, "Immigrants, Industrial Unions, and Social Reconstruction in the United States, 1916–1923," *Labour/ Le Travail* 13 (Spring 1984): 101–14; and H. O'Connor, *Revolution in Seattle* (New York: Monthly Review Press, 1964).

79. M. Hillquit, *New York Call*, September 22, 1919, quoted in A. E. Stevenson et al., *Revolutionary Radicalism: Its History, Purpose and Tactics with an Exposition and Discussion of the Steps Being Taken and Required to Curb It—Report of the Joint Legislative Committee Investigating Seditious Activities of the Senate of the State of New York* (New York: J. B. Lyon and Company, April 24, 1920), 1:557.

80. TIHL, 303.

81. J. Weinstein, *The Decline of Socialism in America, 1912–1925* (New Brunswick, NJ: Rutgers University Press, 1984), 203.

82. A. Bittelman, *Parties and Issues in the Election Campaign* (Chicago: Literature Department of the Workers Party of America, 1924), 5.

83. Jacob Talmon noted similarly of Rosa Luxemburg, who was from Poland yet agitated in Weimar Germany: "'It never seemed to have bothered her that there was something incongruous in the fact that she, only a recently naturalised alien, with a foreign accent, was agitating in a country seething with nationalist passion, for extreme socialist policies and taking up what was by many held as anti-national stances.'" J. Talmon, *The Myth of the Nation and the Vision of Revolution: The Origins of Ideological Polarisation in the Twentieth Century* (London: Secker and Warburg, 1980), 85.

84. TIHL, 306.

85. Epstein, *Jew and Communism*, 70–72.

86. TIHL, 315. Capitals in original.

87. TIHL, 335. Cf. Bell, *Marxian Socialism in the United States*, 3–5.

88. Cf. B. C. Vladeck, "Why Radicalism Has Failed" (speech presented at the Ford Hall Forum, Boston, Massachusetts, January 22, 1933), 13–14, in TAM/037/R-7325/12.

89. A. Bittelman, *Fifteen Years of the Communist Party* (New York: Workers Library, 1934), 8. James Cannon commented favorably on this text in *First Ten Years of American Communism*, 101–4. Cf. Michels, *Fire in Their Hearts*, 217–50.

90. TIHL, 316.

91. Howe, *World of Our Fathers*, 328; and Michels, *Fire in Their Hearts*, 227.

92. TIHL, 330, 331.

93. T. Draper, *Roots of American Communism* (New York: Viking Press, 1957), 190, 206–7.

94. Palmer, *James P. Cannon*, 114.

95. N. Glazer, *The Social Basis of American Communism* (New York: Harcourt, Brace and World, 1961), 40.

96. TIHL, 334, 332, 333.

97. TIHL, 348. Cf. Palmer, *James P. Cannon*, 129.

98. Michels, *Fire in Their Hearts*, 228.

99. B. Gitlow, *I Confess: The Truth About American Communism* (New York: E. P. Dutton, 1940), 133, 153.

100. TIHL, 365; and Palmer, *James P. Cannon*, 152.

101. TIHL, 365, 378, 377.

102. D. Soyer, "Back to the Future: American Jews Visit the Soviet Union in the 1920s and 1930s," *Jewish Social Studies* 6, no. 3 (Spring–Summer 2000): 124.

103. Ibid., 129.

104. TIHL, 385.

105. TIHL, 389. Cf. W. O. McCagg Jr., "Jews in Revolutions: The Hungarian Experience," *Journal of Social History* 6, no. 1 (Autumn 1972): 83.

106. W. Chambers, *Witness* (New York: Random House, 1952), 246.

107. TIHL, 390. Cf. Cannon, *First Ten Years of American Communism*, 76–77.

108. Glazer, *Social Basis of American Communism*, 135. Cf. TIHL, 393.

109. Michels, *Fire in Their Hearts*, 240.

110. Liebman, *Jews and the Left*, 61.

111. Draper, *Roots of American Communism*, 279.

112. Glazer, *Social Basis of American Communism*, 117.

113. G. Charney, *A Long Journey* (Chicago: Quadrangle Books, 1968), 57, 73; and Glazer, *Social Basis of American Communism*, 220n1.

114. T. Draper, *American Communism and Soviet Russia: The Formative Period* (London: Macmillan, 1960), 191.

115. H. Klehr, *Communist Cadre: The Social Background of the American Communist Party Elite* (Stanford, CA: Hoover Institution Press, 1978), 51.

116. Glazer, *Social Basis of American Communism*, 130–31, 146.

117. J. R. Starobin, *American Communism in Crisis, 1943–1957* (Cambridge, MA: Harvard University Press, 1972), 230.

118. M. Rothbard, "Life in the Old Right," *Chronicles* (August 1994), https://www.lewrockwell.com/1970/01/murray-n-rothbard/life-in-the-old-right/.

119. Howe, *World of Our Fathers*, 329.

120. I. Howe and L. Coser, *The American Communist Party: A Critical History* (New York: Da Capo Press, 1974), 236–72; and Glazer, *Social Basis of American Communism*, 138.

121. Liebman, *Jews and the Left*, 65–66; and Epstein, *Jew and Communism*, 95.

122. Palmer, *James P. Cannon*, 163–65.

123. J. R. Barrett, *William Z. Foster and the Tragedy of American Radicalism* (Urbana and Chicago: University of Illinois Press, 1999), 103.

124. P. S. Foner, *The History of the Labor Movement in the United States: TUEL to the End of the Gompers Era* (New York: International Publishers, 1991), 9:107.

125. TIHL, 403.

126. TIHL, 404. Cf. Palmer, *James P. Cannon*, 190. Foster relied on Bittelman's theoretical insights and support for decades. See A. Bittelman, letter to W. Z. Foster, September 20, 1951, in TAM/62.1/3/32.

127. TIHL, 439, 440. Cf. Barrett, *William Z. Foster*, 151; and Draper, *American Communism and Soviet Russia*, 219–29.

128. TIHL, 441, 442. Cf. Barrett, *William Z. Foster*, 152.

129. Draper, *American Communism and Soviet Russia*, 308–12.

130. T. Morgan, *Jay Lovestone: Communist, Anti-Communist, and Spymaster* (New York: Random House, 1999), 80. See also Draper, *American Communism and Soviet Russia*, 401–2; and W. Z. Foster, *From Bryan to Stalin* (New York: International Publishers, 1937), 299–300.

131. TIHL, 524.

132. T. Draper, interview with A. Bittelman, January 20, 1969, in TAM/62.1/3/30; and Draper, *American Communism and Soviet Russia*, 171.

133. TIHL, 543.

134. See, for example, the titles published by Bittelman in New York by the Workers Library Publishers in 1932 and 1933 respectively: *The Communist Party in Action* and *From Left-Socialism to Communism*.

135. TIHL, 563, 567.

136. A. Bittelman and V. J. Jerome, *Leninism: The Only Marxism Today; A Discussion of the Characteristics of Declining Capitalism* (New York: Workers Library, 1934), 64.

137. A. Bittelman, *How Can We Share the Wealth? The Communist Way versus Huey Long* (New York: Workers Library, 1935), 8.

138. TIHL, 579. See also A. Bittelman, *Going Left: The Left Wing Formulates a "Draft for a Program for the Socialist Party of the United States"* (New York: Workers Library, 1936), 38. Cf. E. P. Johanningsmeier, *Forging American Communism: The Life of William Z. Foster* (Princeton, NJ: Princeton University Press, 1994), 273.

139. A. Bittelman, *The Advance of the United Front* (New York: Workers Library, 1934), 5.

140. A. Bittelman, *How to Win Social Justice: Can Coughlin and Lemke Do It?* (New York: Workers Library, 1936), 22.

141. A. Bittelman, *The Townsend Plan* (New York: Workers Library, 1936), 13.

142. Barrett, *William Z. Foster*, 190.

143. TIHL, 575, 579a.

144. R. H. Zieger, *American Workers, American Unions: 1920–1985* (Baltimore, MD: Johns Hopkins University Press, 1986), 42–44.

145. Johanningsmeier, *Forging American Communism*, 275.

146. A. Bittelman, *Break the Economic and Political Sabotage of the Monopolists* (New York: Workers Library, 1937), 5.

147. A. Bittelman, "The Party and the People's Front," in *Party Building and Political Leadership* (New York: Workers Library, 1937), 78, 79.

148. Barrett, *William Z. Foster*, 191; and Johanningsmeier, *Forging American Communism*, 279.

149. Barrett, *William Z. Foster*, 193.

150. Glazer, *Social Basis of American Communism*, 114, 116.

151. TIHL, 623. Cf. Draper, *American Communism and Soviet Russia*, 89.

152. TIHL, 624.

153. Draper, *American Communism and Soviet Russia*, 192; and B. Gitlow, *The Whole of Their Lives* (New York: Charles Scribner, 1948), 130.

154. J. B. S. Hardman, "The Radical Labor Movement," essay typescript, 1932, 32–33, in TAM/050/26/1.

155. Into the 1950s, CPUSA leaders were still writing and talking about the need to "Americanize" the party. See, for example, J. Gates, *The Story of an American Communist* (New York: Thomas Nelson, 1958), 173.

156. Glazer, *Social Basis of American Communism*, 57–62, 158–62.

157. Epstein, *Jew and Communism*, 401.

158. TIHL, 672, 674.

159. TIHL, 675.

160. A. Bittelman, *Jewish Unity for Victory* (New York: Workers Library, 1943), 6.

161. TIHL, 674. Cf. D. E. Lipstadt, *Beyond Belief: The American Press and the Coming of the Holocaust 1933–1945* (New York: Free Press, 1986), 240.

162. TIHL, 680, 675. Cf. I. Deutscher, "Israel's Spiritual Climate," in *The Non-Jewish Jew and Other Essays*, ed. T. Deutscher (London: Oxford University Press, 1968), 112.

163. A. Bittelman, "Current Problems in Our Jewish Work: The Struggle for Peace, Against Anti-Semitism, for a Progressive Culture," essay typescript, October 1949, 5–11, in TAM/62.1/2/12.

164. "Red Leader Seized for Deportation," *New York Times*, January 17, 1948, 1–2.

165. TIHL, 701.

166. "Communists: Gentleman, Very Timid," *Time*, January 26, 1948. See also "Bittelman, Red Leader, Arrested by FBI in Miami for Deportation," *New York Times*, January 17, 1948, 1.

167. TIHL, 738. A. Bittelman, "Bittelman's Proposal to Office Committee on Current Problems," memorandum, May 24, 1944, 2–3, in TAM/62/1/14; A. Bittelman, "Jerusalem, National Independence and Peace," essay typescript, ca. 1949, 1–16, in TAM/62/2/3; and A. Bittelman, letter to President H. S. Truman, 1948, in TAM/62.1/3/26.

168. TIHL, 711.

169. Starobin, *American Communism in Crisis*, 10–11, 224–30. See also A. Bittelman, "The Political Source of Our Theoretical Errors," *The Worker*, July 22, 1945, 13, in TAM/62.1/1/10.

170. For Bittelman's legal papers, see TAM/62.1/3/37.

171. TIHL, 738.

172. TIHL, 735–36. See also CPUSA, "The National Committee of the Communist Party of America Formulates United Front Policies in Mass Struggle for Peace, Civil Liberties, Equal Rights and Economic Security," memorandum, ca. 1954, 1–9, in TAM/62/1/16. Cf. B. Lewis, "Peaceful Transition and the Communist Party, USA, 1949–1958," *Theoretical Review: A Journal of Marxist-Leninist Theory and Discussion* 12 (September–October 1979): 9–20, in TFRB/0182/0182.

173. "Communists: Guilty," *Time*, February 2, 1953.

174. Epstein, *Jew and Communism*, 402.

175. TIHL, 704.

176. TIHL, 723, 833.

177. D. Shannon, *The Decline of American Communism* (New York: Harcourt Brace, 1959), 272–73.

178. TIHL, 1219–21.

179. TIHL, 376–77, 635–36. Bittelman himself had written a Stalinist tract against Trotsky: A. Bittelman, *Trotsky the Traitor* (New York: Workers Library Publishers, 1937), 1–30. This tract was used as evidence in the so-called Dewey Commission, which was initiated in March 1937 by the American Committee for the Defense of Leon Trotsky, an independent, impartial body to ascertain facts about the Moscow trials of Trotsky and his son. See J. Dewey, *The Case of Leon Trotsky: Report of Hearings on the Charges Made Against Him in the Moscow Trials* (London: Secker and Warburg, 1937), 115–17.

180. TIHL, 648, 639.

181. TIHL, 648.

182. TIHL, 898; emphasis in original. An almost identical statement may be found in A. Koestler, "Initiates," in *The God That Failed* [1950], ed. R. Crossman (London: Bantam Books, 1965), 29.

183. TIHL, 656.

184. TIHL, 651.

185. A. Bittelman, letter to Basic Books, May 20, 1968, in TAM/62.1/3/35.

186. TIHL, 654, 670. Bittelman was referring to M. Djilas, *The New Class: An Analysis of the Communist System* (London: Thames and Hudson, 1957).

187. TIHL, 670–71.

188. TIHL, 915, 914.

189. Arthur Koestler explored this question in "Initiates," 40–41.

190. Bittelman even attempted to convince the leaders of the Soviet Union and China. A. Bittelman, letter to N. Khrushchev and M. Tse-Tung, June 23, 1963, in TAM/62.1/3/33.

191. A. Bittelman, *A Communist Views America's Future*, 1960, 1–375, in TAM/62.1/4/4–6. Cf. Starobin, *American Communism in Crisis*, 243n14.

192. "US Reds Oust Theoretician as an 'Anti-Party Revisionist,'" *New York Times*, November 24, 1960, 15; and "Expelled Red Hits Party Leadership," *New York Times*, December 7, 1960, 17.

193. A. Bittelman, letter to L. B. Johnson, January 15, 1965, in TAM/62.1/1/26; and A. Bittelman, letter to CPUSA, February 12, 1971, in TAM/62.1/3/15.

194. See, for example, A. Bittelman, "The Bolshevik Revolution and Its Historic Consequences," typescript, ca. 1967, in TAM/62.1/4/1–3.

195. J. H. M. Laslett and S. M. Lipset, eds., *Failure of a Dream? Essays in the History of American Socialism* (Berkeley: University of California Press, 1974).

196. Harshav, *Language in Time of Revolution*, x.

197. TIHL, 692.

198. *TIHL*.

199. Deutscher, "The Russian Revolution and the Jewish Problem," in *The Non-Jewish Jew and Other Essays*, ed. T. Deutscher (London: Oxford University Press, 1968), 67.

200. W. Cohn, "The Politics of American Jews," *The Jews: Social Patterns of an American Group*, ed. M. Sklare (Glencoe, IL: Free Press, 1958), 614–26.

201. Michels, *Fire in Their Hearts*, 3.

202. H. Burgin, "*History of the Jewish Workers Movement*," trans. anonymous, typescript, November 30, 1914, in TAM/249/1/1, 32.

203. M. Soltes, *The Yiddish Press: An Americanizing Agency* (New York: Columbia University Press, 1924), 24.

204. Michels, *Fire in Their Hearts,* 3–4.

205. G. Sorin, *The Prophetic Minority: American Jewish Immigrant Radicals, 1880–1920* (Bloomington: Indiana University Press, 1985), 70.

206. Such a claim is found in I. Kristol, "The Liberal Tradition," in *American Pluralism and the Jewish Community*, ed. S. M. Lipset (New Brunswick, NJ: Transaction Publishers, 1990), 112. It is refuted in E. Hertz, "Politics: New York," in *The Russian Jew in the United States*, ed. C. S. Bernheimer (Philadelphia: John C. Winston, 1905), 160.

207. Howe, *World of Our Fathers*, 75, 95.

208. J. R. Berkovitz, "The French Revolution and the Jews: Assessing the Cultural Impact," *American Jewish Society Review* 20, no. 1 (1995): 78–86; and P. Pulzer, *Jews and the German State: The Political History of a Minority, 1848–1933* (Oxford: Blackwell, 1992), 82.

209. A. A. Goren, "The Conservative Politics of the Orthodox Press," in *The Politics and Public Culture of American Jews* (Bloomington: Indiana University Press, 1999), 100–109; and M. B. Shapiro, *Between the Yeshiva World and Modern Orthodoxy: The Life and Works of Rabbi Jehiel Jacob Weinberg* (Oxford: Littman Library of Jewish Civilization, 1999), 41.

210. N. Cantor, *The Sacred Chain: A History of the Jews* (New York: Harper Perennial, 1995), 227.

211. D. A. Teutsch, "Reconstructionism and the Public Square: A Multicultural Approach to Judaism in America," in *Jewish Polity and American Civil Society: Communal Agencies and Religious Movements in the American Public Square*, ed. A. Mittelman, J. D. Sarna, and R. Licht (Lanham, MD: Rowman and Littlefield, 2002), 338. See also A. A. Goren, *New York Jews and the Quest for Community: The Kehillah Experiment, 1908–1922* (New York: Columbia University Press, 1970).

212. M. Beer, *Fifty Years of International Socialism* (London: George Allen and Unwin, 1935), 105.

213. See, for example, J. S. Kopstein and J. Wittenberg, "Who Voted Communist? Reconsidering the Social Bases of Radicalism in Interwar Poland," *Slavic Review* 62, no. 1 (Spring 2003): 97.

214. J. Frankel, *Prophecy and Politics: Socialism, Nationalism, and the Russian Jews, 1862–1917* (Cambridge, UK: Cambridge University Press, 1981), 194. See also T. Michels, "Exporting Yiddish Socialism: New York's Role in the Russian Jewish Workers' Movement," *Jewish Social Studies* 16, no. 1 (Fall 2009): 1–26.

215. L. Dinnerstein and D. M. Reimers, *Ethnic Americans: A History of Immigration and Assimilation* (New York: Dodd, Mead and Company, 1987), 60–64.

216. H. May, *The End of American Innocence: A Study of the First Years of Our Own Times, 1912–1917* (Chicago: Quadrangle Books, 1964), 282–83.

217. S. R. Lichter and S. Rothman, *Roots of Radicalism: Jews, Christians, and the New Left* (New York and Oxford: Oxford University Press, 1982), 118.

218. R. Jensen, "The Religious and Occupational Roots of Party Identification: Illinois and Indiana in the 1870s," in *Voters, Parties, and Elections: Quantitative Essays in the History of American Popular Voting Behavior*, ed. J. H. Silbey and S. T. McSeveney (Toronto: Xerox College Publishing, 1972), 167–83.

219. Liebman, *Jews and the Left*, 148–56.

220. Cuddihy, *Ordeal of Civility*, 3–14.

221. S. N. Eisenstadt, *From Generation to Generation: Age Groups and Social Structure* (New York: Free Press of Glencoe, 1956), 173.

222. Harshav, *Language in Time of Revolution*, 8.

223. L. Kaplan, "On Maurice Samuel's Twenty-Fifth Yahrzeit," *Judaism: A Quarterly Journal of Jewish Life and Thought* 46, no. 4 (Fall 1997): 453.

224. M. Samuel, *Jews on Approval* (New York: Liveright Publishers, 1933), 198.

225. Ibid., 12, 9.

226. TIHL, 1053.

227. TIHL, 1066–67.

228. M. Polanyi, "Jewish Problems," *The Political Quarterly* 14, no. 1 (1943): 36.

229. J. M. Zeitz, *White Ethnic New York: Jews, Catholics, and the Shaping of Postwar Politics* (Chapel Hill: University of North Carolina Press, 2007), 117–18.

230. E. Digby Blatzell, "The WASP's Last Gasp," in *The Protestant Establishment Revisited*, ed. and intro. H. G. Schneiderman (New Brunswick, NJ: Transaction Publishers, 2001), 34.

231. L. Trilling, afterword to *The Unpossessed*, ed. T. Slesinger (New York: Basic Books, 1966), 316.

232. E. Lederhendler, "Guides for the Perplexed: Sex, Manners, and Mores for the Yiddish Reader in America," *Modern Judaism* 11, no. 3 (October 1991): 331, 332.

233. Kosak, *Cultures of Opposition*, 82. See also H. R. Diner, *Lower East Side Memories: A Jewish Place in America* (Princeton, NJ: Princeton University Press, 2000), 6.

234. TIHL, 445.

235. É. Durkheim, *The Division of Labor in Society*, trans. G. Simpson (Glencoe, IL: Free Press, 1933), 151.

236. Liebman, *Jews and the Left*, 527–35.

237. B. D. Weinryb, "Jewish Immigration and Accommodation to America," in *The Jews: Social Patterns of an American Group*, ed. M. Sklare (Glencoe, IL: Free Press, 1958), 628n42.

238. L. P. Gartner, "Immigration and the Formation of American Jewry, 1840–1925," in *Jewish Society through the Ages*, ed. H. H. Ben Sasson and S. Ettinger (New York: Schocken Books, 1973), 307–8.

239. TIHL, 1084–85.

240. A. Bittelman, *Program for Survival: The Communist Position on the Jewish Question* (New York: New Century Publishers, 1947), 11, 13.

241. B. Bauer, "The Jewish Question, Brunswick, 1843," in *Karl Marx: Early Writings*, trans. R. Livingstone and G. Benton (London: Penguin Classics, 1992), 212.

242. Durkheim, *Division of Labor in Society.*

243. On the sumptuary legislation in the shtetlach, see G. D. Hundert, *Jews in Poland-Lithuania in the Eighteenth Century: A Genealogy of Modernity* (Berkeley: University of California Press, 2006), 87–95.

244. P. Hayes, "Hobbes's Bourgeois Moderation," *Polity* 33, no. 1 (Autumn 1998): 55; J. Heilbron, *The Rise of Social Theory* (Cambridge, UK: Polity Press, 1995), 72; and M. Weber, *The Protestant Ethic and the Spirit of Capitalism*, trans. T. Parsons (London and New York: Routledge, 2002), 21–22.

245. K. Marx, "On the Jewish Question" [1843], in *Karl Marx: Selected Writings*, 2nd ed., ed. D. McLellan (Oxford: Oxford University Press, 2009), 46–70.

246. "Let us discuss the actual secular Jew, not the sabbath Jew as Bauer does, but the everyday Jew." Ibid., 66.

247. "Thus we recognize in Judaism a general contemporary anti-social element which has been brought to its present height by a historical development which the Jews zealously abetted in its harmful aspects and which now must necessarily disintegrate." *Ibid.*

248. A. Prinz, "New Perspectives on Marx as a Jew," in *Leo Baeck Institute Year Book*, ed. R. Weltsch (London: Horovitz Publishing, 1970), 111, 119, 123–24; D. Fischman, "The Jewish Question About Marx," *Polity* 21, no. 4 (Summer 1989): 760; and E. Silberner, "Was Marx an Anti-Semite?" [1949], in *Essential Papers on Jews and the Left*, ed. E. Mendelsohn (New York: New York University Press, 1997), 368–69.

249. Silberner, "Was Marx an Anti-Semite?," 393–95. See also J. Carlebach, *Karl Marx and the Radical Critique of Judaism* (London: Routledge and Kegan Paul, 1978), 294.

250. K. Marx, "On the Jewish Question," 69, 66.

251. S. Avineri, "Marx and Jewish Emancipation" [1964], in *Essential Papers on Jews and the Left*, ed. E. Mendelsohn (New York: New York University Press, 1997), 404–5.

252. Y. Peled, "From Theology to Sociology: Bruno Bauer and Karl Marx on the Question of Jewish Emancipation," *History of Political Thought* 13, no. 3 (Autumn 1992): 485.

253. On the Jewish dynamics in Trier in the early nineteenth century and the relation of the Marx family thereto, see S. L. Gilman, "Karl Marx and the Secret Language of the Jews," *Modern Judaism* 4, no. 3 (October 1984): 285–86.

254. W. Liebknecht, *Karl Marx: Biographical Memoirs* [1901], trans. E. Unterman (London: Journeyman Press, 1975), 14.

255. Cf. Harshav, *Language in Time of Revolution*, 18–20; and McCagg, "Jews in Revolutions," 95.

256. É. Durkheim, *Socialism and Saint-Simon*, ed. A.W. Gouldner, trans. C. Sattler (London: Routledge and Kegan Paul, 1963), 19.

257. On the link between socialism and multiculturalism, see P. Gottfried, *After Liberalism: Mass Democracy in the Managerial State* (Princeton, NJ, and Oxford: Princeton University Press, 1999), 72–109.

258. TIHL, 108–9.

259. TIHL, 1087.

260. T. Martin, *The Affirmative Action Empire: Nations and Nationalism in the Soviet Union, 1923–1939* (New York: Cornell University Press, 2001), 1.

261. D. Shneer, *Yiddish and the Creation of Soviet Jewish Culture, 1918–1930* (Cambridge, UK: Cambridge University Press, 2004) 2.

262. H. F. Srebrnik, *Dreams of Nationhood: American Jewish Communists and the Soviet Birodizhan Project, 1924–1951* (Boston: Academic Studies Press, 2010). See also "The Flying Reporter," *Yungvarg* (*Little Folks*), 1, no. 1 (May 1937): 3, in ALBA194/1/2.

263. TIHL, 377.

264. TIHL, 378.

265. Cf. J. L. Dekel-Chen, *Farming the Red Land: Jewish Agricultural Colonization and Local Soviet Power, 1924–1942* (New Haven,CT, and London: Yale University Press, 2005).

266. TIHL, 379.

267. J. Veidlinger, *The Moscow State Yiddish Theater: Jewish Culture on the Soviet Stage* (Bloomington: Indiana University Press, 2000), 17.

268. Slezkine, *Jewish Century*, 105–203.

269. A founder and editor in chief of *Di Frayhayt*, Paul Novick, was expelled from the CPUSA for revisionism and Zionism in 1972, but still "affirmed his backing for democratic social-ism and for the Soviet Union 'the way it was during the Lenin period, when Jewish culture flour-ished.'" P. B. Flint, "Paul Novick Is Dead; Editor, 97, Helped Start Yiddish Daily," *New York Times*, August 22, 1989, D23.

270. Martin, *Affirmative Action Empire*, 429.

271. J. Frankel and B. Pinkus, eds. *The Soviet Government and the Jews, 1948–1967: A Documented Study* (Cambridge, UK: Cambridge University Press, 1984) 1–7; and A. Lustiger, *Stalin and the Jews: The Red Book—The Tragedy of the Jewish Anti-Fascist Committee and the Soviet Jews* (New York: Enigma Books, 2003), 195–220.

272. According to Bittelman, the Allies in 1939 did not really want to fight Hitler, but to turn the Third Reich against the Soviet Union; Stalin supposedly refused to fall into the trap. TIHL, 613–16.

273. Glazer, *Social Basis of American Communism*, 165.

274. A. Bittelman, "Stalin: On His Seventieth Birthday," December 1949, 17, in TAM/62.1/2/1.

275. A. Bittelman, "Imperialist Reaction Menaces Achievements of Anti-Fascist Victory," draft article, 1948, 12, in TAM/62/1/23.

276. A. Bittelman, "Ethics and Politics in World Communism," draft article, ca. 1954, 30, in TAM/62.1/1/17.

277. TIHL, 948–49.

278. A. Bittelman, *"Jewish Survival: A Marxist Outlook,"* typescript, 1960–1961, 189, in TAM/62.1/4/12.

279. Ibid., 134.

280. Ibid., 143; emphasis added.

281. Ibid., 189; emphasis in original.

282. R. V. Burks, *The Dynamics of Communism in Eastern Europe* (Princeton, NJ: Princeton University Press, 1961), 150–70; E. Goldhagen, "The Ethnic Consciousness of Early Russian Jewish Socialists," *Judaism* 23, no. 4 (Fall 1974): 483; P. Johnson, *A History of the Jews* (New York: Harper and Row, 1987), 483; and R. Wistrich, *Revolutionary Jews from Marx to Trotsky* (London: Harrap, 1976), 3–22.

283. M. Berkowitz, *The Jewish Self-Image: American and British Perspectives, 1881–1939* (London: Reaktion Books, 2000), 19; emphasis added.

284. W. Herberg, "The Jewish Labor Movement in the United States: Early Years to World War I," *Industrial and Labor Relations Review* 5, no. 4 (July 1952): 523; and M. Rischin, *The Promised City: New York's Jews, 1870–1914* (Cambridge, MA: Harvard University Press, 1962), 168. See also Michels, *Fire in Their Hearts*, 20.

285. Epstein, *Jew and Communism*, 401, 319.

286. Bell, *Marxian Socialism in the United States*, 99.

287. Epstein, *Jew and Communism*, 74.

288. TIHL, 326–27.

289. TIHL, 284–85.

290. TIHL, 304–5.

291. TIHL, 242.

292. P. Lyons, *Philadelphia Communists, 1936–1956* (Philadelphia: Temple University Press, 1982), 74.

293. TIHL, 687.

294. Bittelman, *Jewish Unity for Victory*, 46.

295. Glazer, *Social Basis of American Communism*, 69.

296. See, for example, B.C. Vladeck, letter to L. Marshall, October 15, 1928, in TAM/037/R-7325/8.

297. TIHL, 1048.

298. Michels, *Fire in Their Hearts*, 23.

299. J. Raimondo, *An Enemy of the State: The Life of Murray N. Rothbard* (Amherst, NY: Prometheus Books, 2000), 24, 26, 28.

300. P. Kivisto, "The Decline of the Finnish American Left, 1925–1945," *International Migration Review* 17, no. 1 (Spring 1983): 65–79.

301. Ibid., 80, 84.

302. A similar observation has been made of black radicalism in the South. See R. D. G. Kelley, *Hammer and Hoe: Alabama Communists during the Great Depression* (Chapel Hill and London: University of North Carolina Press, 1990), 99–100, 107.

303. Ibid., 90.

304. Ibid., 80–82; and M. M. Gordon, *Assimilation in American Life—The Role of Race, Religion, and National Origins* (New York: Oxford University Press, 1964), 181.

305. J. T. Kolehmainen, "A Study of Assimilation in a Finnish Community," *American Journal of Sociology* 42, no. 3 (November 1936): 379, 377.

306. W. S. Berlin, *On the Edge of Politics: The Roots of Jewish Political Thought in America* (Westport, CT: Greenwood Press, 1978), 5.

307. W. Herberg, "Socialism, Zionism and Messianic Passion," *Midstream* 2 (Summer 1956): 65. See also Howe, *World of Our Fathers*, 16.

308. Sorin, *Prophetic Minority*, 26.

309. TIHL, 1059.

310. Nineteenth-century antecedents of this tendency are described in I. Singer, *A Religion of Truth, Justice and Peace* (New York: The Amos Society, 1924).

311. TIHL, 1086.

312. TIHL, 1088.

313. E. Manor, *Forward: The Jewish Daily Forward (Forverts) Newspaper: Immigrants, Socialism and Jewish Politics in New York, 1890-1917* (Portland, OR: Sussex Academic Press, 2009), 93–94.

314. Soltes, *Yiddish Press*. See also G. Tyler, *A Vital Voice—100 Years of the Jewish Forward* (New York: Forward Association, 1997).

315. Manor, *Forward*, 94.

316. A. Cahan, *Bleter fun mayn lebn* (New York: Forverts Association, 1926), 3:57, quoted in I. Trunk, "The Cultural Dimension of the American Jewish Labor Movement," in *YIVO Annual of Jewish Social Science*, ed. E. Mendelsohn (New York: YIVO Institute for Jewish Research, 1976), 26:347.

317. A. Cahan, *The Rise of David Levinsky* [1917] (New York: Harper and Row, 1996), 501–2.

318. Manor, *Forward*, 105–7.

319. Ibid., 14. A similar conclusion in relation to Jewish radicalism in interwar Poland was reached by B. K. Johnpoll, *The Politics of Futility: The General Jewish Workers Bund in Poland, 1917-1943* (Ithaca, NY: Cornell University Press, 1967), 269–70.

320. Gordon, *Assimilation in American Life*, 76.

321. Ibid., 97–98.

322. Liebman, *Jews and the Left*, 315.

323. D. Horowitz, *Radical Son: A Journey Through Time* (New York: Free Press, 1997), 42.

324. M. Denning, *The Cultural Front: The Laboring of American Culture in the Twentieth Century* (London and New York: Verso, 1997), xvii.

325. Michels, *Fire in Their Hearts*, 20.

326. On the relationship between perceptions of Jewish left-wing involvement and antisemitism, see W. I. Brustein and R. D. King, "Anti-Semitism as a Response to Perceived Jewish Power: The Case of Bulgaria and Romania before the Holocaust," *Social Forces* 83, no. 2 (December 2004): 691–708; and W.I. Brustein and R. D. King, "A Political Threat Model of Intergroup Violence: Jews in Pre-World War II Germany," *Criminology* 44, no. 4 (2006): 867–91.

327. Quoted in Frankel, *Prophecy and Politics*, 458.

328. TIHL, 875.

329. Z. Bauman, "Assimilation into Exile: The Jew as a Polish Writer," *Poetics Today* 17, no. 4 (Winter 1996): 577.

330. A. Cyrus, A. M. Cohen, and B. C. Vladeck, letter to fellow citizens, October 21, 1935, in TAM/037/R-7325/11; emphasis added.

331. B. C. Vladeck, letter to N. Thomas, June 14, 1934, in TAM/037/R-7325/10.

332. J. Herling, "Vladeck: Man of Faith and Action," 1939, 33, in TAM/037/R-7325/19. Vladeck adhered to this view despite early knowledge of Soviet atrocities.

333. "Half Million See Vladeck Funeral," *New York Times*, November 3, 1938, 23.

334. Herling, "Vladeck: Man of Faith and Action," 25. See also "Aldermen Assail Socialist Members," *New York Times*, July 2, 1919, 15.

335. Frankel, *Prophecy and Politics*, 453.

336. TIHL, 869–71; emphasis added.

337. A. Bittelman, "Speech to the School of Jewish Studies," draft, October 5, 1945, in TAM/62/1/14.

338. I. Amter and S. Van Veen Amter, autobiographical typescript, 1950 and 1965 (revised), 204, in TAM/079/1.

339. Ibid., 116–17.

340. Howe, *World of Our Fathers*, 105.

341. TIHL, 888.

342. TIHL, 888.

343. TIHL, 1047.

344. Liebman, *Jews and the Left*, 444.

345. A. A. Goren, "A Portrait of Ethnic Politics: The Socialists and the 1908 and 1910 Congressional Elections on the East Side," *American Jewish Historical Quarterly* 50, no. 3 (March 1961): 203.

346. Liebman, *Jews and the Left*, 522–26.

347. A. Bittelman, *To Secure Jewish Rights: The Communist Position* (New York: New Century Publishers, 1948), 36–39.

348. S. Avineri, *Moses Hess: Prophet of Communism and Zionism* (New York and London: New York University Press, 1985).

349. See, for example, A. Dowty, "Zionism's Greatest Conceit," *Israel Studies* 3, no. 1 (1998): 1; J. Frankel, "The Roots of Jewish Socialism (1881–1892): From 'Populism' to 'Cosmopolitanism'?" [1988], in *Essential Papers on Jews and the Left*, ed. E. Mendelsohn (New York: New York University Press, 1997), 71–72.

350. Frankel, *Prophecy and Politics*, 453.

351. TIHL, 685.

352. TIHL, 700.

353. A. Bittelman, "The New State of Israel, the Meaning of the Struggle for Its Existence, and Its Historical Significance," draft article, June 11, 1948, 1, in TAM/62/17/1.

354. E. Mendelsohn, *On Modern Jewish Politics* (Oxford: Oxford University Press, 1993), 112.

355. Bittelman, *Jewish Survival*, 150; emphasis in original.

356. TIHL, 888.

357. TIHL, 1287, 1289, 1306, 1308; emphasis in original.

Chapter 2

1. D. D. Moore, *At Home in America: Second Generation New York Jews* (New York: Columbia University Press, 1981), 9–10.

2. Zeitz, *White Ethnic New York*, 183, 107.

3. S. Svonkin, *Jews Against Prejudice: American Jews and the Fight for Civil Liberties* (New York: Columbia University Press, 1997), 8–10.

4. M. Dollinger, *Quest for Inclusion: Jews and Liberalism in Modern America* (Princeton, NJ, and Oxford: Princeton University Press, 2000), 6.

5. The American Jewish Congress had invested in the fraudulent financial schemes of Bernard Madoff. G. Shefler, "Battered American Jewish Congress to Suspend Activities," *Jerusalem Post*, July 18, 2010, 1.

6. "Hails Jewish Congress," *New York Times*, December 15, 1918, 9.

7. D. Philipson, *My Life as an American Jew* (Cincinnati: John G. Kidd & Son, 1941), 172.

8. B. G. Richards, "Where Congress Idea Originated," *Congress Weekly*, April 9, 1943, 12, in AJA361/A4/19.

9. N. W. Cohen, *Not Free to Desist: The American Jewish Committee, 1906–1966* (Philadelphia: The Jewish Publication Society of America, 1972), 91.

10. L. D. Brandeis, letter to L. Marshall, August 31, 1914, in *Letters of Louis D. Brandeis: Progressive and Zionist*, ed. M. I. Urofsky and D. W. Lewy (Albany: State University of New York Press, 1973), 3:294.

11. M. Frommer, "The American Jewish Congress: A History, 1914–1950" (PhD diss., Ohio State University, 1978), 58, 79–83.

12. Ibid., 61.

13. M. I. Urofsky, *A Voice That Spoke for Justice: The Life and Times of Stephen S. Wise* (Albany: State University of New York Press, 1982), 127.

14. Y. Shapiro, *Leadership of the American Zionist Organization, 1897-1930* (Chicago: University of Illinois Press, 1971), 97.

15. O. I. Janowsky, *The Jews and Minority Rights, 1898-1919* (New York: Columbia University Press, 1933), 176.

16. Ibid., 185.

17. M. I. Urofsky, *American Zionism from Herzl to the Holocaust* (Lincoln and London: University of Nebraska Press, 1975), 183, 193.

18. "Louis Marshall Explains," *New York Times*, December 17, 1918, 11. Of course Brandeis had played a role in securing American approval for the Balfour Declaration,

19. "Jews Going to Paris with Bill of Rights," *New York Times*, December 19, 1918, 8.

20. L. Marshall, letter to I. Landman, December 19, 1918, in *Louis Marshall: Champion of Liberty: Selected Papers and Addresses*, ed. C. Reznikoff (Philadelphia: Jewish Publication Society of America, 1957), 2:536.

21. L. Marshall, letter to I. W. Frank, June 3, 1921, in *Louis Marshall, ed.* Reznikoff, 2:556.

22. Cohen, *Not Free to Desist*, 118.

23. H. M. Sachar, *Dreamland: Europeans and Jews in the Aftermath of the Great War* (New York: Alfred A. Knopf, 2002), 46–50.

24. Cohen, *Not Free to Desist*, 122.

25. Frommer, "American Jewish Congress," 173.

26. "Calls Jews to Unite for Palestine Home," *New York Times*, May 22, 1922, 14.

27. Complaints to this effect are found throughout the minutes of the American Jewish Congress's administrative committee in the 1920s in AJHS/I-77/2/2–13. See also S. S. Wise, letter to R. Kesselman, May 8, 1930, in *Stephen S. Wise: Servant of the People—Selected Letters,* ed. C. H. Voss (Philadelphia: Jewish Publication Society of America, 1969), 167.

28. Frommer, "American Jewish Congress," 204–91.

29. See, for example, L. Marshall, letter to S. Ulmer, January 29, 1927, in *Louis Marshall, ed.* Reznikoff, 2:656–59.

30. N. Goldberg, "Economics Trends Among American Jews," *Jewish Affairs* 1, no. 9 (October 1946), 13.

31. E. P. Hutchinson, *Immigrants and Their Children 1850-1950* (New York: John Wiley, 1956), 335–49; and S. Thernstrom, *The Other Bostonians* (Cambridge, MA: Harvard University Press, 1973), 171–75.

32. Liebman, *Jews and the Left*, 361; and H. L. Feingold, *A Midrash on American Jewish History* (Albany: State University of New York Press, 1982), 160.

33. S. Steinberg, *The Academic Melting Pot: Catholics and Jews in American Higher Education* (New York: McGraw-Hill, 1974), 9–10.

34. R. L. Abel, *American Lawyers* (New York: Oxford University Press, 1989), 86.

35. Glazer, "Social Characteristics of American Jews," 15–16; and D. Goldberg and H. Sharp, "Some Characteristics of Detroit Area Jewish and non-Jewish Adults," in *The Jews: Social Patterns of An American Group*, ed. M. Sklare (Glencoe, IL: Free Press, 1958), 107–18.

36. Moore, *At Home in America*, 11.

37. Ibid., 129.

38. I. Goldstein, *Jewish Justice and Conciliation: History of the Jewish Conciliation Board of America, 1930–1968* (New York: KTAV, 1981), 88.

39. See the various papers in M. Sklare, ed., *The Jews: Social Patterns of an American Group* (New York: Free Press, 1958).

40. Moore, *At Home in America*, 89–101.

41. Jewish domination resulted, not incidentally, in increased militancy and radicalism, including intimations of communism, within the United Federation of Teachers (UFT), the New York local of the AFT. See S. Cole, *The Unionization of Teachers: A Case Study of the UFT* (New York: Praeger, 1969), 94–96.

42. Moore, *At Home in America*, 103, 119.

43. L. Lipsky, *Memoirs in Profile* (Philadelphia: Jewish Publication Society of America, 1975), 198.

44. S. S. Wise, letter to H. Morgenthau Sr., July 8, 1912, in *Stephen S. Wise*, ed. Voss, 47–48. See also R. S. Baker, ed., *Woodrow Wilson: Life and Letters—War Leader* (New York: Doubleday, Dorian, 1939), 7:135, 467; and L. Lipsky, *Thirty Years of American Zionism* (New York: Arno Press, 1977), 59.

45. Forman, "Politics of Minority Consciousness," 153. See also Feingold, "American Jewish Liberalism and Jewish Response," 30.

46. S. S. Wise, letter to T. W. Wilson, July 22, 1912, in S. S. Wise, *Challenging Years: The Autobiography of Stephen Wise* (New York: G. P. Putnam's Sons, 1949), 165.

47. Ibid. See also S. S. Wise, letter to B. Moskowitz, June 29, 1928, in *Stephen S. Wise*, ed. Voss, 155.

48. E. M. Hugh-Jones, *Woodrow Wilson and American Liberalism* (New York: Collier Books, 1947), 26, 191–205.

49. L. H. Fuchs, *The Political Behavior of American Jews* (Glencoe, IL: Free Press, 1956), 57–69; and H. L. Feingold, *A Time for Searching: Entering the Mainstream, 1920–1945* (Baltimore, MD: Johns Hopkins University Press, 1992) 198.

50. Frommer, "American Jewish Congress," 497–504.

51. The incident involved a dead Christian girl about whom one state trooper had made an ignorant query about Jewish "ritual murder," which resulted in his suspension and an apology to local Jews from the chief of police. S. S. Friedman, *The Incident at Massena* (New York: Stein and Day, 1978). See also S. S. Wise, letter to J. Shulkin, letter to the mayor of Massena, and letter to J. Warner, September 29, 1928, in *Stephen S. Wise*, ed. Voss, 157–58.

52. Frommer, "American Jewish Congress," 507–8.

53. AJCongress, *The American Jewish Congress: What It Is and What It Does* (New York: AJCongress, 1938), 15, in AJHS/I-77/183/7.

54. S. A. Cohen, *Engineer of the Soul: A Biography of Rabbi J. X. Cohen (1889–1955)* (New York: Bloch Publishing, 1961), 104, in AJHS/P-661/1/7. See also J. X. Cohen, *Jews, Jobs, and Discrimination: A Report on Jewish Non-Employment* (New York: American Jewish Congress, 1937), 31, in AJHS/I-77/182/17.

55. A. Vorspan, "A Disciple of the Wise: Jacob X. Cohen," *Congress Bi-Weekly* 38, no. 7 (May 21, 1971): 14–16, in AJHS/P-661/1/6.

56. Cohen, *Engineer of the Soul*, 103.

57. Cohen, *Engineer of the Soul*, 106. See also "Leaders Hear Cases of Bias Against Jews," *New York Times*, June 28, 1930, 7; "Sees Boycott of Jews," *New York Times*, November 1, 1930, 24; "Score Bias Toward Jews," *New York Times*, April 13, 1931, 26; and "Racial Bias Viewed as Threat to Peace," *New York Times*, February 22, 1932, 20.

58. Cohen, *Not Free to Desist*, 147; "Survey Situation of Jews in World," *New York Times*, October 20, 1930, 44.

59. Wise, *Challenging Years*, 235.

60. A. H. Cohen, *Administrative Report, July 1932 to May 1933, Submitted to the Eleventh (Emergency) Session of the American Jewish Congress* (Washington, DC: American Jewish Congress, May 20–22, 1933), 41, in AJHS/I-77/2/14.

61. Ibid. 49. See also "250,000 Jew Here to Protest Today," *New York Times*, March 27, 1933, 4.

62. B. G. Richards, "Organizing American Jewry," *Jewish Affairs* 2, no. 2 (May 1, 1947): 25, in AJHS/I-77/185/1.

63. Frommer, "American Jewish Congress," 335–36.

64. Ibid., 339–74. See also M. Friedman, *Consumer Boycotts: Effecting Change through the Marketplace and the Media* (London: Routledge, 1999), 138.

65. P. Novick, *The Holocaust in American Life* (Boston and New York: Houghton Mifflin, 2000), 19–59.

66. Lukacs, *Thread of Years*, 296–97.

67. Wise, *Challenging Years,* 224. See also S. S. Wise, letter to F. Frankfurter, January 28, 1936, in *Stephen S. Wise,* ed. Voss, 209–10.

68. Upon his death, Roosevelt was praised glowingly in a written eulogy by the American Jewish Congress, *Roosevelt to the American Jewish Congress, 1882–1945* (New York: American Jewish Congress, 1945), 3–11, in AJHS/I-77/184/23. See also M. Gottlieb, "The Anti-Nazi Boycott Movement in the United States: An Ideological and Sociological Appreciation," *Jewish Social Studies* 35, nos. 3/4 (July–October 1973): 212.

69. W. D. Rubinstein, *The Left, the Right, and the Jews* (London: Croom Helm, 1982), 24.

70. Howe, *World of Our Fathers,* 393.

71. Forman, "Politics of Minority Consciousness."

72. G. H. Gamm, *The Making of New Deal Democrats: Voting Behavior and Realignment in Boston, 1920–1940* (Chicago and London: University of Chicago Press, 1989), 65.

73. E. C. Ladd and C. D. Hadley, *Transformations of the American Party System: Party Coalitions from the New Deal to the 1970s,* 2nd ed. (New York: W. W. Norton, 1978), 115.

74. Gamm, *Making of New Deal Democrats,* 56.

75. B. S. Wenger, *New York Jews and the Great Depression: Uncertain Promise* (New Haven, CT, and London: Yale University Press, 1996), 16–17.

76. Gamm, *Making of New Deal Democrats,* 154–56.

77. Zeitz, *White Ethnic New York,* 94, 140, 194.

78. J. M. Allswang, *The New Deal and American Politics: A Study in Political Change* (New York: John Wiley, 1978), 44. Cf. American Jewish Congress et al., *Father Coughlin: His "Facts" and Arguments* (New York: General Jewish Council, 1939), 1–59, in AJHS/I-77/183/16.

79. P. H. Irons, *The New Deal Lawyers* (Princeton, NJ: Princeton University Press, 1982), 8.

80. See, for example, W. Lasser, *Benjamin V. Cohen: Architect of the New Deal* (New Haven, CT, and London: Yale University Press, 2002), 15–16, 24.

81. Cohen, *Engineer of the Soul,* 108.

82. Cohen, *Jews, Jobs, and Discrimination,* 12. Cohen referred to the Stephens-O'Brien bill, which amended the original 1895 New York State Civil Rights Act. See W. E. B. Du Bois, ed., "Along the Color Line: America, Stephens-O'Brien Bill," *The Crisis: A Record of the Darker Races* (July 1933): 159. The amendment read as follows: "It shall be unlawful for any public utility company, as defined in the public service law, to refuse to employ any person in any capacity in the operation or maintenance of a public service on account of the race, color or religion of such person."

83. Ibid., 27.

84. M. J. Klarman, *From Jim Crow to Civil Rights: The Supreme Court and the Struggle for Racial Equality* (New York: Oxford University Press, 2004), 179.

85. S. I. Rosenman, ed., *The Public Papers and Addresses of Franklin D. Roosevelt, vol. 10, The Call to Battle Stations* (New York: Russell and Russell, 1941), 233–36.

86. S. I. Rosenman, ed., *The Public Papers and Addresses of Franklin D. Roosevelt, vol. 12, The Tide Turns* (New York: Russell and Russell, 1943), 228–32.

87. Rosenman, *Call to Battle Stations,* 234. See also "President Orders an Even Break for Minorities in Defense Jobs," *New York Times,* June 26, 1941, 12.

88. L. Ruchames, *Race, Jobs, and Politics: The Story of FEPC* (New York: Columbia University Press, 1953), 3–21.

89. K. M. Schultz, "The FEPC and the Legacy of the Labor-Based Civil Rights Movement of the 1940s," *Labor History* 49, no. 1 (February 2008): 76.

90. "Jewish Coordinating Committee Approves of Roosevelt's Committee on Job Discrimination," *Jewish Telegraphic Agency,* August 31, 1942, online, July 20, 2011. For the files of the Coordinating Committee, see AJHS/I-169/1/1, 19, 20.

91. M. E. Reed, *Seedtime for the Modern Civil Rights Movement: The President's Committee on Fair Employment Practice, 1941–1946* (Baton Rouge and London: Louisiana State University Press, 1991), 40. See also J. X. Cohen, *Who Discriminates—And How?* (New York: American Jewish Congress, 1945), 12–28, in AJHS/I-77/184/32.

92. Cohen, *Engineer of the Soul*, 117.

93. Schultz, "The FEPC and the Legacy," 75.

94. Reed, *Seedtime*, 253, 258.

95. Ibid., 260.

96. M. R. Konvitz and T. Leskes, *A Century of Civil Rights* (New York and London: Columbia University Press, 1961), 195–96.

97. W. J. Collins, "Race, Roosevelt, and Wartime Production: Fair Employment in World War II Labor Markets," *American Economic Review* 91, no. 1 (March 2001): 274.

98. A. E. Bonfield, "The Origin and Development of American Fair Employment Legislation," *Iowa Law Review* 52, no. 6 (June 1967): 1063.

99. Ibid., 1067.

100. See, for example, American Jewish Congress, "Proposed Bill to Establish a Permanent Federal Civil Rights Commission," *CLSA Reports*, March 22, 1948, 1–5, in AJHS/I-77/29/6; and American Jewish Congress, "Legislative Status of Major Recommendations of President's Committee on Civil Rights," *CLSA Reports*, March 26, 1948, 1–3, in AJHS/I-77/29/3.

101. Dollinger, *Quest for Inclusion*, 145.

102. Reed, *Seedtime*, 206–7, 257.

103. L. C. Kesselman, *The Social Politics of FEPC: A Study in Reform Pressure Movements* (Chapel Hill: University of North Carolina Press, 1948), 106–7.

104. W. Maslow, *The Law and Race Relations* (New York: American Jewish Congress, March 1946), 79, in AJHS/U002/12 (semiprocessed collection).

105. Bonfield, "The Origin and Development," 1074.

106. Cohen, *Engineer of the Soul,* 103.

107. American Jewish Congress, "Materials Available from Commission on Law and Social Action," 1946, in AJHS/I-77/29/4.

108. State of South Carolina, County of Aiken, "Certificate of Birth," July 28, 1942, in AJHS/P-572/8/1; and S. Polier, letter to R. McGill, March 23, 1963, in AJHS/P-572/2/2.

109. S. Polier, letter to F. Frankfurter, July 11, 1932, in AJHS/P-572/8/20.

110. S. Polier, biographical sketch, ca. 1970s, 1–2, in AJHS/P-572/8/2.

111. A. H. Pekelis, "Full Equality in a Free Society: A Program for Jewish Action," in *Law and Social Action: Selected Essays of Alexander H. Pekelis*, ed. M. R. Konvitz (Ithaca, NY: Cornell University Press, 1950), 219, 228.

112. Ibid., 225, 232. See also M. R. Konvitz, "From Jewish Rights to Human Rights," *Congress Monthly* 46, no. 3 (April 1979): 8.

113. W. Maslow and J. B. Robison, "Civil Rights Legislation and the Fight for Equality, 1862–1952," *University of Chicago Law Review* 20, no. 3 (Spring 1953): 397.

114. Laws of the State of New York, 1944, ch. 612, § 3.

115. A. S. Chen, *The Fifth Freedom: Jobs, Politics, and Civil Rights in the United States, 1941–1972* (Princeton, NJ, and Oxford: Princeton University Press, 2009), 96–100.

116. C. C. Burlingham et al., letter to the editor, *New York Times*, February 13, 1945, 22.

117. Chen, *Fifth Freedom*, 100–113.

118. Cohen, *Who Discriminates—And How?*, 11.

119. N. D. Perlman, "Discriminatory and Unfair Employment Practices," February 1944, in AJHS/I-77/26/1. Cf. Laws of the State of New York, 1945, ch. 118.

120. D. Lockard, *Toward Equal Opportunity: A Study of State and Local Antidiscrimination Laws* (New York: Macmillan, 1968) 41. See also W. Maslow, L. Pfeffer, and B. S. Miller, "Check List of State Anti-Discrimination and Anti-Bias Laws," booklet, October 1, 1948, unnumbered, in AJHS/I-77/23/1. Similar lists for the 1950s and 1960s may be found in AJHS/I-77/23/2.

121. American Jewish Congress, "Report of Activities: November-December 1946," *CLSA Reports*, 1946, 1–2, in AJHS/I-77/29/4. See also American Jewish Congress, "Analysis of CLSA Fair Educational Practices Bill for New Jersey," *CLSA Reports*, September 19, 1946, in AJHS/I-77/29/4.

122. Lockard, *Toward Equal Opportunity*, 41–42. Cf. American Jewish Congress, "Consolidated Report of Major Activities: June 1, 1946 through August 31, 1946," 1946, 1–3, in AJHS/I-77/29/4; and American Jewish Congress, "Model Ordinance to Create a Municipal Commission on Group Relations," *CLSA Reports*, September 1947, 1–5, in AJHS/I-77/29/5.

123. American Jewish Congress, "Briefs Filed by the American Jewish Congress, 1945–1955," August 1955, 1–7, in AJHS/I-77/151/4.

124. Svonkin, *Jews Against Prejudice*, 93. See also I. Goldstein, letter to R. F. Wagner Jr., June 21, 1955, 1–2, in AJHS/P-572/3/8: "On behalf of the American Jewish Congress, I express our whole-hearted appreciation for the part you played in establishing a statutory commission on intergroup relations for the City of New York. The American Jewish Congress was the first to propose such a commission and led the campaign for its enactment. We intend to do our utmost to assist and cooperate with the new commission."

125. W. Maslow, A. H. Pekelis, and S. Adelson, "Memorandum in Support of Jurisdiction: *American Jewish Congress v. Lumbermens Casualty Company*," January 31, 1946, 4, 8, in AJHS/I-77/150/1.

126. American Jewish Congress, "Report of Activities," *CLSA Reports*, April 1950, 3, in AJHS/I-77/30/1.

127. Bonfield, "The Origin and Development," 1077.

128. W. Maslow, P. Murray, and A. H. Pollock, "Brief for the American Jewish Congress as *Amicus Curiae: Westminster School Board District of Orange County vs. Gonzalo Mendez*," October 1946, 1–35, in AJHS/U002/12/1 (semiprocessed collection).

129. H. R. Diner, *The Jews of the United States, 1654 to 2000* (Berkeley: University of California Press, 2004), 266.

130. L. E. Berson, *The Negroes and the Jews* (New York: Random House, 1971), 97.

131. Zeitz, *White Ethnic New York*, 147.

132. American Jewish Congress, budget of CLSA, June 1946, in AHJS/I-77/81/16.

133. G. Ivers, *To Build a Wall: American Jews and the Separation of Church and State* (Charlottesville: University Press of Virginia, 1995), 195–96. See also Svonkin, *Jews Against Prejudice*, 84–85, 238–39n24. Pertinent archival documents on the American Jewish Congress's finances may be found in AJHS/I-77/81/16 and AJHS/I-77/96/2.

134. B. Schwartzapfel, "Will Maslow, 99, Pioneer in Fight for Civil Rights," *Forward.com*, March 2, 2007, http://forward.com/news/obituaries/10243/will-maslow-99-pioneer-in-fight-for-civil-rights/; and M. E. Staub, *Torn at the Roots: The Crisis of Jewish Liberalism in Postwar America* (New York: Columbia University Press, 2002), 45.

135. American Jewish Congress, "The Civil Rights Act of 1964," *CLSA Reports*, October 1, 1964, 1–4, in AJHS/I-77/32/5.

136. Bonfield, "The Origin and Development," 1083.

137. American Jewish Congress, memorandum on *American Jewish Congress v. Aramco*, June 30, 1959, 1–4, in AJHS/I-77/162/21.

138. "Aramco's Ban Here on Jews Is Revoked," *New York Times*, July 16, 1959, 1, 14, in AJHS/P-572/2/6. See also R. Cohen, letter to Mrs. Jackie Robinson, July 23, 1959, 1–2, in AJHS/P-572/2/5; R. Cohen, memorandum on *American Jewish Congress v. Aramco*, July 3, 1959, 1–6 in AJHS/P-572/2/6; and R. Cohen, "American Jewish Congress Hails Court Decision in Aramco Case," press release, July 15, 1959, 1–5, in AJHS/I-77/162/25.

139. "State to Appeal Aramco Decision," *New York Times*, July 17, 1959, 23. See also C. J. Lynn, letter to E. A. Carter, July 17, 1959, in AJHS/P-572/2/5.

140. "Aramco's Appeal on Religion Loses," *New York Times*, April 20, 1960, 77. See also M. Stavis, letter to S. Polier, October 3, 1962, in AJHS/P-572/3/1.

141. S. Polier, W. Maslow, and L. Pfeffer, "Brief of Complainant, American Jewish Congress," March 1962, 1–42, in AJHS/I-77/152/2.

142. "Jews Now Hired by Arabian Oil," *New York Times*, July 14, 1963, 39. See also S. Polier, letter to N. D. Rockefeller, May 22, 1959, in AJHS/P-572/2/5.

143. For the relevant files, see AJHS/I-77/150–53. From out of the Aramco episode emerged the American Jewish Congress's long campaign against the Arab League's boycott of Israel, which culminated in the mid-1970s in the passage of federal amendments, coauthored by Maslow, that penalized American companies that adhered to this boycott. See R. Cohen, "Shad Polier Urges Democratic Party Platform Protecting American Citizens Against Religious Discrimination by Arab Countries," *CLSA News*, June 21, 1960, 1–2, in AJHS/I-77/165/35; "Political Parties Hear AJC Hit Arab Boycott," *Congress Bi-Weekly* 27, no. 13 (September 19, 1960): 14; R. Cohen, "The American Jewish Congress vs. the Arab Boycott," *Congress Monthly* 42, no. 6 (June 1975): 9–11; American Jewish Congress, "Resisting the Arab Boycott: A Statement by the American Jewish Congress on President Ford's Executive Order," *Congress Monthly* 43, no. 8 (October 1976): 3; N. Levine, "Challenging Saudi Arabian Discrimination and American Involvement," *Congress Monthly* 48, no. 1 (January 1977): 6–8; and "The Boycott Debate: Where Politics and Trade Meet," *Multinational Monitor* 7, no. 15 (November 1986), http://www.multinationalmonitor.org/hyper/issues/1986/11/debate.html.

144. For a detailed discussion, see Svonkin, *Jews Against Prejudice*, 89–90, 97–107.

145. On the Second Generation's funding and staffing of the NAACP, see H. R. Diner, *In the Almost Promised Land: American Jews and Blacks, 1915–1935* (Westport, CT: Greenwood Press, 1977), 118–63. On American Jewish Congress–NAACP cooperation, see also files in AJHS/P-572/4, for example, American Jewish Congress, "Attacks on NAACP," resolution of the administrative committee, October 21, 1956, 1–6, in AJHS/P-572/4/6.

146. J. B. Robison, ed., *Civil Rights in the United States, 1952: A Balance Sheet of Group Relations* (New York: American Jewish Congress and NAACP, 1952), 80, in AJHS/I-77/185/33.

147. Note, "Exclusion of Negroes from Subsidized Housing Project," *University of Chicago Law Review* 15, no. 3 (Spring 1948): 745–47. For background on the project itself, see J. Schwartz, *The New York Approach: Robert Moses, Urban Liberals, and Redevelopment of the Inner City* (Columbus: Ohio State University Press, 1993), 84–107.

148. American Jewish Congress, "Analysis of Stuyvesant Town Case," *CLSA Reports*, 1950, 1–3, in AJHS/I-77/30/1.

149. I. N. Groner and D. M. Helfeld, "Race Discrimination in Housing," *Yale Law Review* 57, no. 3 (January 1948): 439–40.

150. P. Girvan and F. M. Wozencraft, "Private Attorneys—General: Group Action in the Fight for Civil Liberties," 58, no. 4 *Yale Law Journal* (March 1949): 592.

151. Svonkin, *Jews Against Prejudice*, 104. See also American Jewish Congress, "Significant Activities of CLSA During the Last Year," March 17, 1955, 1–4, in AJHS/P-572/3/8; "Color Line Talks Set on Stuyvesant Town," *New York Times*, June 30, 1950, 15; and T. J. Ruderman, *Stanley M. Isaacs: The Conscience of New York* (New York: Arno Press, 1982), 246.

152. "Stuyvesant Town to Admit Negroes After a Controversy of Seven Years," *New York Times*, August 25, 1950, 1.

153. "Council Passes Bill Barring Bias in All City-Aided Private Housing," *New York Times*, February 17, 1951, 1, 8; "Bill Barring Housing Bias Is Signed by Impellitteri," *New York Times*, March 15, 1951, 6; and Note, "Validity of Municipal Law Barring Discrimination in Private Housing," *Columbia Law Review* 58, no. 5 (May 1958): 728.

154. American Jewish Congress, "Report of Activities," *CLSA Reports*, May–June 1958, 7, in AJHS/I-77/31/1; and R. Cohen, "Negro Winners in Levittown Anti-Bias Fight Hail Agencies Providing Legal Aid," *CLSA News*, July 18, 1960, in AJHS/I-77/165/16.

155. H. J. Gans, *The Levittowners: Ways of Life and Politics in a New Suburban Community* (New York: Pantheon Books, 1967), 371–75. See also R. Cohen, "Banner Year in States' Civil Rights Legislation, American Jewish Congress Study Discloses," *CLSA News*, August 3, 1959, 1–2, in AJHS/I-77/162/28; "Levitt Loses Plea Against Bias Law," *New York Times*, June 14, 1960, 391; and "Jersey Levittown Hires 3 Aides to Smooth Way on Integration," *New York Times*, July 13, 1960, 37.

156. Ibid., 406n27. A case on restrictive covenants in housing (*Shelley v. Kraemer*) in the mid-1940s was the occasion on which the federal government filed an *amicus* brief, "the first time the

United States had gone on record in the Supreme Court broadly condemning all manifestations of racial discrimination." The irony was that "the names of the four Jewish lawyers who wrote the brief were stricken by their Jewish superior" in the Solicitor General's Office, given the bad "look" that such a roster gave to the document. P. Elman, "Solicitor General's Office, Justice Frankfurter, and Civil Rights Litigation, 1946–1960: An Oral History," *Harvard Law Review* 100, no. 4 (February 1987): 819.

157. W. Maslow, "Memorandum of Complaint in Support of the Commission's Jurisdiction: *American Jewish Congress v. Columbia University NYC,*" June 1946, 1–18, in AJHS/I-77/150/2; "Discrimination Charged: Jewish Congress Head Sues to Halt Tax Aid to Columbia," *New York Times*, March 15, 1946, 23; and "Case in Court Bars Action on Columbia," *New York Times*, March 26, 1946, 24.

158. Urofsky, *Voice That Spoke for Justice*, 358.

159. "College Bias Laws Held Undesirable," *New York Times*, June 8, 1948, 27; "City College Bias Case," *New York Times*, April 28, 1949, 30.

160. Model drafts for New York and New Jersey are found in AJHS/I-77/29/4. See also D. Petegorsky, letter to the editor, *New York Times*, January 7, 1948, 24; "Albany Bills Bar Bias in Education," *New York Times*, February 12, 1948, 26; "Draft State Bills on College Policy," *New York Times*, February 24, 1948, 16; and "Dewey Approves College Bias Ban," *New York Times*, April 6, 1948, 15.

161. Maslow, Murray and Pollock, "Brief for the American Jewish Congress."

162. G. M. Lavergne, *Before Brown: Herman Marion Sweatt, Thurgood Marshall, and the Long Road to Justice* (Austin: University of Texas Press, 2010), 37.

163. J. P. Jackson Jr., *Social Scientists for Social Justice: Making the Case against Segregation* (New York and London: New York University Press, 2001), 79–91.

164. P. Strum, *Mendez v. Westminster: School Desegregation and Mexican-American Rights* (Lawrence: University Press of Kansas, 2010), 137–38.

165. Jackson, *Social Scientists for Social Justice*, 91.

166. Strum, *Mendez v. Westminster*, 158.

167. R. Kluger, *Simple Justice: The History of* Brown v. Board of Education *and Black America's Struggle for Equality* (New York: Alfred A. Knopf, 1976). 388–95.

168. Notably, Greenberg filed an *amicus* brief with Joseph B. Robison and Melvin L. Wulf of the American Jewish Congress on behalf of a black plaintiff in the US Supreme Court case *Colorado Commission Against Discrimination v. Continental Air Lines* (October 1962, in AJHS/I-77/152/3). Greenberg's correspondence with Shad Polier from the 1950s can be found in AJHS/P-572/4/6.

169. Jackson, *Social Scientists for Social Justice*, 54, 66–74.

170. N. I. Silber, *With All Deliberate Speed: The Life of Philip Elman* (Ann Arbor: University of Michigan Press, 2004), 13, 191, 232.

171. P. Elman, "Response," *Harvard Law Review* 100, no. 8 (June 1987): 1949.

172. H. L. Weisman et al., *Brief of American Jewish Congress as Amicus Curiae: Brown v. Board of Education of Topeka, Kansas* (New York: Bar Press, October 9, 1952), 2, in AJHS/I-77/150/26. Such invocations were not always successfully persuasive. See, for example, S. Polier, W. Maslow, and L. Pfeffer, "Memorandum of Law on Application for Reconsideration," memorandum to J. E. Conway, November 1956, 1–48, in AJHS/P-572/1/7.

173. R. Cohen, "American Jewish Congress Hails New York City Integration Plan, Pledges Support, Cooperation," press release, September 2, 1960, in AJHS/I-77/165/18.

174. J. de Forest, "The 1958 Harlem School Boycott: Parental Activism and the Struggle for Educational Equity in New York," *Urban Review* 40, no. 1 (2008): 22, 25, 27. See also "South Is Criticized by Jewish Congress," *New York Times*, May 19, 1957, 45.

175. See, for example, E. Roosevelt, letter to J. W. Polier, June 22, 1942, and September 26, 1942; and J. W. Polier, letter to E. Roosevelt, March 23, 1942, in AJHS/P-527/10F1.

176. Quoted in de Forest, "1958 Harlem School Boycott," 36. See also L. Buder, "2 Harlem Schools Called Inferior As Court Frees Two in Boycott," *New York Times*, December 16, 1958, 1.

177. R. Cohen, "American Jewish Congress Hails New York City School Integration Plan, Pledges Support, Cooperation," press release, September 2, 1960, in AJHS/I-77/165/18.

178. de Forest, "1958 Harlem School Boycott," 39.

179. C. S. Stone Jr., letter to S. Polier, June 24, 1964, in AJHS/P-572/7/15.

180. K. B. Clark, *Dark Ghetto: Dilemma of Social Power* [1965] (Middleton, CT: Wesleyan University Press, 1989), 112–17.

181. S. Forman, *Blacks in the Jewish Mind: A Crisis of Liberalism* (New York: New York University Press, 1998), 144.

182. R. D. Kahlenberg, *Tough Liberal: Albert Shanker and the Battles over Schools, Unions, Race, and Democracy* (New York: Columbia University Press, 2007), 67–111.

183. E. J. Sundquist, *Strangers in the Land: Blacks, Jews, Post-Holocaust America* (Cambridge, MA: Harvard University Press, 2005), 344. See also R. E. Tomasson, "Shanker Is Given a 15-Day Sentence in School Strike," *New York Times*, February 4, 1969, 1.

184. C. L. Greenberg, *Troubling the Waters: Black-Jewish Relations in the American Century* (Princeton, NJ: Princeton University Press, 2006), 231.

185. L. Harris and B. E. Swanson, *Black-Jewish Relations in New York City* (New York: Praeger Publishers, 1970), 61–99.

186. A. J. Levine, *"Bad Old Days": The Myth of the 1950s* (New Brunswick, NJ: Transaction Publishers, 2008), 9.

187. I. Rosenwaike, *Population History of New York City* (Syracuse, NY: Syracuse University Press, 1972), 141.

188. R. Polenberg, *Class, Race, and Ethnicity in the United States since 1938* (New York: Viking Press, 1980), 150.

189. N. L. Edelstein, "Jewish Relationship with the Emerging Negro Community in the North," June 23, 1960, 1–11, in AJHS/I-77/45/1.

190. Sundquist, *Strangers in the Land*, 17–94.

191. Zeitz, *White Ethnic New York*, 153.

192. J. T. McGreevy, *Parish Boundaries: The Catholic Encounter with Race in the Twentieth-Century Urban North* (Chicago and London: University of Chicago Press, 1996), 103. See also G. H. Gamm, *Urban Exodus: Why the Jews Left Boston and the Catholics Stayed* (Cambridge, MA: Harvard University Press, 1999), 11–29.

193. M. Cuomo, *Forest Hills Diary: The Crisis of Low-Income Housing* (New York: Vintage Books, 1975), 48–51, 56–59.

194. Dollinger, *Quest for Inclusion*, 186.

195. E. J. Greenfield, "Symposium on Negro-Jewish Tensions," meeting minutes, 1966, 2, in AJHS/P-572/7/4.

196. H. Kaplow, "Jewish Federations, Their Agencies and the Integration Struggle," *Congress Bi-Weekly* 31, no. 13 (September 14, 1964), 3.

197. W. Maslow and R. Cohen, "School Segregation, Northern Style," *Public Affairs Pamphlet* 316 (August 1961): 1–20. See also N. Levine, letter to community relations councils and group relations agencies, June 8, 1961, in AJHS/I-77/45/8.

198. Over this time, CORE was tending toward a black nationalist and segregationist orientation, away from its pacifist, Christian, and integrationist roots. See A. Meier and E. Rudwick, *CORE: A Study in the Civil Rights Movement, 1942–1968* (Chicago: University of Illinois Press, 1975), 205–10.

199. R. Cohen, "Will Maslow Resigns from National Advisory Board of CORE," *News Release*, February 8, 1966, 1–2, in AJHS/I-77/175/73. See also R. Cohen, "Will Maslow Lodges Protest over David Susskind's TV Program 'Negroes and Anti-Semites,'" press release, October 19, 1966, in AJHS/I-77/177/33.

200. Svonkin, *Jews Against Prejudice*, 192.

201. P. S. Berger and J. B. Robison, "Preferential Treatment in the Selective Process," memorandum to members of executive committee, March 10, 1972, 2, in AJHS/I-77/24/3.

202. See, for example, S. L. Shneiderman, "Personal Reports on Soviet Jewry," press release, ca. 1967, 1–4, in TAM/103/34/7.

203. N. Podhoretz, "My Negro Problem—And Ours," *Commentary* (February 1963): 98–101; and J. W. Polier and S. Polier, "Fear Turned to Hatred," *Congress Bi-Weekly* 30, no. 3 (February 18, 1963): 5–6.

204. S. Polier, "The Jew and the Racial Crisis," draft article, July 15, 1964, 1–5, in AJHS/P-572/7/4.

205. O. Pen, interview with S. Polier, trans. from *Jewish Daily Forward*, January 10, 1965, in AJHS/P-572/7/9.

206. S. Polier, letter to L. Granger, January 25, 1957, in AJHS/P-572/5/5.

207. See E. Roosevelt, letter to J. W. Polier, April 14, 1954, in AJHS/P-527/R10F1.

208. J. W. Polier, "Open Letter to the 'Friends': A Critical Analysis of the Quakers' 'Study for Peace in the Middle East,'" *Congress Bi-Weekly* 37, no. 12 (December 4, 1970): 3–6. See also J. W. Polier, "The Malicious UN Resolution on Jerusalem," *Congress Bi-Weekly* 38, no. 10 (October 29, 1971): 4–5.

209. F. Lynn, "More in City are Turning to the Right," *New York Times*, January 15, 1974, 1.

210. L. H. Fuchs, "American Jews and the Presidential Vote," *American Political Science Review* 49 (1955): 393.

211. Forman, "Politics of Minority Consciousness."

212. Zeitz, *White Ethnic New York*, 195.

213. G. Wheatcroft, *The Controversy of Zion: Jewish Nationalism, the Jewish State, and the Unresolved Jewish Dilemma* (New York: Addison Wesley, 1996), 335.

214. J. W. Polier, "Obligations and Commitments," *Congress Bi-Weekly* 37, no. 8 (June 19, 1970): 4.

215. W. Allinsmith and A. Allinsmith, "Religious Affiliation and Politico-Economic Attitude: A Study of Eight Major US Religious Groups," *Public Opinion Quarterly* 12, no. 3 (Autumn 1948): 378.

216. Ibid., 384.

217. S. Goldstein, "Socioeconomic Differentials Among Religious Groups in the United States," *American Journal of Sociology* 74, no. 6 (May 1969): 612–31.

218. N. Glazer and D. P. Moynihan, *Beyond the Melting Pot: The Negroes, Puerto Ricans, Jews, Italians, and Irish of New York City* [1963], 2nd ed. (Cambridge, MA: MIT Press, 1970) 167.

219. Pekelis, "Full Equality in a Free Society," 218–19.

220. Quoted in Cohen, *Not Free to Desist*, 30–31. See also H. Schneiderman, ed., *The American Jewish Year Book* (Philadelphia: Jewish Publication Society of America, 1924), 26:72–73.

221. Urofsky, *Voice That Spoke for Justice*, 27.

222. L. D. Brandeis, "True Americanism" [1915], in *Brandeis on Zionism: A Collection of Addresses and Statements* (Union, NJ: Lawbook Exchange, 1999), 11.

223. L. D. Brandeis, "The Jewish Problem, How to Solve It" [1915], in *Brandeis on Zionism*, 29.

224. M. I. Urofsky, *Louis D. Brandeis: A Life* (New York: Pantheon Books, 2009), 410. See also J. Higham, *Strangers in the Land: Patterns of American Nativism, 1860–1925* (New Brunswick, NJ: Rutgers University Press, 1955), 408n10.

225. H. M. Kallen, *The Struggle for Jewish Unity: An Address by Horace Meyer Kallen before the Eleventh Annual Session of the American Jewish Congress* (New York: Ad Press, May 21, 1933) 8, 3, in AJHS/I-77/181/30. Similar views were expressed by Mordecai Kaplan, the founder of Reconstructionism. See M. M. Kaplan, *Judaism as a Civilization: Toward a Reconstruction of American-Jewish Life* [1934] (New York: Schocken Books, 1967).

226. Pekelis, "Full Equality in a Free Society," 221, 219.

227. W. Herberg, *Protestant, Catholic, Jew: An Essay in American Religious Sociology* (Garden City, NY: Doubleday, 1955), 40.

228. N. Podhoretz, *Making It* (New York: Random House, 1967), 3.

229. "Free Synagogue Guild Hears Rabbi Charge Bias Against Jews," *Flushing Evening News*, December 10, 1930, in AJHS/P-661/1/2.

230. Goldberg, "Economics Trends Among American Jews," 11–17; N. P. McGill, "Some Characteristics of Jewish Youth in New York City," *Jewish Social Survey Quarterly* 14, no. 2 (December 1937): 263.

231. Cohen, *Jews, Jobs, and Discrimination*, 20–23.

232. Diner, *Jews of the United States*, 236.

233. A. Wood, "I Sell My House: One Man's Experience with Suburban Segregation," *Commentary* (November 1958): 383–89.

234. R. H. Bayor, *Neighbors in Conflict: The Irish, Germans, Jews, and Italians in New York City, 1929–1941* (Baltimore, MD: Johns Hopkins University Press, 1978), 20; and H. Broun and G. Britt, *Christians Only: A Study in Prejudice* (New York: Vanguard Press, 1931), 260.

235. Moore, *At Home in America*, 43–45.

236. T. Parsons, "The Sociology of Modern Anti-Semitism" [1942], in *Talcott Parsons on National Socialism*, ed. U. Gerhardt (New York: Aldine de Gruyter, 1993), 143, 146, 139.

237. E. Litt, "Ethnic Status and Political Perspectives," *Midwest Journal of Political Science* 5, no. 3 (August 1961): 282, 280.

238. Cohen, *Not Free to Desist*, 333, 404.

239. American Jewish Congress, "Statement of the American Jewish Congress on the Treatment of Rabble Rousers," *CLSA Reports*, ca. 1946, in AJHS/I-77/29/5.

240. The founder of commercial advertising in the United States, Edward Bernays, was in fact a one-time representative of the American Jewish Committee. Frommer, "American Jewish Congress," 328; and E. L. Bernays, *Propaganda* [1928] (Brooklyn: Ig Publishing, 2005), 147–51.

241. D. S. Siegel and S. Siegel, *Radio and the Jews: The Untold Story of How Radio Influenced the Image of Jews* (New York: Book Hunter Press, 2007), 204–11.

242. Svonkin, *Jews Against Prejudice*, 64.

243. M. Jay, *The Dialectical Imagination: A History of the Frankfurt School and the Institute of Social Research, 1923–1950* (Berkeley: University of California Press, 1973, 1996), 170.

244. T. W. Adorno et al., *The Authoritarian Personality* (New York: Harper and Brothers, 1950), 973.

245. W. Maslow, "Prejudice, Discrimination, and the Law," *Annals of the American Academy of Political and Social Science* 275 (May 1951): 9.

246. W. G. Sumner, *Folkways: A Study of the Sociological Importance of Usages, Manners, Customs, Mores, and Morals* (Boston: Ginn, 1906), 95.

247. G. Myrdal, *An American Dilemma: The Negro Problem and Modern Democracy* [1944] (New Brunswick, NJ: Transaction Publishers, 2009), 2:1023.

248. Maslow, "Prejudice, Discrimination, and the Law," 17.

249. Maslow and Robison, "Civil Rights Legislation," 364.

250. L. Pfeffer, "Sectarianism in the Public Schools," November 11–12, 1946, in Ivers, *To Build a Wall*, 73.

251. C. Wittenstein, interview with G. Ivers, June 2, 1988, in Ivers, *To Build a Wall*, 134–35. See also R. Cohen, "Religious Practices in Public Schools Challenged by American Jewish Congress; Major Test Case May Reach Supreme Court," *CLSA News*, July 22, 1960, in AJHS/I-77/165/41.

252. The Second Generation's social and residential insularity was mocked famously in P. Roth, *Portnoy's Complaint* (London: Jonathan Cape, 1969).

253. G. Lenski, *The Religious Factor: A Sociological Study of Religion's Impact on Politics, Economics, and Family Life* (Garden City, NY: Doubleday, Anchor, 1961), 79.

254. Moore, *At Home in America*, 38.

255. W. Laidlaw, *Population of the City of New York, 1890–1930* (New York: Cities Census Committee, 1932), 275.

256. Moore, *At Home in America*, 30.

257. J. R. Kramer and S. Leventman, *Children of the Gilded Ghetto: Conflict Resolutions of Three Generations of American Jews* (New Haven, CT, and London: Yale University Press, 1961) 11.

258. I. Howe, "A Memoir of the Thirties," in *Steady Work: Essays in the Politics of Democratic Radicalism, 1953–1966* (New York: Harcourt, Brace, 1966), 353.

259. I. Kugler, "*One Eye on the Stars: A Life of a Democratic Socialist; Union Organizer of the Professoriate in America; Secular Humanist; Part of the Jewish People; Devoted to Yiddish Culture*," autobiographical typescript, ca. 1984, 216, in TAM/315/1/59–61.

260. P. I. Rose, *The Ghetto and Beyond: Essays on Jewish Life in America* (New York: Random House, 1969), 9.

261. M. Gold, *Jews Without Money* (New York: Carroll and Graf, 2004), 215.

262. B. Schulberg, *What Makes Sammy Run?* (New York: Vintage Books, 1990), 109. For the Canadian version, see M. Richler, *The Apprenticeship of Duddy Kravitz* [1959] (Toronto: Emblem Editions, 2001).

263. Cuddihy, *Ordeal of Civility*, 142–44.

264. W. Lippmann, "Public Opinion and the American Jew," *American Hebrew*, April 14, 1922, 575.

265. Cohen, *Administrative Report, July 1932 to May 1933*, 80–82.

266. Steinberg, *Academic Melting Pot*, 10–11. See also the personal account of a rather haphazard enrollment at Harvard by the left-wing Jewish journalist George Seldes, in *Witness to a Century: Encounters with the Noted, the Notorious, and the Three SOBs* (New York: Ballantine Books, 1987), 37–42.

267. T. Veblen, *The Higher Learning in America* [1936] (New York Cosimo, 2007), 88.

268. F. Rudolph, *The American College and University: A History* (New York: Knopf, 1962), 289.

269. S. E. Morison, *Three Centuries of Harvard* [1936] (Cambridge, MA: Harvard University Press, 2001) 417.

270. Moore, *At Home in America*, 180; J. Karabel, *The Chosen: The Hidden History of Admission and Exclusion at Harvard, Yale, and Princeton* (New York: Mariner Books, 2005), 98–99; and R. Steel, *Walter Lippmann and the American Century* (New York: Vintage, 1981), 194.

271. L. I. Newman, *A Jewish University in America?* (New York: Bloch Publishing Company, 1923), 19.

272. P. E. Gottfried, *Encounters: My Life with Nixon, Marcuse, and Other Friends and Teachers* (Wilmington, DE: ISI Books, 2009), 21.

273. The Yiddish-speaking Jewish immigrant Harry Wolfson was appointed to Harvard's faculty of arts as early as 1915, teaching in Jewish philosophy and literature. He "never took public stands" and "went out of his way to prevent any embarrassment for Harvard University" on Jewish matters. Wolfson was born in a small village in Russia in 1887, moving with his family to the United States in 1903. His salary was paid externally by the intermarried German Jewish manufacturer and Republican Lucius N. Littauer. See L. S. Feuer, "Recollections of Harry Austryn Wolfson," *American Jewish Archives* 28, no. 1 (April 1976): 33.

274. Newman, *Jewish University in America?*, 11.

275. Moore, *At Home in America*, 180.

276. J. Dorman, *Arguing the World: The New York Intellectuals in Their Own Words* (New York: Free Press, 2000), 50; and J. Heilbrunn, *They Knew They Were Right: The Rise of the Neocons* (New York: Doubleday, 2008), 34.

277. Karabel, *The Chosen*, 134.

278. D. A. Hollinger, *Science, Jews, and Secular Culture: Studies in Mid-Twentieth Century American Intellectual History* (Princeton, NJ: Princeton University Press, 1996), 17–41.

279. A. R. Heinze, *Jews and the American Soul: Human Nature in the Twentieth Century* (Princeton, NJ: Princeton University Press, 2004), 128, 222 *passim*.

280. Rothman and Lichter, *Roots of Radicalism*, 104.

281. Liebman, *Jews and the Left*, 364.

282. Steinberg, *Academic Melting Pot*, 21, 25.

283. A. H. Pekelis, "Private Governments and the Federal Constitution," in *Law and Social Action*, 102–3.

284. D. R. McCoy and R. T. Reutten, *Quest and Response: Minority Rights and the Truman Administration* (Lawrence: University Press of Kansas, 1973), 57. See also P. Roth, *The Facts: A Novelist's Autobiography* (London: Penguin, 1988), 51.

285. Pekelis, "Full Equality in a Free Society," 228.

286. Ibid.

287. Maslow, *Law and Race Relations*, 75, 77; emphasis added.

288. All quotes are from J. Gurock, "The 1913 New York Civil Rights Act," *AJS Review* 1 (1976): 93–120.

289. Bonfield, "The Origin and Development," 1045. Of the ultimately political considerations behind victory in *Brown*, see Elman, "Solicitor General's Office," 829–30, 837, 843.

290. R. A. Epstein, *Forbidden Grounds: The Case Against Employment Discrimination Laws* (Cambridge, MA: Harvard University Press, 1992), xii, 16, 92.

291. Ibid., 93.

292. Maslow, *Law and Race Relations*, 75.

293. P. W. Hogg, *Constitutional Law of Canada: 2010 Student Edition* (Toronto: Carswell, 2010), 21–3, 21–4, 34–1, 34–2, 55–12.

294. American Jewish Congress, "The KKK and State Action," *CLSA Reports*, 1946, in AJHS/ I-77/29/4; American Jewish Congress, "The Patterson Bill to Suppress Racial and Religious Hatred," *CLSA Reports*, September 3, 1946, in AJHS/I-77/29/4; and A. Cohen, "No Protection for Hate-Mongers," news release, 1949, 1–3, in AJHS/I-77/26/7.

295. "The term, 'civil rights bill,' means bill primarily designed to achieve intergroup equality." W. Maslow, "Statement of American Jewish Congress on Civil Rights Bills," July 27, 1955, 1n1, in AJHS/I-77/186/19.

296. The conduct of the Second Generation complicates the recent thesis of Samuel Moyn that human rights do not much predate the 1970s. Moyn defines human rights as categories transcending the nation-state and collective membership. The Second Generation's efforts to decouple bourgeois admission from bourgeois assimilation, however, pointed in the direction of just such a transcendence. Of course the American Jewish Congress and other Jewish groups generally but not always (as in their support for the League of Nations) operated in relation to the state as the locus of sovereignty and apparatus of government, but it is not clear what Moyn means by rights outside such a context, other than as normative assertions by subjective agents. S. Moyn, *The Last Utopia: Human Rights in History* (Cambridge, MA: Harvard University Press, 2010), 11–43.

297. W. Maslow, "The Uses of Law in the Struggle for Equality," August 1955, 306, in AJHS/ I-77/186/15; emphasis added.

298. L. Hartz, *The Liberal Tradition in America* (New York: Harcourt, Brace, 1955).

299. "I certainly proved it. . . . Running on the Socialist ticket I got 60,000 votes, and running on the slogan to 'End Poverty in California' I got 879,000." Quoted in L. A. Harris, *Upton Sinclair: American Rebel* (New York: Crowell, 1975), 351.

300. B. K. Johnpoll, *Pacifist's Progress: Norman Thomas and the Decline of American Socialism* (Chicago: Quadrangle Books, 1970), 175.

301. M. Dubofsky, "Success and Failure of Socialism in New York City, 1900–1918: A Case Study," *Labor History* 9, no. 3 (Autumn 1968): 374.

302. Youth Representative, "Report to the Committee on the YPSL National Plenum Held in Philadelphia, October 14th an 15th, 1939," 1939, 2, in TAM/R-7203–17/9/19. See also Liebman, *Jews and the Left*, 365–74.

303. M. E. Berger, "Behind the Headlines: Fifty Years After Integration Case, Jews Remember Their Crucial Role," *Jewish Telegraphic Agency*, May 11, 2004.

304. R. D. Parmet, *The Master of Seventh Avenue: David Dubinsky and the American Labor Movement* (New York: New York University Press, 2005), 130.

305. Moore, *At Home in America*, 220.

306. Bayor, *Neighbors in Conflict*, 41.

307. Zeitz, *White Ethnic New York*, 95.

308. Moore, *At Home in America*, 221–22, 224. See also W. Spinrad, "New York's Third Party Voter," *Public Opinion Quarterly* 21, no. 4 (Winter 1957–1958): 548–51.

309. C. Quigley, *Tragedy and Hope: A History of the World in Our Time* (New York: Macmillan, 1966), 1244.

310. Allswang, *New Deal and American Politics*, 29–65. See also A. Cohen, *Nothing to Fear: FDR's Inner Circle and the Hundred Days That Created Modern America* (New York: Penguin Press, 2009), 109–32; K. S. Johnson, *Reforming Jim Crow: Southern Politics and the State in the Age Before Brown* (Oxford: Oxford University Press, 2010), 66–90; W. B. Pendergast, *The Catholic Voter in American Politics: The Passing of the Democratic Monolith* (Washington, DC: Georgetown University Press, 1999), 113–14; and A. C. Sutton, *Wall Street and FDR* (New Rochelle, NY: Arlington House Publishers, 1975), 106–42.

311. W. Maslow, "Statement of the American Jewish Congress Presented to the President's Committee on Civil Rights," May 1, 1947, 1, in AJHS/I-77/26/4; emphasis added.

312. P. Gottfried, *Multiculturalism and the Politics of Guilt: Toward a Secular Theocracy* (Columbia and London: University of Missouri Press, 2002), 7.

313. D. Petegorsky, *On Combating Racism* (New York: American Jewish Congress, 1948), 4, in AJHS/I-77/185/8.

314. S. Polier, "Platforms," letter to colleagues, July 29, 1960, 2, in AJHS/I-77/23/1.

315. Svonkin, *Jews Against Prejudice*, 92.

316. Irons, *New Deal Lawyers*, 237.

317. "The New Deal Dispenses a New Brand of Justice to Labor and Industry," *Life* 3, no. 10 (September 6, 1937): 19–23.

318. These letters are found in AJHS/P-572/6/11.

319. S. M. Teles, *The Rise of the Conservative Legal Movement: The Battle for Control of the Law* (Princeton, NJ, and Oxford: Princeton University Press, 2008), 25.

320. Ibid., 45, 24–30.

321. Ibid., 7.

322. W. Maslow, "Statement of the American Jewish Congress Presented to the President's Committee on Civil Rights," May 1, 1947, 9, in AJHS/I-77/26/4.

323. R. Cohen, "Jews Told to Use Religion in Lives at CJA Conference on Jewish Values," September 2, 1960, 3, in AJHS/I-77/165/29.

324. J. Greenberg, *Crusaders in the Courts: How a Dedicated Band of Lawyers Fought for the Civil Rights Revolution* (New York: Basic Books, 1995), 52–53.

325. Kramer and Leventman, *Children of the Gilded Ghetto*, 103–4.

326. M. Sklare, *America's Jews* (New York: Random House, 1971), 120–21.

327. D. Bell, "A Parable of Alienation," *Jewish Frontier* 13, no. 11 (November 1946): 16–18.

328. J. Higham, *Send These to Me: Immigrants in Urban America* (Baltimore, MD: Johns Hopkins University Press, 1984), 155.

329. J. X. Cohen, *The Negro, the Jew, and the FEPC* (New York: American Jewish Congress, 1944) 11, 5–8, in AJHS/P-661/1/2. See also S. Polier, "Why Jews Must Fight for Minorities," November 4, 1949, 1–6, in AJHS/P-572/7/15.

330. R. Cohen, "American Jewish Congress Ends Convention Strengthened and Solidified," press release, June 3, 1960, in AJHS/I-77/165/30.

331. See, for example, B. Ginsberg, *The Fatal Embrace: Jews and the State* (Chicago: University of Chicago Press, 1993), 125–26.

332. Ivers, *To Build a Wall*, 78, 102, 112, 144, 184–85.

333. Quoted in Staub, *Torn at the Roots*, 84.

334. Dollinger, *Quest for Inclusion*, 4–5.

335. Ibid., 173, 184, 165.

336. See, for example, L. Pfeffer, "American Jewish Congress Official Chides Protestants on Church-State Separation," February 1, 1951, in AJHS/I-77/33/1.

337. Dollinger, *Quest for Inclusion*, 79, 130.

338. Glazer and Moynihan, *Beyond the Melting Pot*, 162.

339. Zeitz, *White Ethnic New York*, 11–19.

340. Forman, *Blacks in the Jewish Mind*, 60, 32.

341. Dollinger, *Quest for Inclusion*, 133.

342. E. P. Kaufmann, *The Rise and Fall of Anglo-America* (Cambridge, MA: Harvard University Press, 2004), 11–36.

343. Biale, Galchinsky, and Heschel, *Insider/Outsider*, 1–12.

344. See, for example, W. Maslow, "An Analysis of the Racist Origins of the National Origins Quota System of the Immigration Act of 1924," October 29, 1952, 1–28, in AJHS/I-77/186/1.

345. Svonkin, *Jews Against Prejudice*, 59–60.

346. C. S. Liebman, *The Ambivalent American Jew: Politics, Religion, and Family in American Jewish Life* (Philadelphia: Jewish Publication Society of America, 1973), 24–25.

347. Ibid., 24–25.

348. Zeitz, *White Ethnic New York*, 97.

349. Fuchs, "Americans Jews and the Presidential Vote," 394–95.

350. Both articles quoted and/or translated in "Daily Digest of Public Opinion on Jewish Matters," *Jewish Telegraphic Agency*, July 7, 1926.

351. N. Rotenstreich, "Emancipation and Its Aftermath," in *The Future of the Jewish Community in America*, ed. D. Sidorsky (New York: Basic Books, 1973), 56.

352. M. R. Konvitz, *Separation of Church and State: The First Freedom* (New York: American Jewish Congress, 1949), 44–60, in AJHS/I-77/23/4; and L. Pfeffer, "Statement of American Jewish Congress on Freedom of Religion and Separation of Church and State," October 1955, 1–15, in AJHS/P-572/4/1. For the American Jewish Congress's updates on sundry church-state incidents throughout the country, see AJHS/I-77/195–96.

353. W. Maslow and S. Polier, "Brief of American Jewish Congress as Amicus Curiae [in Feinberg Law case]," October 6, 1949, 1–16, in AJHS/I-77/23/4; and S. Polier, letter to J. P. Lash, March 26, 1947, in AJHS/P-572/1/1.

354. American Jewish Congress, "The Federal Group Libel Bill," *CLSA Reports*, February 1949, 1–10, in AJHS/I-77/26/7; and W. Maslow and B. Diamond, "Brief on Behalf of Petitioners," June 8, 1949, 1–33, in AJHS/I-77/23/4.

355. N. Z. Dershowitz, letter to governing council, June 1980, in AJHS/I-77/29/2.

356. W. Maslow, "Statement of the American Jewish Congress in Submitting Proposed Platform Planks to the National Political Parties," 1948, in AJHS/I-77/26/5.

357. See, for example, S. Welles, "A Jewish Commonwealth NOW," memorandum, May 19, 1947, in AJHS/I-77/185/6; and American Jewish Congress, "For Full Recognition of Israel: An Analysis of United States Diplomatic Practice in Granting De Jure Recognition to Newly-Established Countries," *CLSA Reports*, December 10, 1948, in AJHS/I-77/26/5.

358. C. I. Waxman, *American Aliya: Portrait of an Innovative Migration Movement* (Detroit, MI: Wayne State University Press, 1989), 94–96.

359. D. Petegorsky, "Record in Review" (report presented to Biennial National Convention, New York City, March 31–April 4, 1948), 14, in AJHS/I-77/9/1; emphasis in original.

360. American Jewish Congress, "Lights of Confusion," statement of New England region, June 1953, 1–2, in AJHS/I-77/89/38.

Chapter 3

1. J. Deer et al., eds., "Introduction," *Agenda* 7 (June–July 1981): 1, in TAM/183/13. NB: The *Agenda* newsletters, which were published several times per year during the 1980s, may all be found at the cited archival location.

2. C. Toll, ed., "Beginnings," *Agenda* 1 (Summer 1979): 1.

3. Member of NJA, e-mail to author, August 28, 2011.

4. Member of NJA, e-mail to author, August 28, 2011.

5. An exception to the dearth of research is an undergraduate thesis by E. Nepon, "New Jewish Agenda: The History of an Organization, 1980–1992" (BA thesis, Goddard College, 2006).

6. As the collection has not yet been processed by an archivist, citations include only box numbers. There are no reliable folder numbers. The exact location of any cited material may change in the future.

7. Toll, "Beginnings."

8. W. Novak, "The Breira Story," *Genesis* 2 (March–April 1977): 6.

9. A. J. Wolf, *Unfinished Rabbi: Selected Writings of Arnold Jacob Wolf*, ed. J. S. Wolf (Chicago: Dee, 1998), 245.

10. J. Wertheimer, "Critics of Israel," in *Envisioning Israel: The Changing Ideals and Images of North American Jews*, ed. A. Gal (Detroit, MI: Wayne State University Press, 1996), 405.

11. M. Brettschneider, *Cornerstones of Peace: Jewish Identity Politics and Democratic Theory* (New Brunswick, NJ: Rutgers University Press, 1996), 41. For contemporary criticism of Breira, see R. J. Isaac, "Breira: Council for Judaism," pamphlet, 1977, 1–30, in AJHS/I-250/8. Several years later *Tikkun* magazine came together under Michael Lerner for many of the same reasons and with many of the same goals as NJA. Nonetheless, "there certainly was no formal relationship" between NJA and Lerner. According to Serotta, "*Tikkun*'s political thrust was very similar to NJA but it was aiming to appeal to intellectuals rather than the 'grassroots.'" Member of NJA, e-mail to author, May 6, 2012.

12. Member of NJA, e-mail to author, August 28, 2011.

13. C. Toll, ed., "Statement of Purpose," *Agenda* 1 (Summer 1979): 1.

14. Deer et al., "Introduction."

15. G. Serotta, "Agenda's Dilemma," *Agenda* 3 (April–May 1980): 3.

16. S. Lerner and D. Soyer, letters to the editor, *Agenda* 2 (Winter 1980): 1.

17. A. Layter, "The Third World," *Agenda* 4 (June–July 1980): 2, 4.

18. V. Shemtov, letter to the editor, *Agenda* 6 (October–November 1980): 1.

19. Forman, "Politics of Minority Consciousness," 153.

20. A. Clymer, "Displeasure with Carter Turned Many to Reagan," *New York Times*, November 9, 1980, 28.

21. S. M. Lipset and E. Raab, "The American Jews, the 1984 Elections, and Beyond," in *The New Jewish Politics*, ed. D. J. Elazar (Lanham, MD: University Press of America, 1988), 33.

22. S. M. Lipset and E. Raab, *Jews and the New American Scene* (Cambridge, MA: Harvard University Press, 1995), 165.

23. This was also the year in which many prominent Jewish neoconservative intellectuals left the Democratic Party and went over to the Republicans. Balint, *Running Commentary*, 131.

24. E. Herst, "Agenda's Priorities and Positions," *Agenda* 7 (June–July 1981): 1. Cf. "Delegates to Form Organization as an Alternative to Jewish Group," *New York Times*, December 29, 1980, D8.

25. Interim Council, "Introduction," *Agenda* 7 (June–July 1981): 1. Cf. R. Saidel-Wolk, "New Jewish Group Hopes to Create Progressive-Minded National Membership Organization," *Jewish Telegraphic Agency*, December 25, 1980.

26. J. Bender, ed., "Conference for a New Jewish Agenda for the 1980's," conference catalog, 24–December 28, 1980, 1–40, in TAM/183/3

27. Interim Council, "Questions Frequently Asked About Agenda," *Agenda* 7 (June–July 1981): 2.

28. Member of NJA, e-mail to author, September 5, 2011.

29. G. Serotta, "Agenda's Structure and Ideology," *Agenda* 7 (June–July 1981): 3.

30. Staub, *Torn at the Roots*, 241–79.

31. D. D. Moore, "Jewish Migration to the Sunbelt," in *Shades of the Sunbelt: Essays on Ethnicity, Race, and the Urban South*, ed. R. M. Miller and G. E. Pozzetta (New York: Greenwood Press, 1988), 41.

32. I. M. Sheskin, "Jewish Metropolitan Homelands," *Journal of Cultural Geography* 13, no. 2 (1993): 123–28.

33. NJA, "What's New About New Jewish Agenda," memorandum, early 1981, 1–2, in TAM/183/1.

34. J. McMillian, "You Didn't Have to Be There: Revisiting the New Left Consensus," in *The New Left Revisited*, ed. J. McMillian and P. Buhle (Philadelphia: Temple University Press, 2003), 5.

35. M. Rudd, "Why Were There So Many Jews in SDS? (Or, The Ordeal of Civility)," speech presented to New Mexico Jewish Historical Society, November 2005, http://www.markrudd.com/?about -mark-rudd/why-were-there-so-many-jews-in-sds-or-the-ordeal-of-civility.html.

36. S. R. Lichter and S. Rothman, "Jews on the Left: The Student Movement Reconsidered," *Polity* 14, no. 2 (Winter 1981): 351–52.

37. NJA, "Conference Unity Statement," *Agenda* 7 (June–July 1981): 3.

38. Deer et al., "Introduction," 2.

39. NJA, "Conference Unity Statement."

40. D. Orenstein, "Tisha B'Av—Nagasaki Day," *Agenda* 8 (Autumn 1981): 1.

41. NJA, "Agenda Chapter Update," *Agenda* 9 (Autumn 1981): 3.

42. D. Soyer, "Agenda 'Greets' Reagan on Visit to New York," *Agenda* 10 (Summer 1982): 1, 5; and R. Bernards, "Jewish and Christian Leaders Protest Reagan Award," press release, March 19, 1982, 1–2, in TAM/183/29.

43. D. Soyer, "Argentinian Jewry," *Agenda* 9 (Spring 1982): 1–2.

44. A. LoPresti, "What Do Agenda Members Think?," *Agenda* 8 (Autumn 1981): 6.

45. See, for example, NJA Washington, "Statement Delivered to the Embassy of Israel and the Palestine Liberation Organization," press release, June 8, 1982, 1, in TAM/183/8; NJA, "Jewish Group Urges Israeli Withdrawal from Lebanon," press release, June 11, 1982, 1–2, in TAM/183/8; and NJA Bay Area, "A Jewish Appeal to End Israel's Invasion of Lebanon," *San Francisco Bay Guardian*, June 16, 1982, 9, in TAM/183/8.

46. J. Bloch, "Agenda Protests Invasions of Lebanon—Calls for Israeli-Palestinian Co-Existence," *Agenda* 10 (Summer 1982): 1.

47. See, for example, the score of papers on the Lebanon crisis that were compiled by NJA in its "Discussion Bulletin" of June 1982, in TAM/183/40.

48. J. Bender, statement for Israeli mission to the United Nations, June 18, 1982, in TAM/183/24.

49. M. Reese et al., "Lebanon Splits US Jews," *Newsweek*, July 12, 1982, 32, in TAM/183/8.

50. P. L. Montgomery, "Discord Among US Jews Over Israel Seems to Grow," *New York Times*, July 15, 1982, A16.

51. P. L. Montgomery, "'We Need the Cash,' Begin Says at Bonds Lunch," *New York Times*, June 19, 1982, 7.

52. J. Bloch, "Agenda Protests Invasions of Lebanon," 2. See also S. Koenig, memorandum, June 28, 1982, in TAM/183/8.

53. NJA, "This Is Not the Way!," *New York Times*, June 30, 1982, B4; and NJA, "This Is Not the Way!," *The Jewish Post and Opinion*, July 2, 1982, both in TAM/183/8.

54. D. Goldman, "Agenda's Work for Middle East Peace," *Agenda* 11 (Winter 1983): 6.

55. H. Goldstein, "Case Statement for New Jewish Agenda," survey of fund raising, Fall 1982, 4, 15, in TAM/183/15.

56. R. Bernards, B. Cohen, and J. Dekro, letter to postal inspector, June 11, 1982, in TAM/183/8; and R. Bernards and J. Dekro, "New Jewish Agenda Exposes Fraudulent Letters," press release, July 6, 1982, 1–2, in TAM/183/8.

57. NJA, "Three Rabbis Excommunicate New Jewish Agenda Members," *Agenda* 11 (Winter 1983), 7. See also "Excommunication of Jews Challenged by Rabbis' Group," *New York Times*, November 26, 1982, A21.

58. M. Himmelfarb and D. Singer, eds., *American Jewish Year Book* (Philadelphia: American Jewish Committee, 1986), 86:370.

59. NJA, "National Platform—Adopted November 28, 1982," *Agenda* 13 (Summer 1983): 6, 3.

60. J. Dekro and A. Rose, "New Jewish Agenda Solicitor Training Workshop," memorandum, ca. 1985, 1–13, in TAM/183/12; and member of NJA, e-mail to author, September 21, 2011. NJA's many applications for institutional grants may be found in TAM/183/11.

61. S. T. Rosenthal, *Irreconcilable Differences? The Waning of the American Jewish Love Affair with Israel* (Hanover, PA: University Press of New England, 2001), 36.

62. W. B. Quandt, *Peace Process: American Diplomacy and the Arab-Israeli Conflict since 1967* (Berkeley: University of California Press, 2001), 205–42.

63. E. Noy, ed., *Statistical Abstract of Israel* (Jerusalem: State of Israel, 2006), 57:97.

64. G. Fellman, "Campaign for a Freeze on Settlements," *Agenda* 12 (Spring 1983): 1–2.

65. C. Balka, "NJA Raises West Bank Issue with Federations," *Agenda* 14 (Winter 1984): 1.

66. NJA, "Call for a West Bank Settlement Freeze," *Agenda* 12 (Spring 1983): 1.

67. NJA, "New Jewish Agenda Middle East Program," internal memorandum, 1984, 1–2, in TAM/183/24.

68. C. Balka and R. Bernards, "Joint Israeli-Palestinian Dialogue Touring the US," press release, March 20, 1984, 1–3, in TAM/183/15.

69. B. Chakofsky, "Historic Dialogue: Israeli and Palestinian," *Agenda* 15 (Summer 1984): 1, 3.

70. NJA, "Proposal from Kadima/NJA for Mideast Program/Strategy," memorandum, September 1984, 1–31, in TAM/183/35; D. Yermiya, letter to R. Bernards, November 26, 1984, 1–2, in TAM/183/15; and D. Yermiya and M. Da'wiri, "The Committee Against Racism and for Co-Existence in Israel," memorandum, 1984, 1–2, in TAM/183/15.

71. D. Shevin, "Dov Yermiya—Fighting for Israel's Soul," *Agenda* 17 (Summer 1985): 4.

72. NJA, "Nairobi Conference of Women," *Agenda* 17 (Summer 1985): 7.

73. N. Miller, "Israeli and Jewish Women Hope to Avert Confrontations at NGO Forum," *Jewish Telegraphic Agency*, July 12, 1985, http://www.jta.org/1985/07/12/archive/special-to-the-jta-israeli-and-jewish-women-hope-to-avert-confrontations-at-ngo-forum.

74. C. Balka, "NJA in Nairobi: Women Are Talking," *Agenda* 18 (Autumn 1985): 1, 3.

75. M. Goldman, "Assessment of the Nairobi Conference," *Jewish Telegraphic Agency*, August 8, 1985, http://www.jta.org/1985/08/05/archive/assessment-of-the-nairobi-conference-a-victory-for-women-worldwide.

76. C. Balka and R. Bernards, "New Jewish Agenda's Role at the UN Decade for Women Conference," final report, February 1986, 4–5, in TAM/183/17.

77. Ibid., 1.

78. J. Statman, "The Jewish Human Rights Delegation to Nicaragua," *Agenda* 16 (Winter 1985): 1.

79. K. Freeman, "Members of Mission to Nicaragua Differ over That Government's Policy Toward Its Jewish Community," *Jewish Telegraphic Agency*, September 11, 1984, http://www.jta.org/1984/09/11/archive/members-of-mission-to-nicaragua-differ-over-that-governments-policy-toward-its-jewish-community.

80. Statman, "Jewish Human Rights Delegation to Nicaragua," 6. See also "Jewish Group Voices Support for Nicaragua," *New York Times*, August 18, 1984, 4.

81. M. T. Meyer et al., Report of the Jewish Human Rights Delegation to Nicaragua, original copy, September 6, 1984, 9, 11, in TAM/183/15. See also M. T. Meyer, "American Jews Find No Anti-Semitism in Nicaragua," press release, August 15, 1984, 1, in TAM/183/29.

82. Statman, "Jewish Human Rights Delegation to Nicaragua," 6.

83. "Rabbi Disputes Reagan Point About the Jews in Nicaragua," *New York Times*, March 19, 1986, A4.

84. On the relationship between *Commentary* magazine and the American Jewish Committee, see Abrams, *Commentary Magazine 1945–59*, 44–48.

85. M. Muravchik, S. Alberts, and A. Korenstein, "Sandinista Anti-Semitism and Its Apologists," *Commentary* (September 1986): 25–29.

86. C. J. Aronson, letter to the editor, *Commentary* (January 1987). See also P. Tick, "A Sad Comment on *Commentary*," *Agenda* 21 (Winter 1987): 1, 5, 7.

87. NJA, "Agenda to Aid Central Americans," *Agenda* 18 (Autumn 1985): 4. See also E. Kaufman, "Israel and Central America: Arms Sales and Their Significance," article, February 1989, 29–33, in TAM/183/39.

88. P. Tick, "American Jewish Brigade Answers Nicaragua's Call," press release, October 17, 1985, 1, in TAM/183/15.

89. C. Smith, *Resisting Reagan: The US Central American Peace Movement* (Chicago: University of Chicago Press, 1996), 3–32.

90. H. Cunningham, *God and Caesar at the Rio Grande: Sanctuary and the Politics of Religion* (Minneapolis: University of Minnesota Press, 1995), 65.

91. D. Coyne, "Agenda Promotes Sanctuary Work—Rabbis on Speaking Tour," *Agenda* 19 (Spring 1986): 1. See also Smith, *Resisting Reagan*, 125.

92. NJA, "Sanctuary," press release, spring 1985, 1, in TAM/183/15.

93. R. Bernards, letter to E. Cohen, December 1, 1983, in TAM/183/29; NJA, "The Shalom Seders: Three Original Haggadahs, Compiled by New Jewish Agenda," advertisement, 1983, in TAM/183/29.

94. Coyne, "Agenda Promotes Sanctuary Work," 3.

95. Smith, *Resisting Reagan*, 185.

96. R. Medoff, *Jewish Americans and Political Participation* (Santa Barbara, CA: ABC-CLIO, 2002), 100–101.

97. A. M. Rosenthal, "Jews Must Not Break Bones," *New York Times*, January 26, 1988, A25.

98. N. Glazer, "American Jews and Israel—A Symposium," *Commentary* (February 1988), https://www.commentarymagazine.com/articles/american-jews-and-israel-a-symposium/.

99. Rosenthal, *Irreconcilable Differences?*, 113, 93–115. See also E. Goldstein, "New Jewish Agenda Supports US Direct Talks with PLO," press release, December 16, 1988, 1–2, in TAM/183/17.

100. K. Karabell, "Joining JCRCs," *Agenda* 23 (Winter 1987): 6.

101. E. Goldstein and D. Hurwitz, "No Status Quo Ante," *Agenda* 24 (Spring 1988): 1; and E. Goldstein and D. Hurwitz, "National Jewish Group Urges Positive Response to Palestinians," press release, November 18, 1988, 1, in TAM/183/22.

102. E. Goldstein, "Motivation: New Israel/New Palestine," memorandum, ca. 1990, 2, in TAM/183/40.

103. A. G. Jaffe, "Local Work Promotes Middle East Peace," *Agenda* 24 (Spring 1988): 3.

104. NJA, "Local News," *Agenda in Brief* 1 (August 1988); 1, in TAM/183/13.

105. See, for example, S. Resnick, letter to D. Hurwitz, February 16, 1984, 1–2, in TAM/183/24; D. Steinmetz, "Ann Arbor's Mideast Initiative," *Agenda* 15 (Summer 1984): 3.

106. A. F. K. Organski, *The $36 Billion Bargain: Strategy and Politics in US Assistance to Israel* (New York: Columbia University Press, 1990), 133–52.

107. G. Serotta, "Memorandum on United States Aid to Israel as New Jewish Agenda Issue for Discussion and Action," memorandum, ca. 1987, 1, in TAM/183/17; emphasis in original.

108. E. Goldstein et al., "Internal Discussion Bulletin: US Foreign Policy and Aid to Israel," memorandum, February 1989, 12, in TAM/183/17.

109. Ibid., 16.

110. Member of NJA, e-mail to author, October 14, 2011.

111. Ibid.

112. D. Coyne, "Resignation from Staff," memorandum, April 7, 1988, 1–2, in TAM/183/18.

113. Nepon, "New Jewish Agenda." For scores of funding applications, see TAM/183/11.

114. R. Hurwitz and I. Klepfisz, "New Jewish Agenda Calls for an Immediate Ceasefire in Gulf War," press release, January 21, 1991, 1–2, in TAM/183/22; and J. Milner and D. Spieglman, "Carrying It On: A Report from the New Jewish Agenda Conference on Organizing Against Racism and Anti-Semitism," *Bridges* 3, no. 1 (Spring–Summer 1992): 138–47.

115. A. M. Fisher, "Realignment of the Jewish Vote?," *Political Science Quarterly* 94, no. 1 (Spring 1979): 97–101.

116. D. J. Elazar, *Community and Polity: The Organizational Dynamics of American Jewry* (Philadelphia: The Jewish Publication Society, 1995), 109.

117. Medoff, *Jewish Americans and Political Participation*, 101.

118. Diner, *Jews of the United States*, 327.

119. E. D. Bloch, "One Voice Less for the Jewish Left: New Jewish Agenda, 1981–1993," undated, https://newjewishagenda.files.wordpress.com/2012/01/ethan-bloch.pdf, in Nepon, "New Jewish Agenda"; emphasis added.

120. Staub, *Torn at the Roots*, 6.

121. E. Ginzburg, *Agenda for American Jews* (New York: King's Crown Press, 1950), 80.

122. E. L. Fackenheim, "The Dilemma of Liberal Judaism," *Commentary* (October 1960): 301.

123. G. Lawson, "The Rise and Rise of the Administrative State," *Harvard Law Review* 107, no. 6 (April 1995): 1231–54.

124. R. D. Putnam, *Bowling Alone: The Collapse and Revival of American Community* (New York: Simon and Schuster, 2000), and "*E Pluribus Unum*: Diversity and Community in the Twenty-First Century," *Scandinavian Political Studies* 30, no. 2 (2007): 137–74.

125. Kaufmann, *Rise and Fall of Anglo-America*, 2.

126. C. Lasch, *The Culture of Narcissism: American Life in an Age of Diminishing Expectations* (New York: W. W. Norton, 1979).

127. A. M. Schlesinger Jr., *The Disuniting of America: Reflections on a Multicultural Society* (New York: W. W. Norton, 1998).

128. L. Kochan, *The Jewish Renaissance and Some of Its Discontents* (Manchester, UK: Manchester University Press, 1992), 25–27.

129. Sowell, *Ethnic America*, 98.

130. P. Burstein, "Jewish Educational and Economic Success in the United States: A Search for Explanations," *Sociological Perspectives* 50, no. 2 (2007): 209–14.

131. Lipset and Raab, *Jews and the New American Scene*, 107.

132. Members of NJA, e-mails to author, September 21, 2011, and October 14, 2011.

133. Kramer and Leventman, *Children of the Gilded Ghetto*, 136.

134. S. M. Cohen, *American Assimilation or Jewish Revival?* (Bloomington: Indiana University Press, 1988), 25–42.

135. H. J. Gans, "Symbolic Ethnicity: The Future of Ethnic Groups and Cultures in America," *Ethnic and Racial Studies* 2, no. 1 (January 1979): 7.

136. Liebman and Cohen, *Two Worlds of Judaism*, 19, 53, 55.

137. Cohen, *American Assimilation or Jewish Revival?*, 25–42, 88.

138. C. Goldscheider, *Jewish Continuity and Change: Emerging Patterns in America* (Bloomington: Indiana University Press, 1986), 184.

139. M. Himmelfarb, "Is American Jewry in Crisis?," *Commentary* (March 1969): 34.

140. M. Himmelfarb, "Another Look at the Jewish Vote," *Commentary* (December 1985): 40.

141. S. M. Cohen and C. S. Liebman, "American Jewish Liberalism: Unraveling the Strands," *The Public Opinion Quarterly* 61, no. 3 (Autumn 1997): 419–20.

142. Wald, "Toward a Structural Explanation of Jewish-Catholic Differences in the United States," 111–31.

143. For communal debates on this issue, see Staub, *Torn at the Roots*, 146–52 *passim*.

144. On general American Jewish ritual nonobservance in this period, see Liebman and Cohen, *Two Worlds of Judaism*, 123–28. See also E. I. Wilder, "Socioeconomic Attainment and Expressions of Jewish Identification, 1970 and 1990," *Journal for the Scientific Study of Religion* 35, no. 2 (June 1996): 109–27.

145. Liebman and Cohen, *Two Worlds of Judaism*, 96–109.

146. B. A. Phillips, "Catholic (and Protestant) Israel: The Permutations of Denominational Differences and Identities in Mixed Families," in *Jews, Catholics, and the Burden of History*, ed. Lederhendler, 152.

147. M. Masch, "A Progressive Jewish View," *Agenda* 2 (Winter 1980): 1, 5.

148. E. Willis, letter to the editor, *Agenda* 7 (June–July 1981): 4.

149. NJA, "Statement of Purpose," *Agenda* 13 (November 1982): 1.

150. D. Coyne, "Letter of Self-Introduction from the 'New' Associate Director," ca. 1985, 1–2, in TAM/183/12.

151. D. Coyne, "Welcoming Our Own," *Agenda* 20 (Fall 1986): 1.

152. Cohen, *Dimensions of American Jewish Liberalism*, 34, 1–60.

153. J. Lester, "The Simple Truth About Blacks and Jews," *Reform Judaism* (Summer 1989), in TAM/183/40. Cf. NJA, "The Search for Unity Today: Racism and Anti-Semitism in America," memorandum, ca. 1988, in TAM/183/11.

154. J. S. Woocher, *Sacred Survival: The Civil Religion of American Jews* (Bloomington: Indiana University Press, 1986), 76–80.

155. M. I. Urofsky, *We Are One! American Jewry and Israel* (Garden City, NY: Anchor Press, 1978), 359, 360–61.

156. Ibid., 350, 356.

157. On this counter-motif within the American Jewish imagination, see P. Breines, *Tough Jews: Political Fantasies and the Moral Dilemma of American Jewry* (New York: Basic Books, 1990).

158. Novick, *Holocaust in American Life*, 155, 156.

159. Ibid., 191, 190.

160. R. G. Weisbrod and A. Stein, *Bittersweet Encounter: The Afro-American and the American Jew* (Westport, CT: Negro University Press, 1970), 85–110.

161. Rosenthal, *Irreconcilable Differences?*, xv.

162. See, for example, M. Rudd, *Underground: My Life with SDS and the Weathermen* (New York: William Morrow, 2009), 8; S. Krim, "Ask for a White Cadillac," *Views of a Nearsighted Cannoneer* (London: Alan Ross, 1969), 57, 68; K. Kenniston, *Young Radicals: Notes on Committed Youth* (New York: Harcourt, Brace and World, 1968), 85; and Liebman, *Jews and the Left*, 553.

163. Through the 1980s, prominent neoconservative Jewish intellectuals, many of whom had radical backgrounds, were viewed by members of the isolationist, anti–New Deal Old Right as simply a schism within the Left. M. Friedman, *The Neoconservative Revolution: Jewish Intellectuals and the Shaping of Public Policy* (Cambridge, UK: Cambridge University Press, 2005), 134. See also Gottfried, *Encounters*, 38–40. Given neoconservatives' avowed preference for F. D. Roosevelt over "[s]uch Republican and conservative worthies as Calvin Coolidge, Herbert Hoover, Dwight Eisenhower, and Barry Goldwater," this cavil would seem not baseless. I. Kristol, "The Neoconservative Persuasion: What It Was, and What It Is," *Neoconservatism*, ed. I. Seltzer (London: Atlantic Books, 2004), 34. Early neoconservatives were concerned about and critical of Soviet antisemitism, black radicalism, affirmative action, and left-wing anti-Zionism, yet "had more in common with their liberal Jewish adversaries than with genuine conservatives" on these and other issues. S. E. Shapiro, "Right Turn? Jews and the American Conservative Movement," in *Jews in American Politics*, ed. L. S. Maisel (Lanham, MD: Rowman and Littlefield, 2004), 200.

164. Staub, *Torn at the Roots*, 17.

165. For countless examples of such exchanges, see ibid., 17 *passim*.

166. Liebman, *Jews and the Left*, 561, 574.

167. Rudd, *Underground*, 71–72.

168. Ibid., 23–26.

169. Member of NJA, e-mail to author, October 17, 2011.

170. Rosenblum, letter to the editor, *Agenda* 14 (Winter 1984): 4.

171. B. Chakofsky, "Introduction of Mr. Abdullah Abdullah," speech, November 23, 1985, 1–2, in TAM/183/24.

172. B. Chakofsky, letter to A. Abdullah, February 6, 1986, 1–2, in TAM/183/24.

173. N. Podhoretz, "J'Accuse," *Commentary* (September 1982): 21, 29.

174. Rosenthal, *Irreconcilable Differences?*, 71.

175. NJA, "Statement on Israel's Invasion of Lebanon," June 18, 1982, 1, in TAM/183/8; emphasis added.

176. R. Riechman et al., "A Jewish Plea for the Repair of Lebanon and Israel," June 30, 1982, 1, in TAM/183/24.

177. NJA, "Seek Peace and Pursue It," July 1982, 1, in TAM/183/8; emphasis added.

178. Member of NJA, e-mail to author, August 28, 2011.

179. See, for example, A. Shatz, ed., *Prophets Outcast: A Century of Dissident Jewish Writing about Zionism and Israel* (New York: Nation Books, 2004).

180. A. Waskow, introduction to *The Shalom Seders: Three Haggadahs Compiled by New Jewish Agenda* (New York: Adama Books, 1984), 8. For criticism of this document, see R. Alter, "Revolutionism and the Jews: 2, Appropriating the Religious Tradition," *Commentary* (February 1971): 47–54.

181. A. Waskow, "The Rainbow Seder," in *Shalom Seders*, 33. For the original draft, see A. Waskow, "The Shalom Seder," 1983, 1–44, in TAM/183/29.

182. Waskow, introduction, 10, 9.

183. D. Bartnoff et al., "Seder of the Children of Abraham," *in Shalom Seders*, 45. For the archival copy, see TAM/183/29.

184. Ibid., 56.

185. R. A. Seltzer, "The New Jewish Agenda: Dissent or Disloyalty—Fact Sheet," memorandum, ca. 1989, 2, 11, in TAM/183/11.

186. Member of NJA, e-mail to author, August 28, 2011.

187. Rosenthal, *Irreconcilable Differences?*, 156–69.

188. Cohen, "Did American Jews Really Grow More Distant from Israel, 1983–1993?—A Reconsideration," in *Envisioning Israel*, ed. A. Gal, 371.

189. J. D. Sarna, "Why Are American Jews Abandoning Israel?," *Haaretz*, October 5, 2009.

190. P. Beinart, "The Failure of the American Jewish Establishment," *New York Review of Books*, May 12, 2010, http://www.nybooks.com/articles/2010/06/10/failure-american-jewish-establishment/.

191. N. Novik, *The United States and Israel: Domestic Determinants of a Changing US Commitment* (Boulder, CO, and London: Westview Press and Tel Aviv University, 1986), 11–37.

192. J. J. Goldberg, *Jewish Power: Inside the American Jewish Establishment* (New York: Basic Books, 1996), 266.

193. Lipset and Raab, *Jews and the New American Scene*, 138, 144, 160.

194. Member of NJA, e-mail to author, January 2, 2012.

195. Podhoretz, *Why Are Jews Liberals?*, 282.

Conclusion

1. S. M. Cohen, S. Abrams, and J. Veinstein, *American Jews and the 2008 Presidential Elections: As Democrat and Liberal as Ever?* (New York: New York University, Wagner and Berman Jewish Policy Archive, 2008), 1–32.

2. Podhoretz, *Why Are Jews Liberals?*, 257, 255.

3. Ibid., 294.

4. Ibid., 283, 289, 295.

5. D. Wolpe, "*Why Are Jews Liberals?*—A Commentary Symposium," *Commentary* (September 2009): 44.

6. M. Medved, "*Why Are Jews Liberals?*—A Commentary Symposium," *Commentary* (September 2009): 47.

7. S. Samuels, "Assimilation and Its Discontents," *New York Magazine*, September 28, 2008, http://nymag.com/anniversary/40th/50717/.

8. See, for example, A. M. Dershowitz, *The Vanishing American Jew: In Search of Jewish Identity for the Next Century* (New York: Simon and Schuster, 1998).

9. T. W. Smith, *Jewish Distinctiveness in America: A Statistical Report* (New York: American Jewish Committee, 2005), 52.

10. Ibid., 53.

11. Ibid., 59.

12. Ibid., viii.

13. S. M. Cohen, *A Tale of Two Jewries: The "Inconvenient Truth" for American Jews* (New York: Jewish Life Network/Steinhardt Foundation, 2006), 9. See also A. Pomson, "Jewish Day-School Growth in Toronto: Freeing Policy and Research from the Constraints of Conventional Sociological Wisdom," *Canadian Journal of Education* 27, no. 4 (2002): 379–98.

14. J. D. Sarna, *"Why Are Jews Liberals?*—A Commentary Symposium," *Commentary* (September 2009): 46.

Bibliography

Archival Holdings

Archival documents are cited within the text as follows: Archive name/collection number/box number/folder number (if applicable)

Tamiment Library and Robert F. Wagner Labor Archives (TAM)
New York University, New York City, United States
    Accessed collections:

037	Baruch Charney Vladeck Papers	
050	J. B. S. (Jacob Benjamin Salutsky) Hardman Papers	
062	Alex Bittelman: Things I Have Learned Typescript	
062.1	Alex Bittelman Papers	
079	Israel and Sadie Amter Autobiographical Typescript	
103	Max Schachtman Papers (microfilm R-7203)	
183	New Jewish Agenda Records (unprocessed)	
249	Herzin Bergin Typescript	
315	Israel Kugler Papers	

Abraham Lincoln Brigade Archives (ALBA)
New York University, New York City, United States
    Accessed collections:

194	Benjamin Leider Papers

American Jewish Historical Society Archives (AJHS)
Center for Jewish History, New York City, United States
    Accessed collections:

I-169	Coordinating Committee of Jewish Organizations

Dealing with Employment Discrimination in War Industries Records

I-250	Breira Records
I-77	American Jewish Congress Records
P-527	Justine Wise Polier Papers
P-572	Shad Polier Papers
P-661	Jacob Xenab Cohen Papers

American Jewish Archives (AJA)
Jacob Rader Marcus Center, Cincinnati, United States
    Accessed collections:

361	World Jewish Congress Records
	Series C. Institute of Jewish Affairs

Thomas Fisher Rare Book Library (TFRB)
University of Toronto, Toronto, Canada
    Accessed collections:

0182	Robert S. Kenny Collection

Periodicals

New York Times
Jewish Telegraphic Agency
Time

Archival Sources

American Jewish Congress. *The American Jewish Congress: What It Is and What It Does.* New York: American Jewish Congress, 1938. AJHS/I-77/183/7.

———. "Analysis of CLSA Fair Educational Practices Bill for New Jersey." *CLSA Reports*, September 19, 1946. AJHS/I-77/29/4.

———. "Analysis of Stuyvesant Town Case." *CLSA Reports*, 1950. AJHS/I-77/30/1.

———. "Attacks on NAACP." Resolution of the administrative committee, October 21, 1956. AJHS/P-572/4/6.

———. "Briefs Filed by the American Jewish Congress, 1945–1955." August 1955. AJHS/I-77/151/4.

———. Budget of CLSA. June 1946. AHJS/I-77/81/16.

———. "The Civil Rights Act of 1964." *CLSA Reports*, October 1, 1964. AJHS/I-77/32/5.

———. "Consolidated Report of Major Activities: June 1, 1946 through August 31, 1946." 1946. AJHS/I-77/29/4.

———. "The Federal Group Libel Bill." *CLSA Reports,* February 1949. AJHS/I-77/26/7.

———. "For Full Recognition of Israel: An Analysis of United States Diplomatic Practice in Granting De Jure Recognition to Newly-Established Countries." *CLSA Reports,* December 10, 1948. AJHS/I-77/26/5.

———. "The KKK and State Action." *CLSA Reports,* 1946. AJHS/I-77/29/4.

———. "Legislative Status of Major Recommendations of President's Committee on Civil Rights." *CLSA Reports*, March 26, 1948. AJHS/I-77/29/3.

———. "Lights of Confusion." Statement of New England region, June 1953. AJHS/I-77/89/38.

———. "Materials Available from Commission on Law and Social Action." 1946. AJHS/I-77/29/4.

———. Memorandum on *American Jewish Congress v. Aramco*, June 30, 1959. AJHS/I-77/162/21.

———. "Model Ordinance to Create a Municipal Commission on Group Relations." *CLSA Reports*, September 1947. AJHS/I-77/29/5.

———. "The Patterson Bill to Suppress Racial and Religious Hatred." *CLSA Reports,* September 3, 1946. AJHS/I-77/29/4.

———. "Proposed Bill to Establish a Permanent Federal Civil Rights Commission." *CLSA Reports*, March 22, 1948. AJHS/I-77/29/6

———. "Report of Activities: November-December 1946." *CLSA Reports*, 1946. AJHS/I-77/29/4.

———. "Report of Activities." *CLSA Reports*, April 1950. AJHS/I-77/30/1.

———. "Report of Activities." *CLSA Reports,* May–June 1958. AJHS/I-77/31/1.

———. "Resisting the Arab Boycott: A Statement by the American Jewish Congress on President Ford's Executive Order." *Congress Monthly* 43, no. 8 (October 1976): 3.

———. *Roosevelt to the American Jewish Congress, 1882–1945.* New York: American Jewish Congress, 1945. AJHS/I-77/184/23.

———. "Significant Activities of CLSA During the Last Year." March 17, 1955, 1–4. AJHS/P-572/3/8.

———. "Statement of the American Jewish Congress on the Treatment of Rabble Rousers," *CLSA Reports,* ca. 1946. AJHS/I-77/29/5.

American Jewish Congress, American Jewish Committee, B'Nai B'Rith, and Jewish Labor Committee. *Father Coughlin: His "Facts" and Arguments.* New York: General Jewish Council, 1939. AJHS/I-77/183/16.

Amter, I., and S. Van Veen Amter. Autobiographical typescript, 1950 and 1965 (revised). TAM/079/1.

"Aramco's Ban Here on Jews Is Revoked." *New York Times*, July 16, 1959, 1, 14. AJHS/P-572/2/6.

Balka, C. "NJA in Nairobi: Women Are Talking." *Agenda* 18 (Autumn 1985): 1, 3. TAM/183/13.

——. "NJA Raises West Bank Issue with Federations." *Agenda* 14 (Winter 1984): 1. TAM/183/13.

Balka, C., and R. Bernards. "Joint Israeli-Palestinian Dialogue Touring the US." Press release, March 20, 1984. TAM/183/15.

——. "New Jewish Agenda's Role at the UN Decade for Women Conference." Final report, February 1986. TAM/183/17.

Bartnoff, D., C. Essoyan, M. Liebling, and B. Walt. "Seder of the Children of Abraham." November 15, 1983. TAM/183/29.

Bender, J., ed. "Conference for a New Jewish Agenda for the 1980's." Conference catalogue. December 24–28, 1980. TAM/183/3.

——. Statement for Israeli mission to the United Nations, June 18, 1982. TAM/183/24.

Berger, P. S., and J. B. Robison. "Preferential Treatment in the Selective Process." Memorandum to members of executive committee, March 10, 1972. AJHS/I-77/24/3.

Bernards, R. "Jewish and Christian Leaders Protest Reagan Award." Press release, March 19, 1982. TAM/183/29.

——. Letter to E. Cohen, December 1, 1983. TAM/183/29.

Bernards, R., B. Cohen, and J. Dekro. Letter to postal inspector, June 11, 1982. TAM/183/8.

Bernards, R., and J. Dekro. "New Jewish Agenda Exposes Fraudulent Letters." Press release, July 6, 1982. TAM/183/8.

Bittelman, A. "Bittelman's Proposal to Office Committee on Current Problems." Memorandum, May 24, 1944. TAM/62/1/14.

——. "The Bolshevik Revolution and Its Historic Consequences." Typescript, ca. 1967. TAM/62.1/4/1–3.

——. *"A Communist Views America's Future."* Typescript, 1960. TAM/62.1/4/4–6.

——. "Current Problems in Our Jewish Work: The Struggle for Peace, Against Anti-Semitism, for a Progressive Culture." Essay typescript, October 1949. TAM/62.1/2/12.

——. "Ethics and Politics in World Communism." Draft article, ca. 1954. TAM/62.1/1/17.

——. "Imperialist Reaction Menaces Achievements of Anti-Fascist Victory." Draft article, 1948. TAM/62/1/23.

——. "Jerusalem, National Independence and Peace." Essay typescript, ca. 1949. TAM/62/2/3.

——. *"Jewish Survival: A Marxist Outlook."* Typescript, 1960–1961. TAM/62.1/4/12.

——. Letter to Basic Books, May 20, 1968. TAM/62.1/3/35.

——. Letter to CPUSA, February 12, 1971. TAM/62.1/3/15.

——. Letter to L. B. Johnson, January 15, 1965. TAM/62.1/1/26

——. Letter to N. Khrushchev and M. Tse-Tung, June 23, 1963. TAM/62.1/3/33.

——. Letter to President H. S. Truman, 1948. TAM/62.1/3/26.

——. Letter to W. Z. Foster, September 20, 1951. TAM/62.1/3/32.

——. "The New State of Israel, the Meaning of the Struggle for Its Existence, and Its Historical Significance." Draft article, June 11, 1948. TAM/62/17/1.

——. "The Political Source of Our Theoretical Errors." *The Worker*, July 22, 1945. TAM/62.1/1/10.

———. "Speech to the School of Jewish Studies." Draft, October 5, 1945. TAM/62/1/14.

——. "Stalin: On His Seventieth Birthday." December 1949. TAM/62.1/2/1.

——. *"Things I Have Learned: An Autobiography."* Manuscript, 1962–1963. TAM/62/3–4.

Bloch, J. "Agenda Protests Invasions of Lebanon—Calls for Israeli-Palestinian Co-Existence." *Agenda* 10 (Summer 1982): 1. TAM/183/13.

Burgin, H. *"History of the Jewish Workers Movement."* Translated by anonymous. Typescript, November 30, 1914. TAM/249/1/1, 32.

Chakofsky, B. "Historic Dialogue: Israeli and Palestinian." *Agenda* 15 (Summer 1984): 1, 3. TAM/183/13.

——. "Introduction of Mr. Abdullah Abdullah." Speech, November 23, 1985. TAM/183/24.

——. Letter to A. Abdullah, February 6, 1986. TAM/183/24.

Cohen, A. "No Protection for Hate-Mongers." News release, 1949. AJHS/I-77/26/7.

Cohen, A. H. *Administrative Report, July 1932 to May 1933, Submitted to the Eleventh (Emergency) Session of the American Jewish Congress*. Washington, DC: American Jewish Congress, May 20–22, 1933. AJHS/I-77/2/14.

Cohen, J. X. *Jews, Jobs, and Discrimination: A Report on Jewish Non-Employment*. New York: American Jewish Congress, 1937. AJHS/I-77/182/17.

———. *The Negro, the Jew, and the FEPC*. New York: American Jewish Congress, 1944. AJHS/P-661/1/2.

———. *Who Discriminates—And How?* New York: American Jewish Congress, 1945. AJHS/I-77/184/32.

Cohen, R. "American Jewish Congress Ends Convention Strengthened and Solidified." Press release, June 3, 1960. AJHS/I-77/165/30.

———. "American Jewish Congress Hails Court Decision in Aramco Case." Press release, July 15, 1959. AJHS/I-77/162/25.

———. "American Jewish Congress Hails New York City School Integration Plan, Pledges Support, Cooperation." Press release, September 2, 1960. AJHS/I-77/165/18.

———. "The American Jewish Congress vs. the Arab Boycott." *Congress Monthly* 42, no. 6 (June 1975): 9–11.

———. "Banner Year in States' Civil Rights Legislation, American Jewish Congress Study Discloses." *CLSA News,* August 3, 1959. AJHS/I-77/162/28.

———. "Jews Told to Use Religion in Lives at CJA Conference on Jewish Values." September 2, 1960. AJHS/I-77/165/29.

———. Letter to Mrs. Jackie Robinson, July 23, 1959. AJHS/P-572/2/5.

———. Memorandum on *American Jewish Congress v. Aramco*, July 3, 1959. AJHS/P-572/2/6.

———. "Negro Winners in Levittown Anti-Bias Fight Hail Agencies Providing Legal Aid." *CLSA News,* July 18, 1960. AJHS/I-77/165/16.

———. "Religious Practices in Public Schools Challenged by American Jewish Congress; Major Test Case May Reach Supreme Court." *CLSA News,* July 22, 1960. AJHS/I-77/165/41.

———. "Shad Polier Urges Democratic Party Platform Protecting American Citizens Against Religious Discrimination by Arab Countries." *CLSA News,* June 21, 1960. AJHS/I-77/165/35.

———. "Will Maslow Lodges Protest over David Susskind's TV Program 'Negroes and Anti-Semites.'" Press release, October 19, 1966. AJHS/I-77/177/33.

———. "Will Maslow Resigns from National Advisory Board of CORE." *News release,* February 8, 1966. AJHS/I-77/175/73.

Cohen, S. A. *Engineer of the Soul: A Biography of Rabbi J. X. Cohen (1889–1955)*. New York: Bloch Publishing, 1961. AJHS/P-661/1/7.

Coyne, D. "Agenda Promotes Sanctuary Work—Rabbis on Speaking Tour." *Agenda* 19 (Spring 1986): 1. TAM/183/13.

———. "Letter of Self-Introduction from the 'New' Associate Director." ca. 1985. TAM/183/12.

———. "Resignation from Staff." Memorandum, April 7, 1988. TAM/183/18.

———. "Welcoming Our Own." *Agenda* 20 (Fall 1986): 1. TAM/183/13.

CPUSA. "The National Committee of the Communist Party of America Formulates United Front Policies in Mass Struggle for Peace, Civil Liberties, Equal Rights and Economic Security." Memorandum, ca. 1954. TAM/62/1/16.

Cyrus, A., A. M. Cohen, and B. C. Vladeck. Letter to fellow citizens, October 21, 1935. TAM/037/R-7325/11.

"Daily Digest of Public Opinion on Jewish Matters." *Jewish Telegraphic Agency*, July 7, 1926. Accessed December 4, 2016, at http://www.jta.org/1926/07/07/archive/daily-digest-of-public-opinion-on-jewish-matters-111.

Deer, J., A. Haber, A. Rose, and R. Silverstein, eds. "Introduction." *Agenda* 7 (June–July 1981): 1. TAM/183/13

Dekro, J., and A. Rose. "New Jewish Agenda Solicitor Training Workshop." Memorandum, ca. 1985. TAM/183/12.

Dershowitz, N. Z. Letters to governing council, June 1980. AJHS/I-77/29/2.

Draper, T. Interview with A. Bittelman, January 20, 1969. TAM/62.1/3/30.

Edelstein, N. L. "Jewish Relationship with the Emerging Negro Community in the North." June 23, 1960. AJHS/I-77/45/1.

Fellman, G. "Campaign for a Freeze on Settlements." *Agenda* 12 (Spring 1983): 1–2. TAM/183/13.

"The Flying Reporter." *Yungvarg (Little Folks)* 1, no. 1 (May 1937): 1–3. ALBA194/1/2.

Foster, W. Z. Statement to national committee, April 15, 1951. TAM/62.1/3/14.

"Free Synagogue Guild Hears Rabbi Charge Bias Against Jews." *Flushing Evening News*, December 10, 1930. AJHS/P-661/1/2.

Goldman, D. "Agenda's Work for Middle East Peace." *Agenda* 11 (Winter 1983): 6. TAM/183/13.

Goldstein, E. "Motivation: New Israel/New Palestine." Memorandum, ca. 1990. TAM/183/40.

———. "New Jewish Agenda Supports US Direct Talks with PLO." Press release, December 16, 1988. TAM/183/17.

Goldstein, E., and D. Hurwitz. "National Jewish Group Urges Positive Response to Palestinians." Press release, November 18, 1988. TAM/183/22.

———. "No Status Quo Ante." *Agenda* 24 (Spring 1988): 1. TAM/183/13.

Goldstein, E., D. Hurwitz, L. L. Barrett, and M. Silverberg. "Internal Discussion Bulletin: US Foreign Policy and Aid to Israel." Memorandum, February 1989. TAM/183/17.

Goldstein, H. "Case Statement for New Jewish Agenda." Survey of fund raising, fall 1982. TAM/183/15.

Goldstein, I. Letter to R. F. Wagner Jr., June 21, 1955. AJHS/P-572/3/8.

Greenberg, J., J. B. Robison, and L. W. Melvin. *Colorado Commission Against Discrimination v. Continental Air Lines*, October 1962. AJHS/I-77/152/3.

Greenfield, E. J. "Symposium on Negro-Jewish Tensions." Meeting minutes, 1966. AJHS/P-572/7/4.

Herling, J. "Vladeck: Man of Faith and Action." 1939. TAM/037/R-7325/19.

Herst, E. "Agenda's Priorities and Positions." *Agenda* 7 (June–July 1981): 1. TAM/183/13.

Hardman, J. B. S. "The Radical Labor Movement." Essay typescript, 1932. TAM/050/26/1.

Huber, J. M. Letter to H. Berger, October 5, 1921. TAM/037/R-7325/1.

Hurwitz, R., and I. Klepfisz. "New Jewish Agenda Calls for an Immediate Ceasefire in Gulf War." Press release, January 21, 1991. TAM/183/22.

Interim Council. "Introduction." *Agenda* 7 (June–July 1981): 1. TAM/183/13.

———. "Questions Frequently Asked About Agenda." *Agenda* 7 (June–July 1981): 2. TAM/183/13.

Isaac, R. J. "Breira: Council for Judaism." Pamphlet, 1977. AJHS/I-250/8.

Jaffe, A. G. "Local Work Promotes Middle East Peace." *Agenda* 24 (Spring 1988): 3. TAM/183/13.

Kallen, H. M. *The Struggle for Jewish Unity: An Address by Horace Meyer Kallen before the Eleventh Annual Session of the American Jewish Congress.* New York: Ad Press, May 21, 1933. AJHS/I-77/181/30.

Karabell, K. "Joining JCRCs." *Agenda* 23 (Winter 1987): 6. TAM/183/13.

Kaufman, E. "Israel and Central America: Arms Sales and Their Significance." Draft article. February 1989. TAM/183/39.

Koenig, S. Memorandum, June 28, 1982. TAM/183/8.

Konvitz, M. R. *Separation of Church and State: The First Freedom.* New York: American Jewish Congress. 1949. AJHS/I-77/23/4.

Kugler, I. "*One Eye on the Stars: A Life of a Democratic Socialist; Union Organizer of the Professoriate in America; Secular Humanist; Part of the Jewish People; Devoted to Yiddish Culture.*" Autobiographical typescript, ca. 1984. TAM/315/1/59–61.

Layter, A. "The Third World." *Agenda* 4 (June–July 1980): 2, 4. TAM/183/13.

Lerner, S., and D. Soyer. Letters to the editor. *Agenda* 2 (Winter 1980): 1. TAM/183/13.

Lester, J. "The Simple Truth About Blacks and Jews." *Reform Judaism* (Summer 1989): n.p. TAM/183/40.

Levine, N. Letter to community relations councils and group relations agencies, June 8, 1961. AJHS/I-77/45/8.

Lewis, B. "Peaceful Transition and the Communist Party, USA, 1949–1958." *Theoretical Review: A Journal of Marxist-Leninist Theory and Discussion* 12 (September–October 1979): 9–20. TFRB/0182/0182.

LoPresti, A. "What Do Agenda Members Think?" *Agenda* 8 (Autumn 1981): 6. TAM/183/13.

Lynn, C. J. Letter to E. A. Carter, July 17, 1959. AJHS/P-572/2/5.

Masch, M. "A Progressive Jewish View." *Agenda* 2 (Winter 1980): 1, 5. TAM/183/13.

Maslow, W. "An Analysis of the Racist Origins of the National Origins Quota System of the Immigration Act of 1924." October 29, 1952. AJHS/I-77/186/1.

———. "Memorandum of Complaint in Support of the Commission's Jurisdiction: *American Jewish Congress v. Columbia University NYC.*" June 1946. AJHS/I-77/150/2.

———. "Statement of the American Jewish Congress in Submitting Proposed Platform Planks to the National Political Parties." 1948. AJHS/I-77/26/5.

———. "Statement of American Jewish Congress on Civil Rights Bills." July 27, 1955. AJHS/I-77/186/19.

———. "Statement of the American Jewish Congress Presented to the President's Committee on Civil Rights." May 1, 1947. AJHS/I-77/26/4.

———. "The Uses of Law in the Struggle for Equality." August 1955. AJHS/I-77/186/15.

———. *The Law and Race Relations.* New York: American Jewish Congress, March 1946. AJHS/U002/12 (semiprocessed collection).

Maslow, W., and B. Diamond. "Brief on Behalf of Petitioners." June 8, 1949. AJHS/I-77/23/4.

Maslow, W., P. Murray, and A. H. Pollock. "Brief for the American Jewish Congress as *Amicus Curiae: Westminster School Board District of Orange County vs. Gonzalo Mendez.*" October 1946. AJHS/U002/12/1 (semi-processed collection).

Maslow, W., A. H. Pekelis, and S. Adelson. "Memorandum in Support of Jurisdiction: *American Jewish Congress v. Lumbermens Casualty Company.*" January 31, 1946. AJHS/I-77/150/1.

Maslow, W., L. Pfeffer, and B. S. Miller. "Check List of State Anti-Discrimination and Anti-Bias Laws." Booklet, October 1, 1948. AJHS/I-77/23/1.

Maslow, W., and S. Polier. "Brief of American Jewish Congress as Amicus Curiae [in Feinberg Law case]." October 6, 1949. AJHS/I-77/23/4.

Meyer, M. T. "American Jews Find No Anti-Semitism in Nicaragua." Press release, August 15, 1984. TAM/183/29.

Meyer, M. T., G. Serotta, C. Arnson, A. Blue, D. Cohen, J. Levinson, J. M. Stanman, A. Stern, H. Timerman, R. T. Weisbrot, and J. D. Wurzberg. Report of the Jewish Human Rights Delegation to Nicaragua. Original copy. September 6, 1984. TAM/183/15.

New Jewish Agenda (NJA). "Agenda Chapter Update." *Agenda* 9 (Autumn 1981): 3. TAM/183/13.

———. "Agenda to Aid Central Americans." *Agenda* 18 (Autumn 1985): 4. TAM/183/13.

———. "Call for a West Bank Settlement Freeze." *Agenda* 12 (Spring 1983): 1. TAM/183/13.

———. "Conference Unity Statement." *Agenda* 7 (June–July 1981): 3. TAM/183/13.

———. "Discussion Bulletin." June 1982. TAM/183/40.

———. "Jewish Group Urges Israeli Withdrawal from Lebanon." Press release, June 11, 1982. TAM/183/8.

———. "Local News." *Agenda in Brief* 1 (August 1988): 1. TAM/183/13.

———. "Nairobi Conference of Women." *Agenda* 17 (Summer 1985): 7. TAM/183/13.

———. "National Platform—Adopted November 28, 1982." *Agenda* 13 (Summer 1983): 6, 3. TAM/183/13.

———. "New Jewish Agenda Middle East Program." Internal memorandum, 1984. TAM/183/24.

———. "Proposal from Kadima/NJA for Mideast Program/Strategy." Memorandum, September 1984. TAM/183/35.

———. "Sanctuary." Press release, spring 1985. TAM/183/15.

———. "The Search for Unity Today: Racism and Anti-Semitism in America." Memorandum, ca. 1988. TAM/183/11.

———. "Seek Peace and Pursue It." July 1982. TAM/183/8.

———. "The Shalom Seders: Three Original Haggadahs, Compiled by New Jewish Agenda." Advertisement, 1983. TAM/183/29.

———. "Statement of Purpose." *Agenda* 13 (November 1982): 1. TAM/183/13.

———. "Statement on Israel's Invasion of Lebanon." June 18, 1982. TAM/183/8.

——. "This Is Not the Way!" *New York Times,* June 30, 1982, B4. TAM/183/8.

——. "This Is Not the Way!" *Jewish Post and Opinion,* July 2, 1982, n.p. TAM/183/8.

——. "Three Rabbis Excommunicate New Jewish Agenda Members." *Agenda* 11 (Winter 1983): 7. TAM/183/13.

——. "What's New About New Jewish Agenda." Memorandum, early 1981. TAM/183/1.

NJA Bay Area. "A Jewish Appeal to End Israel's Invasion of Lebanon." *San Francisco Bay Guardian,* June 16, 1982, 9. TAM/183/8.

NJA Washington. "Statement Delivered to the Embassy of Israel and the Palestine Liberation Organization." Press release, June 8, 1982. TAM/183/8.

Orenstein, D. "Tisha B'Av—Nagasaki Day." *Agenda* 8 (Autumn 1981): 1. TAM/183/13.

Pen, O. Interview with S. Polier. Translated from the *Jewish Daily Forward,* January 10, 1965. AJHS/P-572/7/9.

Perlman, N. D. "Discriminatory and Unfair Employment Practices." February 1944. AJHS/I-77/26/1.

Petegorsky, D. *On Combating Racism.* New York: American Jewish Congress, 1948. AJHS/I-77/185/8.

——. "Record in Review." Report presented to Biennial National Convention, New York City, March 31–April 4, 1948. AJHS/I-77/9/1.

Pfeffer, L. "American Jewish Congress Official Chides Protestants on Church-State Separation." February 1, 1951. AJHS/I-77/33/1.

——. "Statement of American Jewish Congress on Freedom of Religion and Separation of Church and State." October 1955. AJHS/P-572/4/1.

Polier, J. W. Letter to E. Roosevelt, March 23, 1942. AJHS/P-527–10F1.

Polier, S. Biographical sketch. c. 1970s. AJHS/P-572/8/2.

——. "The Jew and the Racial Crisis." Draft article, July 15, 1964. AJHS/P-572/7/4.

——. Letter to F. Frankfurter, July 11, 1932. AJHS/P-572/8/20.

——. Letter to J. P. Lash, March 26, 1947. AJHS/P-572/1/1.

——. Letter to L. Granger, January 25, 1957. AJHS/P-572/5/5.

——. Letter to N. D. Rockefeller, May 22, 1959. AJHS/P-572/2/5.

——. Letter to R. McGill, March 23, 1963. AJHS/P-572/2/2.

——. "Platforms." Letter to colleagues, July 29, 1960. AJHS/I-77/23/1.

——. "Why Jews Must Fight for Minorities." November 4, 1949. AJHS/P-572/7/15.

Polier, S., W. Maslow, and L. Pfeffer. "Brief of Complainant, American Jewish Congress." March 1962. AJHS/I-77/152/2.

——. "Memorandum of Law on Application for Reconsideration." Memorandum to J. E. Conway, November 1956. AJHS/P-572/1/7.

Reese, M., P. Cohen, D. Junkin, and S. Zuckerman. "Lebanon Splits US Jews." *Newsweek,* July 12, 1982, 32. TAM/183/8.

Resnick, S. Letter to D. Hurwitz, February 16, 1984. TAM/183/24.

Richards, B. G. "Organizing American Jewry." *Jewish Affairs* 2, no. 2 (May 1, 1947): 25. AJHS/I-77/185/1.

——. "Where Congress Idea Originated." *Congress Weekly,* April 9, 1943. AJA361/A4/19.

Riechman, R., R. Tabak, A. Abromowitz, H. Levitan, H. Pell, J. Dekro, I. Robbin, M. Cohen, M. Kleiner, A. Casper, B. Josephs, A. G. Jaffe, S. Levy, N. Fuchs-Kreimer, D. Harbater, H. Bloom, H. Silverman, and C. Stone. "A Jewish Plea for the Repair of Lebanon and Israel." June 30, 1982. TAM/183/24.

Robison, J. B., ed. *Civil Rights in the United States, 1952: A Balance Sheet of Group Relations.* New York: American Jewish Congress and NAACP, 1952. AJHS/I-77/185/33.

Roosevelt, E. Letter to J. W. Polier, April 14, 1954. AJHS/P-527/R10F1.

——. Letter to J. W. Polier, June 22, 1942 and September 26, 1942. AJHS/P-527/10F1.

Rosenblum, D. Letter to the editor, *Agenda* 14 (Winter 1984): 4. TAM/183/13.

Seltzer, R. A. "The New Jewish Agenda: Dissent or Disloyalty—Fact Sheet." Memorandum, ca. 1989. TAM/183/11.

Serotta, G. "Agenda's Dilemma." *Agenda* 3 (April–May 1980): 3. TAM/183/13.

——. "Agenda's Structure and Ideology." *Agenda* 7 (June–July 1981): 3. TAM/183/13.

———. "Memorandum on United States Aid to Israel as New Jewish Agenda Issue for Discussion and Action." Memorandum, ca. 1987. TAM/183/17.

Shemtov, V. Letter to the editor. *Agenda* 6 (October–November 1980): 1. TAM/183/13.

Shevin, D. "Dov Yermiya—Fighting for Israel's Soul." *Agenda* 17 (Summer 1985): 4. TAM/183/13.

Shneiderman, S. L. "Personal Reports on Soviet Jewry." Press release, ca. 1967. TAM/103/34/7.

Singer, I. *A Religion of Truth, Justice and Peace.* New York: The Amos Society, 1924.

Soyer, D. "Agenda 'Greets' Reagan on Visit to New York." *Agenda* 10 (Summer 1982): 1, 5. TAM/183/13.

———. "Argentinian Jewry." *Agenda* 9 (Spring 1982): 1–2. TAM/183/13.

State of South Carolina, County of Aiken. "Certificate of Birth." July 28, 1942. AJHS/P-572/8/1

Statman, J. "The Jewish Human Rights Delegation to Nicaragua." *Agenda* 16 (Winter 1985): 1. TAM/183/13.

Stavis, M. Letter to S. Polier, October 3, 1962. AJHS/P-572/3/1.

Stone, C. S., Jr. Letter to S. Polier, June 24, 1964. AJHS/P-572/7/15.

Steinmetz, D. "Ann Arbor's Mideast Initiative." *Agenda* 15 (Summer 1984): 3. TAM/183/13.

Tick, P. "American Jewish Brigade Answers Nicaragua's Call." Press release, October 17, 1985. TAM/183/15.

———. "A Sad Comment on *Commentary.*" *Agenda* 21 (Winter 1987): 1, 5, 7. TAM/183/13.

Toll, C., ed. "Beginnings." *Agenda* 1 (Summer 1979): 1. TAM/183/13.

———. "Statement of Purpose." *Agenda* 1 (Summer 1979): 1. TAM/183/13.

Vladeck, B. C. Letter to L. Marshall, October 15, 1928. TAM/037/R-7325/8.

———. Letter to N. Thomas, June 14, 1934. TAM/037/R-7325/10.

———. "Why Radicalism Has Failed." Speech presented at the Ford Hall Forum, Boston, Massachusetts, January 22, 1933. TAM/037/R-7325/12.

Vorspan, A. "A Disciple of the Wise: Jacob X. Cohen," *Congress Bi-Weekly* 38, no. 7 (May 21, 1971): 14–16. AJHS/P-661/1/6.

Waskow, A. "The Shalom Seder." 1983. TAM/183/29.

Weisman, H. L., S. Polier, W. Maslow, and J. B. Robison. *Brief of American Jewish Congress as Amicus Curiae: Brown v. Board of Education of Topeka, Kansas.* New York: Bar Press, October 9, 1952. AJHS/I-77/150/26.

Welles, S. "A Jewish Commonwealth NOW." Memorandum, May 19, 1947. AJHS/I-77/185/6.

Willis, E. Letter to the editor. *Agenda* 7 (June–July 1981): 4. TAM/183/13.

Yermiya, D., and M. Da'wiri. "The Committee Against Racism and for Co-Existence in Israel." Memorandum, 1984. TAM/183/15.

Yermiya, D. Letter to R. Bernards, November 26, 1984. TAM/183/15.

Youth Representative. "Report to the Committee on the YPSL National Plenum Held in Philadelphia, October 14th and 15th, 1939." 1939. TAM/R-7203–17/9/19.

Primary Sources

Adam, P. *Vues d'Amérique.* 10th ed. Paris: Librairie Paul Ollendorff, 1906.

Aronson, C. J. Letter to the editor. *Commentary* (January 1987). Accessed October 12, 2011, at https://www.commentarymagazine.com/articles/sandinista-anti-semitism/.

Baker, R. S., ed. *Woodrow Wilson: Life and Letters—War Leader.* 8 vols. New York: Doubleday, Dorian, 1939.

Bauer, B. "The Jewish Question, Brunswick, 1843." In *Karl Marx: Early Writings,* translated by R. Livingstone and G. Benton, 211–34. London: Penguin Classics, 1992.

Beinart, P. "The Failure of the American Jewish Establishment." *New York Review of Books,* May 12, 2010. Accessed January 16, 2012, at http://www.nybooks.com/articles/2010/06/10/failure-american-jewish-establishment/.

Berger, M. E. "Behind the Headlines: Fifty Years After Integration Case, Jews Remember Their Crucial Role." *Jewish Telegraphic Agency*, May 11, 2004. Accessed November 30, 2016, at http://www.jta.org/2004/05/11/archive/behind-the-headlines-50-years-after-integration-case-jews-remember-their-crucial-role-by-matthew-e.

Bernays, E. L. *Propaganda* [1928]. Brooklyn: Ig Publishing, 2005.

Bittelman, A. *The Advance of the United Front*. New York: Workers Library Publishers, 1934.

——. *Break the Economic and Political Sabotage of the Monopolists*. New York: Workers Library, 1937.

——. *The Communist Party in Action*. New York: Workers Library Publishers, 1932.

——. *Fifteen Years of the Communist Party*. New York: Workers Library Publishers, 1934.

——. *From Left-Socialism to Communism*. New York: Workers Library Publishers, 1933.

——. *Going Left: The Left Wing Formulates a "Draft for a Program for the Socialist Party of the United States"*. New York: Workers Library, 1936.

——. *How Can We Share the Wealth? The Communist Way versus Huey Long*. New York: Workers Library, 1935.

——. *How to Win Social Justice: Can Coughlin and Lemke Do It?* New York: Workers Library, 1936.

——. *Jewish Unity for Victory*. New York: Workers Library Publishers, 1943.

——. *Parties and Issues in the Election Campaign*. Chicago: Literature Department of the Workers Party of America, 1924.

——. "The Party and the People's Front." In *Party Building and Political Leadership*, New York: Workers Library, 1937.

——. *Program for Survival: The Communist Position on the Jewish Question*. New York: New Century Publishers, 1947.

——. *To Secure Jewish Rights: The Communist Position*. New York: New Century Publishers, 1948.

——. *The Townsend Plan*. New York: Workers Library Publishers, 1936.

——. *Trotsky the Traitor*. New York: Workers Library Publishers, 1937.

Bittelman, A., and V. J. Jerome. *Leninism: The Only Marxism Today; A Discussion of the Characteristics of Declining Capitalism*. New York: Workers Library Publishers, 1934.

Bloch, E. D. "One Voice Less for the Jewish Left: New Jewish Agenda, 1981–1993." N.d. Accessed November 29, 2016, at https://newjewishagenda.files.wordpress.com/2012/01/ethan-bloch.pdf.

"The Boycott Debate: Where Politics and Trade Meet." *Multinational Monitor* 7, no. 15 (November 1986). Accessed July 5, 2011, at http://www.multinationalmonitor.org/hyper/issues/1986/11/debate.html.

Brandeis, L. D. *Brandeis on Zionism: A Collection of Addresses and Statements*. Union, NJ: Lawbook Exchange, 1999.

Buder, L. "2 Harlem Schools Called Inferior as Court Frees Two in Boycott." *New York Times*, December 16, 1958, 1.

Burlingham, C. C., G. W. Alger, B. Flexner, E. M. Herrick, O. G. Villard, and W. N. Seymour. Letter to the editor. *New York Times*, February 13, 1945, 22.

Cahan, A. *Bleter fun mayn lebn*. 5 vols. New York: Forverts Association, 1926.

Cannon, J. *The First Ten Years of American Communism—Report of a Participant*. New York: Pathfinder, 1973.

Carpenter, N. *Immigrants and Their Children, 1920: A Study Based on Census Statistics Relative to the Foreign Born and Native White of Foreign or Mixed Parentage*. Washington, DC: Government Printing Office, 1927.

Charney, G. *A Long Journey*. Chicago: Quadrangle Books, 1968.

Clymer, A. "Displeasure with Carter Turned Many to Reagan." *New York Times*, November 9, 1980, 28.

Cohen, S. M. *American Assimilation or Jewish Revival?* Bloomington: Indiana University Press, 1988.

——. *The Dimensions of American Jewish Liberalism*. New York: American Jewish Committee, Institute of Human Relations, 1989.

——. *The 1984 National Survey of American Jews: Political and Social Outlooks*. New York: American Jewish Committee, Institute of Human Relations, 1984.

————. *A Tale of Two Jewries: The "Inconvenient Truth" for American Jews.* New York: Jewish Life Network/Steinhardt Foundation, 2006.

Cohen, S. M., S. Abrams, and J. Veinstein. *American Jews and the 2008 Presidential Elections: As Democrat and Liberal As Ever?* New York: New York University, Wagner and Berman Jewish Policy Archive, 2008.

Cuomo, M. *Forest Hills Diary: The Crisis of Low-Income Housing.* New York: Vintage Books, 1975.

DeLeon, S., and N. Fine, eds. *American Labor Year Book.* New York: Rand School of Social Science, 1929.

Dewey, J. *The Case of Leon Trotsky: Report of Hearings on the Charges Made Against Him in the Moscow Trials.* London: Secker and Warburg, 1937.

Dorman, J. *Arguing the World: The New York Intellectuals in Their Own Words.* New York: Free Press, 2000.

Du Bois, W. E. B., ed. "Along the Color Line: America, Stephens-O'Brien Bill." *The Crisis: A Record of the Darker Races* (July 1933): 159.

Elman, P. "Response." *Harvard Law Review* 100, no. 8 (June 1987): 1949–57.

Elman, P. "Solicitor General's Office, Justice Frankfurter, and Civil Rights Litigation, 1946–1960: An Oral History." *Harvard Law Review* 100, no. 4 (February 1987): 817–52.

Fackenheim, E. L. "The Dilemma of Liberal Judaism." *Commentary* (October 1960): 301.

Flint, P. B. "Paul Novick Is Dead; Editor, 97, Helped Start Yiddish Daily." *New York Times*, August 22, 1989, D23.

Foster, W. Z. *From Bryan to Stalin.* New York: International Publishers, 1937.

Freeman, K. "Members of Mission to Nicaragua Differ over That Government's Policy Toward Its Jewish Community." *Jewish Telegraphic Agency*, September 11, 1984. Accessed October 12, 2011, at http://www.jta.org/1984/09/11/archive/members-of-mission-to-nicaragua-differ -over-that-governments-policy-toward-its-jewish-community.

Gates, J. *The Story of an American Communist.* New York: Thomas Nelson, 1958.

Gitlow, B. *I Confess: The Truth About American Communism.* New York: E. P. Dutton, 1940.

————. *The Whole of Their Lives.* New York: Charles Scribner, 1948.

Glazer, N. "American Jews and Israel—A Symposium." *Commentary* (February 1988). Accessed October 15, 2011, at https://www.commentarymagazine.com/articles/american-jews-and -israel-a-symposium/.

————. "Social Characteristics of American Jews, 1654–1954." In *American Jewish Year Book,* edited by M. Fine and J. Sloan. 3–41. Philadelphia: Jewish Publication Society of America, 1955.

Gold, M. *Jews Without Money.* New York: Carroll and Graf, 2004.

Goldberg, N. "Economic Trends Among American Jews." *Jewish Affairs* 1, no. 9 (October 1946): 1–19.

Goldman, M. "Assessment of the Nairobi Conference." *Jewish Telegraphic Agency*, August 8, 1985. Accessed October 11, 2011, at http://www.jta.org/1985/08/05/archive/assessment-of-the -nairobi-conference-a-victory-for-women-worldwide.

Gompers, S. *Seventy Years of Life and Labour: An Autobiography.* London: Hurst and Blackett, 1923.

Gottfried, P. *Encounters: My Life with Nixon, Marcuse, and Other Friends and Teachers.* Wilmington, DE: ISI Books, 2009.

Himmelfarb, M., and D. Singer, eds. *American Jewish Year Book.* Philadelphia: American Jewish Committee, 1986.

Horowitz, D. *Radical Son: A Journey Through Time.* New York: Free Press, 1997.

Kaplow, H. "Jewish Federations, Their Agencies and the Integration Struggle." *Congress Bi-Weekly* 31, no. 13 (September 14, 1964): 3.

Konvitz, M. R. "From Jewish Rights to Human Rights." *Congress Monthly* 46, no. 3 (April 1979): 8.

Konvitz, M. R., and T. Leskes. *A Century of Civil Rights.* New York and London: Columbia University Press, 1961.

Kopeloff, I. "First Days in America," translated by L. Wolf. In *Voices from the Yiddish: Essays, Memoirs, Diaries,* edited by I. Howe and E. Greenberg, 193–201. Ann Arbor: University of Michigan Press, 1972.

Krim, S. "Ask for a White Cadillac." In *Views of a Nearsighted Cannoneer*, 55–72. London: Alan Ross, 1969.

Laidlaw, W. *Population of the City of New York, 1890–1930*. New York: Cities Census Committee, 1932.

Levine, N. "Challenging Saudi Arabian Discrimination and American Involvement." *Congress Monthly* 48, no. 1 (January 1977): 6–8.

Lippmann, W. "Public Opinion and the American Jew." *American Hebrew*, April 14, 1922, 575.

Lipsky, L. *Thirty Years of American Zionism*. New York: Arno Press, 1977.

Lynn, F. "More in City Are Turning to the Right." *New York Times*, January 15, 1974, 1.

Marx, K. "On the Jewish Question" [1843]. In *Karl Marx: Selected Writings*, 2nd ed., edited by D. McLellan, 46–70. Oxford: Oxford University Press, 2009.

Maslow, W. "Prejudice, Discrimination, and the Law." *Annals of the American Academy of Political and Social Science* 275 (May 1951): 9–17.

Maslow, W., and R. Cohen. *School Segregation, Northern Style*. New York: Public Affairs Committee, 1961.

Maslow, W., and J. B. Robison. "Civil Rights Legislation and the Fight for Equality, 1862–1952." *University of Chicago Law Review* 20, no. 3 (Spring 1953): 363–413.

McGill, N. P. "Some Characteristics of Jewish Youth in New York City." *Jewish Social Survey Quarterly* 14, no. 2 (December 1937): 251–72.

Medved, M. "*Why Are Jews Liberals?*—A Commentary Symposium." *Commentary* (September 2009): 47.

Miller, N. "Israeli and Jewish Women Hope to Avert Confrontations at NGO Forum." *Jewish Telegraphic Agency*, July 12, 1985. Accessed October 11, 2011, at http://www.jta.org/1985/07/12/archive/special-to-the-jta-israeli-and-jewish-women-hope-to-avert-confrontations-at-ngo-forum.

Montgomery, P. L. "Discord Among US Jews Over Israel Seems to Grow." *New York Times*, July 15, 1982, A16.

———. "'We Need the Cash,' Begin Says at Bonds Lunch." *New York Times*, June 19, 1982, 7.

Muravchik, M., S. Alberts, and A. Korenstein. "Sandinista Anti-Semitism and Its Apologists." *Commentary* (September 1986): 25–29.

National Liberal Immigration League. *The Immigrant Jew in America*. Edited by E. J. James. New York: B. F. Buck, 1907.

"The New Deal Dispenses a New Brand of Justice to Labor and Industry." *Life* 3, no. 10 (September 6, 1937): 19–23.

Newman, L. I. *A Jewish University in America?* New York: Bloch Publishing Company, 1923.

Note. "Exclusion of Negroes from Subsidized Housing Project." *University of Chicago Law Review* 15, no. 3 (Spring 1948): 745–47.

———. "Validity of Municipal Law Barring Discrimination in Private Housing." *Columbia Law Review* 58, no. 5 (May 1958): 728–35.

Novak, W. "The Breira Story." *Genesis* 2 (March–April 1977): 6–10.

Noy, E., ed. *Statistical Abstract of Israel*. Jerusalem: State of Israel, 2006.

Pekelis, A. H. "Full Equality in a Free Society: A Program for Jewish Action." In *Law and Social Action: Selected Essays of Alexander H. Pekelis*, edited by M. R. Konvitz, 218–59. Ithaca, NY: Cornell University Press, 1950.

Petegorsky, D. Letter to the editor. *New York Times*, January 7, 1948, 24.

Philipson, D. *My Life as an American Jew*. Cincinnati, OH: John G. Kidd & Son, 1941.

Podhoretz, N. "J'Accuse." *Commentary* (September 1982): 21–31.

———. *Making It*. New York: Random House, 1967.

———. "My Negro Problem—And Ours." *Commentary* (February 1963): 93–101.

Polier, J. W. "The Malicious UN Resolution on Jerusalem." *Congress Bi-Weekly* 38, no. 10 (October 29, 1971): 4–5.

———. "Obligations and Commitments." *Congress Bi-Weekly* 37, no. 8 (June 19, 1970): 4.

———. "Open Letter to the 'Friends': A Critical Analysis of the Quakers' 'Study for Peace in the Middle East.'" *Congress Bi-Weekly* 37, no. 12 (December 4, 1970): 3–6.

Polier, J. W., and S. Polier. "Fear Turned to Hatred." *Congress Bi-Weekly* 30, no. 3 (February 18, 1963): 5–6.

"Political Parties Hear AJC Hit Arab Boycott." *Congress Bi-Weekly* 27, no. 13 (September 19, 1960): 14.

Potter, B. "The Jewish Community." In *Life and Labor of the People in London*, edited by C. Booth, 564–90. London: Macmillan, 1902.

Reznikoff, C., ed. *Louis Marshall: Champion of Liberty; Selected Papers and Addresses*. 2 vols. Philadelphia: Jewish Publication Society of America, 1957.

Riis, J. A. *How the Other Half Lives: Studies Among the Tenements of New York*. New York: Dover, 1971.

Rosenthal, A. M. "Jews Must Not Break Bones." *New York Times*, January 26, 1988, A25.

Rosenwaike, I. *Population History of New York City*. Syracuse, NY: Syracuse University Press, 1972.

Roskolenko, H. *The Time That Was Then: The Lower East Side, 1900–1914; An Intimate Chronicle*. New York: Dial Press, 1971.

Roth, P. *The Facts: A Novelist's Autobiography*. London: Penguin, 1988.

Rothbard, M. "Life in the Old Right." *Chronicles* (August 1994). Accessed February 10, 2009, at https://www.lewrockwell.com/1970/01/murray-n-rothbard/life-in-the-old-right/.

Rudd, M. *Underground: My Life with SDS and the Weathermen*. New York: William Morrow, 2009.

———. "Why Were There So Many Jews in SDS? (Or, The Ordeal of Civility)." Speech presented to New Mexico Jewish Historical Society, November 2005. Accessed October 6, 2011, http://www.markrudd.com/?about-mark-rudd/why-were-there-so-many-jews-in-sds-or-the-ordeal-of-civility.html.

Saidel-Wolk, R. "New Jewish Group Hopes to Create Progressive-Minded National Membership Organization." *Jewish Telegraphic Agency*, December 25, 1980. Accessed September 26, 2011, at http://www.jta.org/1980/12/26/archive/new-jewish-group-hopes-to-create-progressive-minded-national-membership-organization.

Samuel, M. *Jews on Approval*. New York: Liveright Publishers, 1933.

Samuels, S. "Assimilation and Its Discontents." *New York Magazine*, September 28, 2008. Accessed March 9, 2010, http://nymag.com/anniversary/40th/50717/.

———. "Why Are Jews Liberals?—A Commentary Symposium." *Commentary* (September 2009): 46.

Sarna, J. D. "Why Are American Jews Abandoning Israel?" *Haaretz*, October 5, 2009. Accessed November 1, 2011, at http://www.haaretz.com/jewish/news/why-are-american-jews-abandoning-israel-1.6652.

Schneiderman, H., ed. *The American Jewish Year Book 5685*. Philadelphia: Jewish Publication Society of America, 1924.

Schulberg, B. *What Makes Sammy Run?* New York: Vintage Books, 1990.

Schwartzapfel, B. "Will Maslow, 99, Pioneer in Fight for Civil Rights." *Forward.com*, March 2, 2007. Accessed July 1, 2011, at http://forward.com/news/obituaries/10243/will-maslow-99-pioneer-in-fight-for-civil-rights/.

Shefler, G. "Battered American Jewish Congress to Suspend Activities." *Jerusalem Post*, July 18, 2010, 1.

Smith, T.W. *Jewish Distinctiveness in America: A Statistical Report*. New York: American Jewish Committee, 2005.

Stevenson, A. E., A. L. Frothingham, S. A. Berger, and E. A. Barnes. *Revolutionary Radicalism: Its History, Purpose and Tactics with an Exposition and Discussion of the Steps Being Taken and Required to Curb It—Report of the Joint Legislative Committee Investigating Seditious Activities of the Senate of the State of New York*. 4 vols. New York: J. B. Lyon and Company, April 24, 1920.

Tomasson, R. E. "Shanker Is Given a 15-Day Sentence in School Strike." *New York Times*, February 4, 1969, 1.

Trachtenberg, A., ed. *The American Labor Year Book 1917–1918*. New York: Rand School of Social Science, 1918.

Urofsky, M. I., and D. W. Lewy, eds. *Letters of Louis D. Brandeis: Progressive and Zionist*. 5 vols. Albany: State University of New York Press, 1973.

Voss, C. H., ed. *Stephen S. Wise: Servant of the People—Selected Letters*. Philadelphia: Jewish Publication Society of America, 1969.

Waskow, A. Introduction to *The Shalom Seders: Three Haggadahs Compiled by New Jewish Agenda.* New York: Adama Books, 1984.

Weidman, J. *I Can Get It for You Wholesale.* New York: Modern Library, 1937.

Weizmann, C. *The Letters and Papers of Chaim Weizmann.* 23 vols. Edited by M. W. Weisgal. London: Oxford University Press, 1971.

Wise, S.S. *Challenging Years: The Autobiography of Stephen Wise.* New York: G.P. Putnam's Sons, 1949.

Wolf, A. J. *Unfinished Rabbi: Selected Writings of Arnold Jacob Wolf.* Edited by J. S. Wolf. Chicago: Dee, 1998.

Wolman, L. *The Growth of American Trade Unions, 1880-1923.* New York: National Bureau of Economic Research, 1924.

Wolpe, D. "*Why Are Jews Liberals?*—A Commentary Symposium." *Commentary* (September 2009): 44.

Wood, A. "I Sell My House: One Man's Experience with Suburban Segregation." *Commentary* (November 1958): 383–89.

Secondary Sources

Abel, R. L. *American Lawyers.* New York: Oxford University Press, 1989.

Abrams, N. *Commentary Magazine 1945-59.* London and Portland, OR: Vallentine Mitchell, 2007.

———. *Norman Podhoretz and Commentary Magazine: The Rise and Fall of the Neocons.* New York: Continuum, 2010.

Adorno, T. W., E. Frenkel-Brunswik, and D. Levinson. *The Authoritarian Personality.* New York: Harper and Brothers, 1950.

Alexander, M. "Exile and Alienation in America." *American Jewish History* 90, no. 2 (June 2002): 165–69.

———. *Jazz Age Jews.* Princeton, NJ: Princeton University Press, 2001.

Allinsmith, W., and A. Allinsmith. "Religious Affiliation and Politico-Economic Attitude: A Study of Eight Major US Religious Groups." *Public Opinion Quarterly* 12, no. 3 (Autumn 1948): 377–89.

Allswang, J. M. *The New Deal and American Politics: A Study in Political Change.* New York: John Wiley, 1978.

Alter, R. "Revolutionism and the Jews: 2, Appropriating the Religious Tradition." *Commentary* (February 1971): 47–54.

Avineri, S. "Marx and Jewish Emancipation" [1964]. In *Essential Papers on Jews and the Left,* edited by E. Mendelsohn, 402–9. New York: New York University Press, 1997.

———. *Moses Hess: Prophet of Communism and Zionism.* New York and London: New York University Press, 1985.

Bailin, I. B. "Socialist Activities Among the Jews." In *The American Labor Year Book, 1916,* edited by A. L. Trachtenberg, 138–40. New York: Rand School of Social Research, 1916.

Balint, B. *Running Commentary: The Contentious Magazine That Transformed the Jewish Left into the Neoconservative Right.* New York: Public Affairs, 2010.

Baltzell, E. D. "The WASP's Last Gasp." In *The Protestant Establishment Revisited,* edited and introduced by H. G. Schneiderman, 33–43. New Brunswick, NJ: Transaction Publishers, 2001.

Barrett, J. R. *William Z. Foster and the Tragedy of American Radicalism.* Urbana and Chicago: University of Illinois Press, 1999.

Barzun, J. *From Dawn to Decadence: 500 Years of Western Cultural Life, 1500 to the Present.* New York: Perennial, 2001.

Bauman, Z. "Assimilation into Exile: The Jew as a Polish Writer." *Poetics Today* 17, no. 4 (Winter 1996): 569–97.

Bayor, R. H. *Neighbors in Conflict: The Irish, Germans, Jews, and Italians in New York City, 1929-1941.* Baltimore, MD: Johns Hopkins University Press, 1978.

Beer, M. *Fifty Years of International Socialism.* London: George Allen and Unwin, 1935.

Bell, D. *Marxian Socialism in the United States*. Princeton, NJ: Princeton University Press, 1967.

———. "A Parable of Alienation." *Jewish Frontier* 13, no. 11 (November 1946): 12–19.

Benson, L. "Ethnocultural Groups and Political Parties." In *Voters, Parties, and Elections: Quantitative Essays in the History of American Popular Voting Behavior*, edited by J. H. Silbey and S. T. McSeveney, 83–98. Lexington, MA: Xerox College Publishing, 1972.

Bercuson, D. J. *Confrontation at Winnipeg: Labour, Industrial Relations, and the General Strike*. Kingston, ON: McGill-Queen's University Press, 1974.

Berkovitz, J. R. "The French Revolution and the Jews: Assessing the Cultural Impact." *American Jewish Society Review* 20, no. 1 (1995): 25–86.

Berkowitz, M. *The Jewish Self-Image: American and British Perspectives, 1881–1939*. London: Reaktion Books, 2000.

Berlin, I. *Chaim Weizmann*. London: Weidenfeld and Nicolson, 1958.

Berlin, W. S. *On the Edge of Politics: The Roots of Jewish Political Thought in America*. Westport, CT: Greenwood Press, 1978.

Berson, L. E. *The Negroes and the Jews*. New York: Random House, 1971.

Biale, D., M. Galchinsky, and S. Heschel. *Insider/Outsider: American Jews and Multiculturalism*. Berkeley: University of California Press, 1998.

Bonfield, A. E. "The Origin and Development of American Fair Employment Legislation." *Iowa Law Review* 52, no. 6 (June 1967): 1043–92.

Breines, P. *Tough Jews: Political Fantasies and the Moral Dilemma of American Jewry*. New York: Basic Books, 1990.

Brettschneider, M. *Cornerstones of Peace: Jewish Identity Politics and Democratic Theory*. New Brunswick, NJ: Rutgers University Press, 1996, 41.

Broun, H., and G. Britt. *Christians Only: A Study in Prejudice*. New York: Vanguard Press, 1931.

Brustein, W. I., and R. D. King. "Anti-Semitism as a Response to Perceived Jewish Power: The Case of Bulgaria and Romania before the Holocaust." *Social Forces* 83, no. 2 (December 2004): 691–708.

———. "A Political Threat Model of Intergroup Violence: Jews in Pre-World War II Germany." *Criminology* 44, no. 4 (2006): 867–91.

Burks, R. V. *The Dynamics of Communism in Eastern Europe*. Princeton, NJ: Princeton University Press, 1961.

Burstein, P. "Jewish Educational and Economic Success in the United States: A Search for Explanations." *Sociological Perspectives* 50, no. 2 (2007): 209–28.

Cahan, A. *The Rise of David Levinsky* [1917]. New York: Harper and Row, 1996.

Cantor, N. *The Sacred Chain: A History of the Jews*. New York: Harper Perennial, 1995.

Carlebach, J. *Karl Marx and the Radical Critique of Judaism*. London: Routledge and Kegan Paul, 1978.

Chambers, W. *Witness*. New York: Random House, 1952.

Chen, A. S. *The Fifth Freedom: Jobs, Politics, and Civil Rights in the United States, 1941–1972*. Princeton, NJ, and Oxford: Princeton University Press, 2009.

Clark, K. B. *Dark Ghetto: Dilemma of Social Power* [1965]. Middleton, CT: Wesleyan University Press, 1989.

Cohen, A. *Nothing to Fear: FDR's Inner Circle and the Hundred Days That Created Modern America*. New York: Penguin Press, 2009.

Cohen, N. W. *Not Free to Desist: The American Jewish Committee, 1906–1966*. Philadelphia: The Jewish Publication Society of America, 1972.

Cohen, S. M., and C. S. Liebman. "American Jewish Liberalism: Unraveling the Strands." *Public Opinion Quarterly* 61, no. 3 (Autumn 1997): 405–30.

Cohn, W. "The Politics of American Jews." In *The Jews: Social Patterns of an American Group*, edited by M. Sklare, 614–26. Glencoe, IL: Free Press, 1958.

Cole, S. *The Unionization of Teachers: A Case Study of the UFT*. New York: Praeger, 1969.

Collins, W.J. "Race, Roosevelt, and Wartime Production: Fair Employment in World War II Labor Markets." *American Economic Review* 91, no. 1 (March 2001): 272–86.

Cuddihy, J. M. *The Ordeal of Civility: Freud, Marx, Lévi-Strauss and the Jewish Struggle with Modernity.* New York: Basic Books, 1974.

Cunningham, H. *God and Caesar at the Rio Grande: Sanctuary and the Politics of Religion.* Minneapolis: University of Minnesota Press, 1995.

Daly, J. "Crime in Late Imperial Russia." *Journal of Modern History* 74, no. 1 (March 2002): 62–100.

De Forest, J. "The 1958 Harlem School Boycott: Parental Activism and the Struggle for Educational Equity in New York." *Urban Review* 40, no. 1 (2008): 21–41.

Dekel-Chen, J.L. *Farming the Red Land: Jewish Agricultural Colonization and Local Soviet Power, 1924–1942.* New Haven, CT, and London: Yale University Press, 2005.

Denning, M. *The Cultural Front: The Laboring of American Culture in the Twentieth Century.* London and New York: Verso, 1997.

Dershowitz, A. M. *The Vanishing American Jew: In Search of Jewish Identity for the Next Century.* New York: Simon and Schuster, 1998.

Deutscher, I. *The Non-Jewish Jew and Other Essays.* Edited by T. Deutscher. London: Oxford University Press, 1968.

Diner, H. R. *In the Almost Promised Land: American Jews and Blacks, 1915–1935.* Westport, CT: Greenwood Press, 1977.

———. *The Jews of the United States, 1654 to 2000.* Berkeley: University of California Press, 2004.

———. *Lower East Side Memories: A Jewish Place in America.* Princeton, NJ: Princeton University Press, 2000.

Dinnerstein, L. *Anti-Semitism in America.* New York and Oxford: Oxford University Press, 1994.

Dinnerstein, L., and D. M. Reimers. *Ethnic Americans: A History of Immigration and Assimilation.* New York: Dodd, Mead, 1987.

Djilas, M. *The New Class: An Analysis of the Communist System.* London: Thames and Hudson, 1957.

Dollinger, M. *Quest for Inclusion: Jews and Liberalism in Modern America.* Princeton, NJ, and Oxford: Princeton University Press, 2000.

Dowty, A. "Zionism's Greatest Conceit." *Israel Studies* 3, no. 1 (1998): 1–23.

Draper, T. *American Communism and Soviet Russia: The Formative Period.* London: Macmillan, 1960.

———. *Roots of American Communism.* New York: Viking Press, 1957.

Dubofsky, M. "Success and Failure of Socialism in New York City, 1900–1918: A Case Study." *Labor History* 9, no. 3 (Autumn 1968): 361–75.

Durkheim, É. *The Division of Labor in Society.* Translated by G. Simpson. Glencoe, IL: Free Press, 1933.

———. *Socialism and Saint-Simon.* Edited by A. W. Gouldner. Translated by C. Sattler. London: Routledge and Kegan Paul, 1963.

Dwork, D. "Health Considerations of Immigrant Jews on the Lower East Side of New York: 1880–1914." *Medical History* 25, no. 1 (January 1981): 1–40.

Edwards, P. K. *Strikes in the United States, 1881–1974.* Oxford: Basil Blackwell, 1981.

Eisenstadt, S. N. *From Generation to Generation: Age Groups and Social Structure.* New York: Free Press of Glencoe, 1956.

Elazar, D. J. *Community and Polity: The Organizational Dynamics of American Jewry.* Philadelphia: The Jewish Publication Society, 1995.

Epstein, M. *The Jew and Communism: The Story of Early Communist Victories and Ultimate Defeats in the Jewish Community, USA, 1919–1941.* New York: Trade Union Sponsoring Committee, 1959.

———. *Jewish Labor in the USA: An Industrial, Political and Cultural History of the Jewish Labor Movement.* 2 vols. New York: Ktav Publishing House, 1969.

Epstein, R. A. *Forbidden Grounds: The Case Against Employment Discrimination Laws.* Cambridge, MA: Harvard University Press, 1992.

Feingold, H. L. "American Jewish Liberalism and Jewish Response." *Contemporary Jewry* 9, no. 1 (September 1987): 19–45.

———. *A Midrash on American Jewish History.* Albany: State University of New York Press, 1982.

———. *A Time for Searching: Entering the Mainstream, 1920–1945.* Baltimore, MD: Johns Hopkins University Press, 1992.

Feuer, L. S. "Recollections of Harry Austryn Wolfson." *American Jewish Archives* 28, no. 1 (April 1976): 25–50.

Fine, N. *Labor and Farmer Parties in the United States: 1828–1928.* New York: Russell and Russell, 1961.

Fischman, D. "The Jewish Question About Marx." *Polity* 21, no. 4 (Summer 1989): 760.

Fisher, A. M. "Realignment of the Jewish Vote?" *Political Science Quarterly* 94, no. 1 (Spring 1979): 97–116.

Foner, P. S. *The History of the Labor Movement in the United States.* 10 vols. New York: International Publishers, 1991.

Forman, I. N. "The Politics of Minority Consciousness." In *Jews in American Politics*, edited by L. S. Maisel, 142–59. Lanham, MD: Rowman and Littlefield, 2004.

Forman, S. *Blacks in the Jewish Mind: A Crisis of Liberalism.* New York: New York University Press, 1998.

Frankel, J. *Prophecy and Politics: Socialism, Nationalism, and the Russian Jews, 1862–1917.* Cambridge, UK: Cambridge University Press, 1981.

———. "The Roots of 'Jewish Socialism' (1881–1892): From 'Populism' to 'Cosmopolitanism'?" [1988]. In *Essential Papers on Jews and the Left*, edited by E. Mendelsohn, 58–77. New York: New York University Press, 1997.

Frankel, J., and B. Pinkus, eds. *The Soviet Government and the Jews, 1948–1967: A Documented Study.* Cambridge, UK: Cambridge University Press, 1984.

Friedman, M(onroe). *Consumer Boycotts: Effecting Change through the Marketplace and the Media.* London: Routledge, 1999.

Friedman, M(urray). *The Neoconservative Revolution: Jewish Intellectuals and the Shaping of Public Policy.* Cambridge, UK: Cambridge University Press, 2005.

Friedman, S. S. *The Incident at Massena.* New York: Stein and Day, 1978.

Frommer, M. "The American Jewish Congress: A History, 1914–1950." PhD diss., Ohio State University, 1978.

Fuchs, L. H. "American Jews and the Presidential Vote." *American Political Science Review* 49 (1955): 385–401.

———. *The Political Behavior of American Jews.* Glencoe, IL: Free Press, 1956.

Gamm, G. H. *The Making of New Deal Democrats: Voting Behavior and Realignment in Boston, 1920–1940.* Chicago and London: University of Chicago Press, 1989.

———. *Urban Exodus: Why the Jews Left Boston and the Catholics Stayed.* Cambridge, MA: Harvard University Press, 1999.

Gans, H. J. *The Levittowners: Ways of Life and Politics in a New Suburban Community.* New York: Pantheon Books, 1967.

———. "Symbolic Ethnicity: The Future of Ethnic Groups and Cultures in America." *Ethnic and Racial Studies* 2, no. 1 (January 1979): 1–20.

Gartner, L. P. "Immigration and the Formation of American Jewry, 1840–1925." In *Jewish Society through the Ages*, edited by H. H. Ben Sasson and S. Ettinger, 297–312. New York: Schocken Books, 1973.

Gelman, A. *Red State, Blue State, Rich State, Poor State: Why Americans Vote the Way They Do.* Princeton, NJ: Princeton University Press, 2008.

Gilman, S. L. "Karl Marx and the Secret Language of the Jews." *Modern Judaism* 4, no. 3 (October 1984): 275–94.

Ginsberg, B. *The Fatal Embrace: Jews and the State.* Chicago: University of Chicago Press, 1993.

Ginzburg, E. *Agenda for American Jews.* New York: King's Crown Press, 1950.

Girard, F., and B. Perry. *The Socialist Labor Party of America, 1876–1991: A Short History.* Philadelphia: Livra Books, 1993.

Girvan, P., and F. M. Wozencraft. "Private Attorneys—General: Group Action in the Fight for Civil Liberties." *Yale Law Journal* 58, no. 4 (March 1949): 574–98.

Glazer, N. *The Social Basis of American Communism*. New York: Harcourt, Brace and World, 1961.

Glazer, N., and D. P. Moynihan. *Beyond the Melting Pot: The Negroes, Puerto Ricans, Jews, Italians, and Irish of New York City* [1963]. 2nd ed. Cambridge, MA: MIT Press, 1970.

Godley, A. *Jewish Immigrant Entrepreneurship in New York and London, 1880–1914*. New York: Palgrave, 2001.

Goldberg, D., and H. Sharp. "Some Characteristics of Detroit Area Jewish and non-Jewish Adults." In *The Jews: Social Patterns of An American Group*, edited by M. Sklare, 107–118. New York: Free Press, 1958.

Goldberg, J. J. *Jewish Power: Inside the American Jewish Establishment*. New York: Basic Books, 1996.

Goldhagen, E. "The Ethnic Consciousness of Early Russian Jewish Socialists." *Judaism* 23, no. 4 (Fall 1974): 479–96.

Goldscheider, C. *Jewish Continuity and Change: Emerging Patterns in America*. Bloomington: Indiana University Press, 1986.

Goldstein, I. *Jewish Justice and Conciliation: History of the Jewish Conciliation Board of America, 1930–1968*. New York: KTAV, 1981.

Goldstein, S. "Socioeconomic Differentials Among Religious Groups in the United States." *American Journal of Sociology* 74, no. 6 (May 1969): 612–31.

Gordon, M. M. *Assimilation in American Life—The Role of Race, Religion, and National Origins*. New York: Oxford University Press, 1964.

Goren, A. A. "The Conservative Politics of the Orthodox Press." In *The Politics and Public Culture of American Jews, 100–109*. Bloomington: Indiana University Press, 1999.

———. *New York Jews and the Quest for Community: The Kehillah Experiment, 1908–1922*. New York: Columbia University Press, 1970.

———. "A Portrait of Ethnic Politics: The Socialists and the 1908 and 1910 Congressional Elections on the East Side." *American Jewish Historical Quarterly* 50, no. 3 (March 1961): 202–38.

Gottfried, P. *After Liberalism: Mass Democracy in the Managerial State*. Princeton, NJ, and Oxford: Princeton University Press, 1999.

———. *Multiculturalism and the Politics of Guilt: Toward a Secular Theocracy*. Columbia and London: University of Missouri Press, 2002.

Gottlieb, M. "The Anti-Nazi Boycott Movement in the United States: An Ideological and Sociological Appreciation." *Jewish Social Studies* 35, nos. 3/4 (July–October 1973): 198–227.

Grebler, L. *Housing Market Behavior in a Declining Area*. New York: Columbia University Press, 1952.

Greenberg, C. L. *Troubling the Waters: Black-Jewish Relations in the American Century*. Princeton, NJ: Princeton University Press, 2006.

Greenberg, J. *Crusaders in the Courts: How a Dedicated Band of Lawyers Fought for the Civil Rights Revolution*. New York: Basic Books, 1995.

Groner, I. N., and D. M. Helfeld. "Race Discrimination in Housing." *Yale Law Review* 57, no. 3 (January 1948): 426–58.

Gurock, J. "The 1913 New York Civil Rights Act." *AJS Review* 1 (1976): 93–120.

Harris, L., and B. E. Swanson. *Black-Jewish Relations in New York City*. New York: Praeger Publishers, 1970.

Harris, L. A. *Upton Sinclair: American Rebel*. New York: Crowell, 1975.

Harshav, B. *Language in Time of Revolution*. Berkeley: University of California Press, 1993.

Hartz, L. *The Liberal Tradition in America*. New York: Harcourt, Brace, 1955.

Hayes, P. "Hobbes's Bourgeois Moderation." *Polity* 33, no. 1 (Autumn 1998): 53–74.

Heilbron, J. *The Rise of Social Theory*. Cambridge, UK: Polity Press, 1995.

Heilbrunn, J. *They Knew They Were Right: The Rise of the Neocons*. New York: Doubleday, 2008.

Heinze, A. R. *Jews and the American Soul: Human Nature in the Twentieth Century*. Princeton, NJ: Princeton University Press, 2004.

Herberg, W. "The Jewish Labor Movement in the United States: Early Years to World War I." *Industrial and Labor Relations Review* 5, no. 4 (July 1952): 501–23.

———. *Protestant, Catholic, Jew: An Essay in American Religious Sociology.* Garden City, NY: Doubleday, 1955.

———. "Socialism, Zionism and Messianic Passion." *Midstream* 2 (Summer 1956): 65–74.

Hertz, E. "Politics: New York." In *The Russian Jew in the United States: Studies of Social Conditions in New York, Philadelphia, and Chicago, with a Description of Rural Settlements*, edited by C. S. Bernheimer, 255–69. Philadelphia: John C. Winston, 1905.

Higham, J. *Send These to Me: Immigrants in Urban America.* Baltimore, MD: Johns Hopkins University Press, 1984.

———. *Strangers in the Land: Patterns of American Nativism, 1860–1925.* New Brunswick, NJ: Rutgers University Press, 1955.

Hillquit, M. *History of Socialism in the United States.* New York and London: Funk and Wagnalls, 1903.

Himmelfarb, M. "Another Look at the Jewish Vote." *Commentary* (December 1985): 39–44.

———. "Is American Jewry in Crisis?" *Commentary* (March 1969): 33–42.

Hogg, P. W. *Constitutional Law of Canada: 2010 Student Edition.* Toronto: Carswell, 2010.

Hollinger, D. A. *Science, Jews, and Secular Culture: Studies in Mid-Twentieth Century American Intellectual History.* Princeton, NJ: Princeton University Press, 1996.

Howe, I. *Steady Work: Essays in the Politics of Democratic Radicalism, 1953–1966.* New York: Harcourt, Brace, 1966.

———. *World of Our Fathers: The Journey of East European Jews to America and the Life They Found and Made.* New York: Simon and Shuster, 1976.

Howe, I., and L. Coser. *The American Communist Party: A Critical History.* New York: Da Capo Press, 1974.

Hugh-Jones, E. M. *Woodrow Wilson and American Liberalism.* New York: Collier Books, 1947.

Hundert, G. D. *Jews in Poland-Lithuania in the Eighteenth Century: A Genealogy of Modernity.* Berkeley: University of California Press, 2006.

Hutchinson, E. P. *Immigrants and Their Children 1850–1950.* New York: John Wiley, 1956.

Irons, P. H. *The New Deal Lawyers.* Princeton, NJ: Princeton University Press, 1982.

Ivers, G. *To Build a Wall: American Jews and the Separation of Church and State.* Charlottesville: University Press of Virginia, 1995.

Jackson, J. P., Jr. *Social Scientists for Social Justice: Making the Case against Segregation.* New York and London: New York University Press, 2001.

Janowsky, O. I. *The Jews and Minority Rights, 1898–1919.* New York: Columbia University Press, 1933.

Jay, M. *The Dialectical Imagination: A History of the Frankfurt School and the Institute of Social Research, 1923–1950.* Berkeley: University of California Press, 1973, 1996.

Jensen, R. "The Religious and Occupational Roots of Party Identification: Illinois and Indiana in the 1870s." In *Voters, Parties, and Elections: Quantitative Essays in the History of American Popular Voting Behavior*, edited by J. H. Silbey and S. T. McSeveney, 167–83. Toronto: Xerox College Publishing, 1972.

Johanningsmeier, E. P. *Forging American Communism: The Life of William Z. Foster.* Princeton, NJ: Princeton University Press, 1994.

Johnpoll, B. K. *Pacifist's Progress: Norman Thomas and the Decline of American Socialism.* Chicago: Quadrangle Books, 1970.

———. *The Politics of Futility: The General Jewish Workers Bund in Poland, 1917–1943.* Ithaca, NY: Cornell University Press, 1967.

Johnson, K. S. *Reforming Jim Crow: Southern Politics and the State in the Age Before Brown.* Oxford: Oxford University Press, 2010.

Johnson, P. *A History of the Jews.* New York: Harper and Row, 1987.

Kahan, A. "Economic Opportunities and Some Pilgrims' Progress: Jewish Immigrants from Eastern Europe in the US, 1890–1914." *Journal of Economic History* 38, no. 1 (March 1978): 235–51.

Kaplan, L. "On Maurice Samuel's Twenty-Fifth Yahrzeit." *Judaism: A Quarterly Journal of Jewish Life and Thought* 46, no. 4 (Fall 1997): 453–64.

Kaplan, M. M. *Judaism as a Civilization: Toward a Reconstruction of American-Jewish Life* [1934]. New York: Schocken Books, 1967.

Karabel, J. *The Chosen: The Hidden History of Admission and Exclusion at Harvard, Yale, and Princeton.* New York: Mariner Books, 2005.

Karady, V. *The Jews of Europe in the Modern Era: A Socio-Historical Outline.* Budapest and New York: Central European University Press, 2004.

Katz, J. *Exclusiveness and Tolerance: Studies in Jewish-Gentile Relations in Medieval and Modern Times.* New York: Oxford University Press, 1962.

Kaufmann, E. P. *The Rise and Fall of Anglo-America.* Cambridge, MA: Harvard University Press, 2004.

Kelley, R. D. G. *Hammer and Hoe: Alabama Communists during the Great Depression.* Chapel Hill and London: University of North Carolina Press, 1990.

Kenniston, K. *Young Radicals: Notes on Committed Youth.* New York: Harcourt, Brace and World, 1968.

Kesselman, L. C. *The Social Politics of FEPC: A Study in Reform Pressure Movements.* Chapel Hill: University of North Carolina Press, 1948.

Kessner, T. *The Golden Door: Italian and Jewish Immigrant Mobility in New York City, 1880–1915.* New York: Oxford University Press, 1977.

King, R. D., and M. F. Weiner. "Group Position, Collective Threat, and American Anti-Semitism." *Social Problems* 54, no. 1 (2007): 47–77.

Kivisto, P. "The Decline of the Finnish American Left, 1925–1945." *International Migration Review* 17, no. 1 (Spring 1983): 65–94.

Klarman, M. J. *From Jim Crow to Civil Rights: The Supreme Court and the Struggle for Racial Equality.* New York: Oxford University Press, 2004.

Klehr, H. *Communist Cadre: The Social Background of the American Communist Party Elite.* Stanford, CA: Hoover Institution Press, 1978.

Kluger, R. *Simple Justice: The History of* Brown v. Board of Education *and Black America's Struggle for Equality.* New York: Alfred A. Knopf, 1976.

Kochan, L. *The Jewish Renaissance and Some of Its Discontents.* Manchester, UK: Manchester University Press, 1992.

Koestler, A. "Initiates." In *The God That Failed* [1950], edited by R. Crossman, 11–66. London: Bantam Books, 1965.

Kolehmainen, J. T. "A Study of Assimilation in a Finnish Community." *American Journal of Sociology* 42, no. 3 (November 1936): 371–82.

Kopstein, J. S., and J. Wittenberg. "Who Voted Communist? Reconsidering the Social Bases of Radicalism in Interwar Poland." *Slavic Review* 62, no. 1 (Spring 2003): 87–109.

Kosak, H. *Cultures of Opposition: Jewish Immigrant Workers, New York City, 1881–1905.* Albany: State University of New York Press, 2000.

Kramer, J. K., and S. Leventman. *Children of the Gilded Ghetto: Conflict Resolutions of Three Generations of American Jews.* New Haven, CT, and London: Yale University Press, 1961.

Kristol, I. "The Liberal Tradition." In *American Pluralism and the Jewish Community*, edited by S. M. Lipset, 109–16. New Brunswick, NJ: Transaction Publishers, 1990.

———. "The Neoconservative Persuasion: What It Was, and What It Is." In *Neoconservatism*, edited by I. Seltzer, 33–37. London: Atlantic Books, 2004.

Kuznets, S. "Immigration of Russian Jews to the United States: Background and Structure." In *Perspectives in American History*, edited by D. Fleming and B. Bailyn, 35–126. Cambridge, MA: Harvard University Press, 1975.

Ladd, E. C., and C. D. Hadley. *Transformations of the American Party System: Party Coalitions from the New Deal to the 1970s.* 2nd ed. New York: W. W. Norton, 1978.

Lasch, C. *The Culture of Narcissism: American Life in an Age of Diminishing Expectations*. New York: W. W. Norton, 1979.

Laslett, J. H. M., and LS. M. ipset, eds. *Failure of a Dream? Essays in the History of American Socialism*. Berkeley: University of California Press, 1974.

Lasser, W. *Benjamin V. Cohen: Architect of the New Deal*. New Haven, CT, and London: Yale University Press, 2002.

Lavergne, G. M. *Before Brown: Herman Marion Sweatt, Thurgood Marshall, and the Long Road to Justice*. Austin: University of Texas Press, 2010.

Lawson, G. "The Rise and Rise of the Administrative State." *Harvard Law Review* 107, no. 6 (April 1995): 1231–54.

Lederhendler, E. "Guides for the Perplexed: Sex, Manners, and Mores for the Yiddish Reader in America." *Modern Judaism* 11, no. 3 (October 1991): 321–41.

———, ed. *Jews, Catholics, and the Burden of History*. Oxford: Oxford University Press, 2005.

Lenski, G. *The Religious Factor: A Sociological Study of Religion's Impact on Politics, Economics, and Family Life*. Garden City, NY: Doubleday Anchor, 1961.

Levey, G. B. "The Liberalism of American Jews—Has It Been Explained?" *British Journal of Political Science* 26, no. 3 (July 1996): 369–401.

———. "Toward a Theory of Disproportionate American Jewish Liberalism." In *Values, Interests and Identity: Jews and Politics in a Changing World*, edited by P. Y. Medding, 64–85. *Studies in Contemporary Jewry*. Oxford: Oxford University Press, 1995.

Levine, A. J. *"Bad Old Days": The Myth of the 1950s*. New Brunswick, NJ: Transaction Publishers, 2008.

Lichter, S. R., and S. Rothman. "Jews on the Left: The Student Movement Reconsidered." *Polity* 14, no. 2 (Winter 1981): 347–66.

———. *Roots of Radicalism: Jews, Christians and the New Left*. New York: Oxford University Press, 1982.

Liebknecht, W. *Karl Marx: Biographical Memoirs* [1901]. Translated by E. Unterman. London: Journeyman Press, 1975.

Liebman, A. *Jews and the Left*. New York: John Wiley and Sons, 1979.

Liebman, C. S., and S. M. Cohen. *The Ambivalent American Jew: Politics, Religion, and Family in American Jewish Life*. Philadelphia: Jewish Publication Society of America, 1973.

———. *Two Worlds of Judaism: The Israeli and American Experiences*. New Haven, CT: Yale University Press, 1990.

Lipset, S. M., and E. Raab. "The American Jews, the 1984 Elections, and Beyond." In *The New Jewish Politics*, edited by D. J. Elazar, 33–56. Lanham, MD: University Press of America, 1988.

———. *Jews and the New American Scene*. Cambridge, MA: Harvard University Press, 1995.

Lipsky, L. *Memoirs in Profile*. Philadelphia: Jewish Publication Society of America, 1975.

Lipstadt, D. E. *Beyond Belief: The American Press and the Coming of the Holocaust 1933–1945*. New York: Free Press, 1986.

Litt, E. "Ethnic Status and Political Perspectives." *Midwest Journal of Political Science* 5, no. 3 (August 1961): 276–83.

Lockard, D. *Toward Equal Opportunity: A Study of State and Local Antidiscrimination Laws*. New York: Macmillan, 1968.

Lukacs, J. *A Thread of Years*. New Haven, CT, and London: Yale University Press, 1998.

Lustiger, A. *Stalin and the Jews: The Red Book—The Tragedy of the Jewish Anti-Fascist Committee and the Soviet Jews*. New York: Enigma Books, 2003.

Lyons, P. *Philadelphia Communists, 1936–1956*. Philadelphia: Temple University Press, 1982.

Manor, E. *Forward: The Jewish Daily Forward (Forverts) Newspaper: Immigrants, Socialism and Jewish Politics in New York, 1890–1917*. Portland, OR: Sussex Academic Press, 2009.

Marks, G., and M. Burbank. "Immigrant Support for the American Socialist Party, 1912 and 1920." *Social Science History* 14, no. 2 (Summer 1990): 175–202.

Martin, T. *The Affirmative Action Empire: Nations and Nationalism in the Soviet Union, 1923–1939*. New York: Cornell University Press, 2001.

May, H. *The End of American Innocence: A Study of the First Years of Our Own Times, 1912–1917*. Chicago: Quadrangle Books, 1964.

McCagg, W. O., Jr. "Jews in Revolutions: The Hungarian Experience." *Journal of Social History* 6, no. 1 (Autumn 1972): 78–105.

McCoy, D. R., and R. T. Reutten. *Quest and Response: Minority Rights and the Truman Administration*. Lawrence: University Press of Kansas, 1973.

McGreevy, J. T. *Parish Boundaries: The Catholic Encounter with Race in the Twentieth-Century Urban North*. Chicago and London: University of Chicago Press, 1996.

McMillian, J. "You Didn't Have to Be There: Revisiting the New Left Consensus." In *The New Left Revisited*, edited by J. McMillian and P. Buhle, 1–8. Philadelphia: Temple University Press, 2003.

McSeveney, S. T. *The Politics of Depression: Political Behavior in the Northeast, 1893–1896*. New York: Oxford University Press, 1972.

Medoff, R. *Jewish Americans and Political Participation*. Santa Barbara, CA: ABC-CLIO, 2002.

Meier, A., and E. Rudwick. *CORE: A Study in the Civil Rights Movement, 1942–1968*. Chicago: University of Illinois Press, 1975.

Mendelsohn, E. Introduction to *Essential Papers on Jews and the Left*, edited by J. Reinharz and A. Shapira, 1–18. New York and London: New York University Press, 1997.

———. *On Modern Jewish Politics*. Oxford: Oxford University Press, 1993.

Michels, T. "Exporting Yiddish Socialism: New York's Role in the Russian Jewish Workers' Movement." *Jewish Social Studies* 16, no. 1 (Fall 2009): 1–26.

———. *A Fire in Their Hearts: Yiddish Socialists in New York*. Cambridge, MA: Harvard University Press, 2005.

Milner, J., and D. Spieglman. "Carrying It On: A Report from the New Jewish Agenda Conference on Organizing Against Racism and Anti-Semitism." *Bridges* 3, no. 1 (Spring–Summer 1992): 138–47.

Model, S. W. "Italian and Jewish Intergenerational Mobility: New York, 1910." *Social Science History* 12, no. 1 (Spring 1988): 31–48.

Montgomery, D. "Immigrants, Industrial Unions, and Social Reconstruction in the United States, 1916–1923." *Labour/Le Travail* 13 (Spring 1984): 101–14.

Moore, D. D. *At Home in America: Second Generation New York Jews*. New York: Columbia University Press, 1981.

———. "Jewish Migration to the Sunbelt." In *Shades of the Sunbelt: Essays on Ethnicity, Race, and the Urban South*, edited by R. M. Miller and G. E. Pozzetta, 41–52. New York: Greenwood Press, 1988.

Morgan, T. *Jay Lovestone: Communist, Anti-Communist, and Spymaster*. New York: Random House, 1999.

Morison, S. E. *Three Centuries of Harvard* [1936]. Cambridge, MA: Harvard University Press, 2001.

Myrdal, G. *An American Dilemma: The Negro Problem and Modern Democracy* [1944]. 2 vols. New Brunswick, NJ: Transaction Publishers, 2009.

Nepon, E. "New Jewish Agenda: The History of an Organization, 1980–1992." BA thesis, Goddard College, 2006.

Novick, P. *The Holocaust in American Life*. Boston and New York: Houghton Mifflin, 2000.

Novik, N. *The United States and Israel: Domestic Determinants of a Changing US Commitment*. Boulder, CO, and London: Westview Press and Tel Aviv University, 1986.

O'Connor, H. *Revolution in Seattle*. New York: Monthly Review Press, 1964.

Organski, A. F. K. *The $36 Billion Bargain: Strategy and Politics in US Assistance to Israel*. New York: Columbia University Press, 1990.

Palmer, B. D. *James P. Cannon and the Origins of the American Revolutionary Left, 1890–1928*. Urbana and Chicago: University of Illinois Press, 2007.

Parmet, R. D. *The Master of Seventh Avenue: David Dubinsky and the American Labor Movement*. New York: New York University Press, 2005.

Parsons, T. "The Sociology of Modern Anti-Semitism" [1942]. In *Talcott Parsons on National Socialism*, edited by U. Gerhardt, 101–22. New York: Aldine de Gruyter, 1993.

Peled, Y. "From Theology to Sociology: Bruno Bauer and Karl Marx on the Question of Jewish Emancipation." *History of Political Thought* 13, no. 3 (Autumn 1992): 463–85.

Pendergast, W. B. *The Catholic Voter in American Politics: The Passing of the Democratic Monolith*. Washington, DC: Georgetown University Press, 1999.

Perrier, H. "Le mouvement ouvrier aux États-Unis et al guerre, 1889–1919." *Le Mouvement social* 147 (April–June 1989): 27–50.

———. "The Socialists and the Working Class in New York: 1890–1896." *Labor History* 22, no. 4 (Fall 1981): 485–511.

Phillips, B. A. "Catholic (and Protestant) Israel: The Permutations of Denominational Differences and Identities in Mixed Families." In *Jews, Catholics, and the Burden of History*, edited by E. Lederhendler, 132–53. *Studies in Contemporary Jewry*. Oxford: Oxford University Press, 2005.

Podhoretz, N. *Why Are Jews Liberals?* New York: Doubleday, 2009.

Polanyi, M. "Jewish Problems." *Political Quarterly* 14, no. 1 (1943): 33–45.

Polenberg, R. *Class, Race, and Ethnicity in the United States since 1938*. New York: Viking Press, 1980.

Pomson, A. "Jewish Day-School Growth in Toronto: Freeing Policy and Research from the Constraints of Conventional Sociological Wisdom." *Canadian Journal of Education* 27, no. 4 (2002): 379–98.

Prinz, A. "New Perspectives on Marx as a Jew." In *Leo Baeck Institute Year Book*, edited by R. Weltsch, 107–24. London: Horovitz Publishing, 1970.

Pulzer, P. *Jews and the German State: The Political History of a Minority, 1848–1933*. Oxford: Blackwell, 1992.

Putnam, R. D. *Bowling Alone: The Collapse and Revival of American Community*. New York: Simon and Schuster, 2000.

———. "*E Pluribus Unum*: Diversity and Community in the Twenty-First Century." *Scandinavian Political Studies* 30, no. 2 (2007): 137–74.

Quandt, W. B. *Peace Process: American Diplomacy and the Arab-Israeli Conflict since 1967*. Berkeley: University of California Press, 2001.

Quigley, C. *Tragedy and Hope: A History of the World in Our Time*. New York: Macmillan, 1966.

Raimondo, J. *An Enemy of the State: The Life of Murray N. Rothbard*. Amherst, NY: Prometheus Books, 2000.

Rappaport, J. *Hands Across the Sea: Jewish Immigrants and World War I*. Lanham, MD: Hamilton Books, 2005.

Reed, M. E. *Seedtime for the Modern Civil Rights Movement: The President's Committee on Fair Employment Practice, 1941–1946*. Baton Rouge and London: Louisiana State University Press, 1991.

Richler, M. *The Apprenticeship of Duddy Kravitz* [1959]. Toronto: Emblem Editions, 2001.

Rischin, M. *The Promised City: New York's Jews, 1870–1914*. Cambridge, MA: Harvard University Press, 1962.

Rogoff, H. *An East Side Epic: The Life and Work of Meyer London*. New York: Vanguard Press, 1930.

Rose, P. I. *The Ghetto and Beyond: Essays on Jewish Life in America*. New York: Random House, 1969.

Rosenman, S. I., ed. *The Public Papers and Addresses of Franklin D. Roosevelt: The Call to Battle Stations*. New York: Russell and Russell, 1941.

———. *The Public Papers and Addresses of Franklin D. Roosevelt: The Tide Turns*. New York: Russell and Russell, 1943.

Rosenthal, S. T. *Irreconcilable Differences? The Waning of the American Jewish Love Affair with Israel*. Hanover, PA: University Press of New England, 2001.

Rotenstreich, N. "Emancipation and Its Aftermath." In *The Future of the Jewish Community in America*, edited by D. Sidorsky, 46–61. New York: Basic Books, 1973.

Roth, P. *Portnoy's Complaint*. London: Jonathan Cape, 1969.

Rubinow, I. "Economic and Industrial Conditions: New York." In *The Russian Jew in the United States: Studies of Social Conditions in New York, Philadelphia, and Chicago, with a Description of Rural Settlements*, edited by C. S. Bernheimer, 103–21. Philadelphia: John C. Winston, 1905.

Rubinstein, W. D. *The Left, the Right, and the Jews*. London: Croom Helm, 1982.

Ruchames, L. *Race, Jobs, and Politics: The Story of FEPC*. New York: Columbia University Press, 1953.

Ruderman, T. J. *Stanley M. Isaacs: The Conscience of New York*. New York: Arno Press, 1982.

Rudolph, F. *The American College and University: A History*. New York: Knopf, 1962.

Ruppin, A. *The Jews in the Modern World*. London: Macmillan, 1934.

Sachar, H. M. *Dreamland: Europeans and Jews in the Aftermath of the Great War*. New York: Alfred A. Knopf, 2002.

Sarna, J. D., ed. *The American Jewish Experience*. New York: Holmes and Meier, 1986.

———. "The Myth of No Return: Jewish Return Migration to Eastern Europe, 1881–1914." *American Jewish History* 71, no. 2 (December 1981): 256–68.

Schlesinger, A. M., Jr. *The Disuniting of America: Reflections on a Multicultural Society*. New York: W. W. Norton, 1998.

Schultz, K. M. "The FEPC and the Legacy of the Labor-Based Civil Rights Movement of the 1940s," *Labor History* 49, no. 1 (February 2008): 71–92.

Schwartz, J. *The New York Approach: Robert Moses, Urban Liberals, and Redevelopment of the Inner City*. Columbus: Ohio State University Press, 1993.

Scruton, R. *A Short History of Modern Philosophy: From Descartes to Wittgenstein*. London and New York: Routledge, 2002.

Seldes, G. *Witness to a Century: Encounters with the Noted, the Notorious, and the Three SOBs*. New York: Ballantine Books, 1987.

Shannon, D. *The Decline of American Communism*. New York: Harcourt Brace, 1959.

Shapira, A. "Labour Zionism and the October Revolution." *Journal of Contemporary History* 24, no. 4 (October 1989): 623–56.

Shapiro, M. B. *Between the Yeshiva World and Modern Orthodoxy: The Life and Works of Rabbi Jehiel Jacob Weinberg*. Oxford: Littman Library of Jewish Civilization, 1999.

Shapiro, S. E. "Right Turn? Jews and the American Conservative Movement." In *Jews in American Politics*, edited by L. S. Maisel, 196–211. Lanham, MD: Rowman and Littlefield, 2004.

Shapiro, Y. *Leadership of the American Zionist Organization, 1897–1930*. Chicago: University of Illinois Press, 1971.

Shatz, A., ed. *Prophets Outcast: A Century of Dissident Jewish Writing about Zionism and Israel*. New York: Nation Books, 2004.

Sheskin, I. M. "Jewish Metropolitan Homelands." *Journal of Cultural Geography* 13, no. 2 (1993): 119–32.

Shneer, D. *Yiddish and the Creation of Soviet Jewish Culture, 1918–1930*. Cambridge, UK: Cambridge University Press, 2004.

Siegel, D. S., and S. Siegel. *Radio and the Jews: The Untold Story of How Radio Influenced the Image of Jews*. New York: Book Hunter Press, 2007.

Silber, N. I. *With All Deliberate Speed: The Life of Philip Elman*. Ann Arbor: University of Michigan Press, 2004.

Silberner, E. "Was Marx an Anti-Semite?" [1949]. In *Essential Papers on Jews and the Left*, edited by E. Mendelsohn, 361–401. New York: New York University Press, 1997.

Sklare, M. *America's Jews*. New York: Random House, 1971.

———, ed. *The Jews: Social Patterns of an American Group*. Glencoe, IL: Free Press, 1958.

Slezkine, Y. *The Jewish Century*. Princeton, NJ: Princeton University Press, 2004.

Smith, C. *Resisting Reagan: The US Central American Peace Movement*. Chicago: University of Chicago Press, 1996.

Soltes, M. *The Yiddish Press: An Americanizing Agency*. New York: Columbia University Press, 1924.

Sorin, G. *The Prophetic Minority: American Jewish Immigrant Radicals, 1880–1920*. Bloomington: Indiana University Press, 1985.

Sowell, T. *Ethnic America: A History*. New York: Basic Books, 1981.

Soyer, D. "Back to the Future: American Jews Visit the Soviet Union in the 1920s and 1930s." *Jewish Social Studies* 6, no. 3 (Spring–Summer 2000): 124–59.

———. "Class Conscious Workers as Immigrant Entrepreneurs: The Ambiguity of Class among Eastern European Jewish Immigrants to the United States at the Turn of the Twentieth Century." *Labor History* 42, no. 1 (2001): 45–59.

Spinrad, W. "New York's Third Party Voter." *Public Opinion Quarterly* 21, no. 4 (Winter 1957–1958): 548–51.

Srebrnik, H. F. *Dreams of Nationhood: American Jewish Communists and the Soviet Birodizhan Project, 1924–1951*. Boston: Academic Studies Press, 2010.

Starobin, J. R. *American Communism in Crisis, 1943–1957*. Cambridge, MA: Harvard University Press, 1972.

Staub, M. E. *Torn at the Roots: The Crisis of Jewish Liberalism in Postwar America*. New York: Columbia University Press, 2002.

Steel, R. *Walter Lippmann and the American Century*. New York: Vintage, 1981.

Steinberg, S. *The Academic Melting Pot: Catholics and Jews in American Higher Education*. New York: McGraw-Hill, 1974.

Strum, P. *Mendez v. Westminster: School Desegregation and Mexican-American Rights*. Lawrence: University Press of Kansas, 2010.

Sumner, W. G. *Folkways: A Study of the Sociological Importance of Usages, Manners, Customs, Mores, and Morals*. Boston: Ginn, 1906.

Sundquist, E. J. *Strangers in the Land: Blacks, Jews, Post-Holocaust America*. Cambridge, MA: Harvard University Press, 2005.

Sutton, A. C. *Wall Street and FDR*. New Rochelle, NY: Arlington House Publishers, 1975.

Svonkin, S. *Jews Against Prejudice: American Jews and the Fight for Civil Liberties*. New York: Columbia University Press, 1997.

Szajkowski, Z. *Jews, Wars, and Communism: The Attitude of American Jews to World War I, the Russian Revolutions of 1917, and Communism (1914–1945)*. New York: Ktav Publishing House, 1972.

Talmon, J. *The Myth of the Nation and the Vision of Revolution: The Origins of Ideological Polarisation in the Twentieth Century*. London: Secker and Warburg, 1980.

Teles, S. M. *The Rise of the Conservative Legal Movement: The Battle for Control of the Law*. Princeton, NJ, and Oxford: Princeton University Press, 2008.

Teutsch, D. A. "Reconstructionism and the Public Square: A Multicultural Approach to Judaism in America." In *Jewish Polity and American Civil Society: Communal Agencies and Religious Movements in the American Public Square*, edited by A. Mittelman, J.D. Sarna and R. Licht, 337–62. Lanham, MD: Rowman and Littlefield, 2002.

Thernstrom, S. *The Other Bostonians*. Cambridge: Harvard University Press, 1973.

Tobias, H. J. *The Jewish Bund in Russia: From Its Origins to 1905*. Stanford, CA: Stanford University Press, 1972.

Trilling, L. Afterword to *The Unpossessed*, edited by T. Slesinger, 311–33. New York: Basic Books, 1966.

Trunk, I. "The Cultural Dimension of the American Jewish Labor Movement." In *YIVO Annual of Jewish Social Science*, edited by E. Mendelsohn, 26:342–93. New York: YIVO Institute for Jewish Research, 1976.

Tyler, G. *A Vital Voice—100 Years of the Jewish "Forward"*. New York: Forward Association, 1997.

Urofsky, M. I. *American Zionism from Herzl to the Holocaust*. Lincoln and London: University of Nebraska Press, 1975.

———. *Louis D. Brandeis: A Life*. New York: Pantheon Books, 2009.

———. *A Voice That Spoke for Justice: The Life and Times of Stephen S. Wise*. Albany: State University of New York Press, 1982.

———. *We Are One! American Jewry and Israel.* Garden City, NY: Anchor Press, 1978.

Veblen, T. *The Higher Learning in America* [1936]. New York Cosimo, 2007.

Veidlinger, J. *The Moscow State Yiddish Theater: Jewish Culture on the Soviet Stage.* Bloomington: Indiana University Press, 2000.

Wald, K. D. "Toward a Structural Explanation of Jewish-Catholic Differences in the United States." In *Jews, Catholics, and the Burden of History*, edited by E. Lederhendler, 111–31. *Studies in Contemporary Jewry.* Oxford: Oxford University Press, 2005.

Waxman, C. I. *American Aliya: Portrait of an Innovative Migration Movement.* Detroit, MI: Wayne State University Press, 1989.

Weber, M. *The Protestant Ethic and the Spirit of Capitalism.* Translated by T. Parsons. London and New York: Routledge, 2002.

Weeks, T. "Polish-Jewish Relations 1903–1914: The View from the Chancellery." *Canadian Slavonic Papers* 40, nos. 3/4 (September–December 1998): 233–49.

Weinryb, B. D. "Jewish Immigration and Accommodation to America." In *The Jews: Social Patterns of an American Group*, edited by M. Sklare, 4–22, 627–29. Glencoe, IL: Free Press, 1958.

Weinstein, J. *The Decline of Socialism in America, 1912–1925.* New Brunswick, NJ: Rutgers University Press, 1984.

Weisbrod, R. G., and A. Stein. *Bittersweet Encounter: The Afro-American and the American Jew.* Westport, CT: Negro University Press, 1970.

Wenger, B. S. *New York Jews and the Great Depression: Uncertain Promise.* New Haven, CT, and London: Yale University Press, 1996.

Wertheimer, J. "Critics of Israel." In *Envisioning Israel: The Changing Ideals and Images of North American Jews*, edited by A. Gal, 397–419. Detroit, MI: Wayne State University Press, 1996.

Wheatcroft, G. *The Controversy of Zion: Jewish Nationalism, the Jewish State, and the Unresolved Jewish Dilemma.* New York: Addison Wesley, 1996.

Wilder, E. I. "Socioeconomic Attainment and Expressions of Jewish Identification, 1970 and 1990." *Journal for the Scientific Study of Religion* 35, no. 2 (June 1996): 109–27.

Wistrich, R. *Revolutionary Jews from Marx to Trotsky.* London: Harrap, 1976.

Woocher, J. S. *Sacred Survival: The Civil Religion of American Jews.* Bloomington: Indiana University Press, 1986.

Zeitz, J. M. *White Ethnic New York: Jews, Catholics, and the Shaping of Postwar Politics.* Chapel Hill: University of North Carolina Press, 2007.

Zieger, R. H. *American Workers, American Unions: 1920–1985.* Baltimore, MD: Johns Hopkins University Press, 1986.

Index